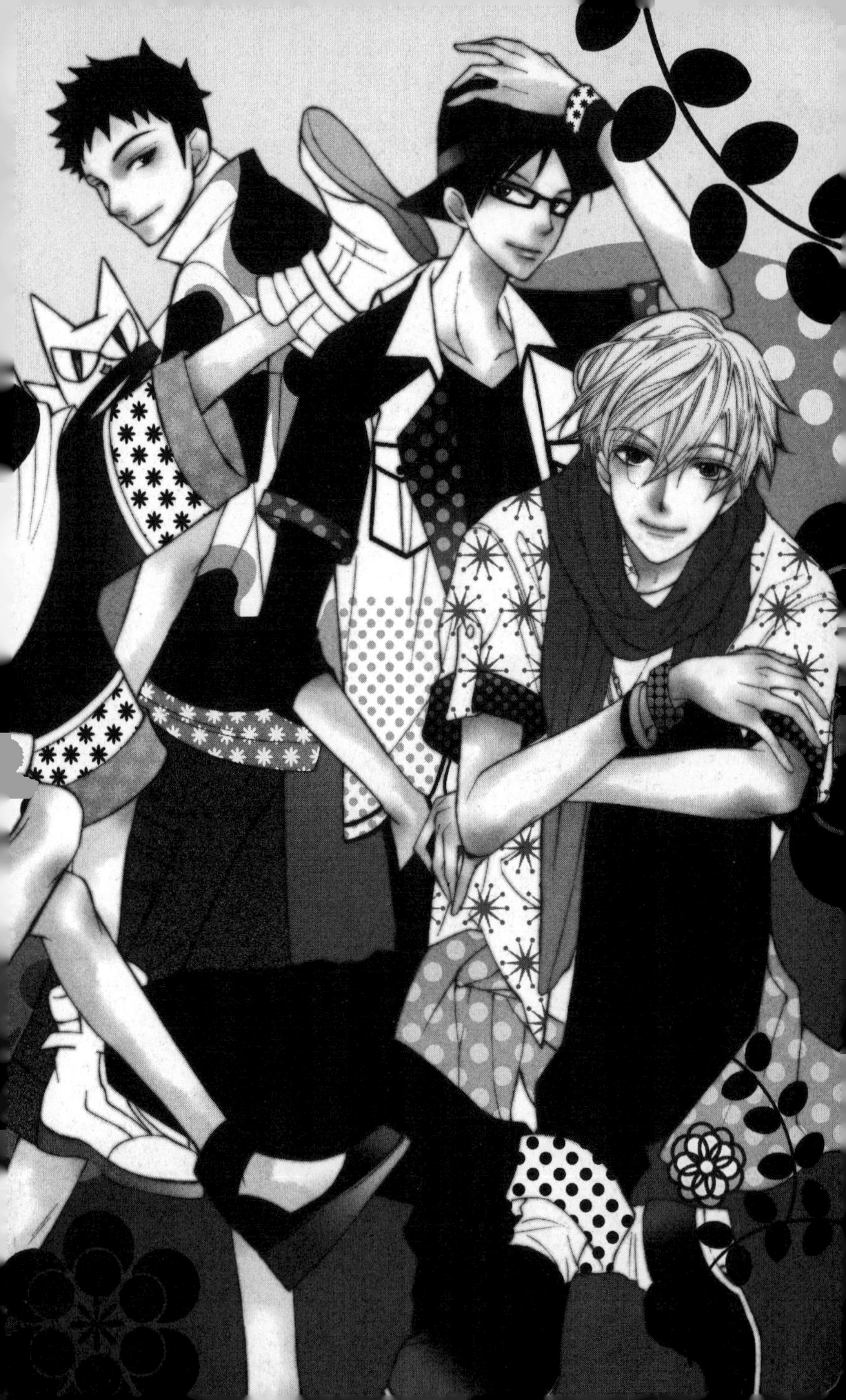

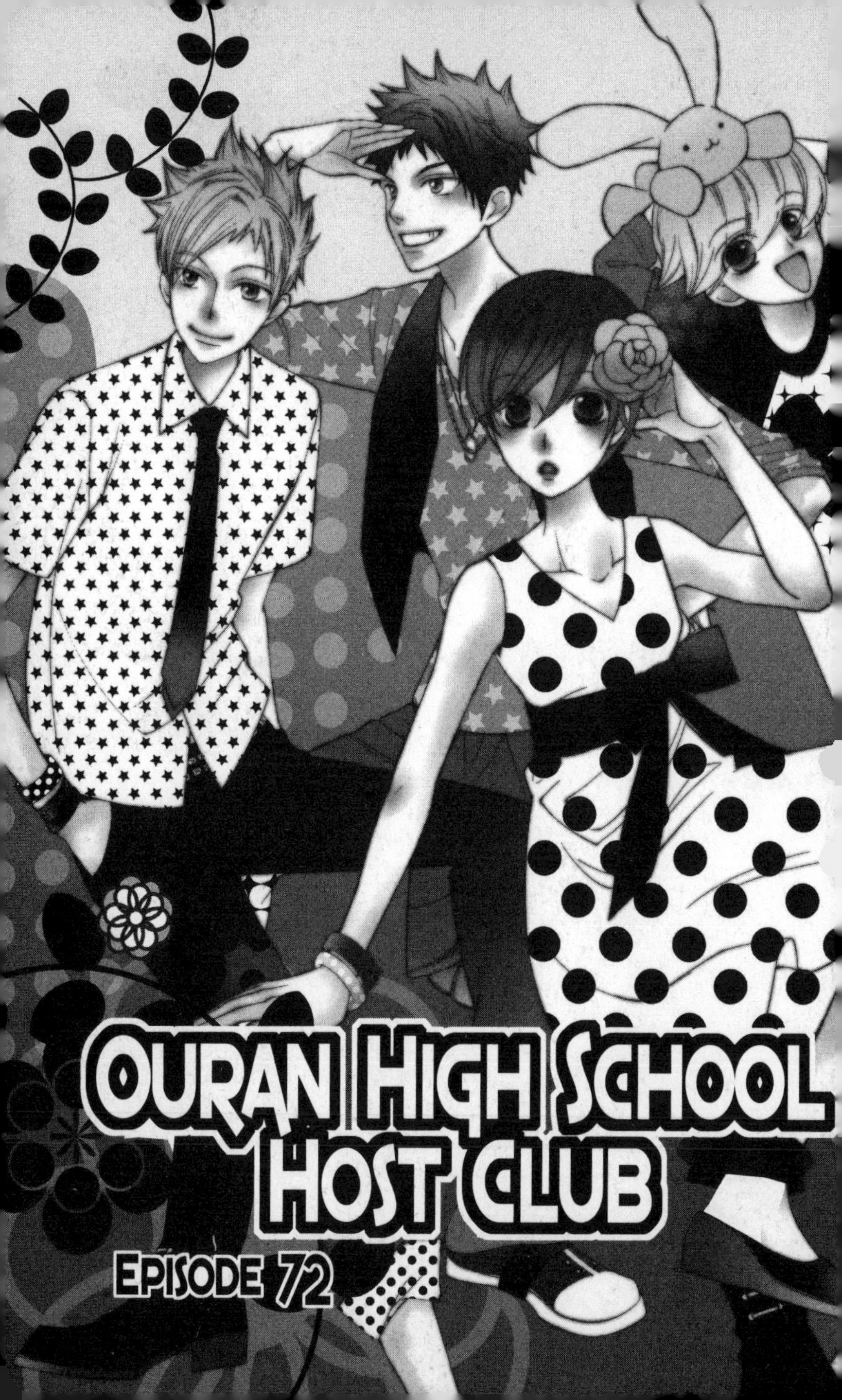
OURAN HIGH SCHOOL
HOST CLUB
EPISODE 72

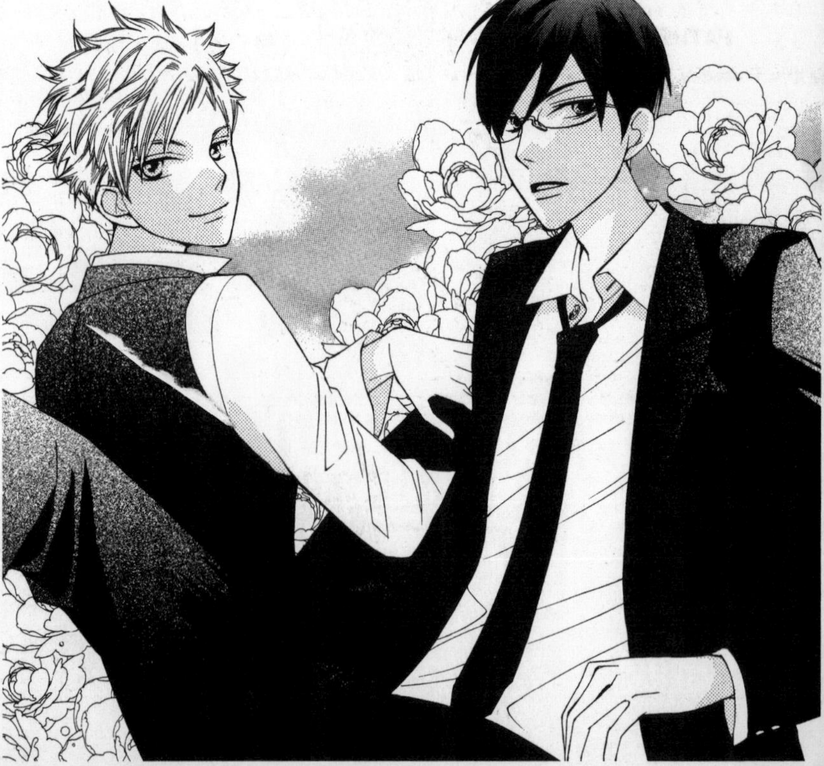

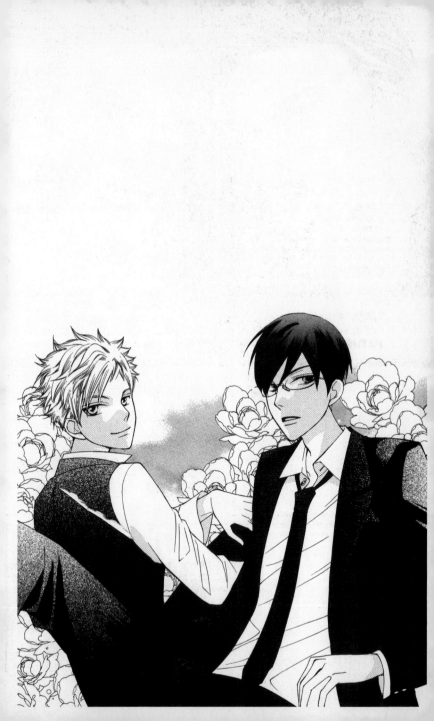

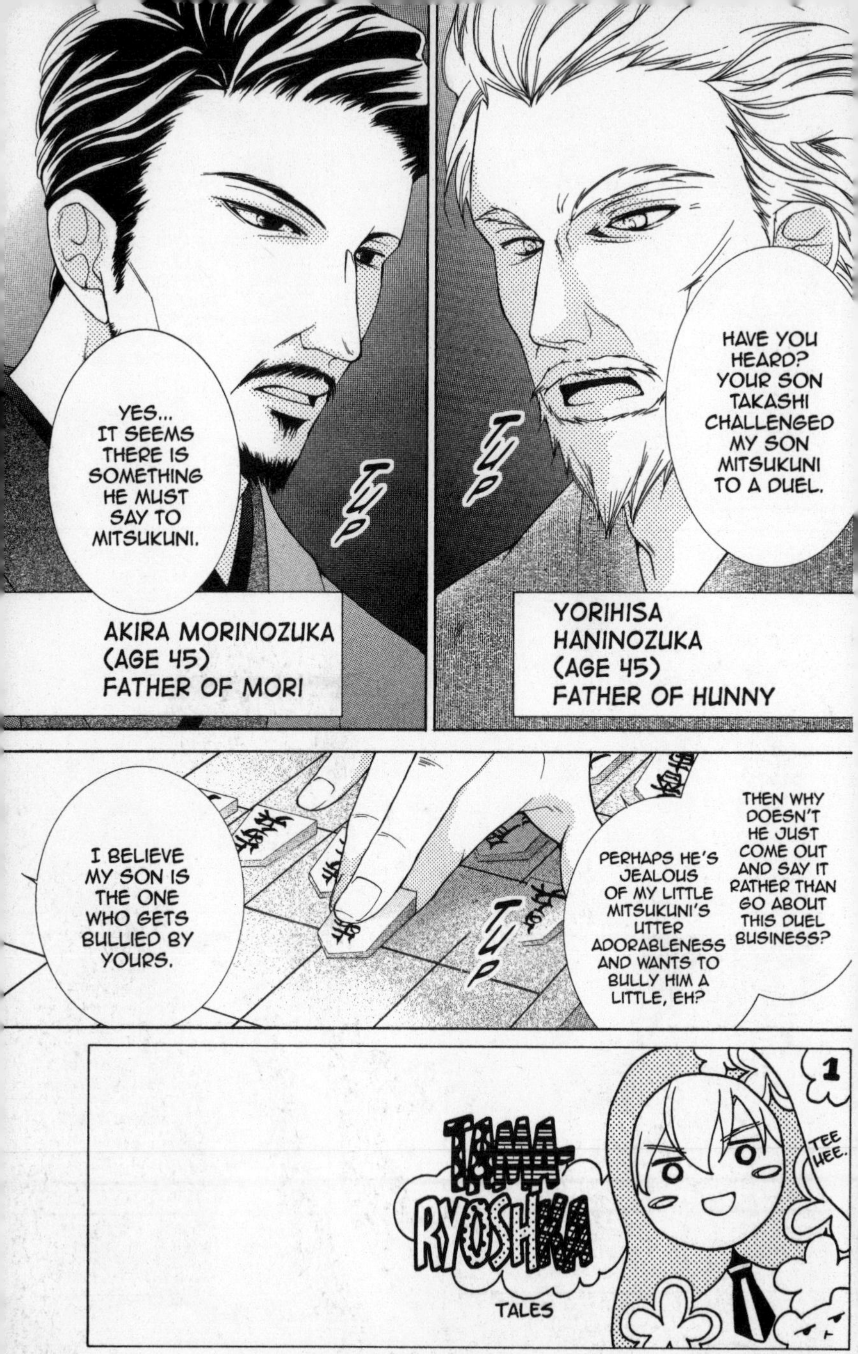
HAVE YOU HEARD? YOUR SON TAKASHI CHALLENGED MY SON MITSUKUNI TO A DUEL.
TUP
YORIHISA HANINOZUKA (AGE 45) FATHER OF HUNNY
YES... IT SEEMS THERE IS SOMETHING HE MUST SAY TO MITSUKUNI.
TUP
AKIRA MORINOZUKA (AGE 45) FATHER OF MORI
THEN WHY DOESN'T HE JUST COME OUT AND SAY IT RATHER THAN GO ABOUT THIS DUEL BUSINESS?
PERHAPS HE'S JEALOUS OF MY LITTLE MITSUKUNI'S UTTER ADORABLENESS AND WANTS TO BULLY HIM A LITTLE, EH?
TUP
I BELIEVE MY SON IS THE ONE WHO GETS BULLIED BY YOURS.
1
TEE HEE.
TAMA-RYOSHKA
TALES

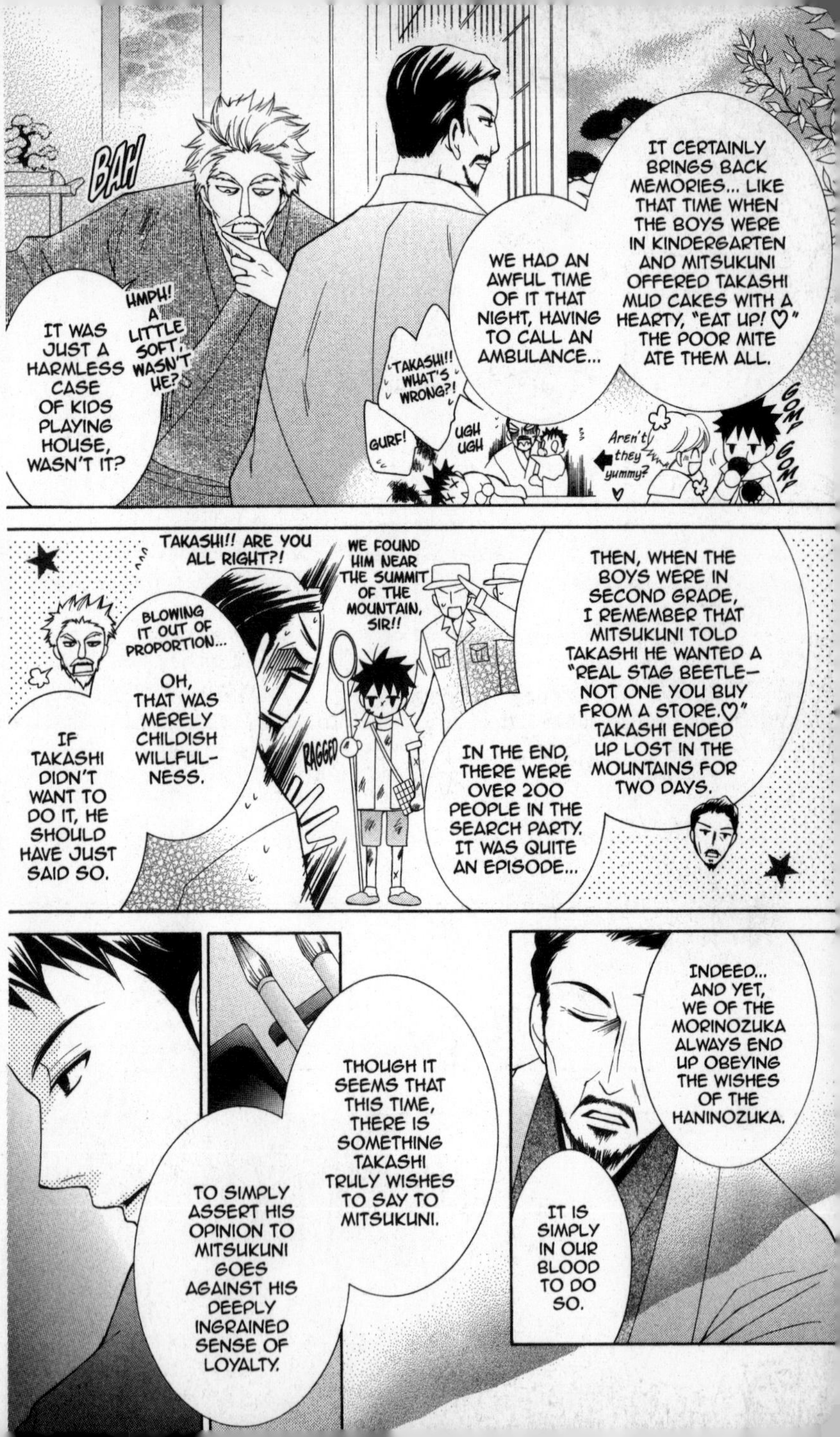

IT CERTAINLY BRINGS BACK MEMORIES... LIKE THAT TIME WHEN THE BOYS WERE IN KINDERGARTEN AND MITSUKUNI OFFERED TAKASHI MUD CAKES WITH A HEARTY, "EAT UP! ♡" THE POOR MITE ATE THEM ALL.
WE HAD AN AWFUL TIME OF IT THAT NIGHT, HAVING TO CALL AN AMBULANCE...
GOM! GOM!
Aren't they yummy? ♡
UGH UGH
TAKASHI!! WHAT'S WRONG?!
GURF!
BAH
HMPH! A LITTLE SOFT, WASN'T HE?
IT WAS JUST A HARMLESS CASE OF KIDS PLAYING HOUSE, WASN'T IT?
THEN, WHEN THE BOYS WERE IN SECOND GRADE, I REMEMBER THAT MITSUKUNI TOLD TAKASHI HE WANTED A "REAL STAG BEETLE—NOT ONE YOU BUY FROM A STORE.♡" TAKASHI ENDED UP LOST IN THE MOUNTAINS FOR TWO DAYS.
WE FOUND HIM NEAR THE SUMMIT OF THE MOUNTAIN, SIR!!
IN THE END, THERE WERE OVER 200 PEOPLE IN THE SEARCH PARTY. IT WAS QUITE AN EPISODE...
TAKASHI!! ARE YOU ALL RIGHT?!
RAGGED
BLOWING IT OUT OF PROPORTION...
OH, THAT WAS MERELY CHILDISH WILLFUL-NESS.
IF TAKASHI DIDN'T WANT TO DO IT, HE SHOULD HAVE JUST SAID SO.
INDEED... AND YET, WE OF THE MORINOZUKA ALWAYS END UP OBEYING THE WISHES OF THE HANINOZUKA.
IT IS SIMPLY IN OUR BLOOD TO DO SO.
THOUGH IT SEEMS THAT THIS TIME, THERE IS SOMETHING TAKASHI TRULY WISHES TO SAY TO MITSUKUNI.
TO SIMPLY ASSERT HIS OPINION TO MITSUKUNI GOES AGAINST HIS DEEPLY INGRAINED SENSE OF LOYALTY.

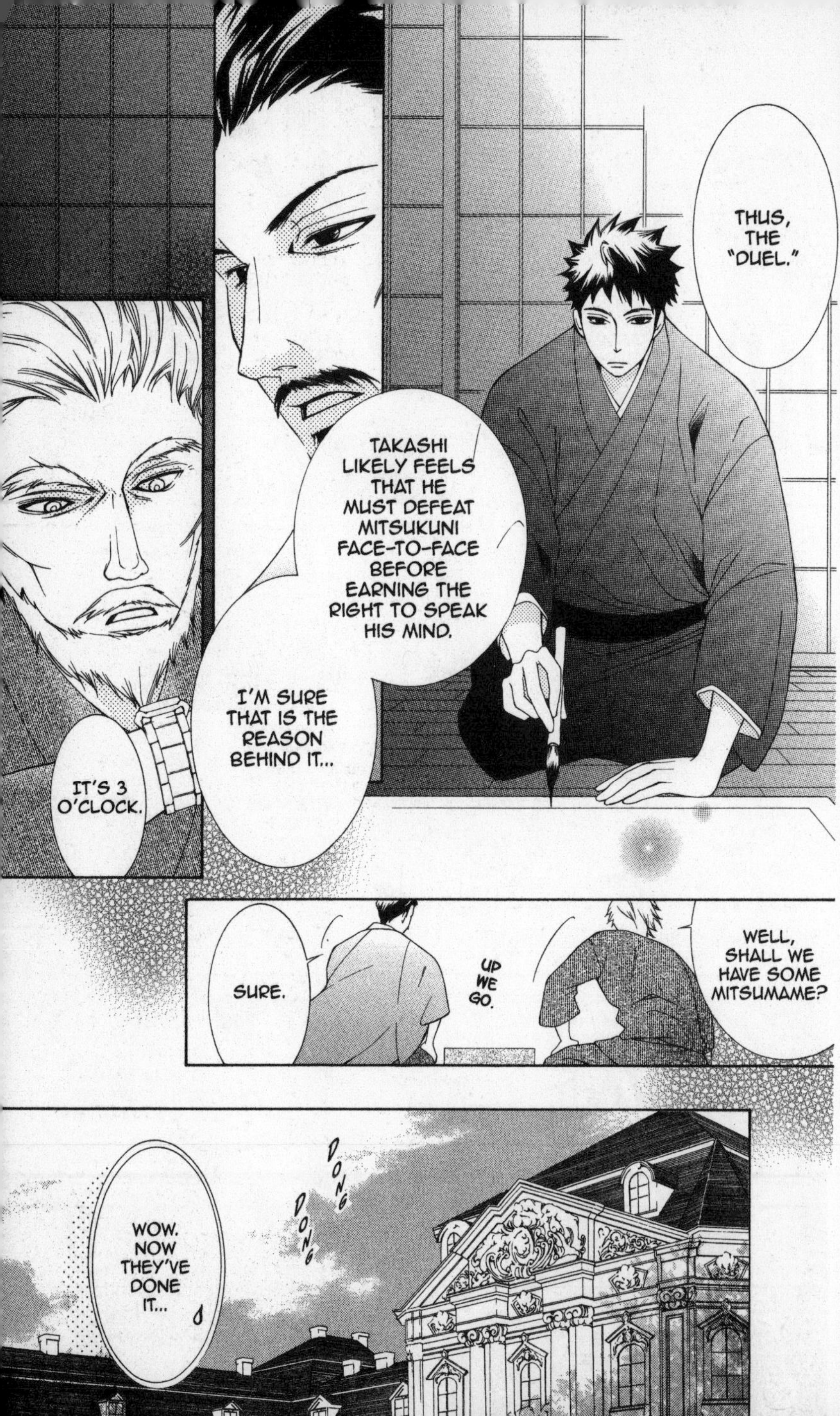
THUS, THE "DUEL."
TAKASHI LIKELY FEELS THAT HE MUST DEFEAT MITSUKUNI FACE-TO-FACE BEFORE EARNING THE RIGHT TO SPEAK HIS MIND.
I'M SURE THAT IS THE REASON BEHIND IT...
IT'S 3 O'CLOCK.
WELL, SHALL WE HAVE SOME MITSUMAME?
UP WE GO.
SURE.
DONG
DONG
WOW. NOW THEY'VE DONE IT...

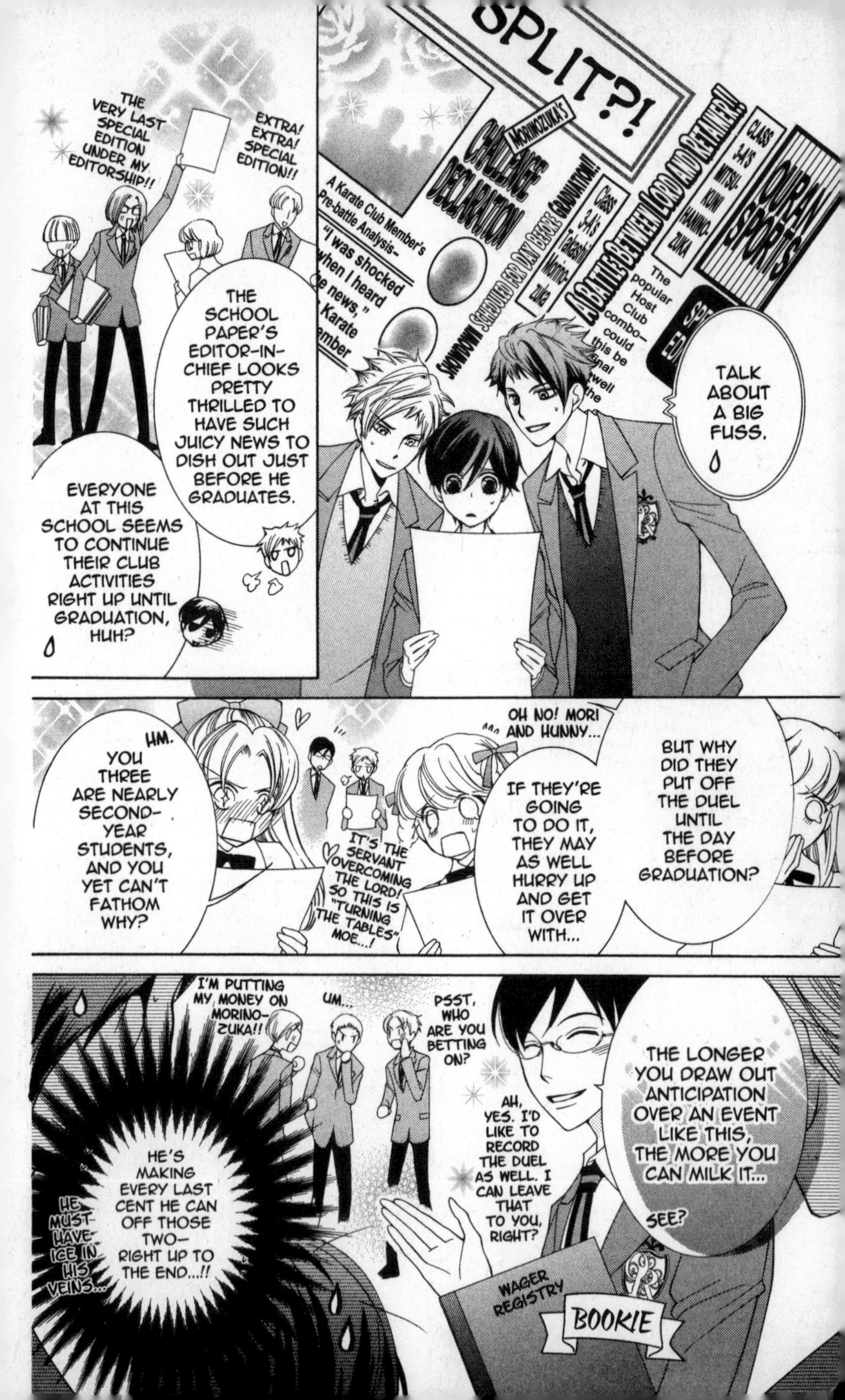
SPLIT?!
OURAN SPORTS
CLASS 3-A's
A BATTLE BETWEEN LORD AND RETAINER!!
Class 3-A's Morinozuka Takashi
SHOWDOWN SCHEDULED FOR DAY BEFORE GRADUATION!
MORINOZUKA'S CHALLENGE DECLARATION
A Karate Club Member's Pre-battle Analysis–
"I was shocked when I heard the news," Karate member
The popular Host Club combo– could this be
TALK ABOUT A BIG FUSS.
EXTRA! EXTRA! SPECIAL EDITION!!
THE VERY LAST SPECIAL EDITION UNDER MY EDITORSHIP!!
THE SCHOOL PAPER'S EDITOR-IN-CHIEF LOOKS PRETTY THRILLED TO HAVE SUCH JUICY NEWS TO DISH OUT JUST BEFORE HE GRADUATES.
EVERYONE AT THIS SCHOOL SEEMS TO CONTINUE THEIR CLUB ACTIVITIES RIGHT UP UNTIL GRADUATION, HUH?
BUT WHY DID THEY PUT OFF THE DUEL UNTIL THE DAY BEFORE GRADUATION?
OH NO! MORI AND HUNNY...
IF THEY'RE GOING TO DO IT, THEY MAY AS WELL HURRY UP AND GET IT OVER WITH...
IT'S THE SERVANT OVERCOMING THE LORD! SO THIS IS "TURNING THE TABLES" MOE...!
HM.
YOU THREE ARE NEARLY SECOND-YEAR STUDENTS, AND YOU YET CAN'T FATHOM WHY?
THE LONGER YOU DRAW OUT ANTICIPATION OVER AN EVENT LIKE THIS, THE MORE YOU CAN MILK IT...
SEE?
AH, YES. I'D LIKE TO RECORD THE DUEL AS WELL. I CAN LEAVE THAT TO YOU, RIGHT?
PSST, WHO ARE YOU BETTING ON?
UM...
I'M PUTTING MY MONEY ON MORINOZUKA!!
WAGER REGISTRY
BOOKIE
HE'S MAKING EVERY LAST CENT HE CAN OFF THOSE TWO–RIGHT UP TO THE END...!!
HE MUST HAVE ICE IN HIS VEINS...

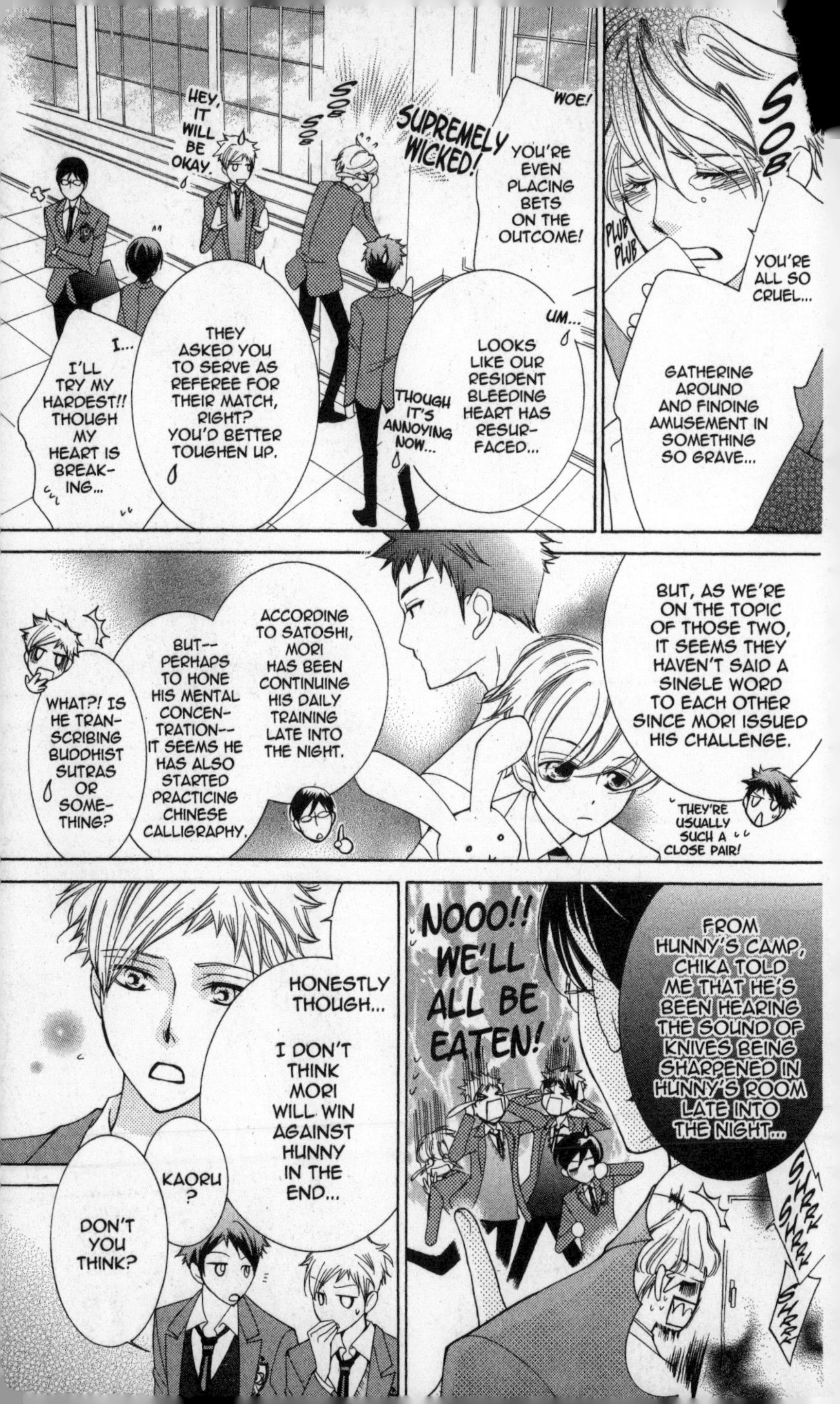
SOB
PLUB PLUB
YOU'RE ALL SO CRUEL...
GATHERING AROUND AND FINDING AMUSEMENT IN SOMETHING SO GRAVE...
WOE!
YOU'RE EVEN PLACING BETS ON THE OUTCOME!
SUPREMELY WICKED!
SOB SOB
HEY, IT WILL BE OKAY.
UM...
LOOKS LIKE OUR RESIDENT BLEEDING HEART HAS RESURFACED...
THOUGH IT'S ANNOYING NOW...
THEY ASKED YOU TO SERVE AS REFEREE FOR THEIR MATCH, RIGHT? YOU'D BETTER TOUGHEN UP.
I...
I'LL TRY MY HARDEST!! THOUGH MY HEART IS BREAKING...
BUT, AS WE'RE ON THE TOPIC OF THOSE TWO, IT SEEMS THEY HAVEN'T SAID A SINGLE WORD TO EACH OTHER SINCE MORI ISSUED HIS CHALLENGE.
THEY'RE USUALLY SUCH A CLOSE PAIR!
ACCORDING TO SATOSHI, MORI HAS BEEN CONTINUING HIS DAILY TRAINING LATE INTO THE NIGHT.
BUT-- PERHAPS TO HONE HIS MENTAL CONCENTRATION-- IT SEEMS HE HAS ALSO STARTED PRACTICING CHINESE CALLIGRAPHY.
WHAT?! IS HE TRANSCRIBING BUDDHIST SUTRAS OR SOMETHING?
FROM HUNNY'S CAMP, CHIKA TOLD ME THAT HE'S BEEN HEARING THE SOUND OF KNIVES BEING SHARPENED IN HUNNY'S ROOM LATE INTO THE NIGHT...
SHRK SHRK SHRK
NOOO!! WE'LL ALL BE EATEN!
HONESTLY THOUGH...
I DON'T THINK MORI WILL WIN AGAINST HUNNY IN THE END...
KAORU?
DON'T YOU THINK?

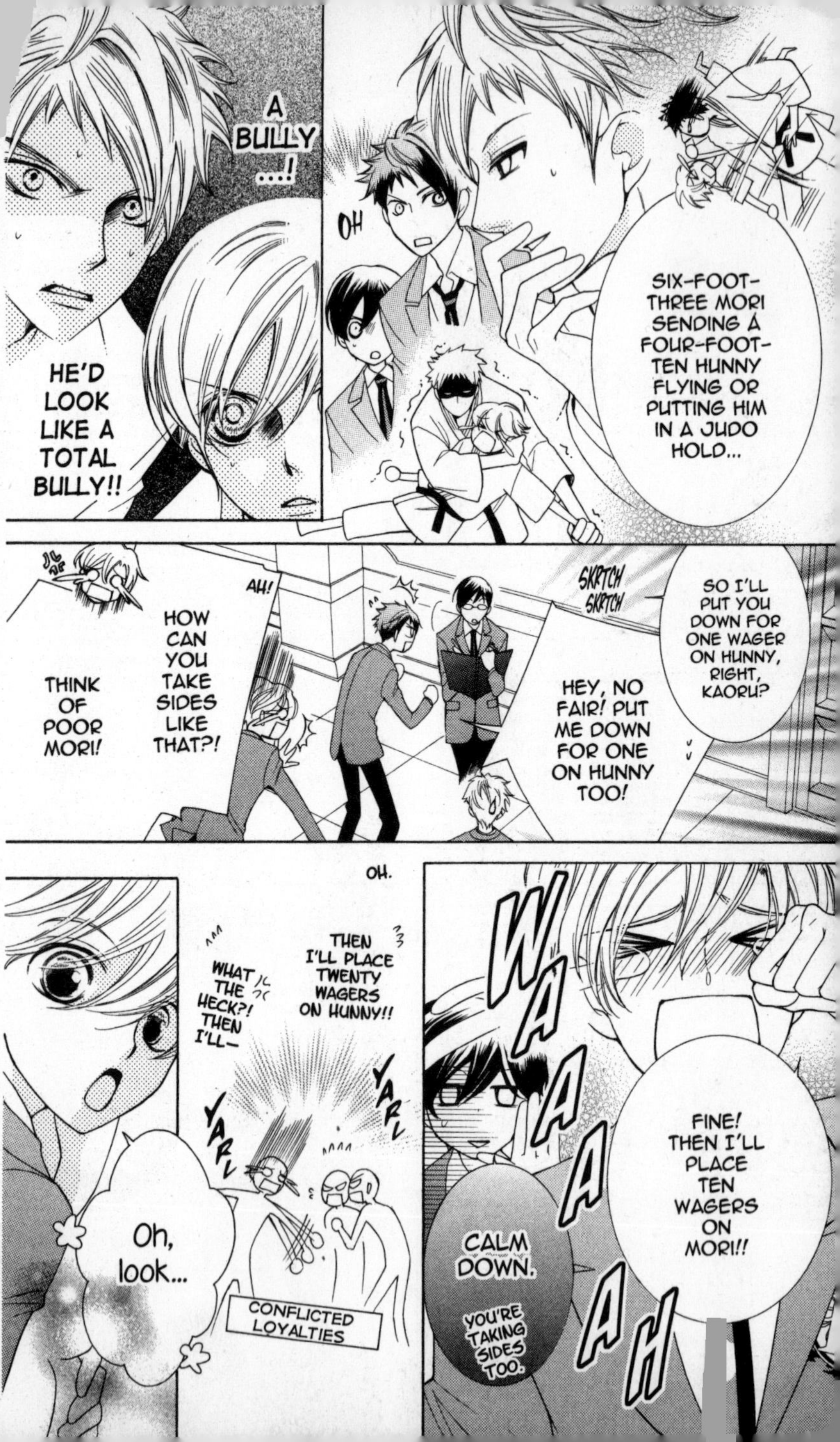
SIX-FOOT-THREE MORI SENDING A FOUR-FOOT-TEN HUNNY FLYING OR PUTTING HIM IN A JUDO HOLD...
OH
A BULLY ...!
HE'D LOOK LIKE A TOTAL BULLY!!
SO I'LL PUT YOU DOWN FOR ONE WAGER ON HUNNY, RIGHT, KAORU?
SKRTCH SKRTCH
HEY, NO FAIR! PUT ME DOWN FOR ONE ON HUNNY TOO!
AH!
HOW CAN YOU TAKE SIDES LIKE THAT?!
THINK OF POOR MORI!
WAAAAAH
FINE! THEN I'LL PLACE TEN WAGERS ON MORI!!
CALM DOWN.
YOU'RE TAKING SIDES TOO.
OH.
THEN I'LL PLACE TWENTY WAGERS ON HUNNY!!
WHAT THE HECK?! THEN I'LL—
CONFLICTED LOYALTIES
Oh, look...

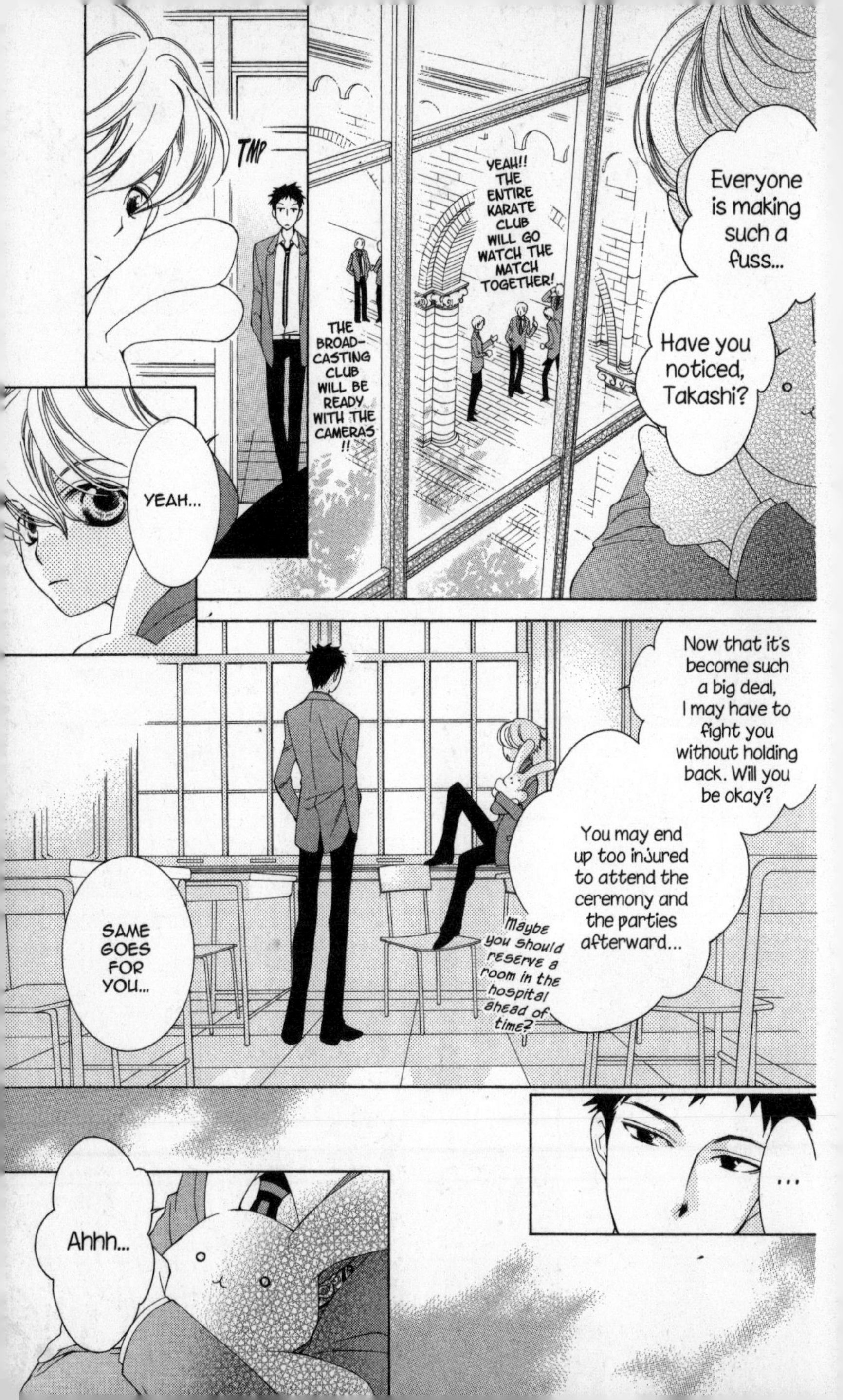
Everyone is making such a fuss...
Have you noticed, Takashi?
YEAH!! THE ENTIRE KARATE CLUB WILL GO WATCH THE MATCH TOGETHER!
THE BROADCASTING CLUB WILL BE READY WITH THE CAMERAS!!
TMP
YEAH...
Now that it's become such a big deal, I may have to fight you without holding back. Will you be okay?
You may end up too injured to attend the ceremony and the parties afterward...
Maybe you should reserve a room in the hospital ahead of time?
SAME GOES FOR YOU...
...
Ahhh...

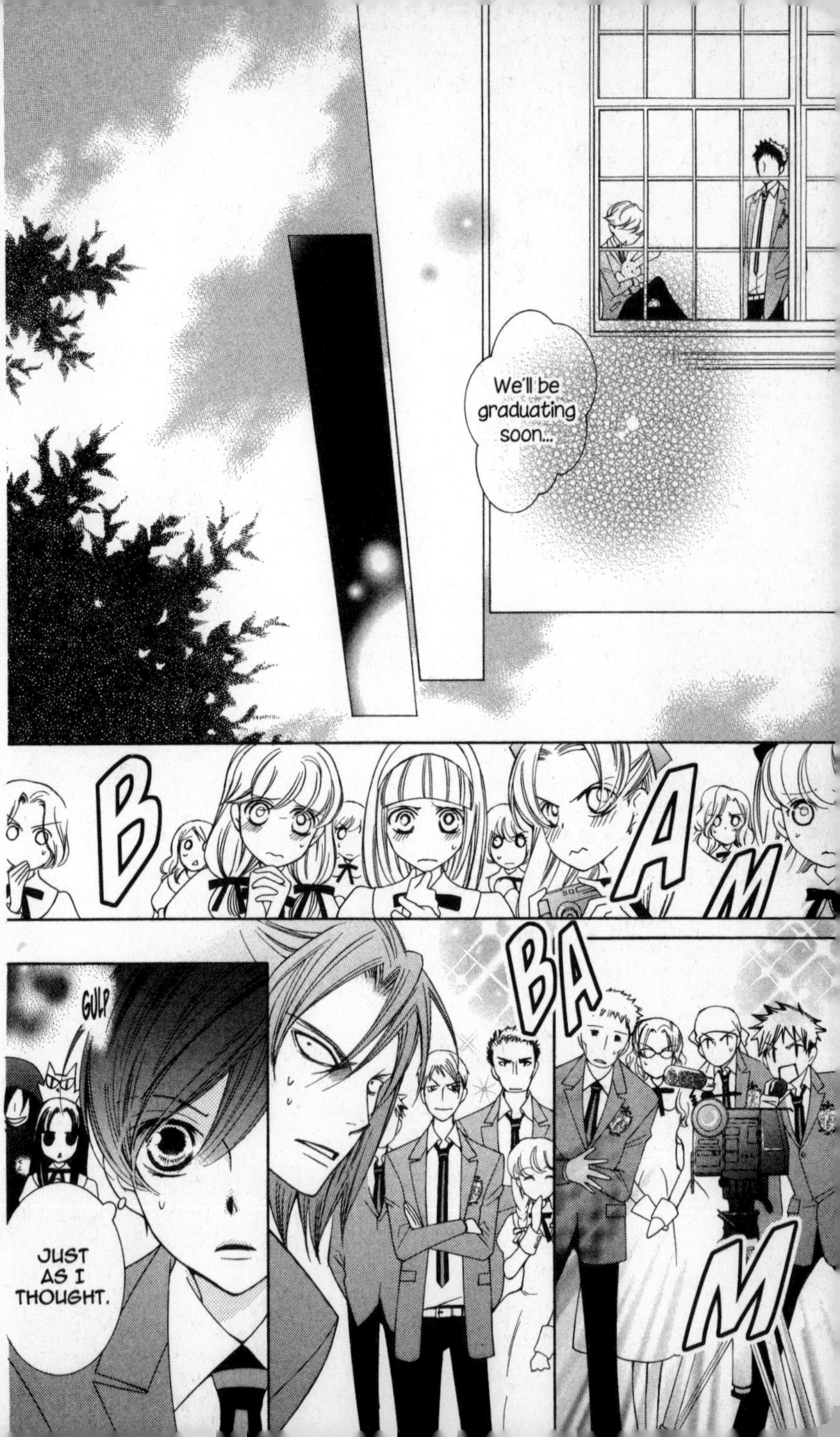
We'll be graduating soon...
BAM
BAM
GULP
JUST AS I THOUGHT.

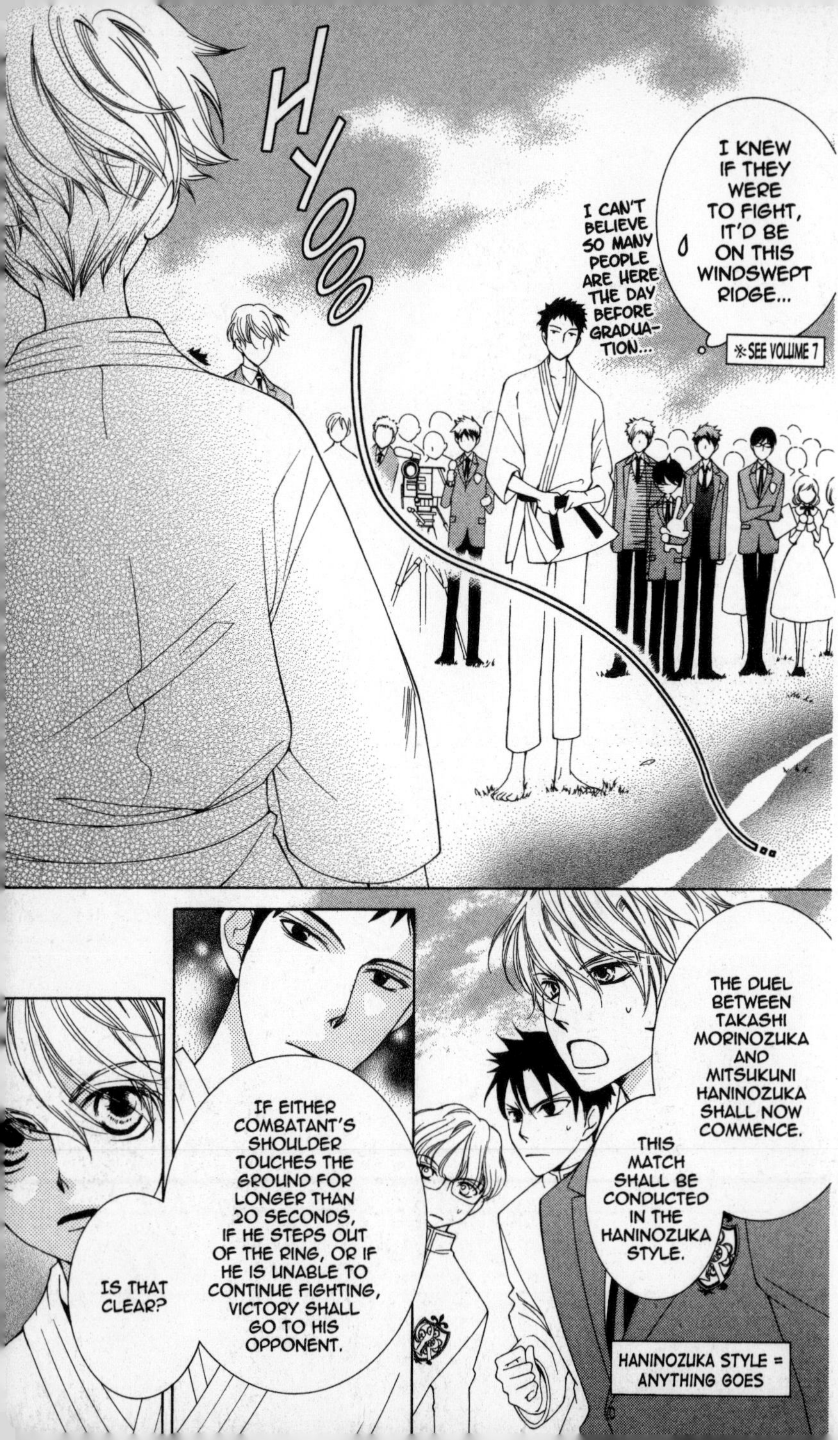
I KNEW IF THEY WERE TO FIGHT, IT'D BE ON THIS WINDSWEPT RIDGE...
※SEE VOLUME 7
I CAN'T BELIEVE SO MANY PEOPLE ARE HERE THE DAY BEFORE GRADUATION...
HYOOO
THE DUEL BETWEEN TAKASHI MORINOZUKA AND MITSUKUNI HANINOZUKA SHALL NOW COMMENCE.
THIS MATCH SHALL BE CONDUCTED IN THE HANINOZUKA STYLE.
HANINOZUKA STYLE = ANYTHING GOES
IF EITHER COMBATANT'S SHOULDER TOUCHES THE GROUND FOR LONGER THAN 20 SECONDS, IF HE STEPS OUT OF THE RING, OR IF HE IS UNABLE TO CONTINUE FIGHTING, VICTORY SHALL GO TO HIS OPPONENT.
IS THAT CLEAR?

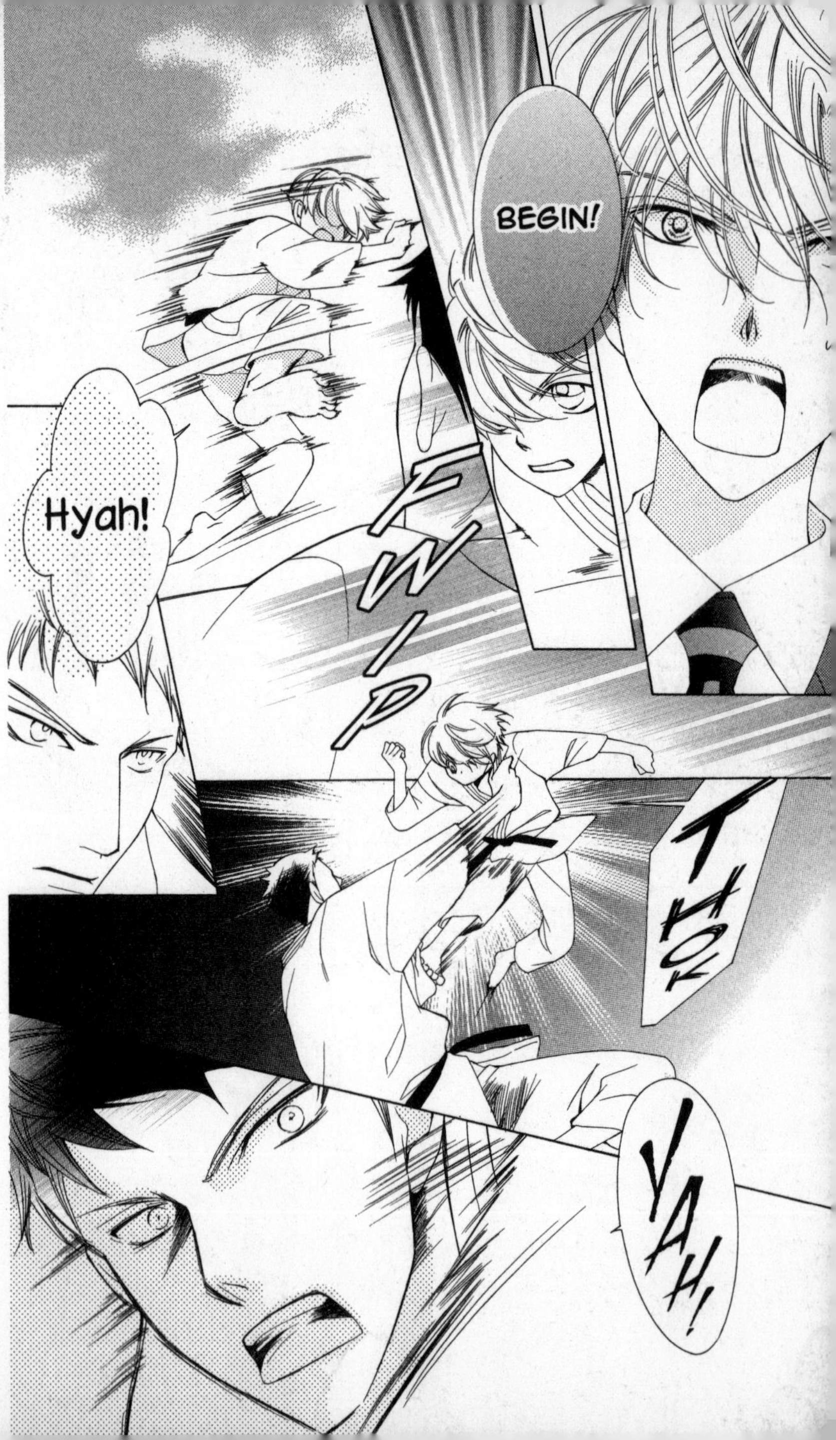
BEGIN!
FWIP
Hyah!
THOK
YAH!

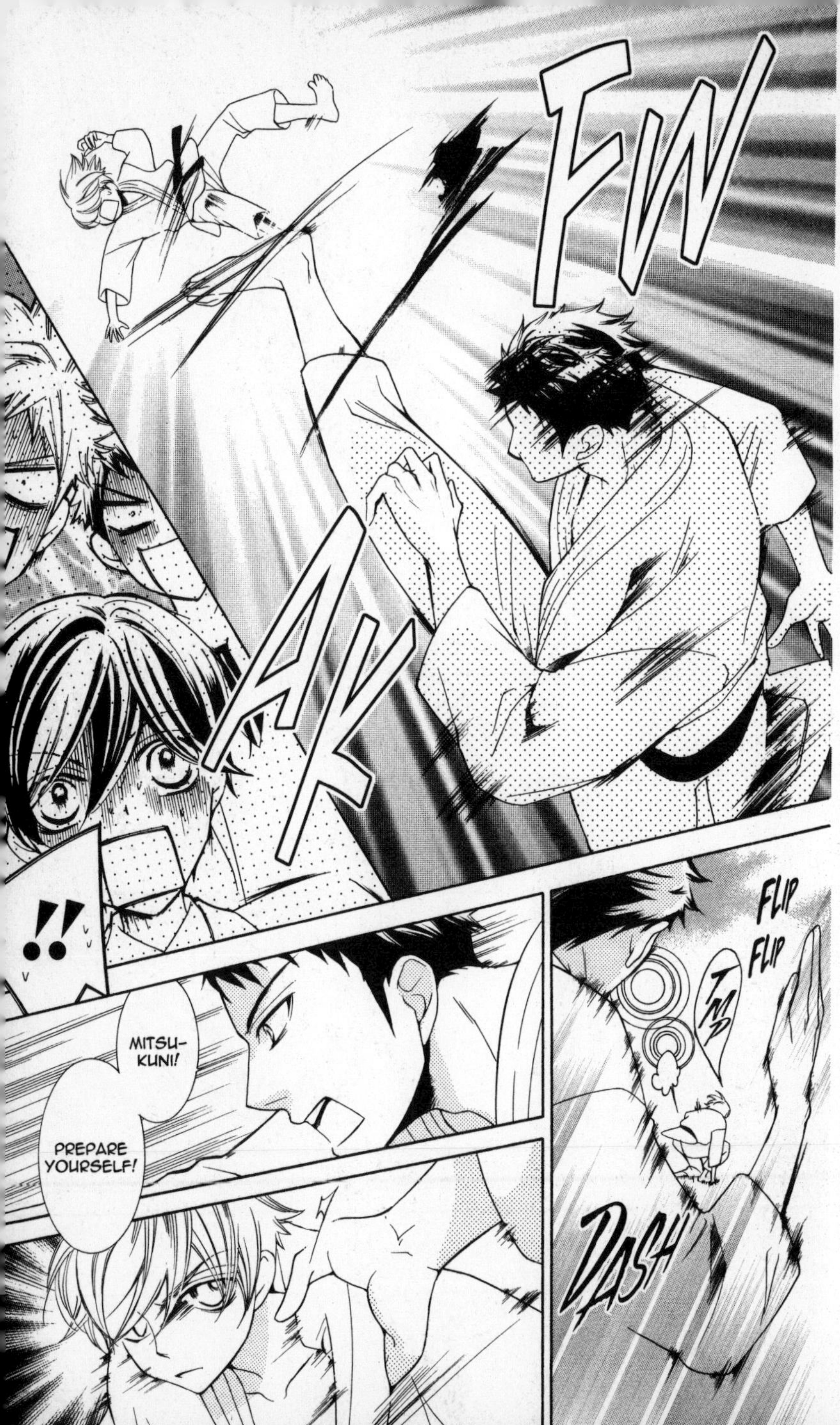
FW
AK
!!
FLIP
FLIP
DASH
MITSU-KUNI!
PREPARE YOURSELF!

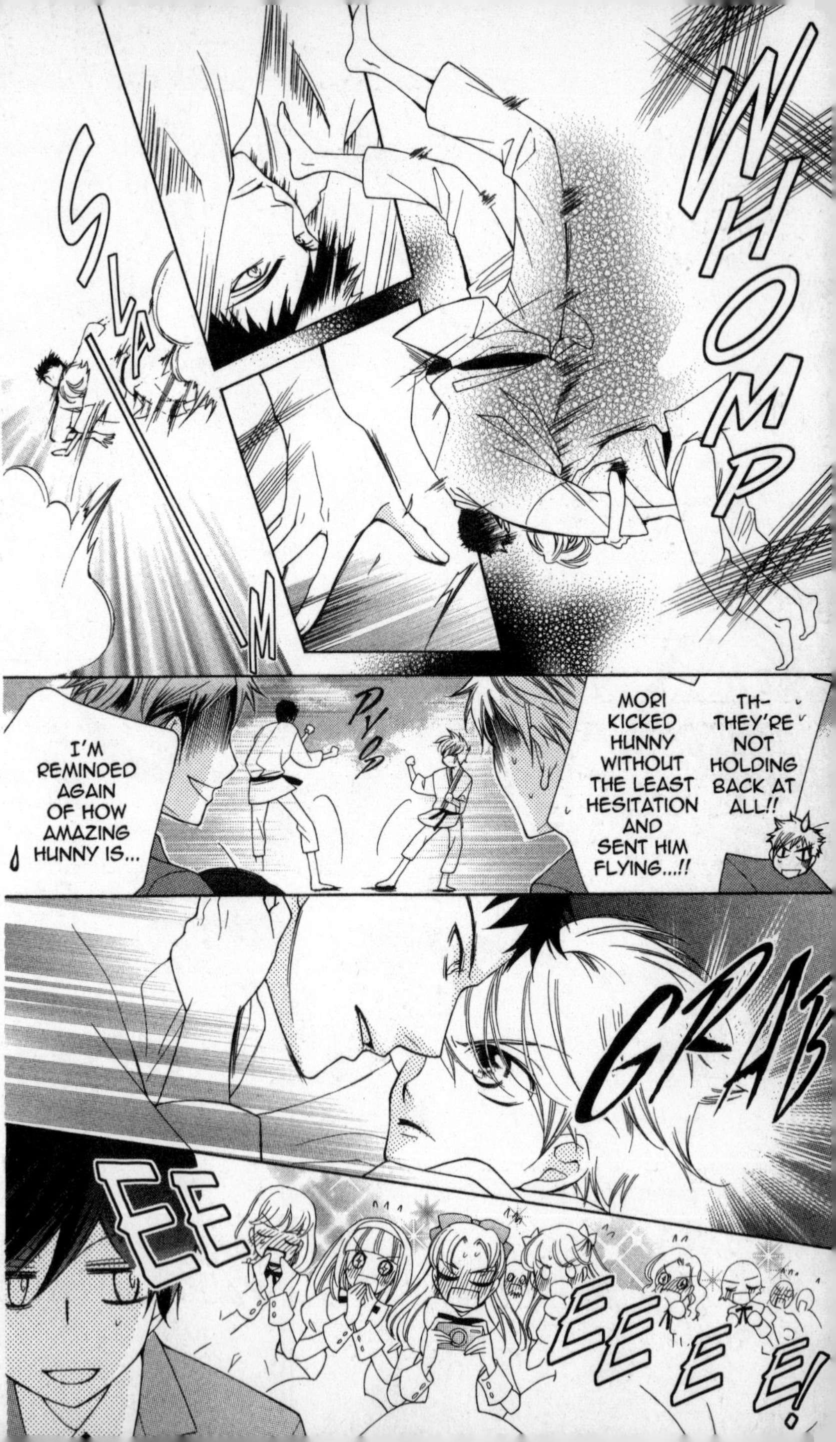
WHOMP
SLAM
TH-THEY'RE NOT HOLDING BACK AT ALL!!
MORI KICKED HUNNY WITHOUT THE LEAST HESITATION AND SENT HIM FLYING...!!
I'M REMINDED AGAIN OF HOW AMAZING HUNNY IS...
GRAB
EEEEEEE!

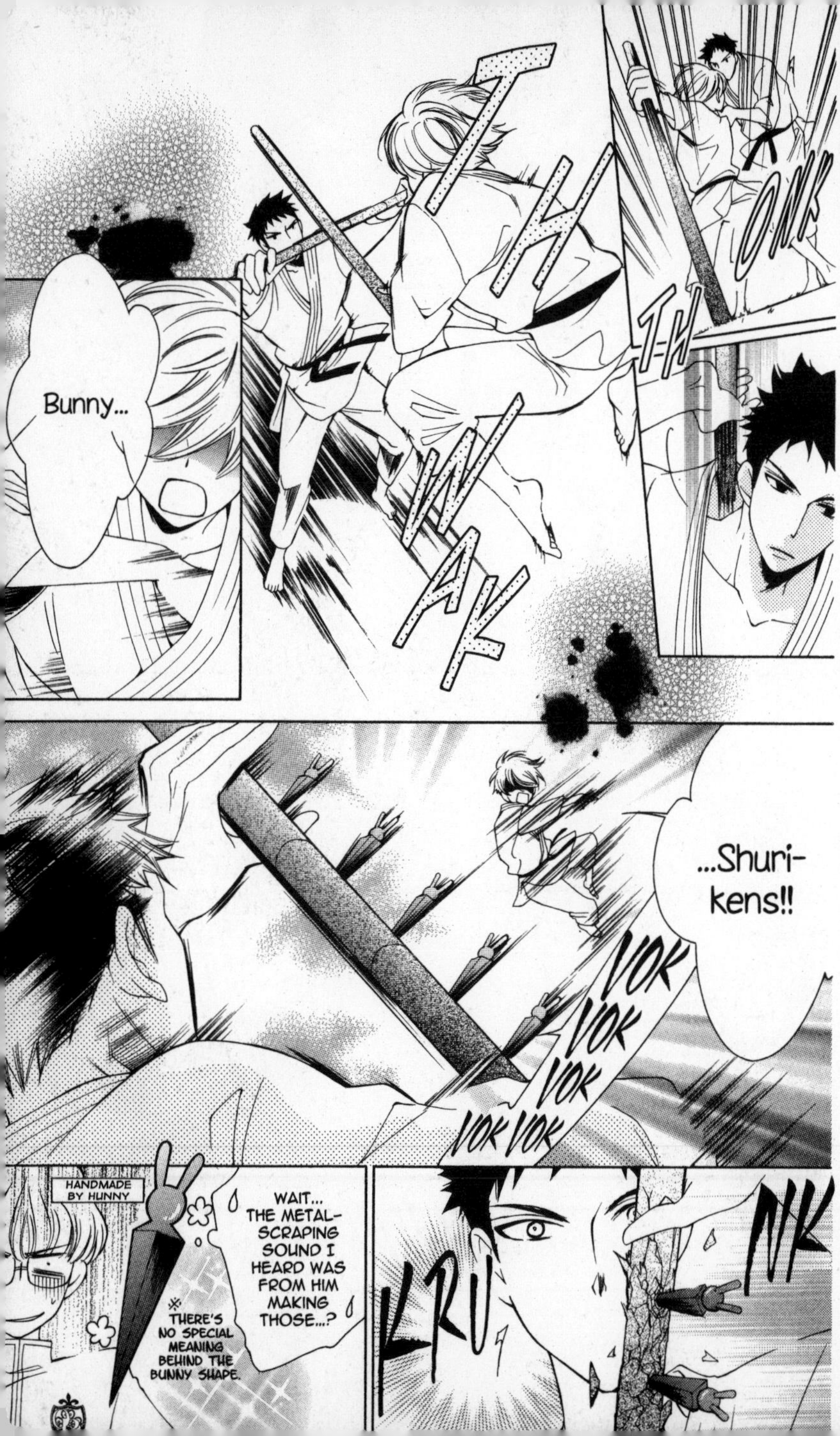
THONK
THWAK
Bunny...
...Shuri-kens!!
VOK VOK VOK VOK VOK
KRUNK
WAIT... THE METAL-SCRAPING SOUND I HEARD WAS FROM HIM MAKING THOSE...?
HANDMADE BY HUNNY
※ THERE'S NO SPECIAL MEANING BEHIND THE BUNNY SHAPE.

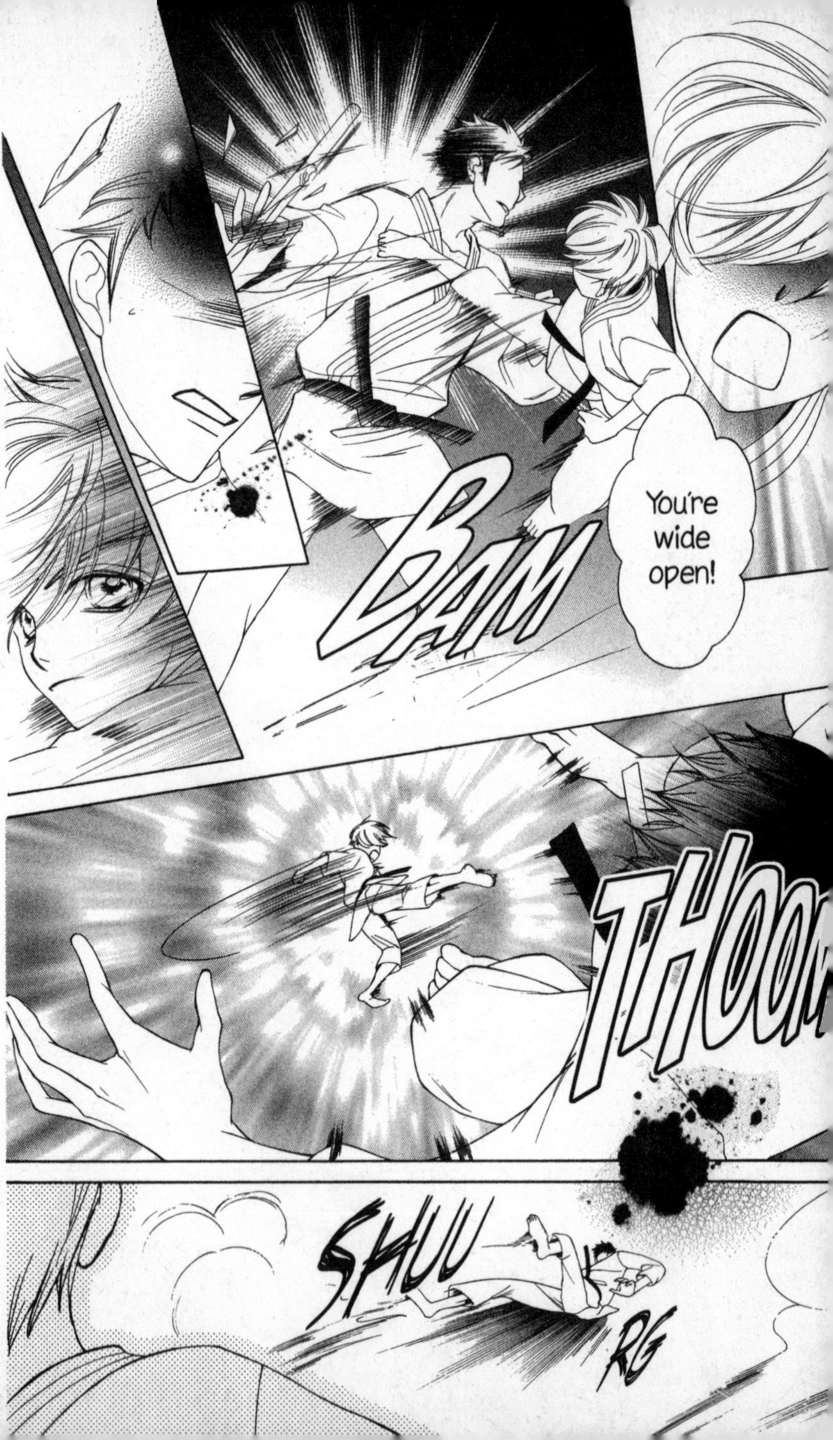
You're wide open!
BAM
THOO
SHUU
RG

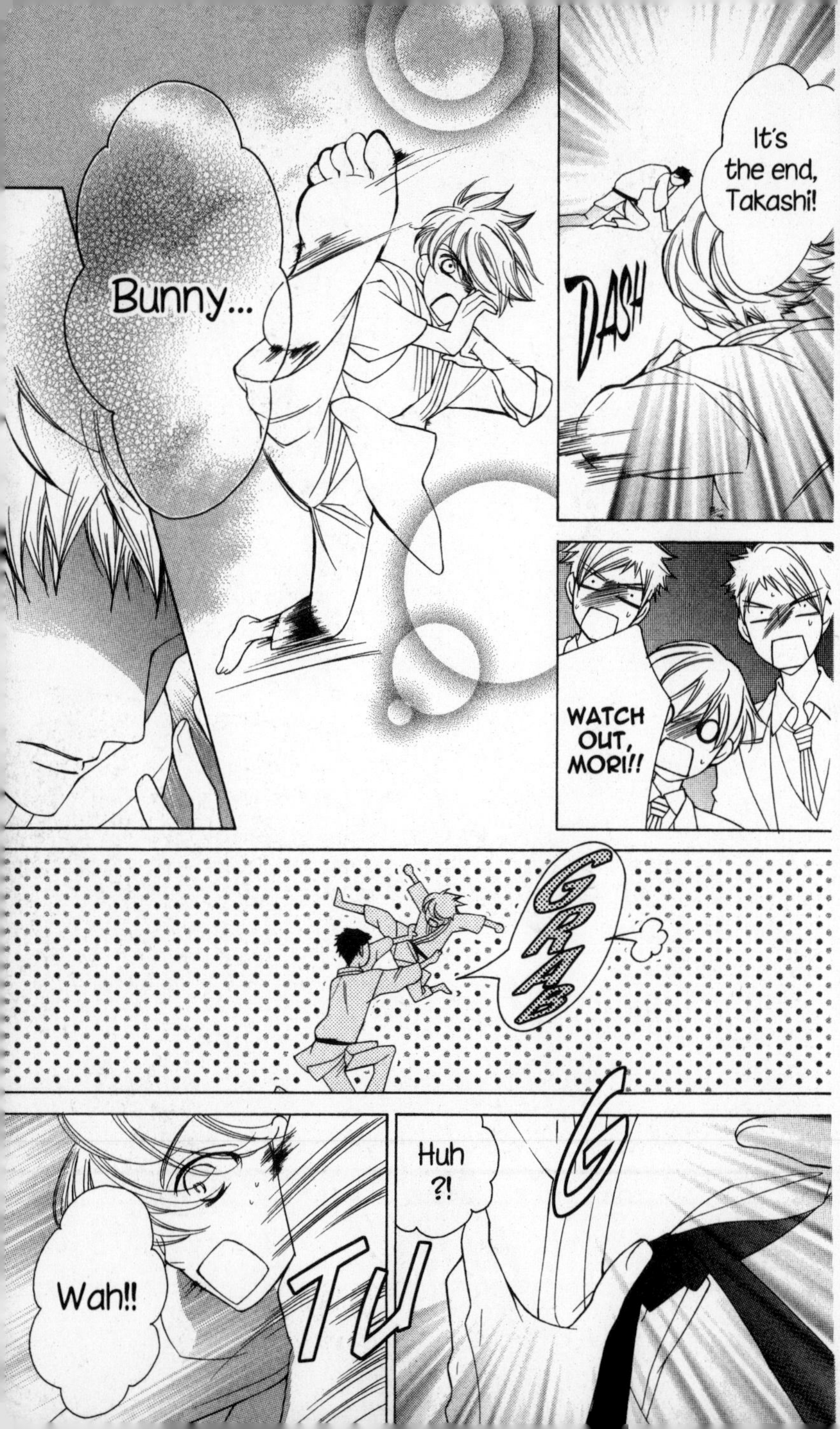
It's the end, Takashi!
DASH
WATCH OUT, MORI!!
Bunny...
GRAB
Huh ?!
G
TU
Wah!!

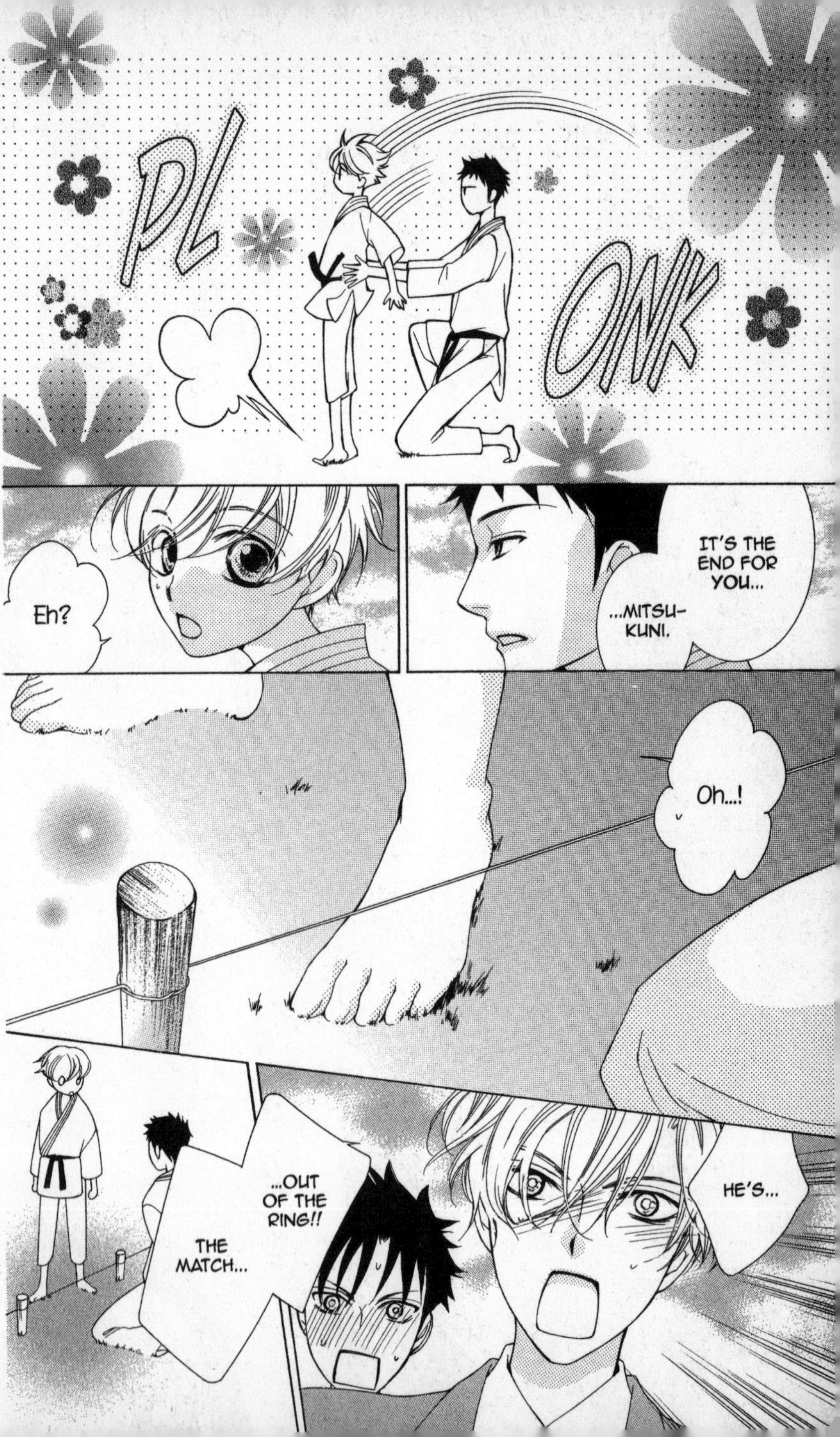
PL
ONK
IT'S THE END FOR YOU...
...MITSU-KUNI.
Eh?
Oh...!
HE'S...
...OUT OF THE RING!!
THE MATCH...

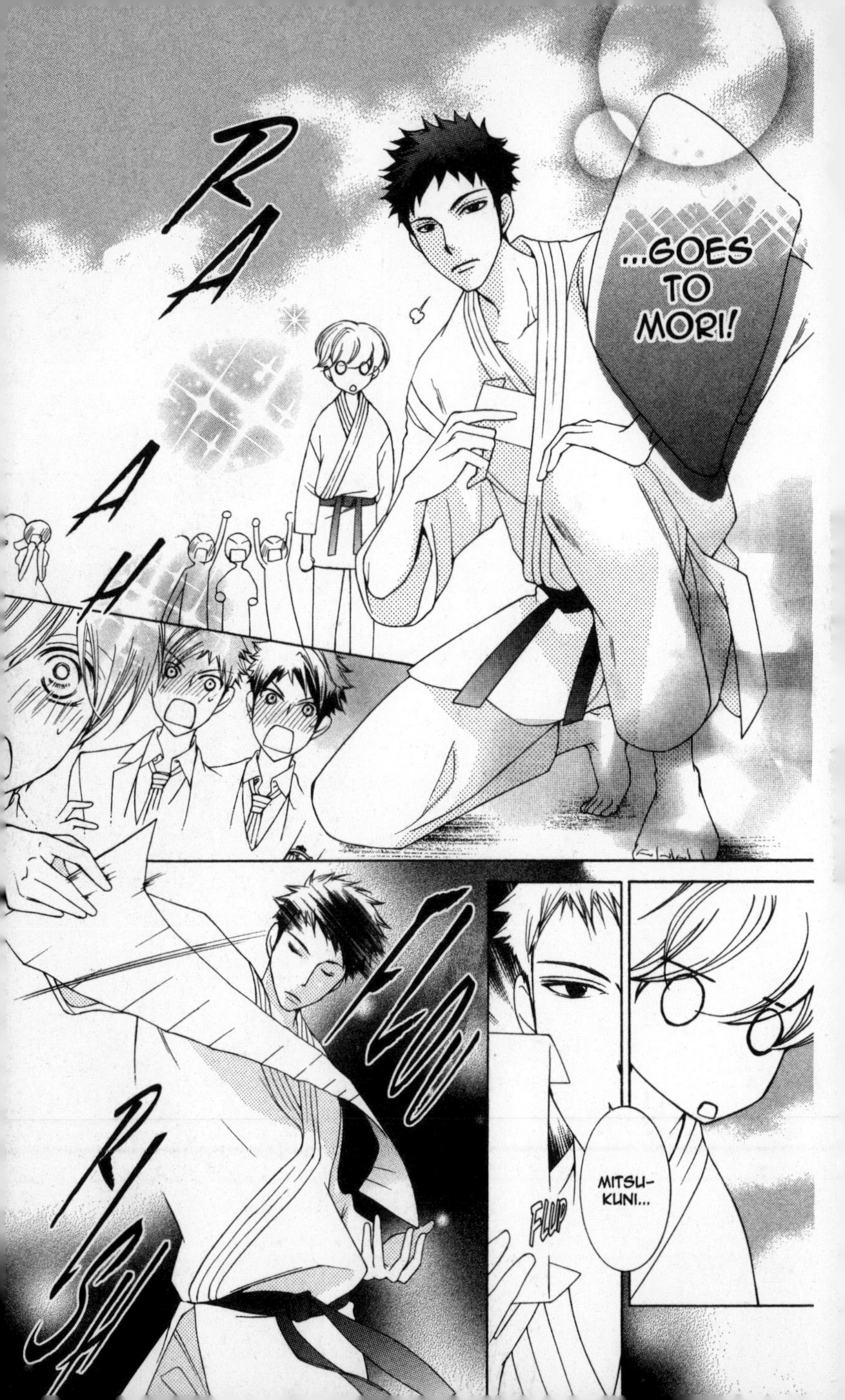
...GOES TO MORI!
RAAAH
MITSU-KUNI...
FLUP
FWOO
RRISH

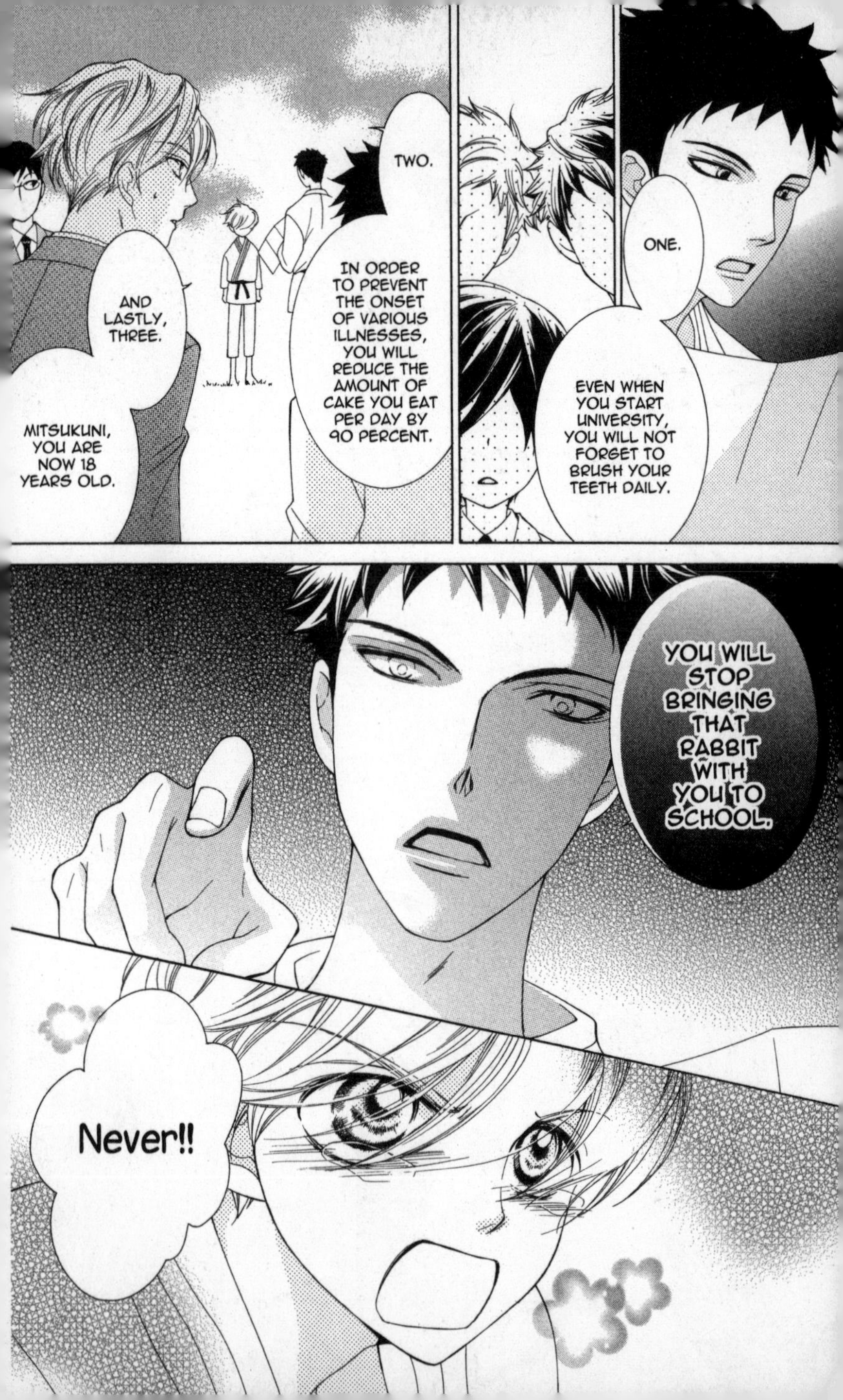
ONE.
EVEN WHEN YOU START UNIVERSITY, YOU WILL NOT FORGET TO BRUSH YOUR TEETH DAILY.
TWO.
IN ORDER TO PREVENT THE ONSET OF VARIOUS ILLNESSES, YOU WILL REDUCE THE AMOUNT OF CAKE YOU EAT PER DAY BY 90 PERCENT.
AND LASTLY, THREE.
MITSUKUNI, YOU ARE NOW 18 YEARS OLD.
YOU WILL STOP BRINGING THAT RABBIT WITH YOU TO SCHOOL.
Never!!

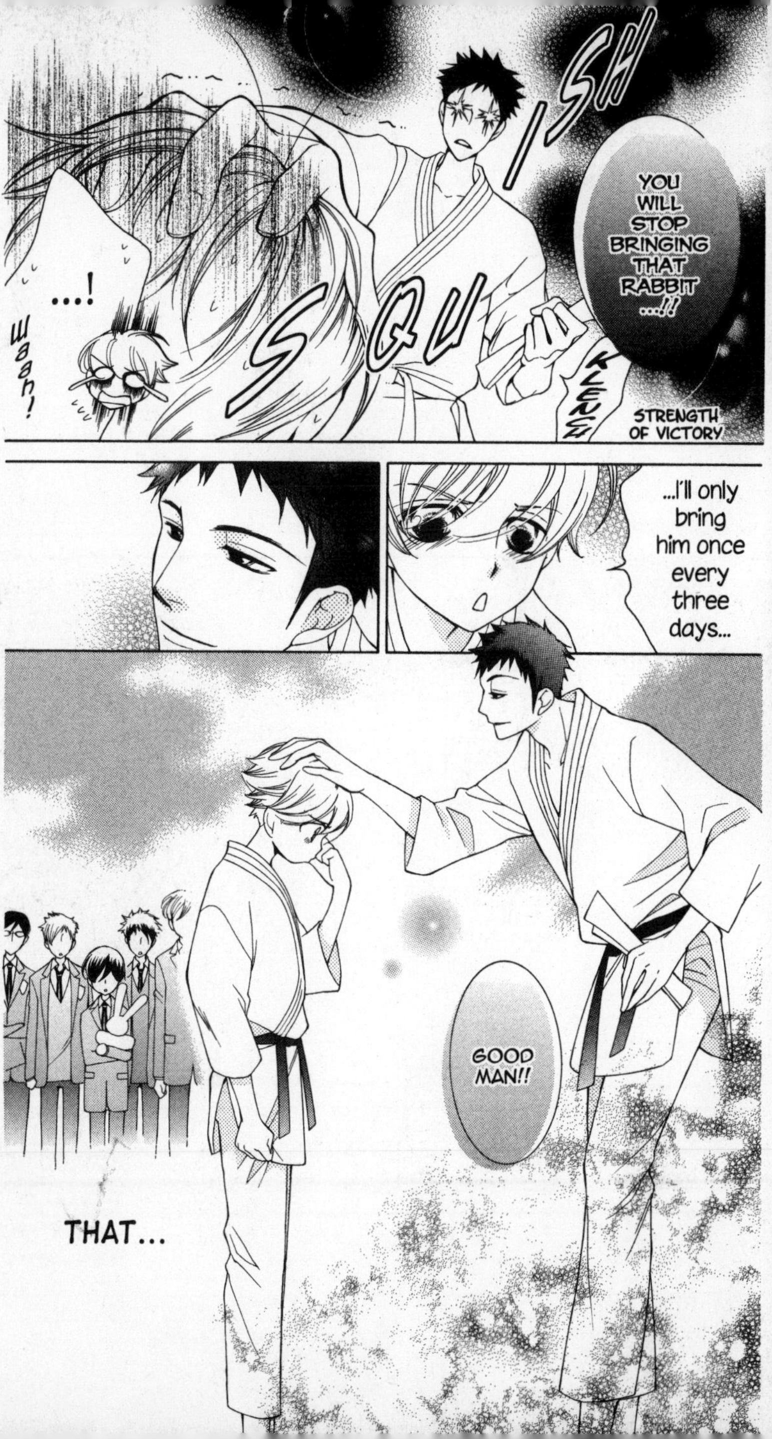
ISH
YOU WILL STOP BRINGING THAT RABBIT ...!!
KLENCH
STRENGTH OF VICTORY
SQU
...!
Waah!
...I'll only bring him once every three days...
GOOD MAN!!
THAT...

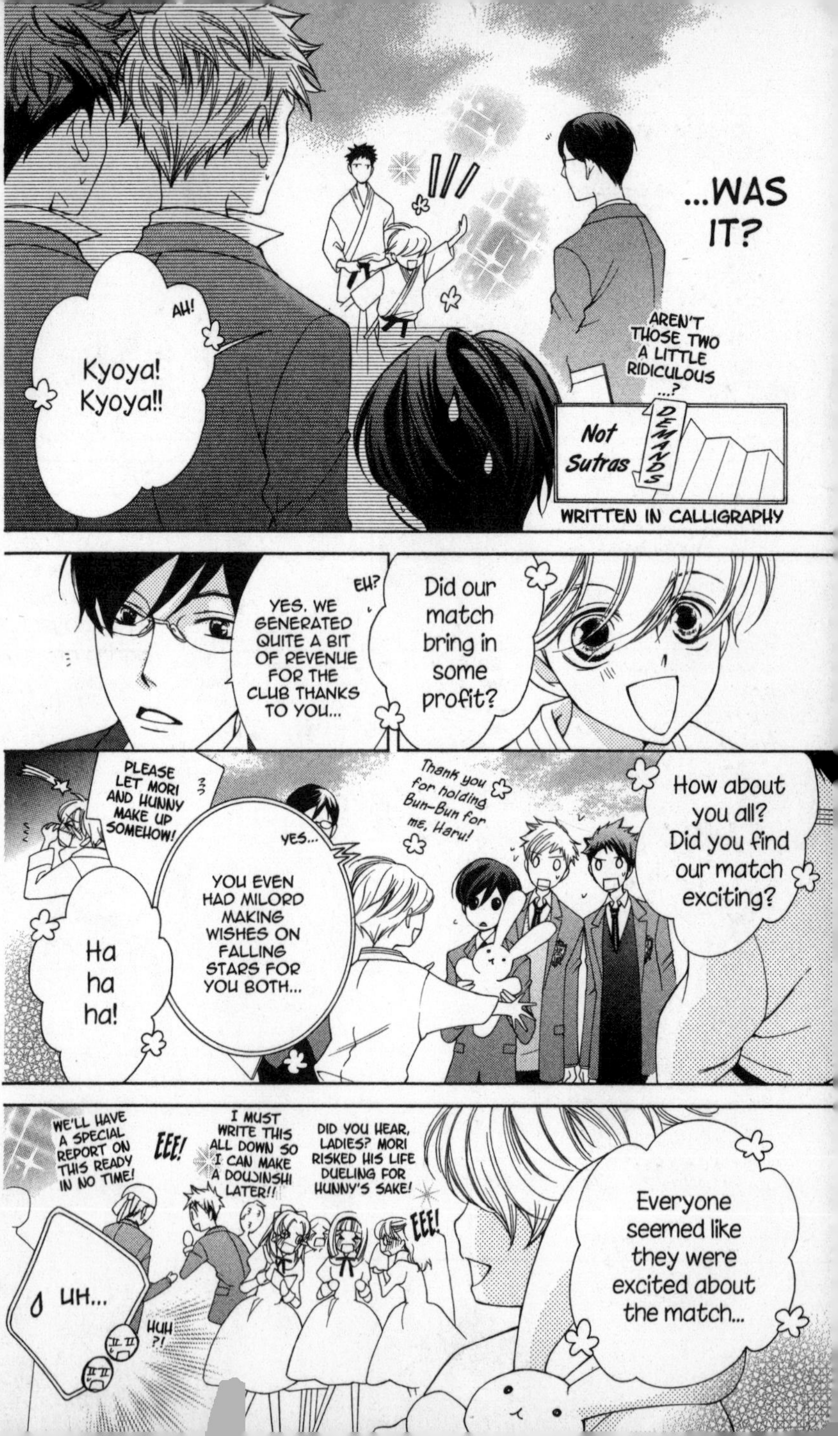
...WAS IT?
AREN'T THOSE TWO A LITTLE RIDICULOUS ...?
Not Sutras
DEMANDS
WRITTEN IN CALLIGRAPHY
AH!
Kyoya! Kyoya!!
Did our match bring in some profit?
EH?
YES. WE GENERATED QUITE A BIT OF REVENUE FOR THE CLUB THANKS TO YOU...
How about you all? Did you find our match exciting?
Thank you for holding Bun-Bun for me, Haru!
YES...
YOU EVEN HAD MILORD MAKING WISHES ON FALLING STARS FOR YOU BOTH...
PLEASE LET MORI AND HUNNY MAKE UP SOMEHOW!
Ha ha ha!
Everyone seemed like they were excited about the match...
EEE!
DID YOU HEAR, LADIES? MORI RISKED HIS LIFE DUELING FOR HUNNY'S SAKE!
I MUST WRITE THIS ALL DOWN SO I CAN MAKE A DOUJINSHI LATER!!
EEE!
WE'LL HAVE A SPECIAL REPORT ON THIS READY IN NO TIME!
HUH ?!
UH...

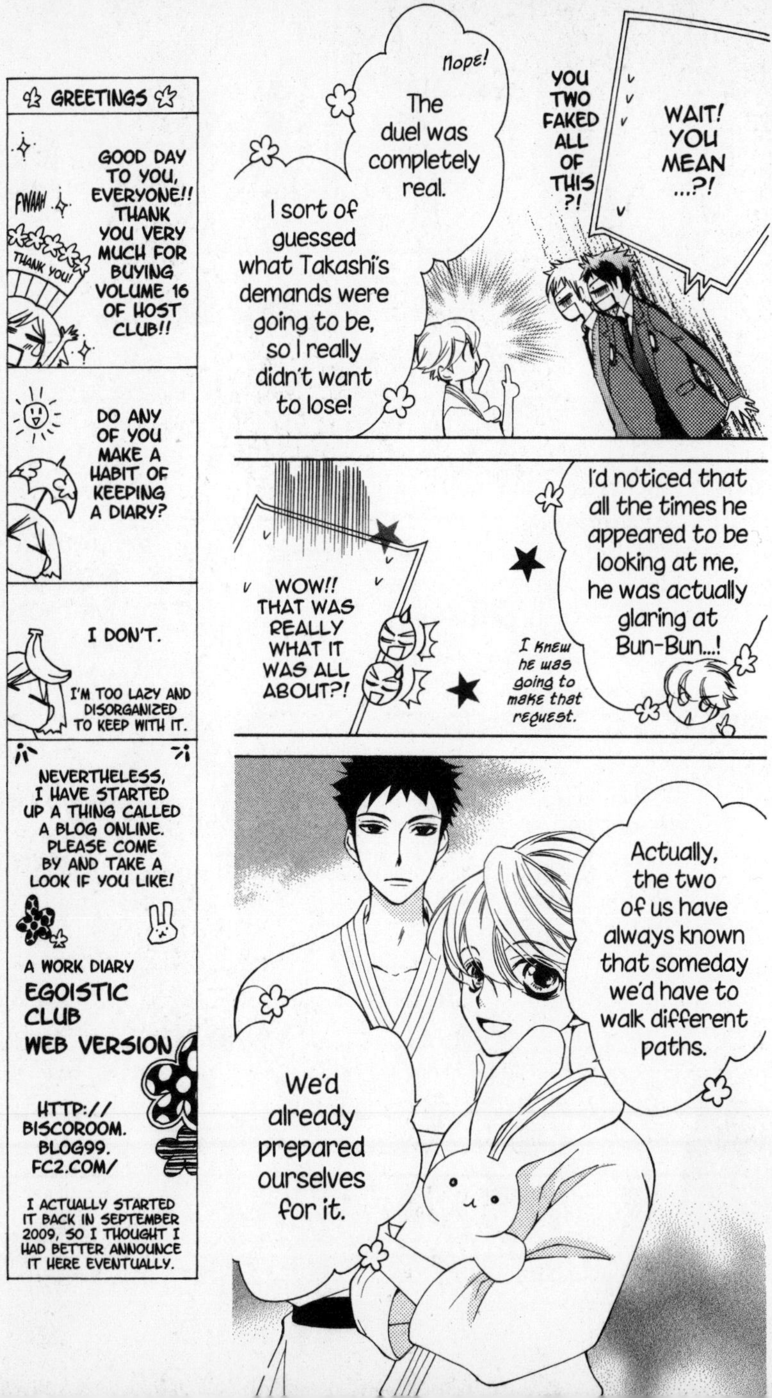
WAIT! YOU MEAN ...?!
YOU TWO FAKED ALL OF THIS?!
Nope!
The duel was completely real.
I sort of guessed what Takashi's demands were going to be, so I really didn't want to lose!
I'd noticed that all the times he appeared to be looking at me, he was actually glaring at Bun-Bun...!
I knew he was going to make that request.
WOW!! THAT WAS REALLY WHAT IT WAS ALL ABOUT?!
Actually, the two of us have always known that someday we'd have to walk different paths.
We'd already prepared ourselves for it.

GREETINGS

GOOD DAY TO YOU, EVERYONE!! THANK YOU VERY MUCH FOR BUYING VOLUME 16 OF HOST CLUB!!

FWAAH

THANK YOU!

DO ANY OF YOU MAKE A HABIT OF KEEPING A DIARY?

I DON'T.

I'M TOO LAZY AND DISORGANIZED TO KEEP WITH IT.

NEVERTHELESS, I HAVE STARTED UP A THING CALLED A BLOG ONLINE. PLEASE COME BY AND TAKE A LOOK IF YOU LIKE!

A WORK DIARY

EGOISTIC CLUB WEB VERSION

HTTP://BISCOROOM.BLOG99.FC2.COM/

I ACTUALLY STARTED IT BACK IN SEPTEMBER 2009, SO I THOUGHT I HAD BETTER ANNOUNCE IT HERE EVENTUALLY.

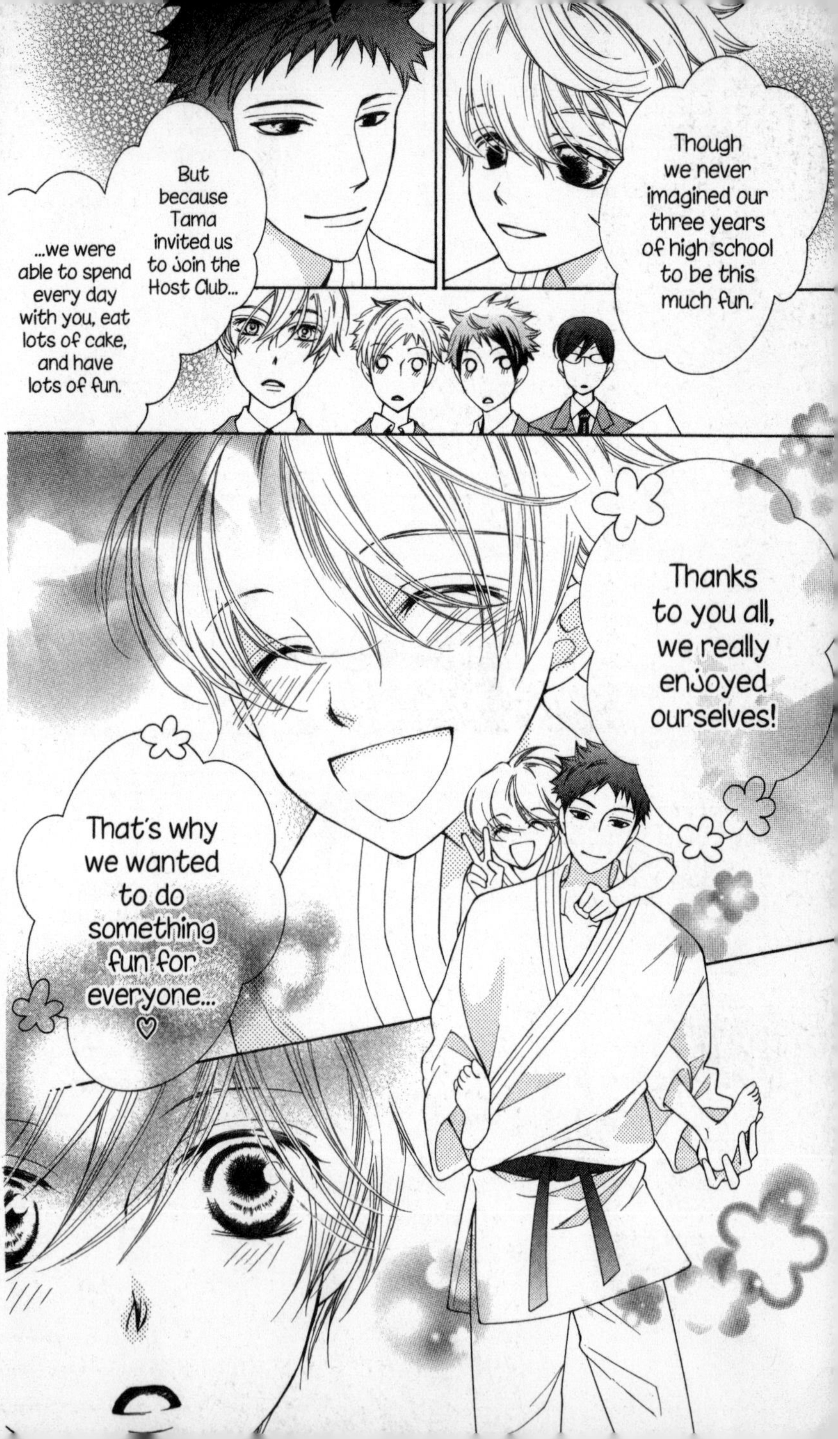

Though we never imagined our three years of high school to be this much fun.
But because Tama invited us to join the Host Club...
...we were able to spend every day with you, eat lots of cake, and have lots of fun.
Thanks to you all, we really enjoyed ourselves!
That's why we wanted to do something fun for everyone... ♡

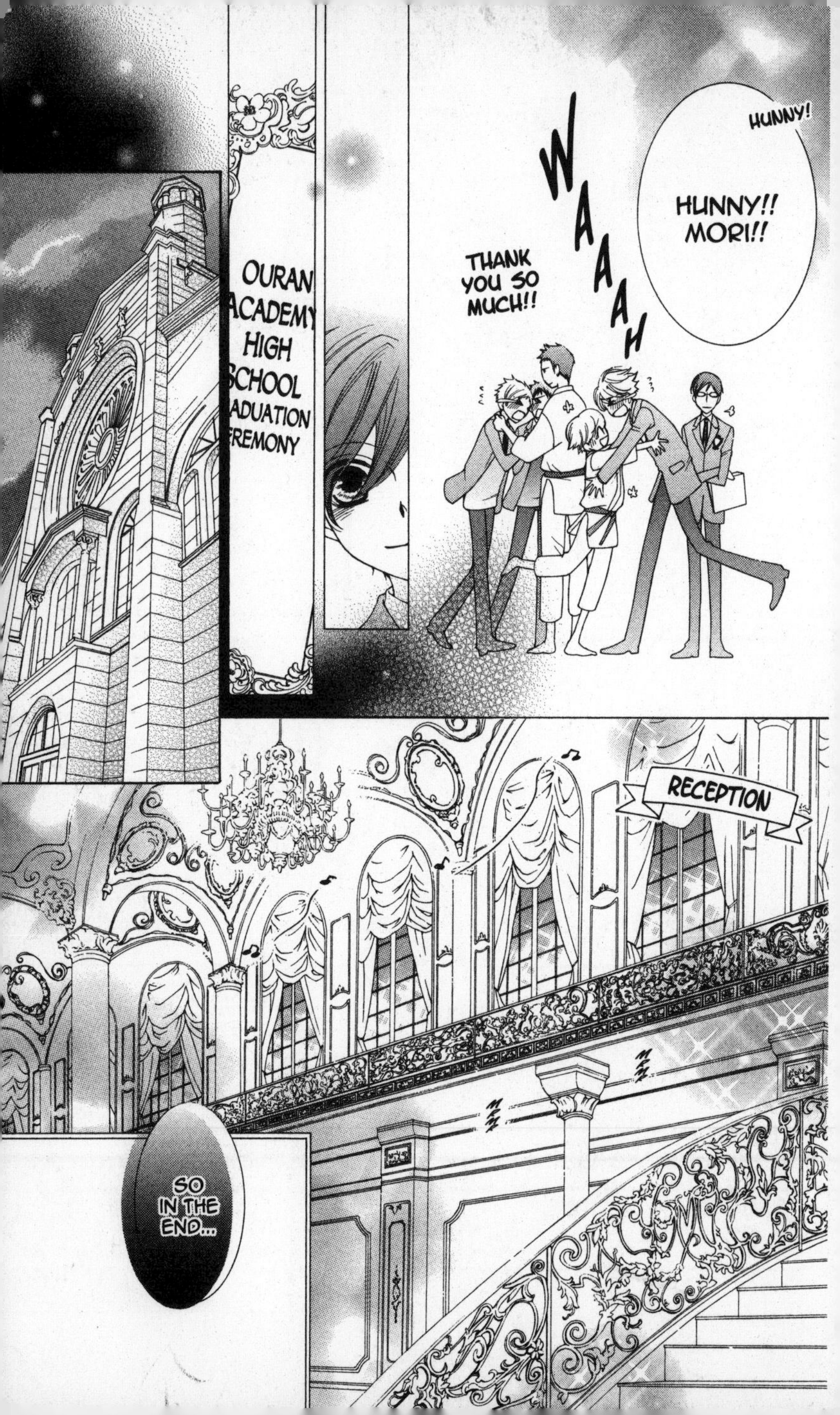
HUNNY!
HUNNY!! MORI!!
WAAAAH
THANK YOU SO MUCH!!
OURAN ACADEMY HIGH SCHOOL
ADUATION
EREMONY
RECEPTION
SO IN THE END...

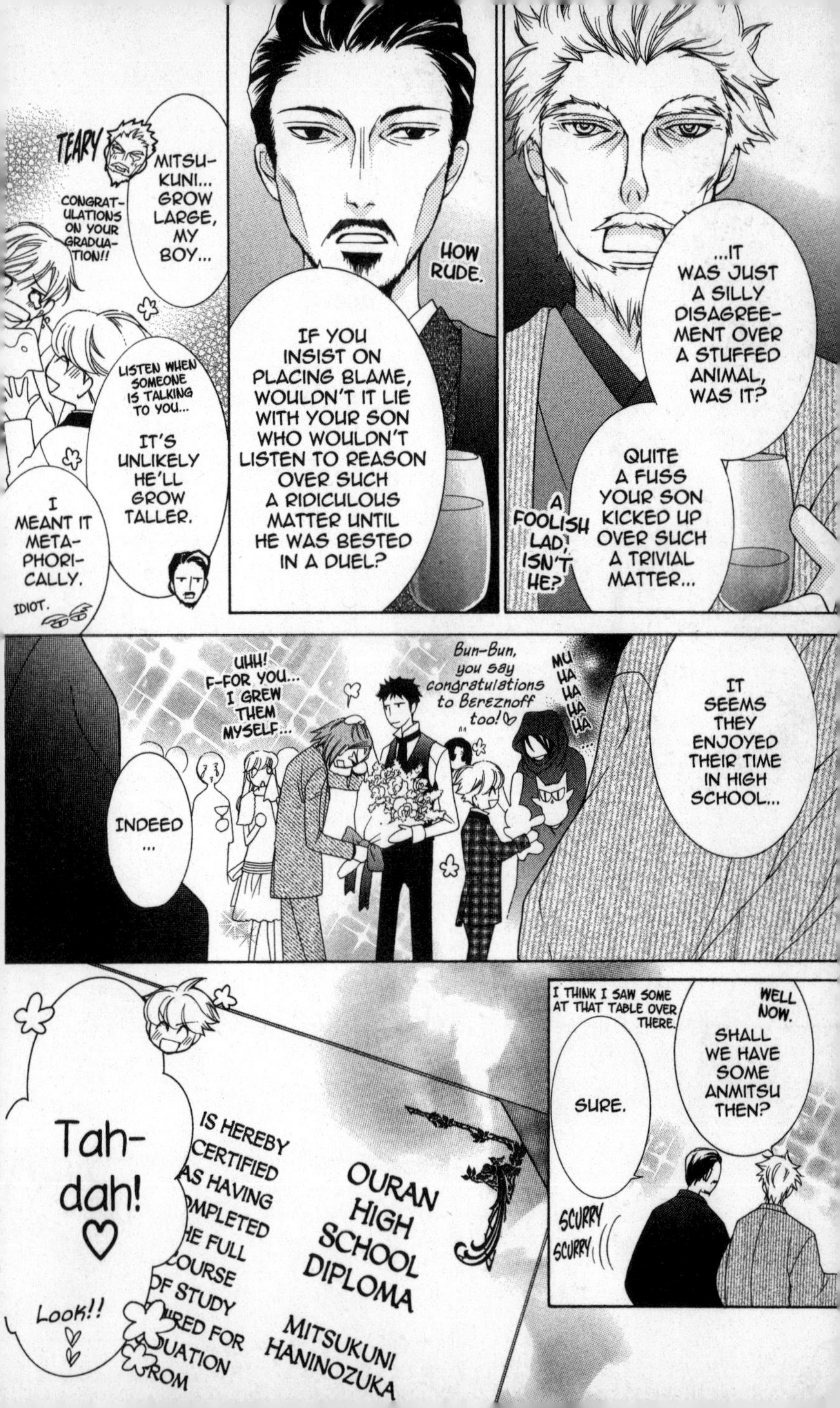
...IT WAS JUST A SILLY DISAGREEMENT OVER A STUFFED ANIMAL, WAS IT?
QUITE A FUSS YOUR SON KICKED UP OVER SUCH A TRIVIAL MATTER...
A FOOLISH LAD, ISN'T HE?
HOW RUDE.
IF YOU INSIST ON PLACING BLAME, WOULDN'T IT LIE WITH YOUR SON WHO WOULDN'T LISTEN TO REASON OVER SUCH A RIDICULOUS MATTER UNTIL HE WAS BESTED IN A DUEL?
TEARY
MITSUKUNI... GROW LARGE, MY BOY...
CONGRATULATIONS ON YOUR GRADUATION!!
LISTEN WHEN SOMEONE IS TALKING TO YOU...
IT'S UNLIKELY HE'LL GROW TALLER.
I MEANT IT METAPHORICALLY.
IDIOT.
IT SEEMS THEY ENJOYED THEIR TIME IN HIGH SCHOOL...
MU HA HA HA HA
Bun-Bun, you say congratulations to Bereznoff too!♡
UHH! F-FOR YOU... I GREW THEM MYSELF...
INDEED...
WELL NOW. SHALL WE HAVE SOME ANMITSU THEN?
I THINK I SAW SOME AT THAT TABLE OVER THERE.
SURE.
SCURRY SCURRY
Tah-dah! ♡
Look!! ♡
OURAN HIGH SCHOOL DIPLOMA
MITSUKUNI HANINOZUKA
IS HEREBY CERTIFIED AS HAVING OMPLETED HE FULL COURSE OF STUDY IRED FOR UATION ROM

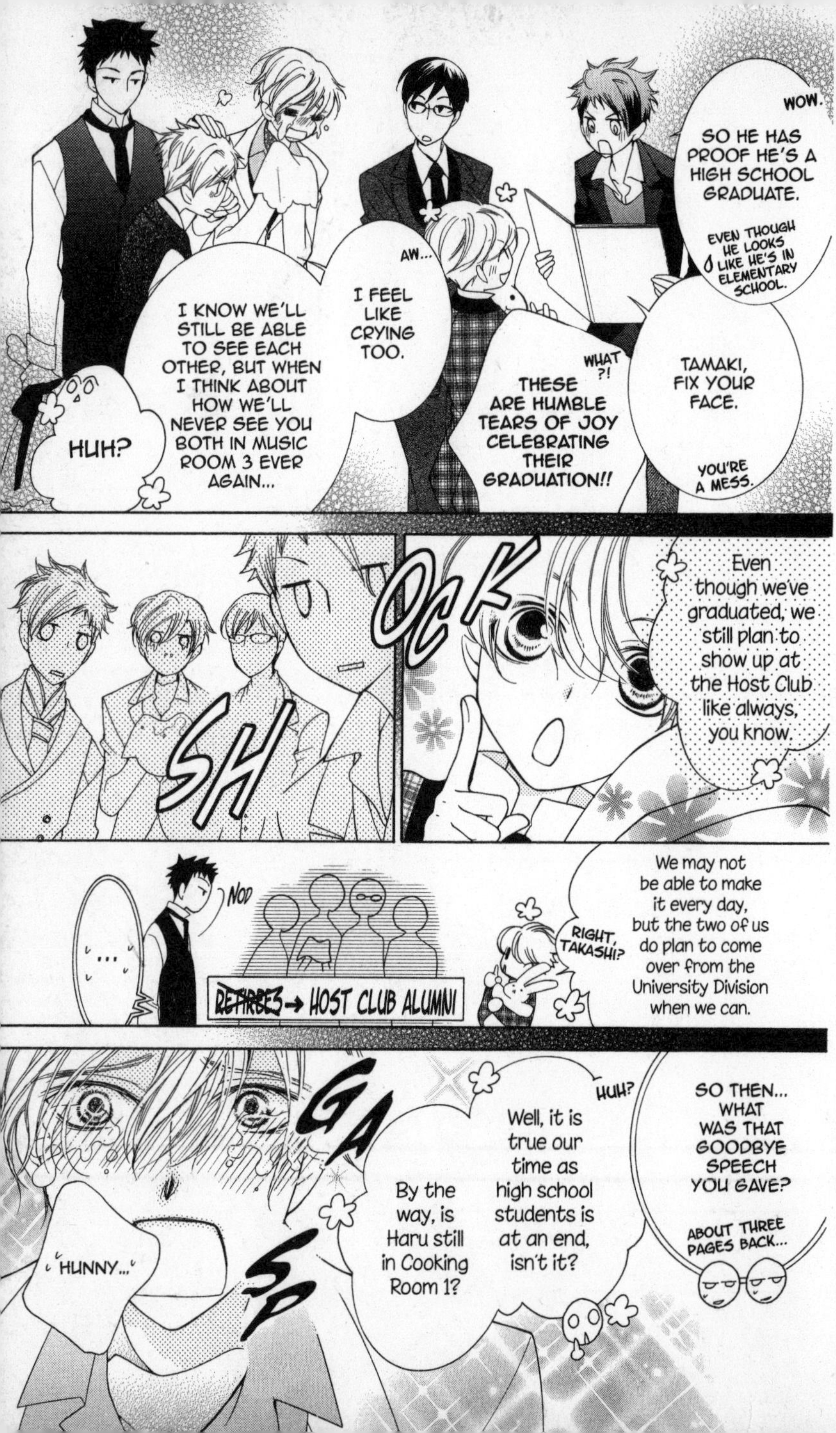
WOW.
SO HE HAS PROOF HE'S A HIGH SCHOOL GRADUATE.
EVEN THOUGH HE LOOKS LIKE HE'S IN ELEMENTARY SCHOOL.
TAMAKI, FIX YOUR FACE.
YOU'RE A MESS.
WHAT?!
THESE ARE HUMBLE TEARS OF JOY CELEBRATING THEIR GRADUATION!!
AW...
I FEEL LIKE CRYING TOO.
I KNOW WE'LL STILL BE ABLE TO SEE EACH OTHER, BUT WHEN I THINK ABOUT HOW WE'LL NEVER SEE YOU BOTH IN MUSIC ROOM 3 EVER AGAIN...
HUH?
Even though we've graduated, we still plan to show up at the Host Club like always, you know.
OCK
SH
We may not be able to make it every day, but the two of us do plan to come over from the University Division when we can.
RIGHT, TAKASHI?
NOD
...
~~RETIREES~~ → HOST CLUB ALUMNI
SO THEN... WHAT WAS THAT GOODBYE SPEECH YOU GAVE?
ABOUT THREE PAGES BACK...
HUH?
Well, it is true our time as high school students is at an end, isn't it?
By the way, is Haru still in Cooking Room 1?
GA
SP
"HUNNY..."

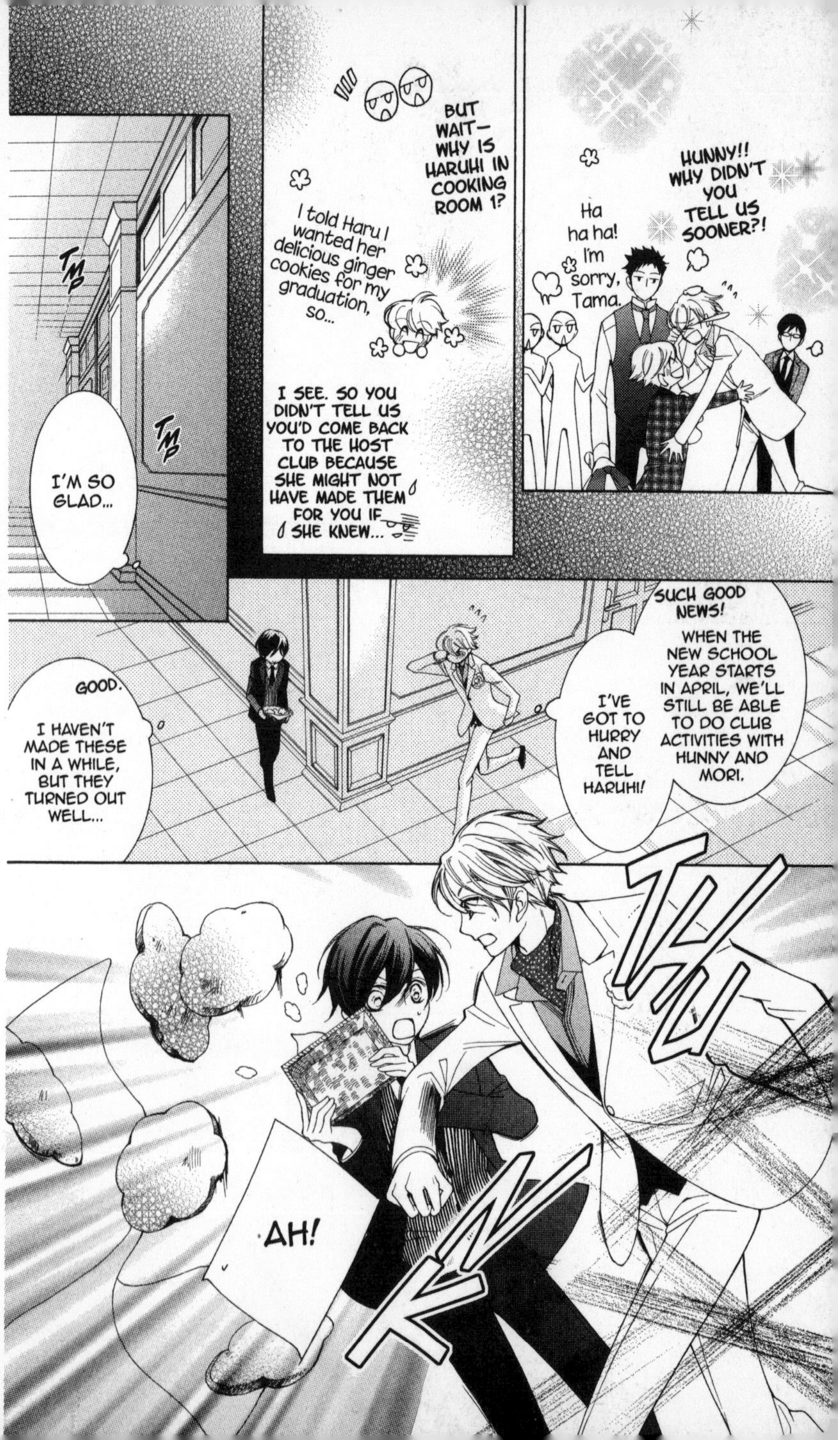
HUNNY!! WHY DIDN'T YOU TELL US SOONER?!
Ha ha ha! I'm sorry, Tama.
BUT WAIT— WHY IS HARUHI IN COOKING ROOM 1?
I told Haru I wanted her delicious ginger cookies for my graduation, so...
I SEE. SO YOU DIDN'T TELL US YOU'D COME BACK TO THE HOST CLUB BECAUSE SHE MIGHT NOT HAVE MADE THEM FOR YOU IF SHE KNEW...
TMP
TMP
I'M SO GLAD...
SUCH GOOD NEWS!
WHEN THE NEW SCHOOL YEAR STARTS IN APRIL, WE'LL STILL BE ABLE TO DO CLUB ACTIVITIES WITH HUNNY AND MORI.
I'VE GOT TO HURRY AND TELL HARUHI!
GOOD.
I HAVEN'T MADE THESE IN A WHILE, BUT THEY TURNED OUT WELL...
THUNK
AH!

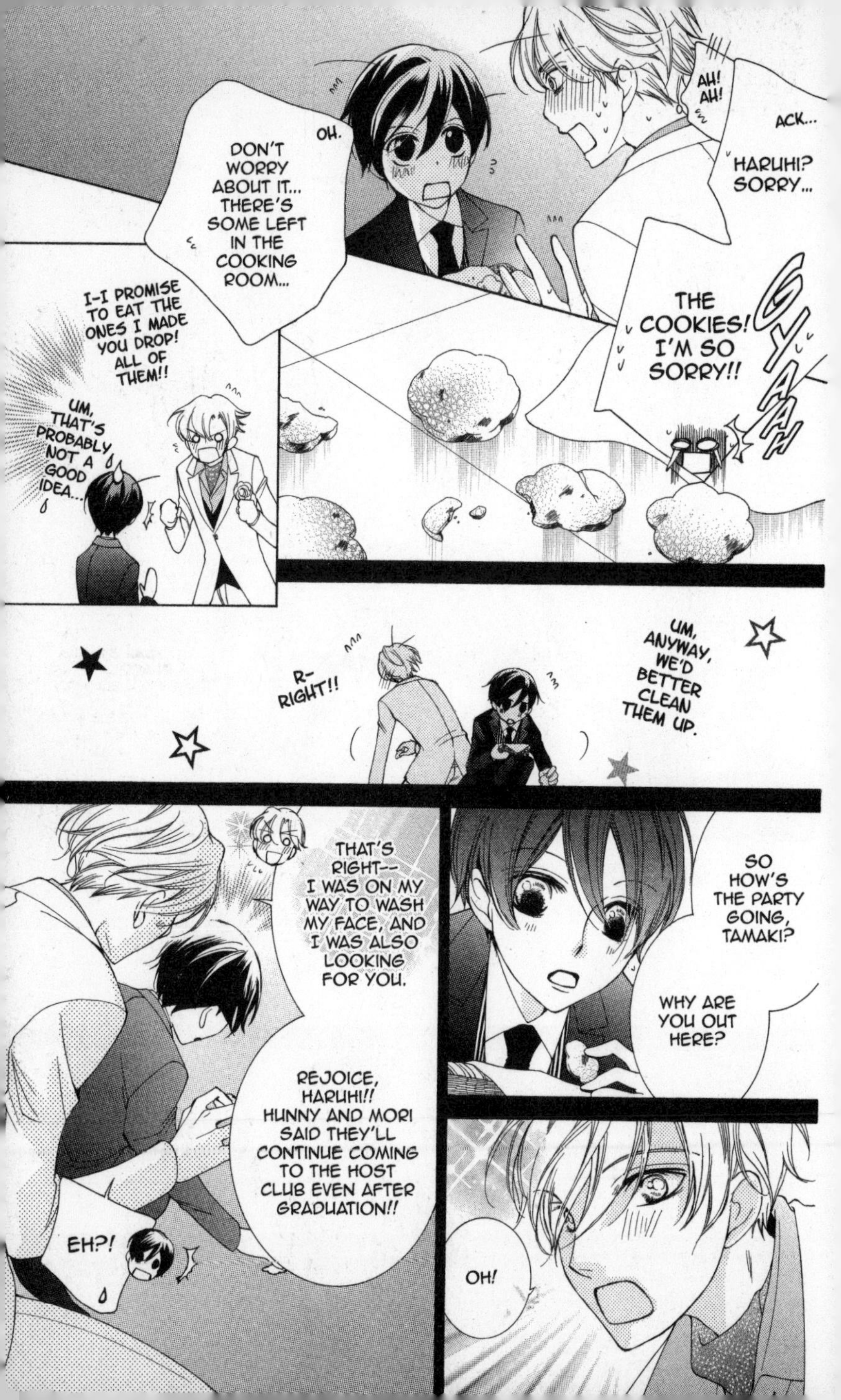
AH! AH!
ACK...
HARUHI? SORRY...
GYAAAH
THE COOKIES! I'M SO SORRY!!
OH.
DON'T WORRY ABOUT IT... THERE'S SOME LEFT IN THE COOKING ROOM...
I-I PROMISE TO EAT THE ONES I MADE YOU DROP! ALL OF THEM!!
UM, THAT'S PROBABLY NOT A GOOD IDEA...
UM, ANYWAY, WE'D BETTER CLEAN THEM UP.
R-RIGHT!!
SO HOW'S THE PARTY GOING, TAMAKI?
WHY ARE YOU OUT HERE?
OH!
THAT'S RIGHT-- I WAS ON MY WAY TO WASH MY FACE, AND I WAS ALSO LOOKING FOR YOU.
REJOICE, HARUHI!! HUNNY AND MORI SAID THEY'LL CONTINUE COMING TO THE HOST CLUB EVEN AFTER GRADUATION!!
EH?!

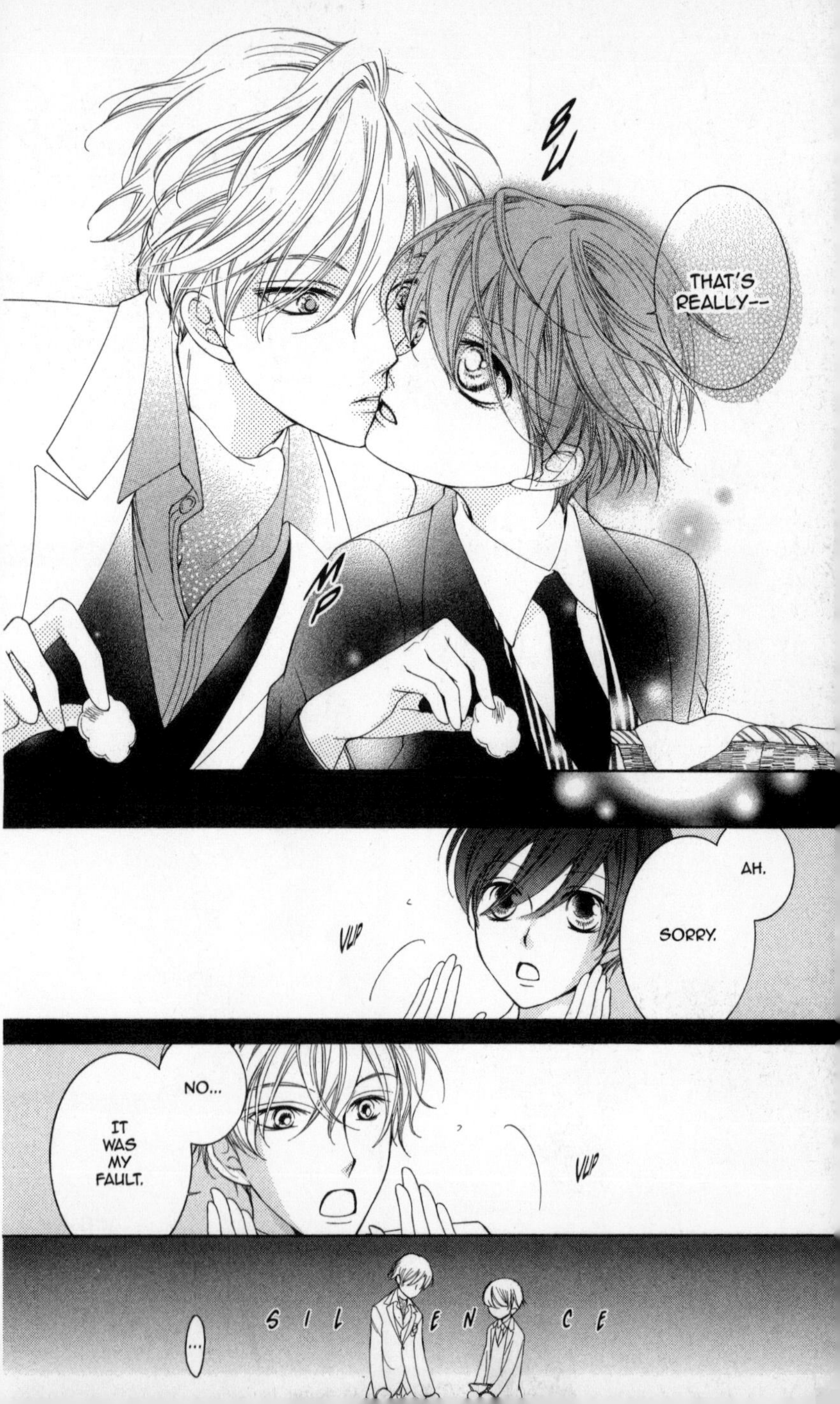

BU
THAT'S REALLY--
MP
AH.
SORRY.
VUP
NO...
IT WAS MY FAULT.
VUP
...
SILENCE

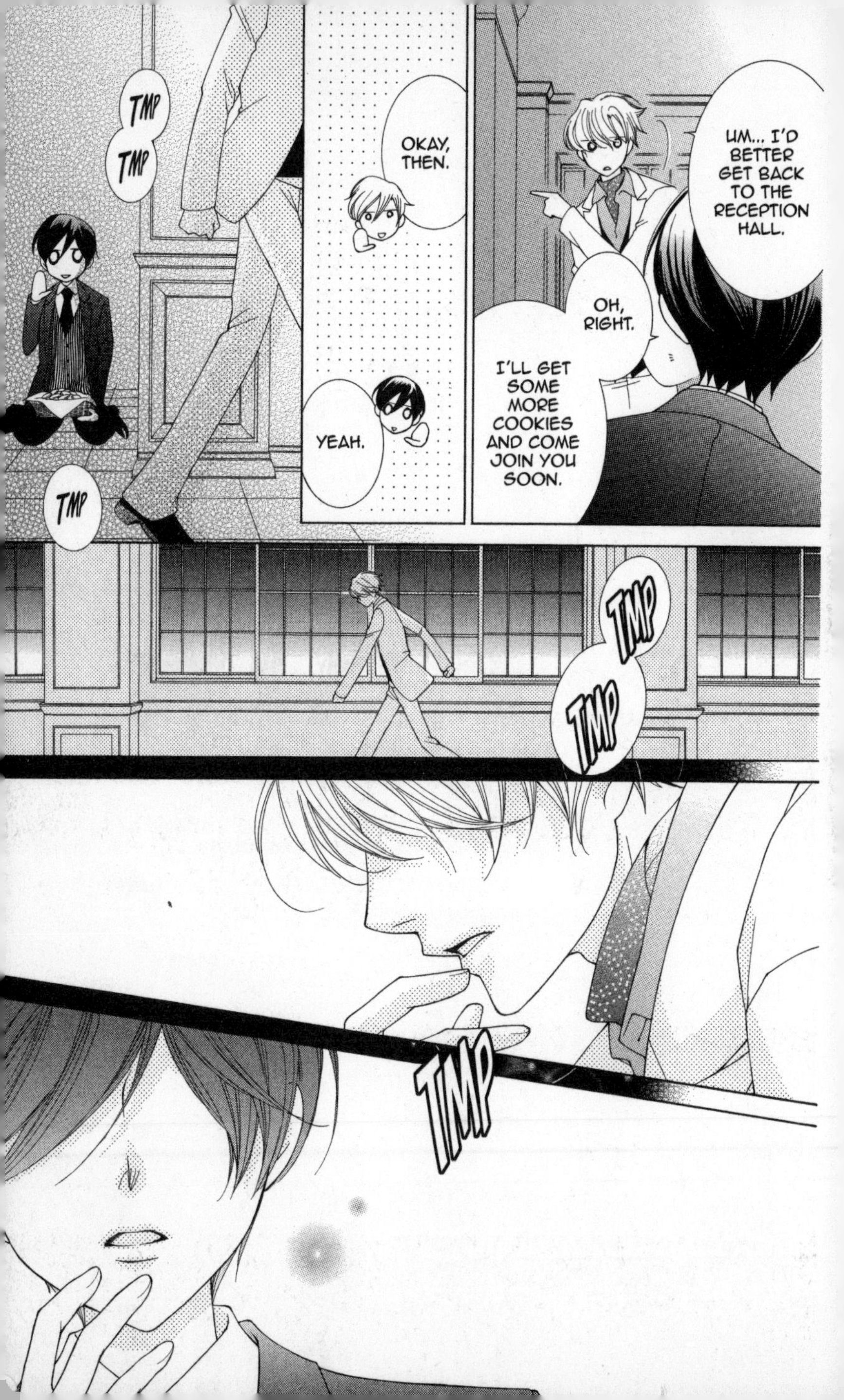
UM... I'D BETTER GET BACK TO THE RECEPTION HALL.
OH, RIGHT.
I'LL GET SOME MORE COOKIES AND COME JOIN YOU SOON.
OKAY, THEN.
YEAH.
TMP
TMP
TMP
TMP
TMP
TMP

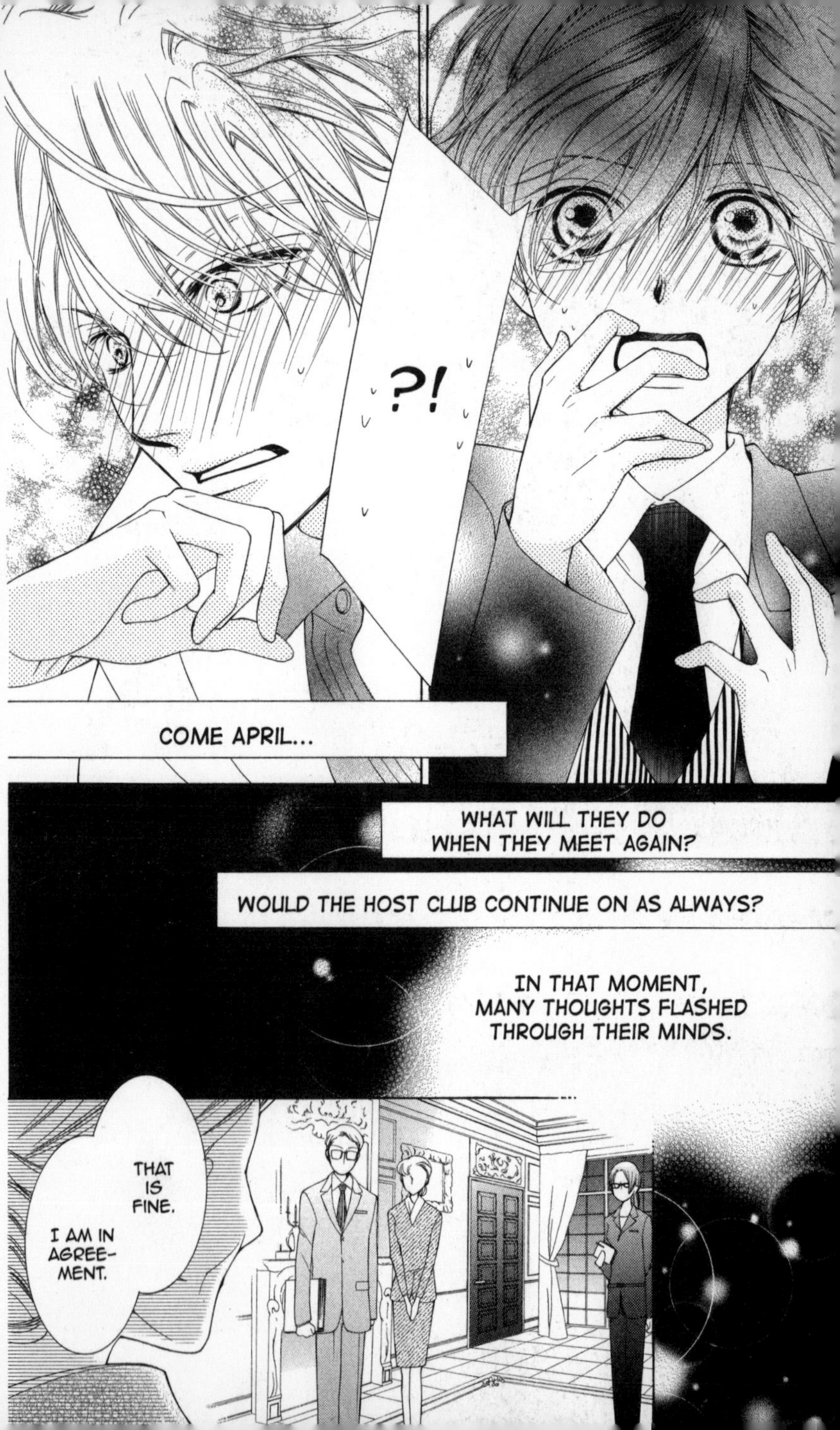
?!
COME APRIL...
WHAT WILL THEY DO WHEN THEY MEET AGAIN?
WOULD THE HOST CLUB CONTINUE ON AS ALWAYS?
IN THAT MOMENT, MANY THOUGHTS FLASHED THROUGH THEIR MINDS.
THAT IS FINE.
I AM IN AGREE-MENT.

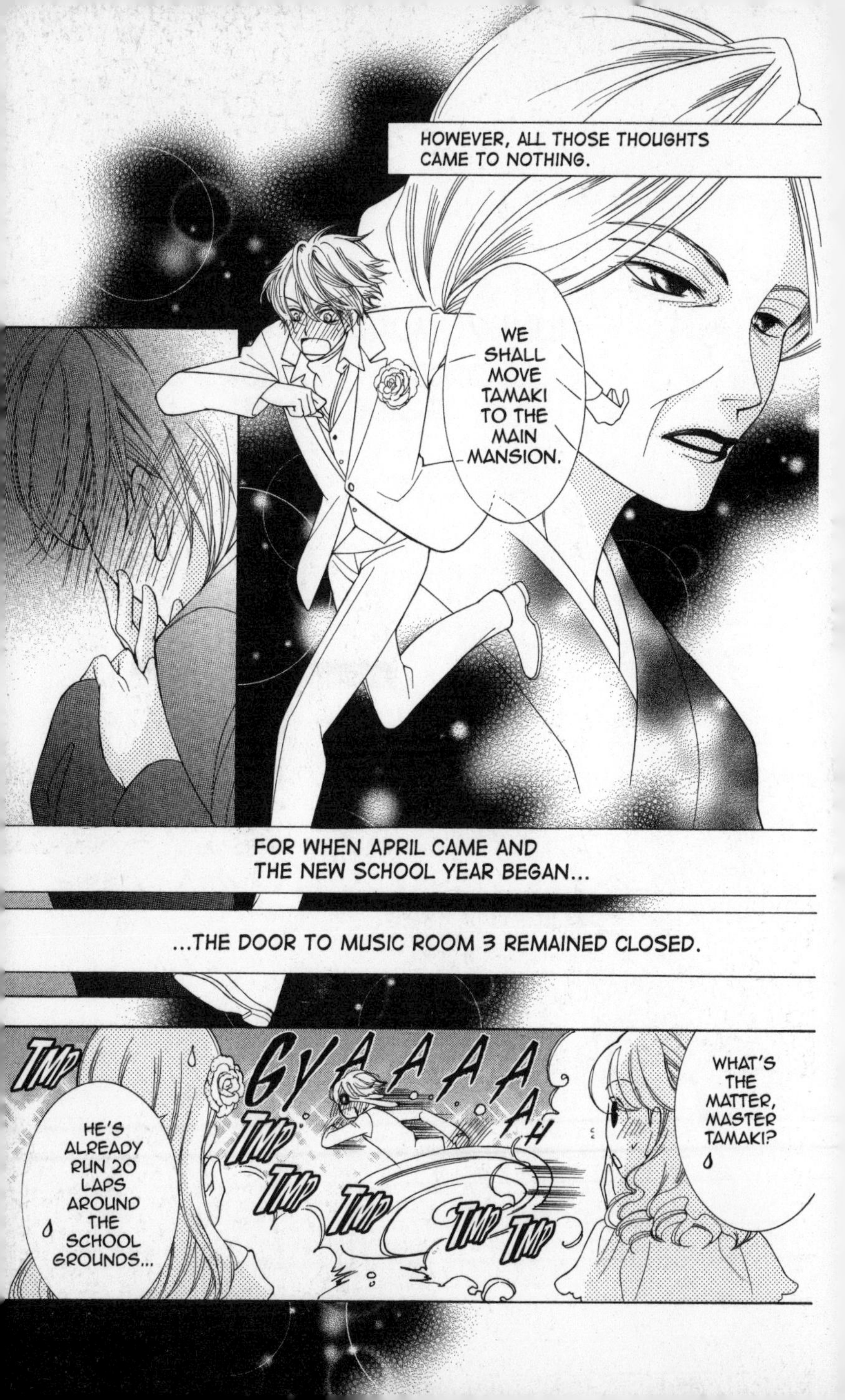

HOWEVER, ALL THOSE THOUGHTS CAME TO NOTHING.
WE SHALL MOVE TAMAKI TO THE MAIN MANSION.
FOR WHEN APRIL CAME AND THE NEW SCHOOL YEAR BEGAN...
...THE DOOR TO MUSIC ROOM 3 REMAINED CLOSED.
WHAT'S THE MATTER, MASTER TAMAKI?
GYAAAAAH
TMP TMP TMP TMP TMP TMP TMP
HE'S ALREADY RUN 20 LAPS AROUND THE SCHOOL GROUNDS...

GUEST ROOM: FAXES

SPECIAL THANKS TO EMIKO NAKANO!! (2ND TIME!)

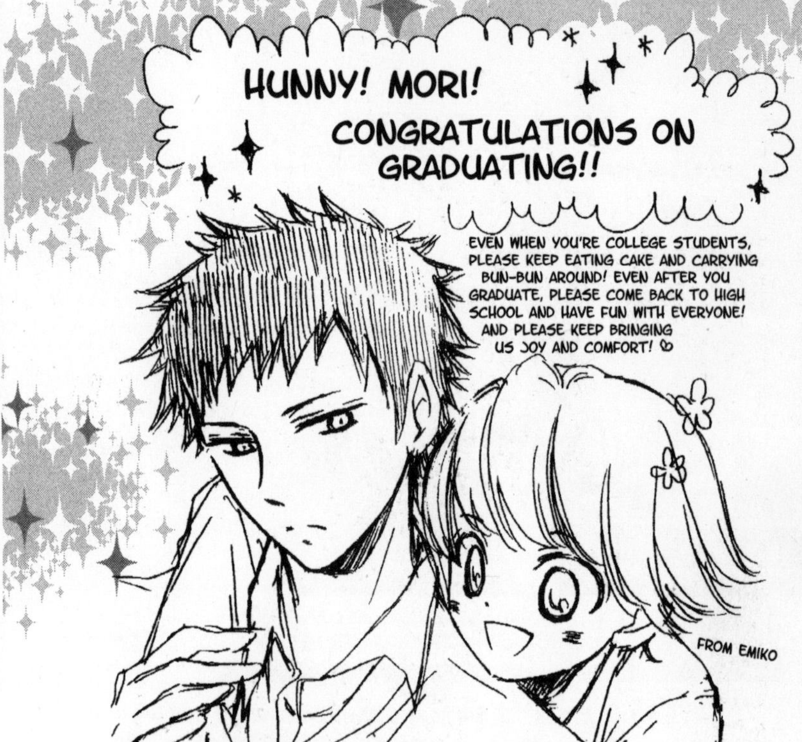

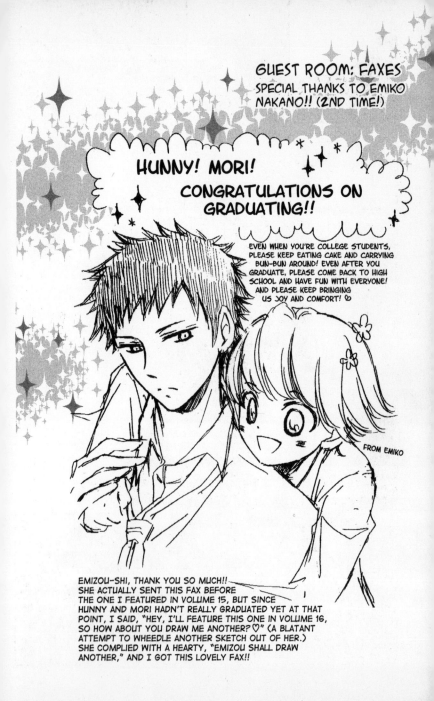

HUNNY! MORI! CONGRATULATIONS ON GRADUATING!!
EVEN WHEN YOU'RE COLLEGE STUDENTS, PLEASE KEEP EATING CAKE AND CARRYING BUN-BUN AROUND! EVEN AFTER YOU GRADUATE, PLEASE COME BACK TO HIGH SCHOOL AND HAVE FUN WITH EVERYONE! AND PLEASE KEEP BRINGING US JOY AND COMFORT! ♡
FROM EMIKO

EMIZOU-SHI, THANK YOU SO MUCH!! SHE ACTUALLY SENT THIS FAX BEFORE THE ONE I FEATURED IN VOLUME 15, BUT SINCE HUNNY AND MORI HADN'T REALLY GRADUATED YET AT THAT POINT, I SAID, "HEY, I'LL FEATURE THIS ONE IN VOLUME 16, SO HOW ABOUT YOU DRAW ME ANOTHER? ♡" (A BLATANT ATTEMPT TO WHEEDLE ANOTHER SKETCH OUT OF HER.) SHE COMPLIED WITH A HEARTY, "EMIZOU SHALL DRAW ANOTHER," AND I GOT THIS LOVELY FAX!!

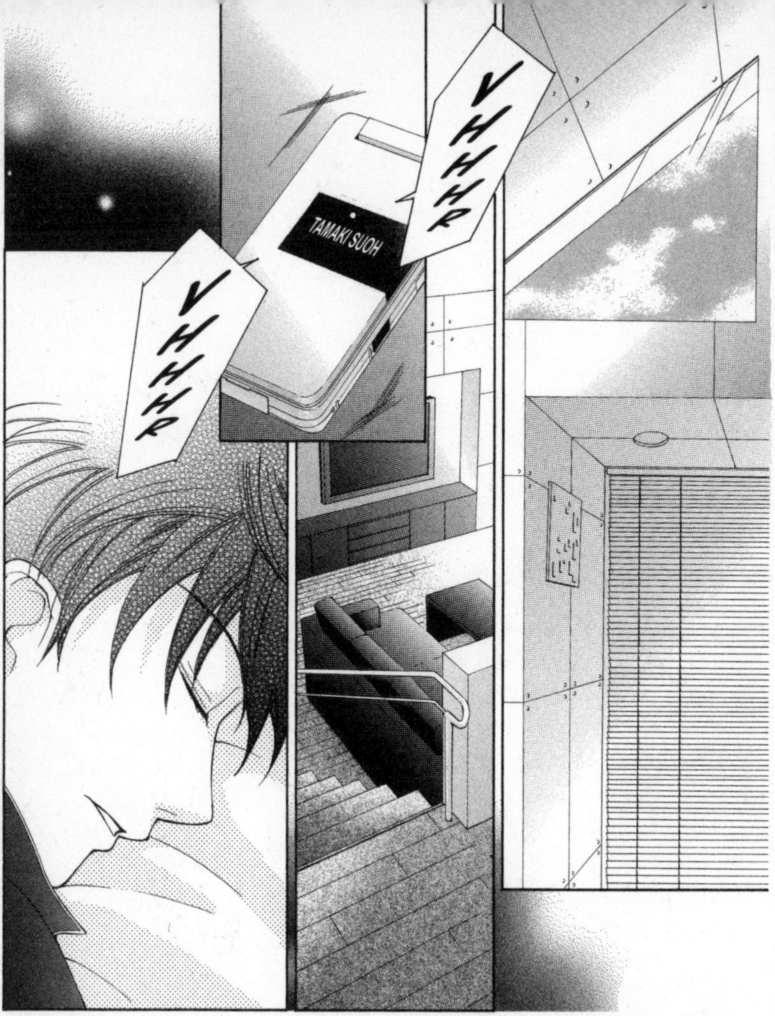
VHHHHR
TAMAKI SUOH
VHHHHR

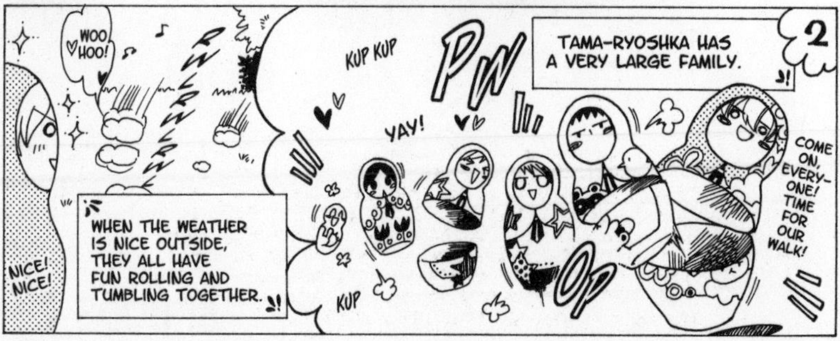
2
TAMA-RYOSHKA HAS A VERY LARGE FAMILY.
COME ON, EVERYONE! TIME FOR OUR WALK!
PW
YAY!
KUP KUP
KUP
WHEN THE WEATHER IS NICE OUTSIDE, THEY ALL HAVE FUN ROLLING AND TUMBLING TOGETHER.
WOO HOO!
NICE! NICE!

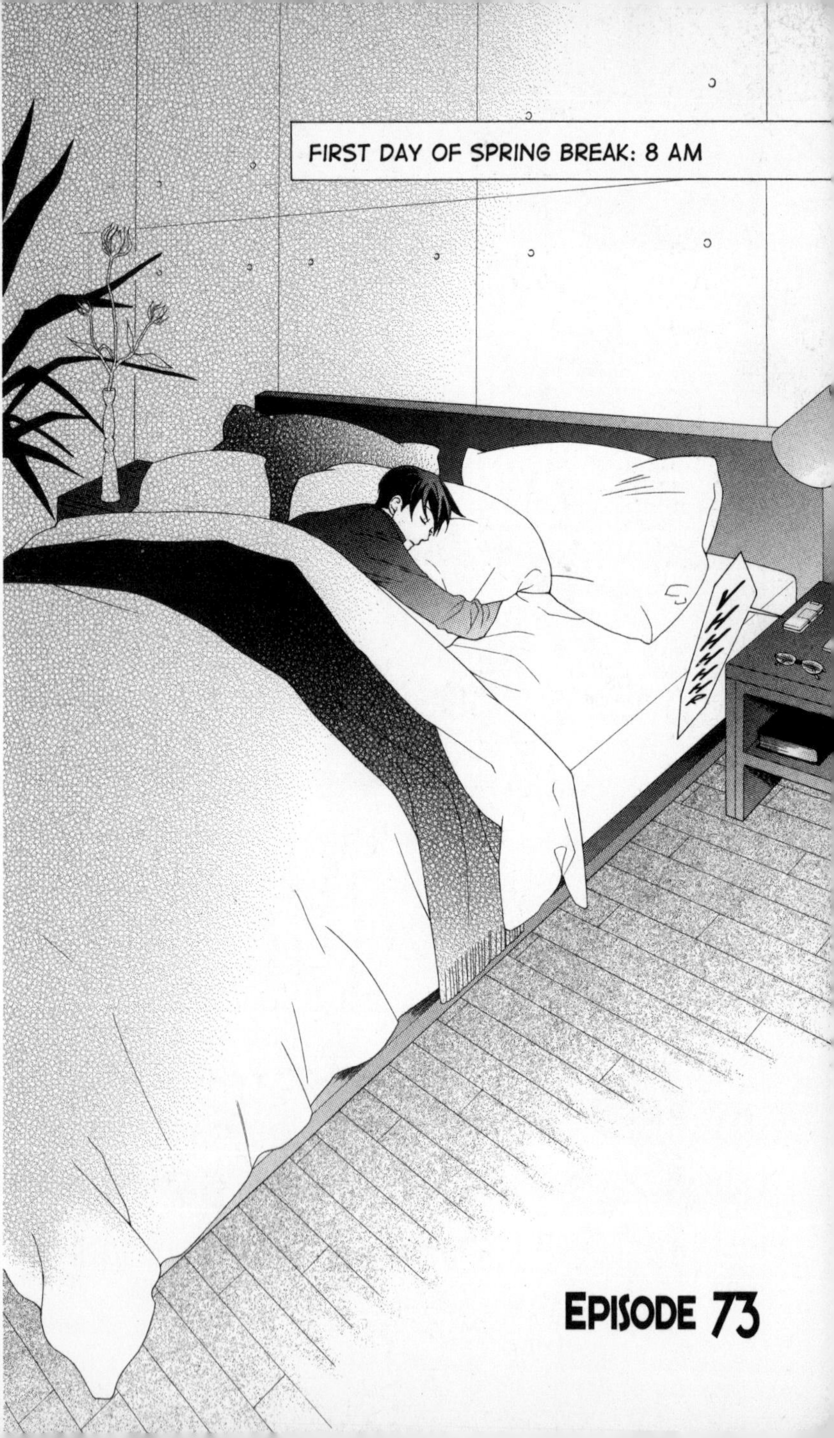
FIRST DAY OF SPRING BREAK: 8 AM
VHHHHHR
EPISODE 73

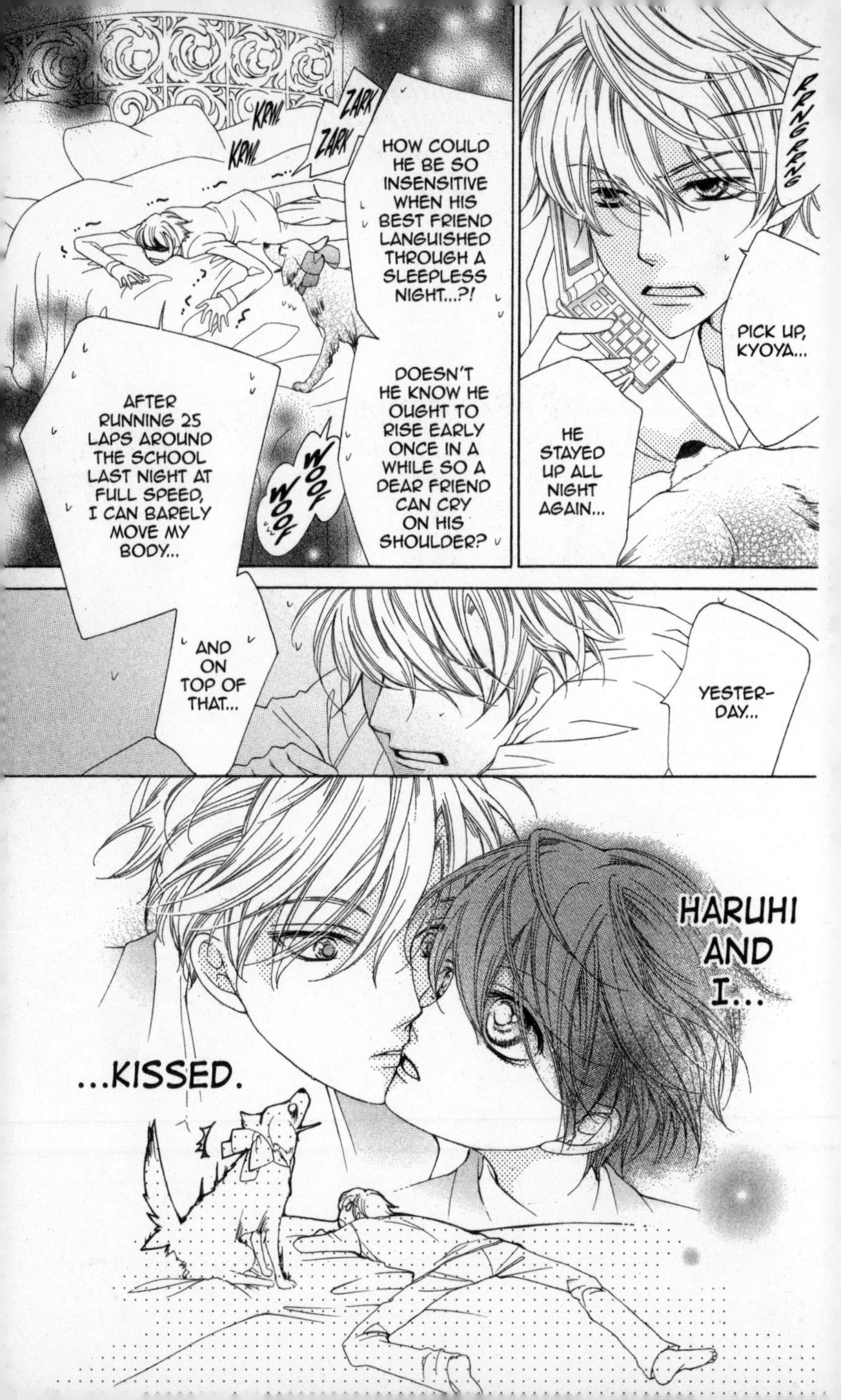
RRNG RRNG
PICK UP, KYOYA...
HE STAYED UP ALL NIGHT AGAIN...
ZARK ZARK
KRWL KRWL
HOW COULD HE BE SO INSENSITIVE WHEN HIS BEST FRIEND LANGUISHED THROUGH A SLEEPLESS NIGHT...?!
DOESN'T HE KNOW HE OUGHT TO RISE EARLY ONCE IN A WHILE SO A DEAR FRIEND CAN CRY ON HIS SHOULDER?
WOOF WOOF
AFTER RUNNING 25 LAPS AROUND THE SCHOOL LAST NIGHT AT FULL SPEED, I CAN BARELY MOVE MY BODY...
YESTER-DAY...
AND ON TOP OF THAT...
HARUHI AND I...
...KISSED.

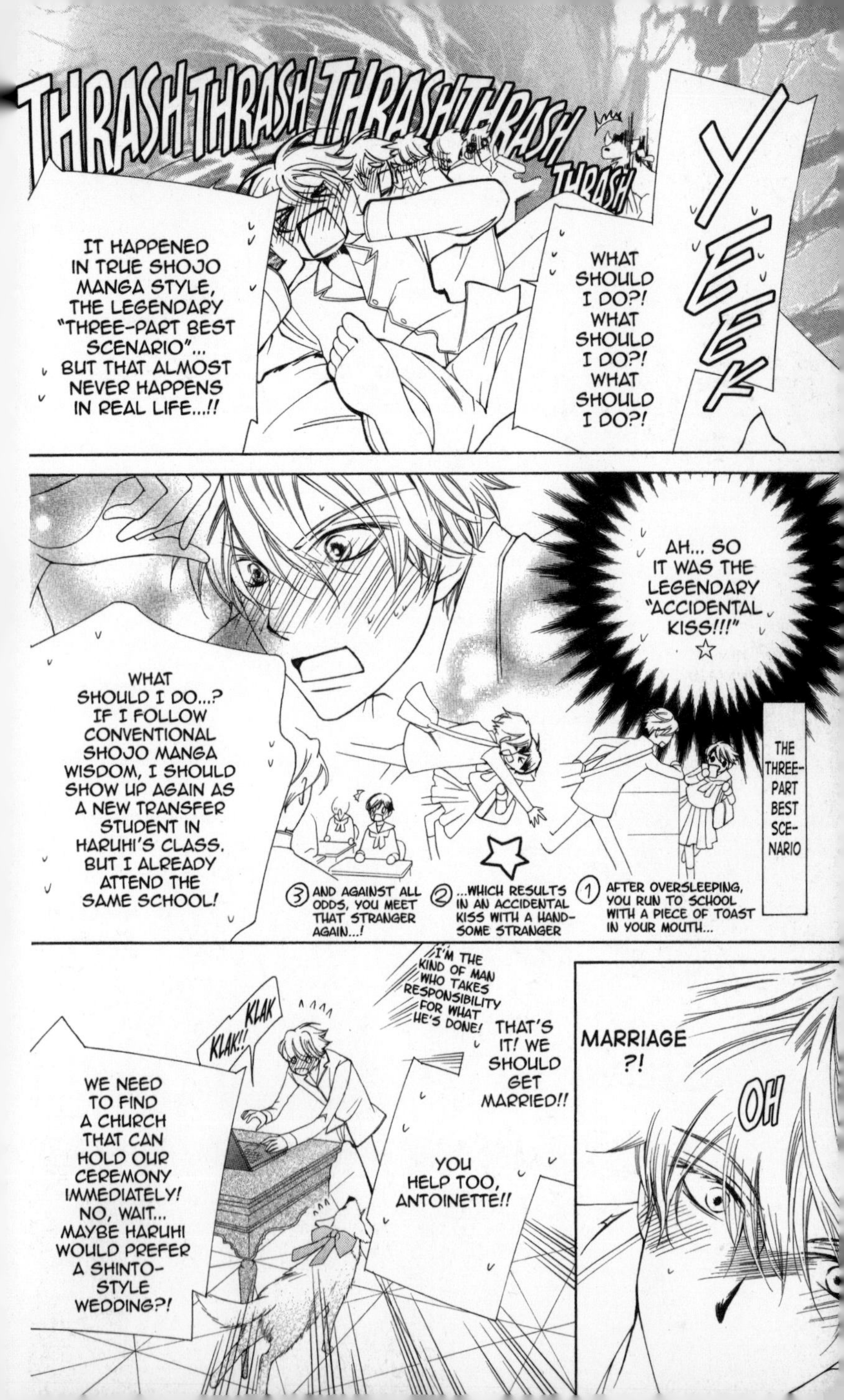
YEEEK
THRASH THRASH THRASH THRASH THRASH
WHAT SHOULD I DO?! WHAT SHOULD I DO?! WHAT SHOULD I DO?!
IT HAPPENED IN TRUE SHOJO MANGA STYLE, THE LEGENDARY "THREE-PART BEST SCENARIO"... BUT THAT ALMOST NEVER HAPPENS IN REAL LIFE...!!
AH... SO IT WAS THE LEGENDARY "ACCIDENTAL KISS!!!" ☆
THE THREE-PART BEST SCENARIO
① AFTER OVERSLEEPING, YOU RUN TO SCHOOL WITH A PIECE OF TOAST IN YOUR MOUTH...
② ...WHICH RESULTS IN AN ACCIDENTAL KISS WITH A HANDSOME STRANGER
③ AND AGAINST ALL ODDS, YOU MEET THAT STRANGER AGAIN...!
WHAT SHOULD I DO...? IF I FOLLOW CONVENTIONAL SHOJO MANGA WISDOM, I SHOULD SHOW UP AGAIN AS A NEW TRANSFER STUDENT IN HARUHI'S CLASS. BUT I ALREADY ATTEND THE SAME SCHOOL!
MARRIAGE?!
OH
I'M THE KIND OF MAN WHO TAKES RESPONSIBILITY FOR WHAT HE'S DONE!
THAT'S IT! WE SHOULD GET MARRIED!!
KLAK KLAK!!
YOU HELP TOO, ANTOINETTE!!
WE NEED TO FIND A CHURCH THAT CAN HOLD OUR CEREMONY IMMEDIATELY! NO, WAIT... MAYBE HARUHI WOULD PREFER A SHINTO-STYLE WEDDING?!

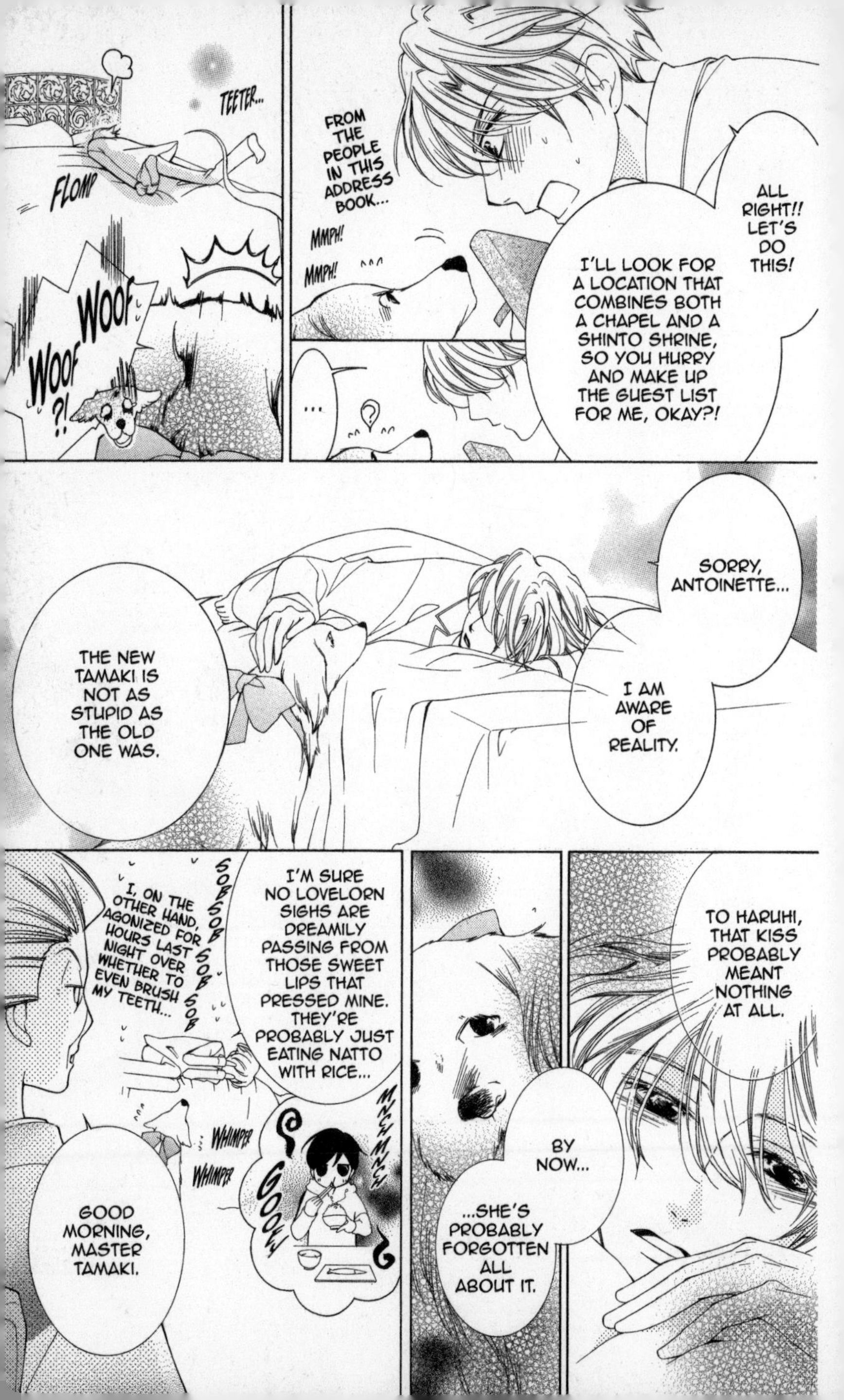
ALL RIGHT!! LET'S DO THIS!
FROM THE PEOPLE IN THIS ADDRESS BOOK...
MMPH!
MMPH!
I'LL LOOK FOR A LOCATION THAT COMBINES BOTH A CHAPEL AND A SHINTO SHRINE, SO YOU HURRY AND MAKE UP THE GUEST LIST FOR ME, OKAY?!
...
TEETER...
FLOMP
WOOF
WOOF
?!
SORRY, ANTOINETTE...
I AM AWARE OF REALITY.
THE NEW TAMAKI IS NOT AS STUPID AS THE OLD ONE WAS.
TO HARUHI, THAT KISS PROBABLY MEANT NOTHING AT ALL.
BY NOW...
...SHE'S PROBABLY FORGOTTEN ALL ABOUT IT.
I'M SURE NO LOVELORN SIGHS ARE DREAMILY PASSING FROM THOSE SWEET LIPS THAT PRESSED MINE. THEY'RE PROBABLY JUST EATING NATTO WITH RICE...
MNCH MNCH
GOOOH
SOB SOB SOB SOB SOB
I, ON THE OTHER HAND, AGONIZED FOR HOURS LAST NIGHT OVER WHETHER TO EVEN BRUSH MY TEETH...
WHIMPER
WHIMPER
GOOD MORNING, MASTER TAMAKI.

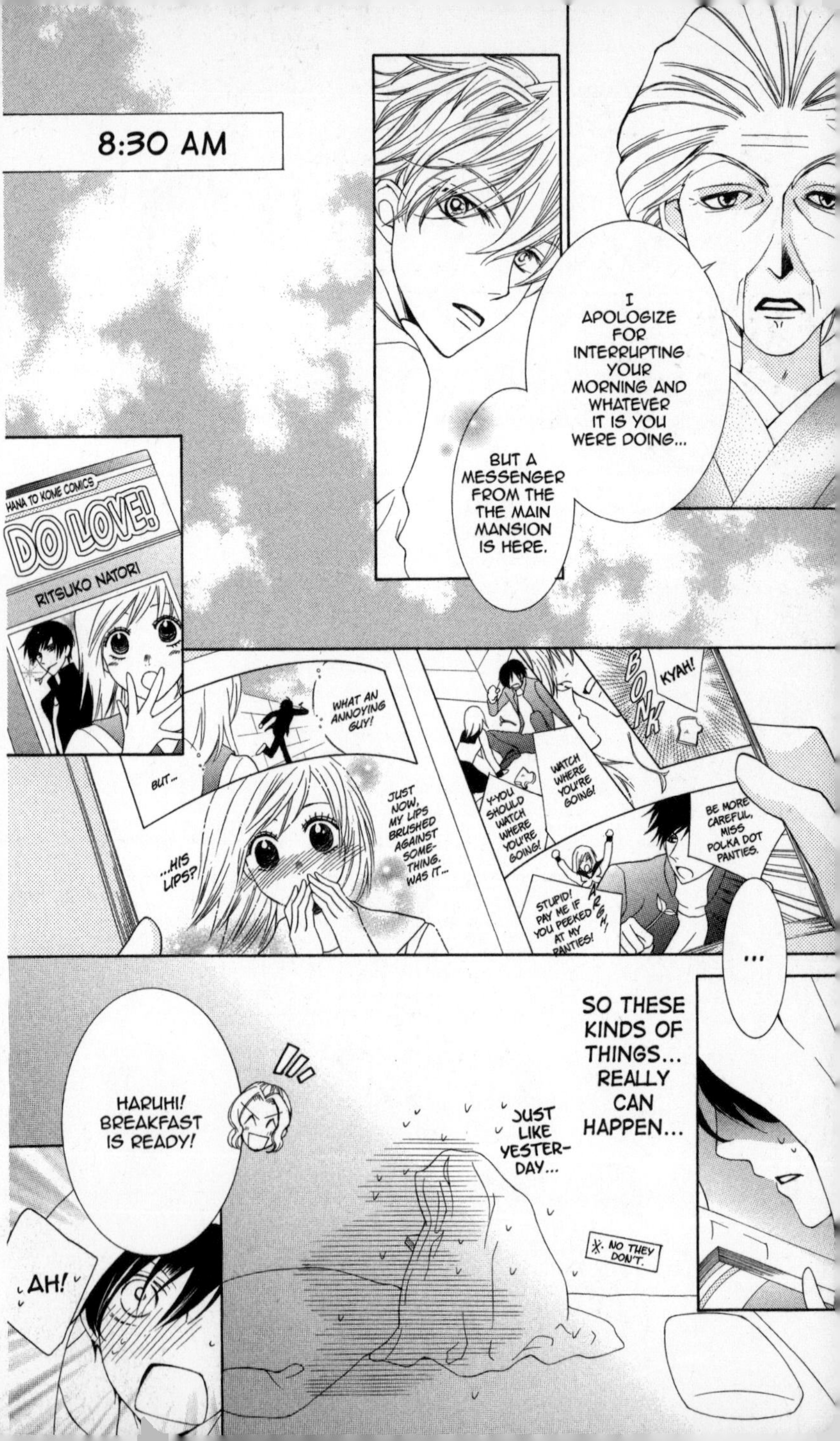
I APOLOGIZE FOR INTERRUPTING YOUR MORNING AND WHATEVER IT IS YOU WERE DOING...
BUT A MESSENGER FROM THE THE MAIN MANSION IS HERE.
8:30 AM
KYAH!
BONK
WATCH WHERE YOU'RE GOING!
Y-YOU SHOULD WATCH WHERE YOU'RE GOING!
BE MORE CAREFUL, MISS POLKA DOT PANTIES.
STUPID! PAY ME IF YOU PEEKED AT MY PANTIES!
ARGH!
WHAT AN ANNOYING GUY!
BUT...
JUST NOW, MY LIPS BRUSHED AGAINST SOMETHING. WAS IT...
...HIS LIPS?
HANA TO KOME COMICS
DO LOVE!
RITSUKO NATORI
...
SO THESE KINDS OF THINGS... REALLY CAN HAPPEN...
JUST LIKE YESTER-DAY...
※. NO THEY DON'T.
HARUHI! BREAKFAST IS READY!
AH!

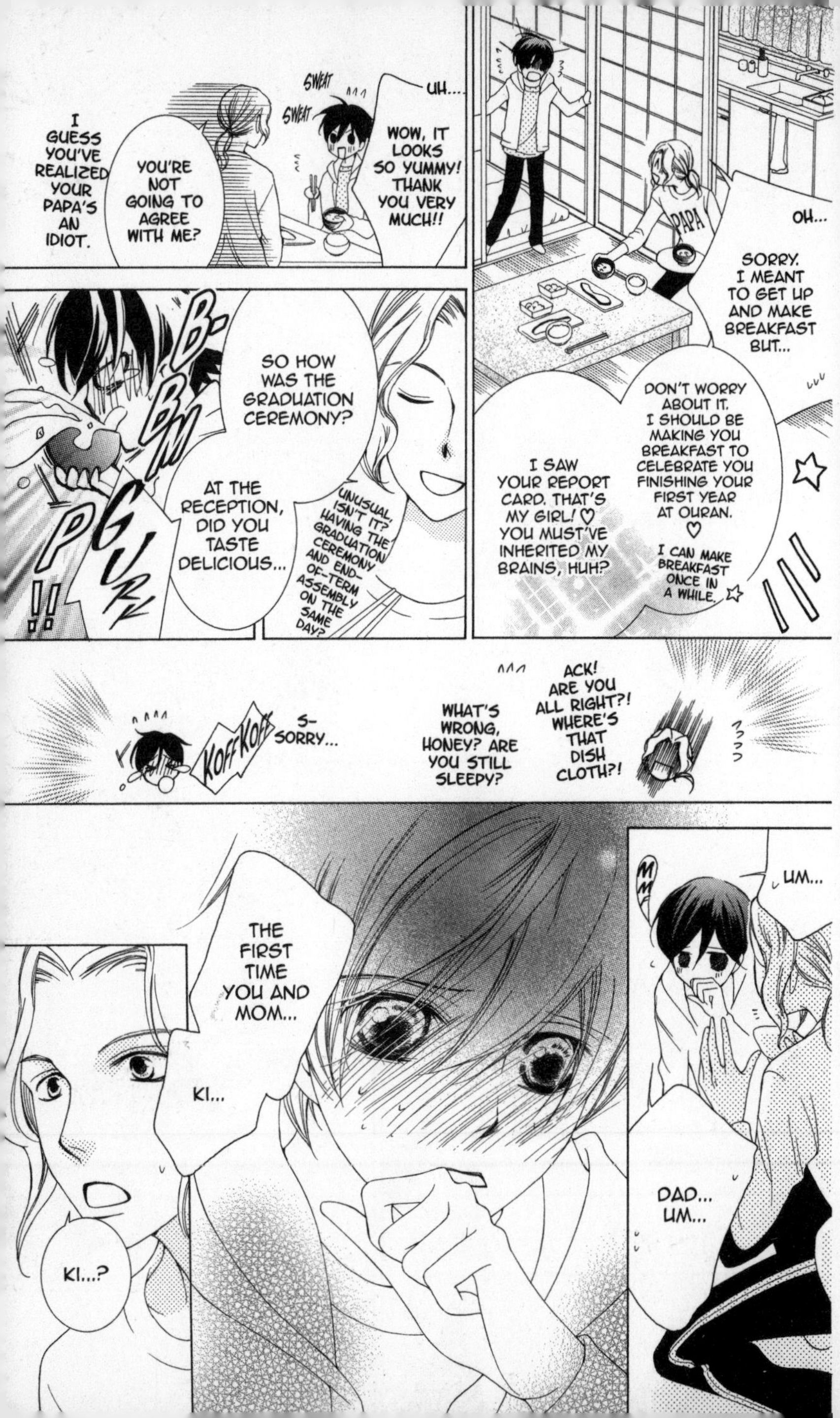
OH...
SORRY. I MEANT TO GET UP AND MAKE BREAKFAST BUT...
DON'T WORRY ABOUT IT. I SHOULD BE MAKING YOU BREAKFAST TO CELEBRATE YOU FINISHING YOUR FIRST YEAR AT OURAN. ♡
I CAN MAKE BREAKFAST ONCE IN A WHILE. ☆
I SAW YOUR REPORT CARD. THAT'S MY GIRL! ♡ YOU MUST'VE INHERITED MY BRAINS, HUH?
UH...
WOW, IT LOOKS SO YUMMY! THANK YOU VERY MUCH!!
SWEAT
SWEAT
YOU'RE NOT GOING TO AGREE WITH ME?
I GUESS YOU'VE REALIZED YOUR PAPA'S AN IDIOT.
SO HOW WAS THE GRADUATION CEREMONY?
UNUSUAL, ISN'T IT? HAVING THE GRADUATION CEREMONY AND END-OF-TERM ASSEMBLY ON THE SAME DAY?
AT THE RECEPTION, DID YOU TASTE DELICIOUS...
GURK
P!!
ACK! ARE YOU ALL RIGHT?! WHERE'S THAT DISH CLOTH?!
WHAT'S WRONG, HONEY? ARE YOU STILL SLEEPY?
S-SORRY...
KOFF KOFF
UM...
DAD... UM...
THE FIRST TIME YOU AND MOM...
KI...
KI...?

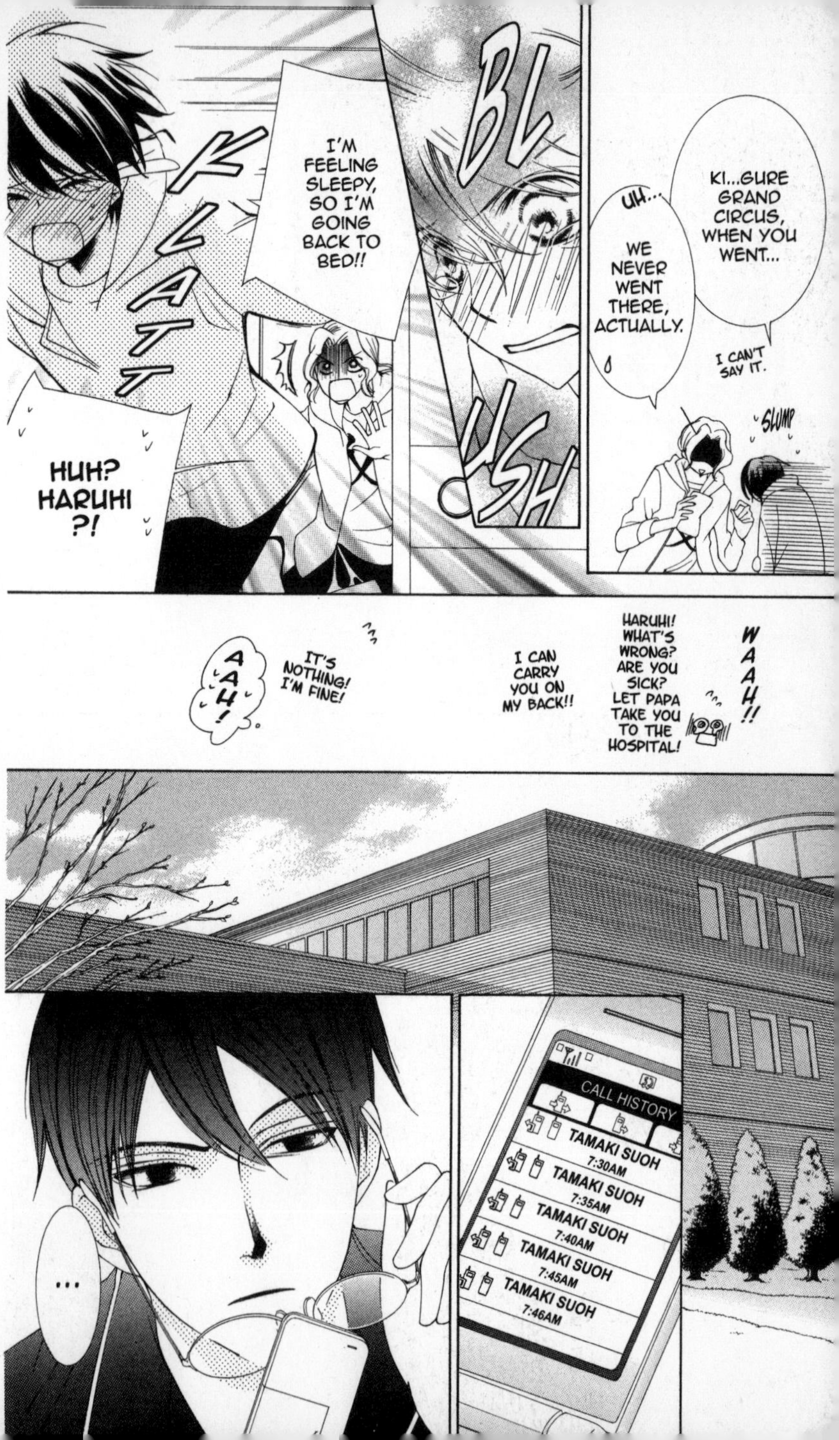
KI...GURE GRAND CIRCUS, WHEN YOU WENT...
I CAN'T SAY IT.
UH...
WE NEVER WENT THERE, ACTUALLY.
SLUMP
BLUSH
I'M FEELING SLEEPY, SO I'M GOING BACK TO BED!!
KLATTT
HUH? HARUHI?!
WAAAH!!
HARUHI! WHAT'S WRONG? ARE YOU SICK? LET PAPA TAKE YOU TO THE HOSPITAL!
I CAN CARRY YOU ON MY BACK!!
IT'S NOTHING! I'M FINE!
AAH!
CALL HISTORY
TAMAKI SUOH
7:30AM
TAMAKI SUOH
7:35AM
TAMAKI SUOH
7:40AM
TAMAKI SUOH
7:45AM
TAMAKI SUOH
7:46AM
...

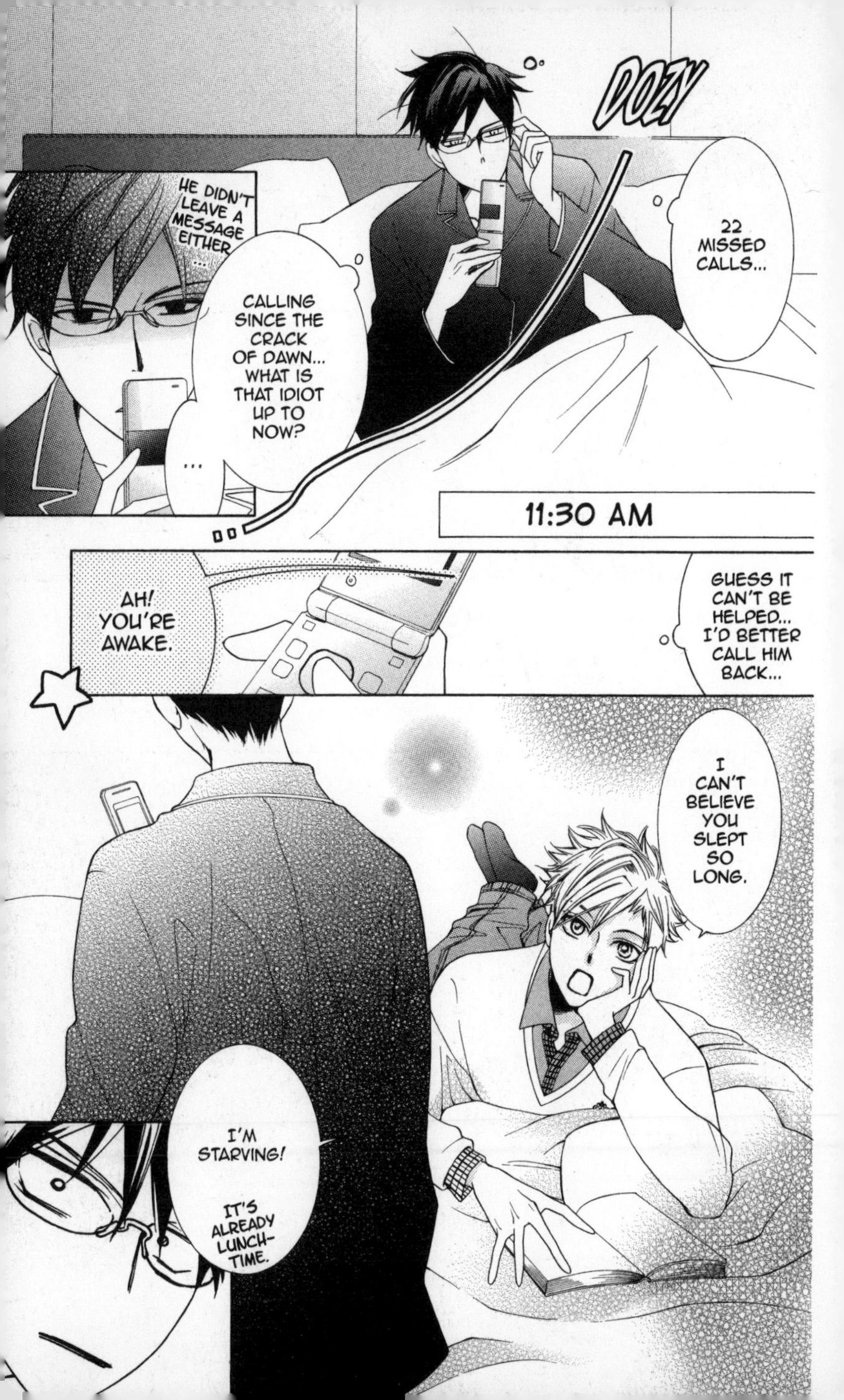
DOZY
22 MISSED CALLS...
HE DIDN'T LEAVE A MESSAGE EITHER...
CALLING SINCE THE CRACK OF DAWN... WHAT IS THAT IDIOT UP TO NOW?
...
11:30 AM
GUESS IT CAN'T BE HELPED... I'D BETTER CALL HIM BACK...
AH! YOU'RE AWAKE.
I CAN'T BELIEVE YOU SLEPT SO LONG.
I'M STARVING!
IT'S ALREADY LUNCH-TIME.

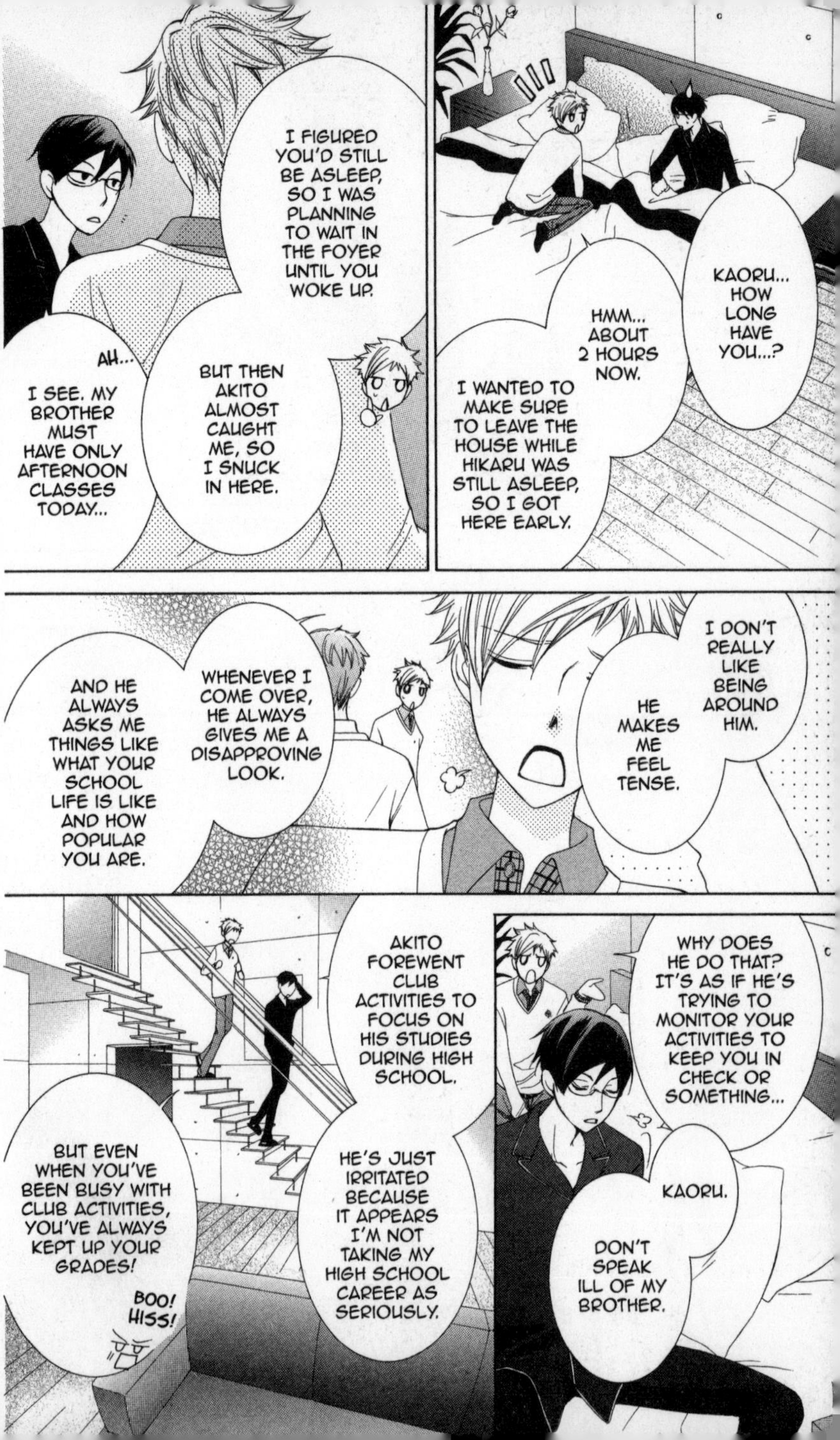
KAORU... HOW LONG HAVE YOU...?
HMM... ABOUT 2 HOURS NOW.
I WANTED TO MAKE SURE TO LEAVE THE HOUSE WHILE HIKARU WAS STILL ASLEEP, SO I GOT HERE EARLY.
I FIGURED YOU'D STILL BE ASLEEP, SO I WAS PLANNING TO WAIT IN THE FOYER UNTIL YOU WOKE UP.
BUT THEN AKITO ALMOST CAUGHT ME, SO I SNUCK IN HERE.
AH...
I SEE. MY BROTHER MUST HAVE ONLY AFTERNOON CLASSES TODAY...
I DON'T REALLY LIKE BEING AROUND HIM.
HE MAKES ME FEEL TENSE.
WHENEVER I COME OVER, HE ALWAYS GIVES ME A DISAPPROVING LOOK.
AND HE ALWAYS ASKS ME THINGS LIKE WHAT YOUR SCHOOL LIFE IS LIKE AND HOW POPULAR YOU ARE.
WHY DOES HE DO THAT? IT'S AS IF HE'S TRYING TO MONITOR YOUR ACTIVITIES TO KEEP YOU IN CHECK OR SOMETHING...
KAORU.
DON'T SPEAK ILL OF MY BROTHER.
AKITO FOREWENT CLUB ACTIVITIES TO FOCUS ON HIS STUDIES DURING HIGH SCHOOL.
HE'S JUST IRRITATED BECAUSE IT APPEARS I'M NOT TAKING MY HIGH SCHOOL CAREER AS SERIOUSLY.
BUT EVEN WHEN YOU'VE BEEN BUSY WITH CLUB ACTIVITIES, YOU'VE ALWAYS KEPT UP YOUR GRADES!
BOO! HISS!

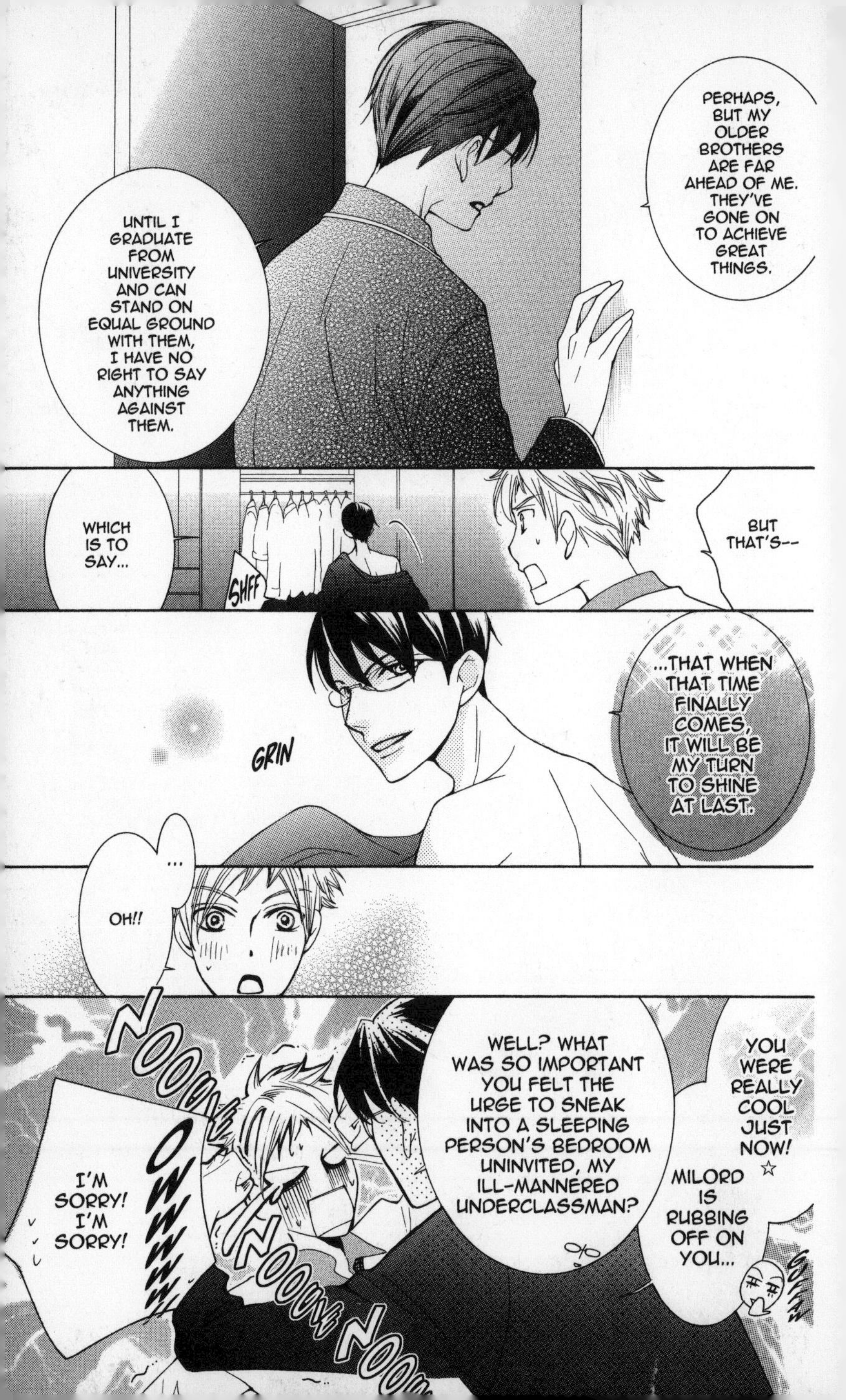
PERHAPS, BUT MY OLDER BROTHERS ARE FAR AHEAD OF ME. THEY'VE GONE ON TO ACHIEVE GREAT THINGS.
UNTIL I GRADUATE FROM UNIVERSITY AND CAN STAND ON EQUAL GROUND WITH THEM, I HAVE NO RIGHT TO SAY ANYTHING AGAINST THEM.
BUT THAT'S--
WHICH IS TO SAY...
SHFF
...THAT WHEN THAT TIME FINALLY COMES, IT WILL BE MY TURN TO SHINE AT LAST.
GRIN
...
OH!!
YOU WERE REALLY COOL JUST NOW! ☆
MILORD IS RUBBING OFF ON YOU...
WELL? WHAT WAS SO IMPORTANT YOU FELT THE URGE TO SNEAK INTO A SLEEPING PERSON'S BEDROOM UNINVITED, MY ILL-MANNERED UNDERCLASSMAN?
I'M SORRY! I'M SORRY!

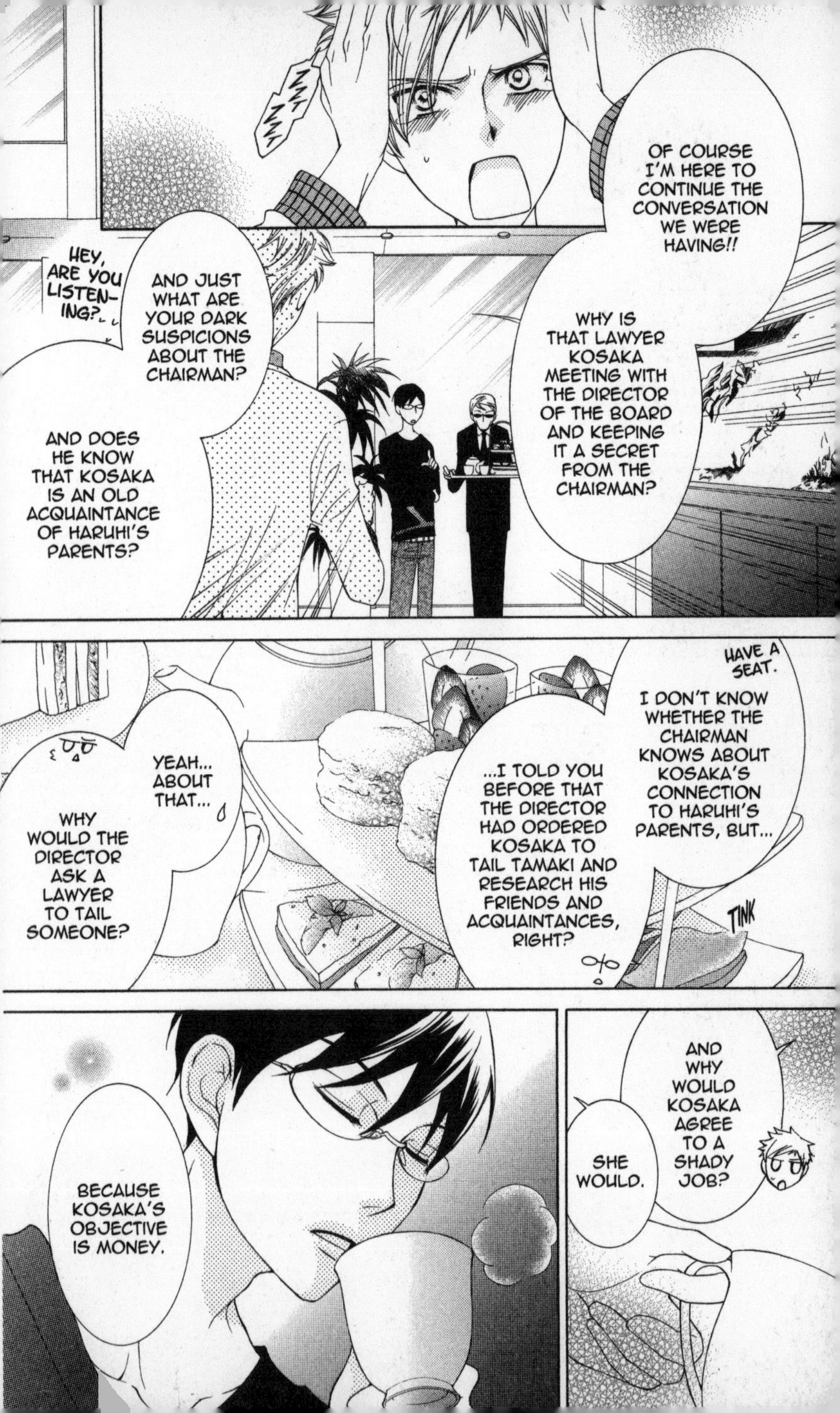
OF COURSE I'M HERE TO CONTINUE THE CONVERSATION WE WERE HAVING!!
WHY IS THAT LAWYER KOSAKA MEETING WITH THE DIRECTOR OF THE BOARD AND KEEPING IT A SECRET FROM THE CHAIRMAN?
AND JUST WHAT ARE YOUR DARK SUSPICIONS ABOUT THE CHAIRMAN?
HEY, ARE YOU LISTENING?
AND DOES HE KNOW THAT KOSAKA IS AN OLD ACQUAINTANCE OF HARUHI'S PARENTS?
HAVE A SEAT.
I DON'T KNOW WHETHER THE CHAIRMAN KNOWS ABOUT KOSAKA'S CONNECTION TO HARUHI'S PARENTS, BUT...
TINK
...I TOLD YOU BEFORE THAT THE DIRECTOR HAD ORDERED KOSAKA TO TAIL TAMAKI AND RESEARCH HIS FRIENDS AND ACQUAINTANCES, RIGHT?
YEAH... ABOUT THAT...
WHY WOULD THE DIRECTOR ASK A LAWYER TO TAIL SOMEONE?
AND WHY WOULD KOSAKA AGREE TO A SHADY JOB?
SHE WOULD.
BECAUSE KOSAKA'S OBJECTIVE IS MONEY.

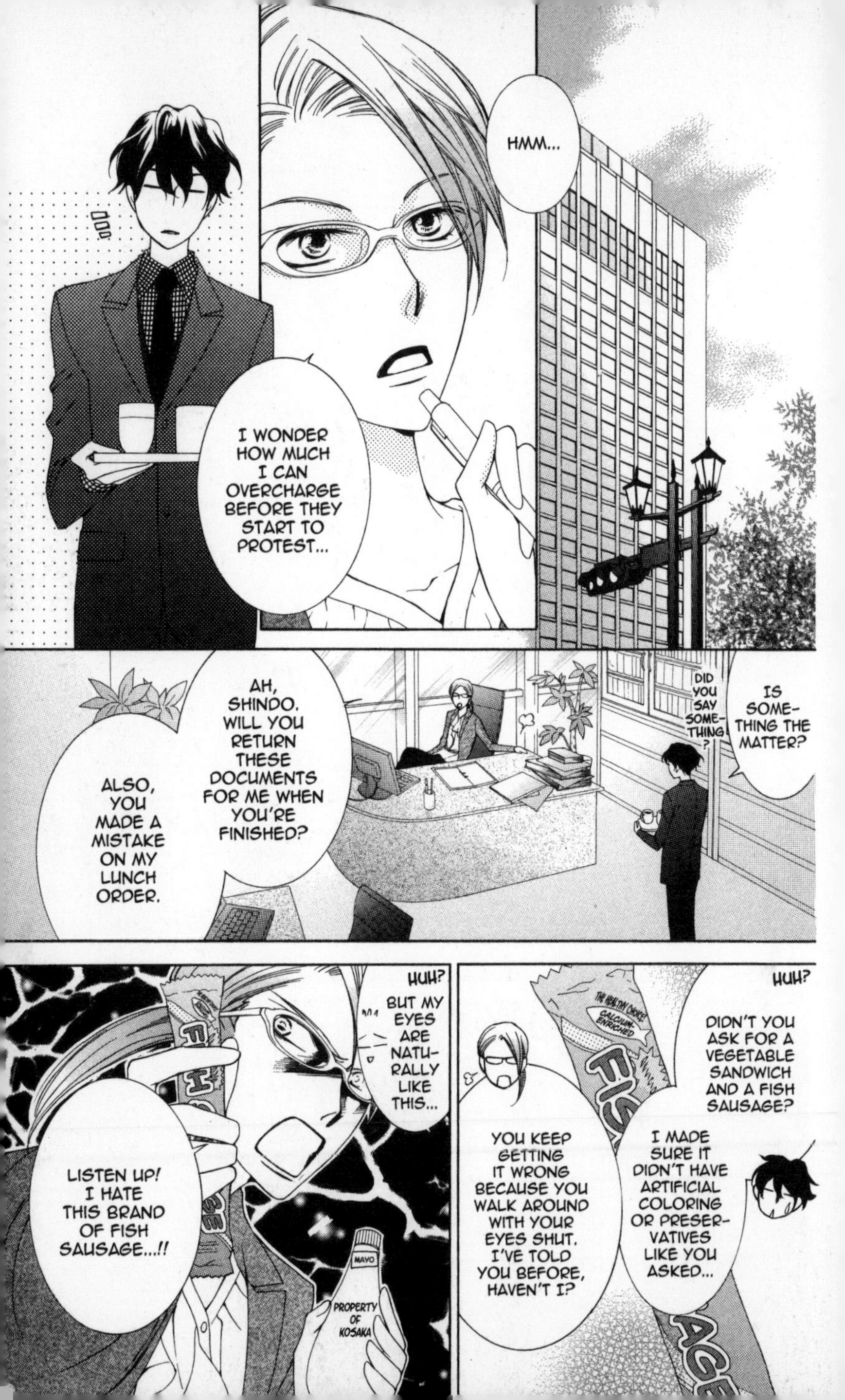
HMM...
I WONDER HOW MUCH I CAN OVERCHARGE BEFORE THEY START TO PROTEST...
IS SOME-THING THE MATTER?
DID YOU SAY SOME-THING?
AH, SHINDO. WILL YOU RETURN THESE DOCUMENTS FOR ME WHEN YOU'RE FINISHED?
ALSO, YOU MADE A MISTAKE ON MY LUNCH ORDER.
HUH?
DIDN'T YOU ASK FOR A VEGETABLE SANDWICH AND A FISH SAUSAGE?
THE HEALTHY CHOICE! CALCIUM-ENRICHED
I MADE SURE IT DIDN'T HAVE ARTIFICIAL COLORING OR PRESER-VATIVES LIKE YOU ASKED...
YOU KEEP GETTING IT WRONG BECAUSE YOU WALK AROUND WITH YOUR EYES SHUT. I'VE TOLD YOU BEFORE, HAVEN'T I?
HUH?
BUT MY EYES ARE NATU-RALLY LIKE THIS...
LISTEN UP! I HATE THIS BRAND OF FISH SAUSAGE...!!
MAYO
PROPERTY OF KOSAKA

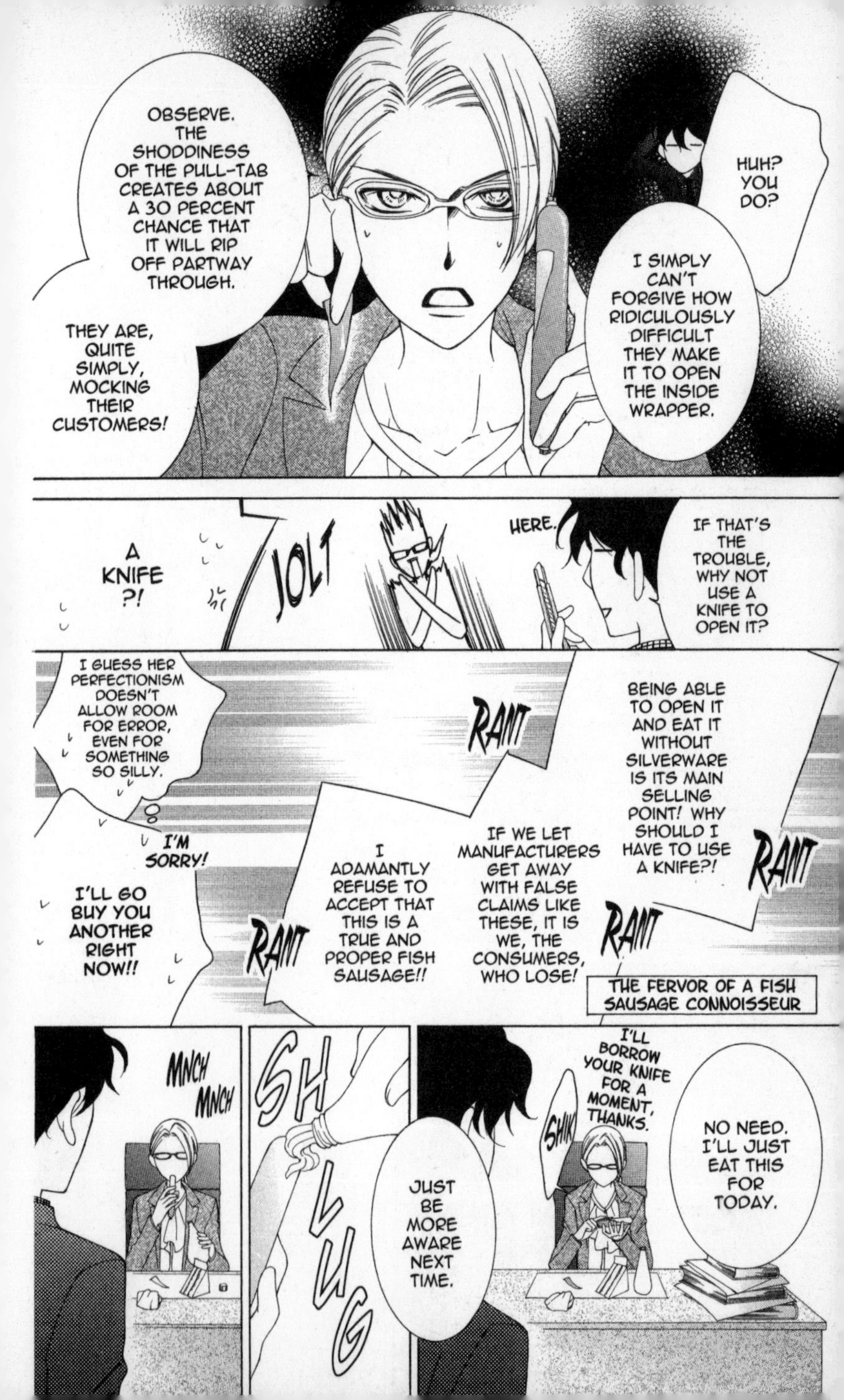
HUH? YOU DO?
I SIMPLY CAN'T FORGIVE HOW RIDICULOUSLY DIFFICULT THEY MAKE IT TO OPEN THE INSIDE WRAPPER.
OBSERVE. THE SHODDINESS OF THE PULL-TAB CREATES ABOUT A 30 PERCENT CHANCE THAT IT WILL RIP OFF PARTWAY THROUGH.
THEY ARE, QUITE SIMPLY, MOCKING THEIR CUSTOMERS!
IF THAT'S THE TROUBLE, WHY NOT USE A KNIFE TO OPEN IT?
HERE.
JOLT
A KNIFE?!
BEING ABLE TO OPEN IT AND EAT IT WITHOUT SILVERWARE IS ITS MAIN SELLING POINT! WHY SHOULD I HAVE TO USE A KNIFE?!
RANT
RANT
RANT
IF WE LET MANUFACTURERS GET AWAY WITH FALSE CLAIMS LIKE THESE, IT IS WE, THE CONSUMERS, WHO LOSE!
I ADAMANTLY REFUSE TO ACCEPT THAT THIS IS A TRUE AND PROPER FISH SAUSAGE!!
RANT
I GUESS HER PERFECTIONISM DOESN'T ALLOW ROOM FOR ERROR, EVEN FOR SOMETHING SO SILLY.
I'M SORRY!
I'LL GO BUY YOU ANOTHER RIGHT NOW!!
THE FERVOR OF A FISH SAUSAGE CONNOISSEUR
NO NEED. I'LL JUST EAT THIS FOR TODAY.
I'LL BORROW YOUR KNIFE FOR A MOMENT, THANKS.
SHIK
JUST BE MORE AWARE NEXT TIME.
SHLUG
MNCH MNCH

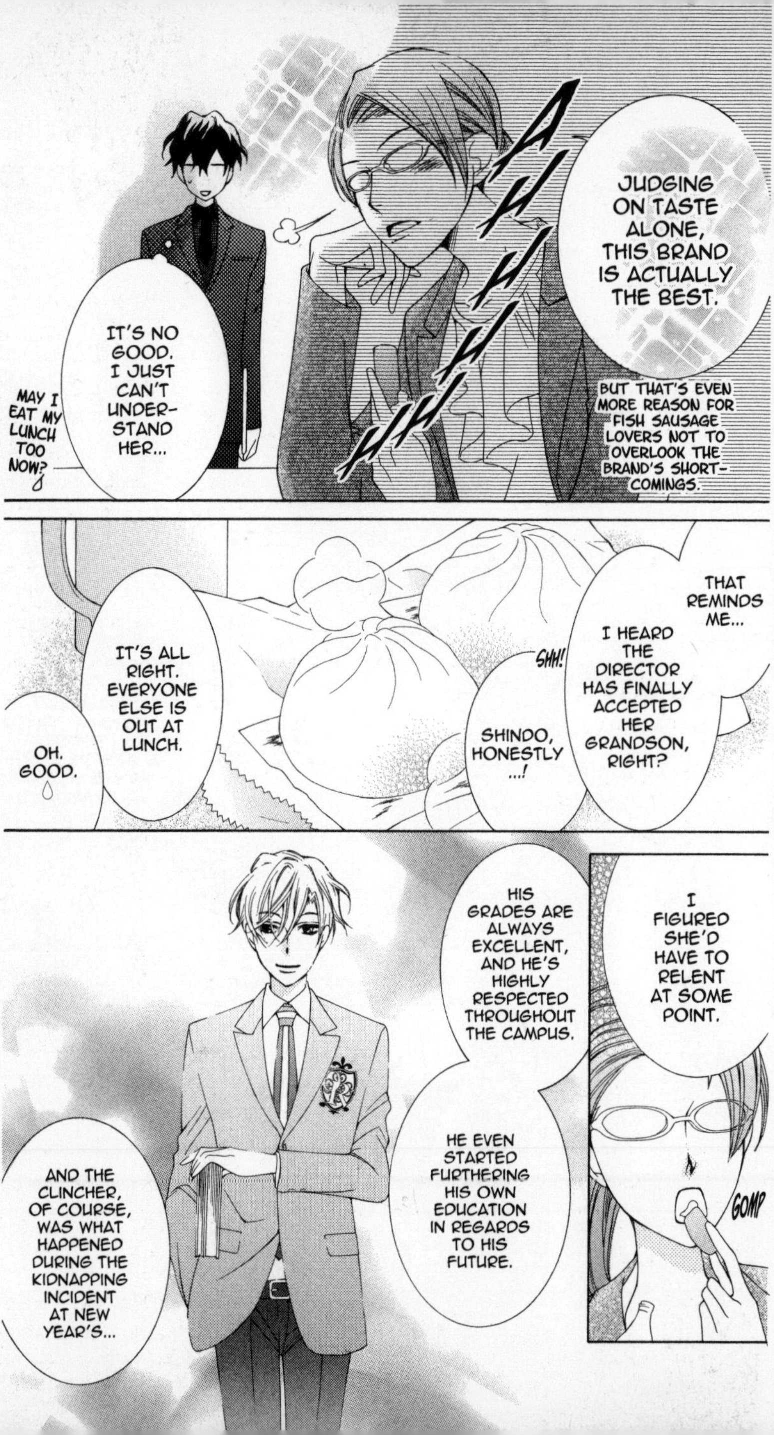
JUDGING ON TASTE ALONE, THIS BRAND IS ACTUALLY THE BEST.
BUT THAT'S EVEN MORE REASON FOR FISH SAUSAGE LOVERS NOT TO OVERLOOK THE BRAND'S SHORT-COMINGS.
IT'S NO GOOD. I JUST CAN'T UNDER-STAND HER...
MAY I EAT MY LUNCH TOO NOW?
THAT REMINDS ME...
I HEARD THE DIRECTOR HAS FINALLY ACCEPTED HER GRANDSON, RIGHT?
SHH!
SHINDO, HONESTLY...!
IT'S ALL RIGHT. EVERYONE ELSE IS OUT AT LUNCH.
OH. GOOD.
I FIGURED SHE'D HAVE TO RELENT AT SOME POINT.
GOMP
HIS GRADES ARE ALWAYS EXCELLENT, AND HE'S HIGHLY RESPECTED THROUGHOUT THE CAMPUS.
HE EVEN STARTED FURTHERING HIS OWN EDUCATION IN REGARDS TO HIS FUTURE.
AND THE CLINCHER, OF COURSE, WAS WHAT HAPPENED DURING THE KIDNAPPING INCIDENT AT NEW YEAR'S...

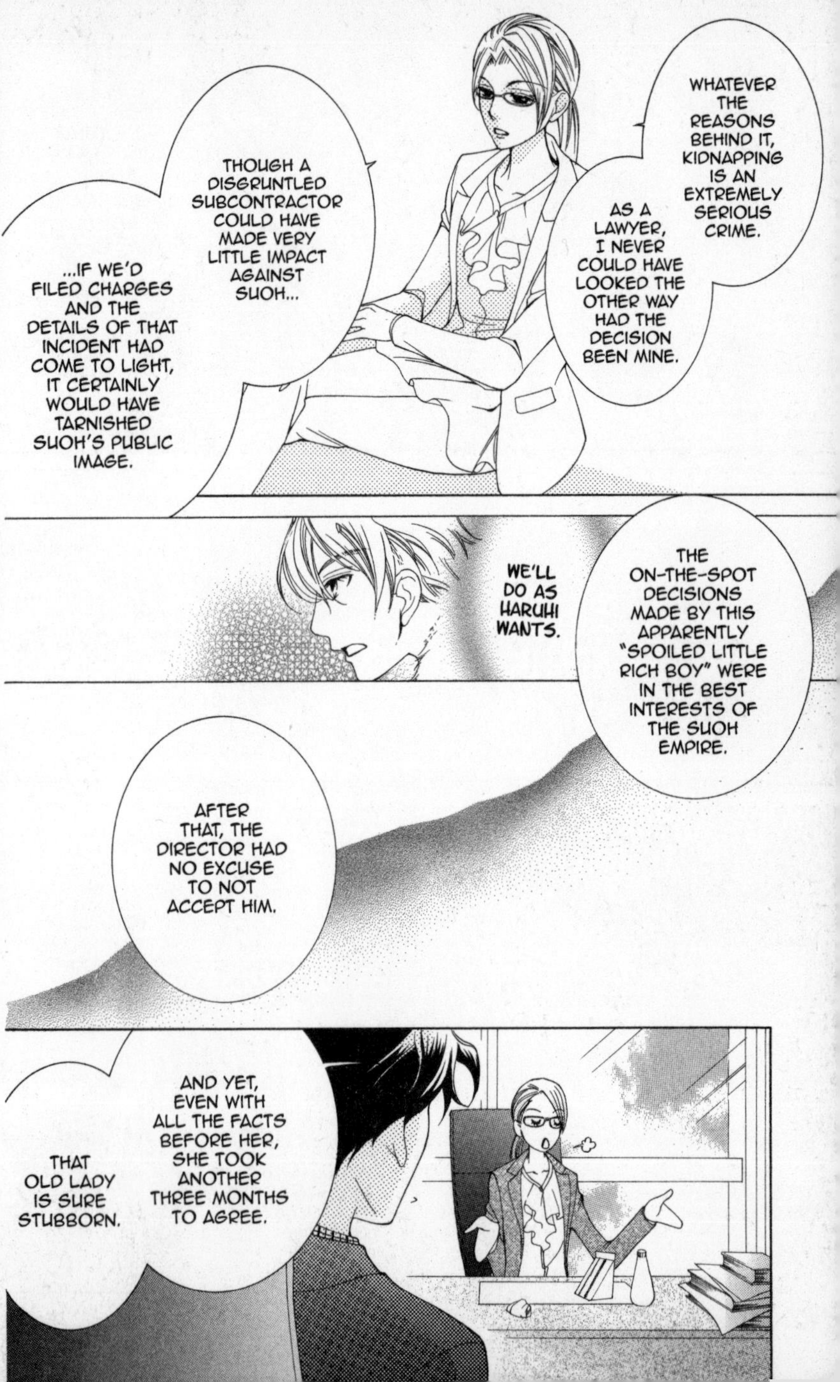
WHATEVER THE REASONS BEHIND IT, KIDNAPPING IS AN EXTREMELY SERIOUS CRIME.
AS A LAWYER, I NEVER COULD HAVE LOOKED THE OTHER WAY HAD THE DECISION BEEN MINE.
THOUGH A DISGRUNTLED SUBCONTRACTOR COULD HAVE MADE VERY LITTLE IMPACT AGAINST SUOH...
...IF WE'D FILED CHARGES AND THE DETAILS OF THAT INCIDENT HAD COME TO LIGHT, IT CERTAINLY WOULD HAVE TARNISHED SUOH'S PUBLIC IMAGE.
THE ON-THE-SPOT DECISIONS MADE BY THIS APPARENTLY "SPOILED LITTLE RICH BOY" WERE IN THE BEST INTERESTS OF THE SUOH EMPIRE.
WE'LL DO AS HARUHI WANTS.
AFTER THAT, THE DIRECTOR HAD NO EXCUSE TO NOT ACCEPT HIM.
AND YET, EVEN WITH ALL THE FACTS BEFORE HER, SHE TOOK ANOTHER THREE MONTHS TO AGREE.
THAT OLD LADY IS SURE STUBBORN.

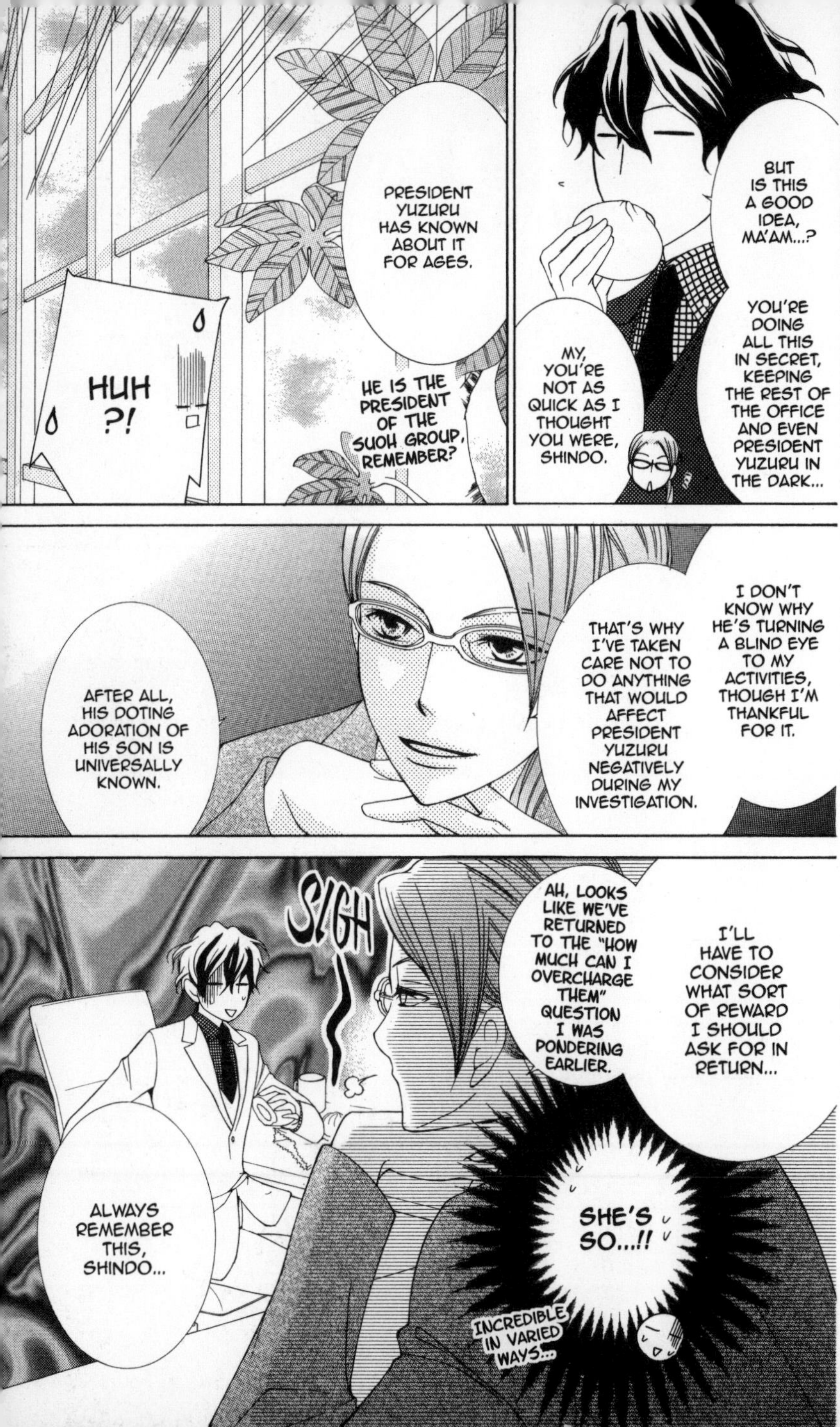
BUT IS THIS A GOOD IDEA, MA'AM...?
YOU'RE DOING ALL THIS IN SECRET, KEEPING THE REST OF THE OFFICE AND EVEN PRESIDENT YUZURU IN THE DARK...
MY, YOU'RE NOT AS QUICK AS I THOUGHT YOU WERE, SHINDO.
PRESIDENT YUZURU HAS KNOWN ABOUT IT FOR AGES.
HE IS THE PRESIDENT OF THE SUOH GROUP, REMEMBER?
HUH ?!
I DON'T KNOW WHY HE'S TURNING A BLIND EYE TO MY ACTIVITIES, THOUGH I'M THANKFUL FOR IT.
THAT'S WHY I'VE TAKEN CARE NOT TO DO ANYTHING THAT WOULD AFFECT PRESIDENT YUZURU NEGATIVELY DURING MY INVESTIGATION.
AFTER ALL, HIS DOTING ADORATION OF HIS SON IS UNIVERSALLY KNOWN.
I'LL HAVE TO CONSIDER WHAT SORT OF REWARD I SHOULD ASK FOR IN RETURN...
AH, LOOKS LIKE WE'VE RETURNED TO THE "HOW MUCH CAN I OVERCHARGE THEM" QUESTION I WAS PONDERING EARLIER.
SIGH
SHE'S SO...!!
ALWAYS REMEMBER THIS, SHINDO...
INCREDIBLE IN VARIED WAYS...

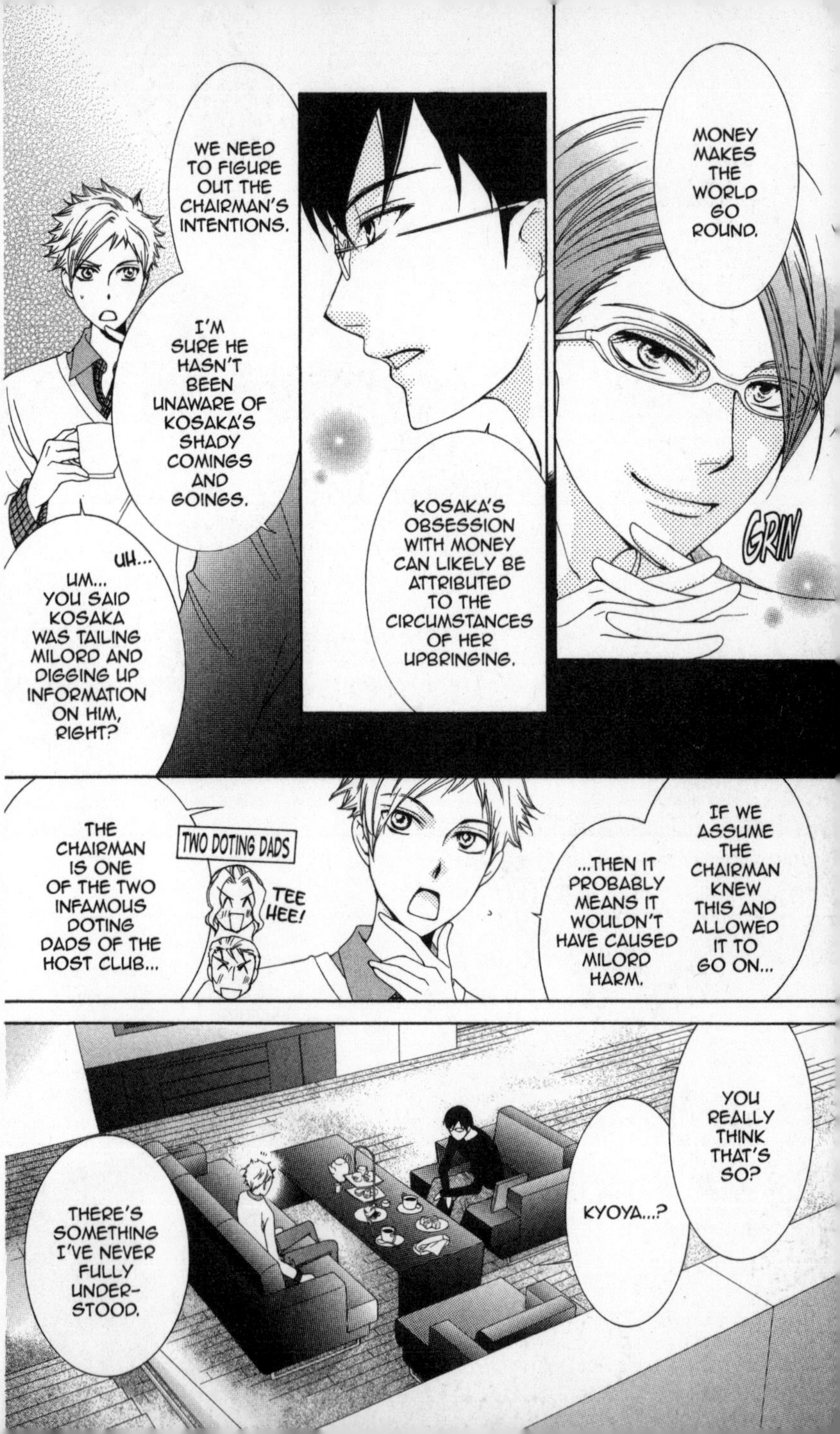
MONEY MAKES THE WORLD GO ROUND.
GRIN
KOSAKA'S OBSESSION WITH MONEY CAN LIKELY BE ATTRIBUTED TO THE CIRCUMSTANCES OF HER UPBRINGING.
WE NEED TO FIGURE OUT THE CHAIRMAN'S INTENTIONS.
I'M SURE HE HASN'T BEEN UNAWARE OF KOSAKA'S SHADY COMINGS AND GOINGS.
UH...
UM... YOU SAID KOSAKA WAS TAILING MILORD AND DIGGING UP INFORMATION ON HIM, RIGHT?
IF WE ASSUME THE CHAIRMAN KNEW THIS AND ALLOWED IT TO GO ON...
...THEN IT PROBABLY MEANS IT WOULDN'T HAVE CAUSED MILORD HARM.
TWO DOTING DADS
TEE HEE!
THE CHAIRMAN IS ONE OF THE TWO INFAMOUS DOTING DADS OF THE HOST CLUB...
YOU REALLY THINK THAT'S SO?
KYOYA...?
THERE'S SOMETHING I'VE NEVER FULLY UNDER-STOOD.

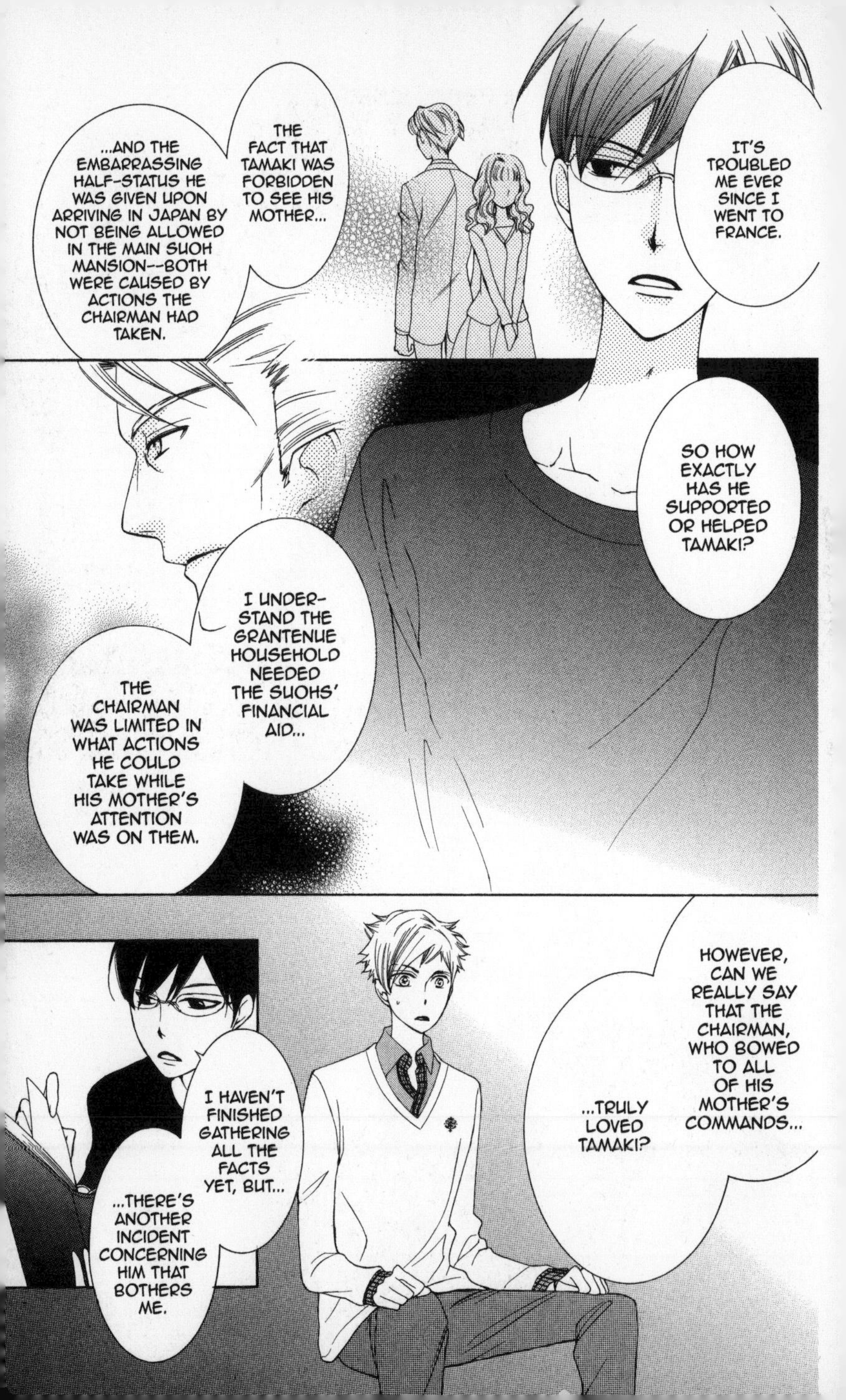
IT'S TROUBLED ME EVER SINCE I WENT TO FRANCE.
THE FACT THAT TAMAKI WAS FORBIDDEN TO SEE HIS MOTHER...
...AND THE EMBARRASSING HALF-STATUS HE WAS GIVEN UPON ARRIVING IN JAPAN BY NOT BEING ALLOWED IN THE MAIN SUOH MANSION--BOTH WERE CAUSED BY ACTIONS THE CHAIRMAN HAD TAKEN.
SO HOW EXACTLY HAS HE SUPPORTED OR HELPED TAMAKI?
I UNDER-STAND THE GRANTENUE HOUSEHOLD NEEDED THE SUOHS' FINANCIAL AID...
THE CHAIRMAN WAS LIMITED IN WHAT ACTIONS HE COULD TAKE WHILE HIS MOTHER'S ATTENTION WAS ON THEM.
HOWEVER, CAN WE REALLY SAY THAT THE CHAIRMAN, WHO BOWED TO ALL OF HIS MOTHER'S COMMANDS...
...TRULY LOVED TAMAKI?
I HAVEN'T FINISHED GATHERING ALL THE FACTS YET, BUT...
...THERE'S ANOTHER INCIDENT CONCERNING HIM THAT BOTHERS ME.

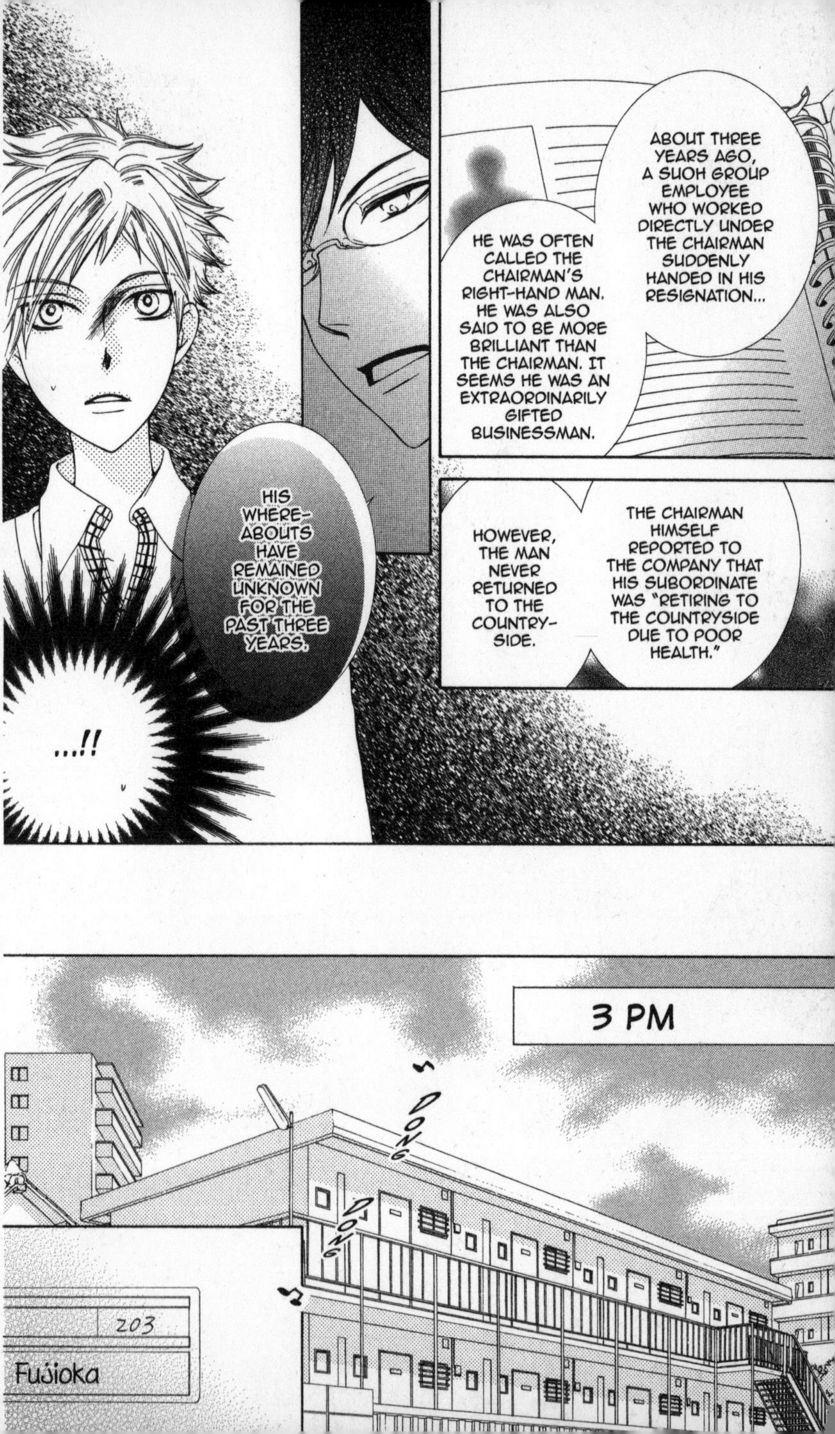
ABOUT THREE YEARS AGO, A SUOH GROUP EMPLOYEE WHO WORKED DIRECTLY UNDER THE CHAIRMAN SUDDENLY HANDED IN HIS RESIGNATION...
HE WAS OFTEN CALLED THE CHAIRMAN'S RIGHT-HAND MAN. HE WAS ALSO SAID TO BE MORE BRILLIANT THAN THE CHAIRMAN. IT SEEMS HE WAS AN EXTRAORDINARILY GIFTED BUSINESSMAN.
THE CHAIRMAN HIMSELF REPORTED TO THE COMPANY THAT HIS SUBORDINATE WAS "RETIRING TO THE COUNTRYSIDE DUE TO POOR HEALTH."
HOWEVER, THE MAN NEVER RETURNED TO THE COUNTRY-SIDE.
HIS WHERE-ABOUTS HAVE REMAINED UNKNOWN FOR THE PAST THREE YEARS.
...!!
3 PM
DONG
DONG
203
Fujioka

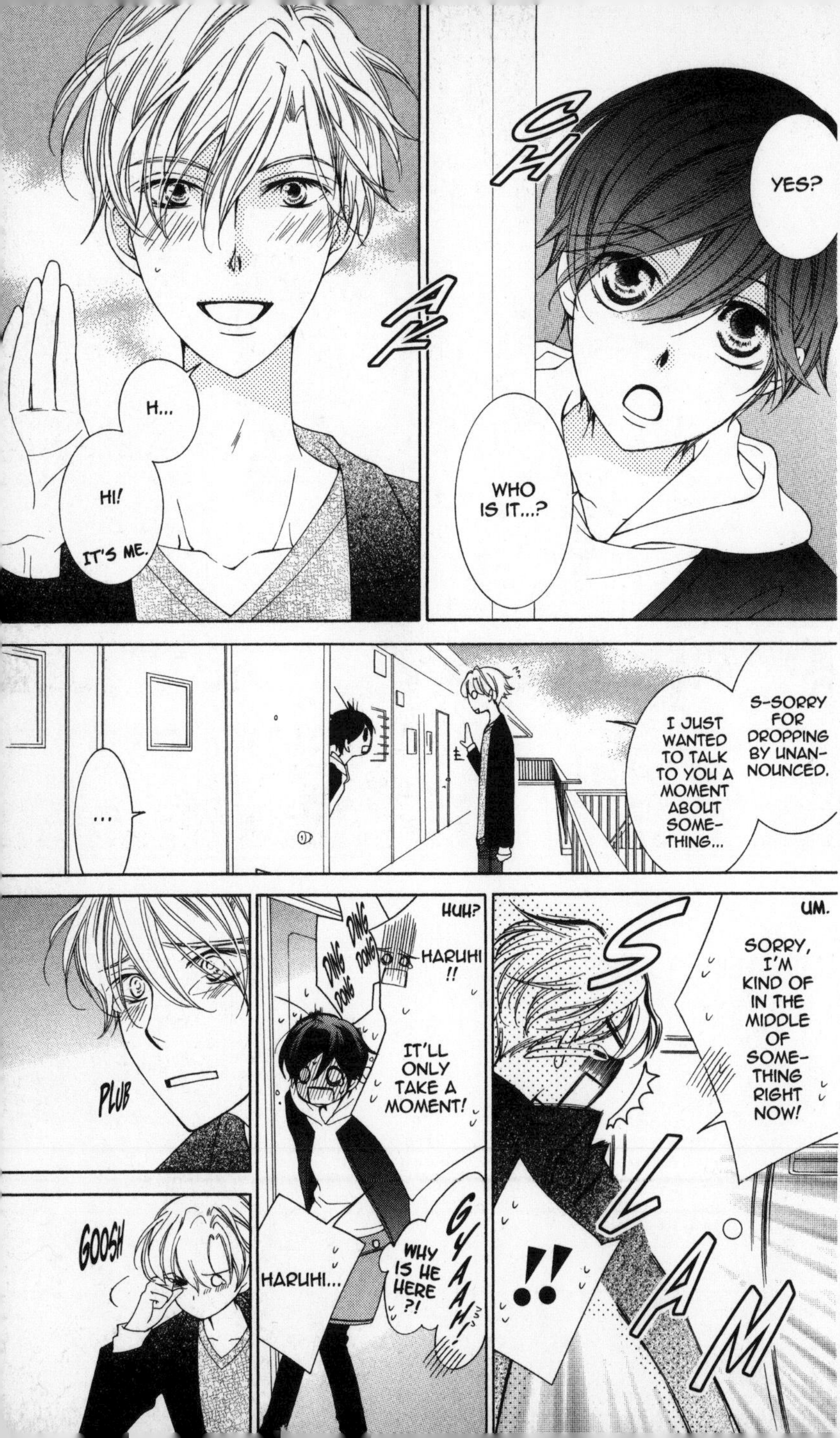
CHAK
YES?
WHO IS IT...?
H...
HI!
IT'S ME.
S-SORRY FOR DROPPING BY UNANNOUNCED.
I JUST WANTED TO TALK TO YOU A MOMENT ABOUT SOMETHING...
...
UM.
SORRY, I'M KIND OF IN THE MIDDLE OF SOMETHING RIGHT NOW!
SLAM
!!
HUH?
HARUHI!!
DING DONG DING DONG
IT'LL ONLY TAKE A MOMENT!
GYAAAH!
WHY IS HE HERE?!
HARUHI...
PLUB
GOOSH

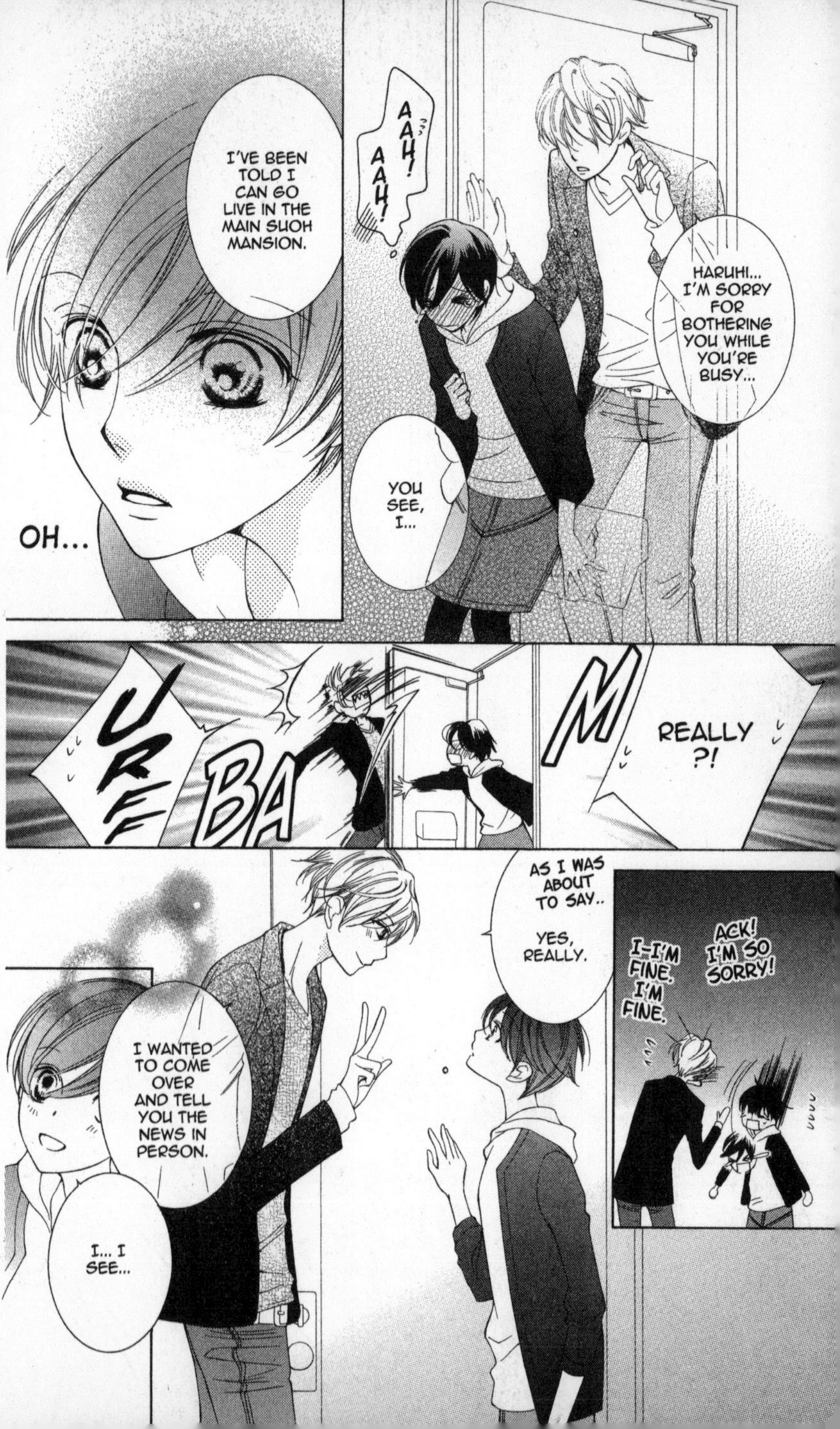
AAH! AAH!
HARUHI... I'M SORRY FOR BOTHERING YOU WHILE YOU'RE BUSY...
YOU SEE, I...
I'VE BEEN TOLD I CAN GO LIVE IN THE MAIN SUOH MANSION.
OH...
REALLY ?!
M
BA
URFF
ACK! I'M SO SORRY!
I-I'M FINE. I'M FINE.
AS I WAS ABOUT TO SAY..
YES, REALLY.
I WANTED TO COME OVER AND TELL YOU THE NEWS IN PERSON.
I... I SEE...

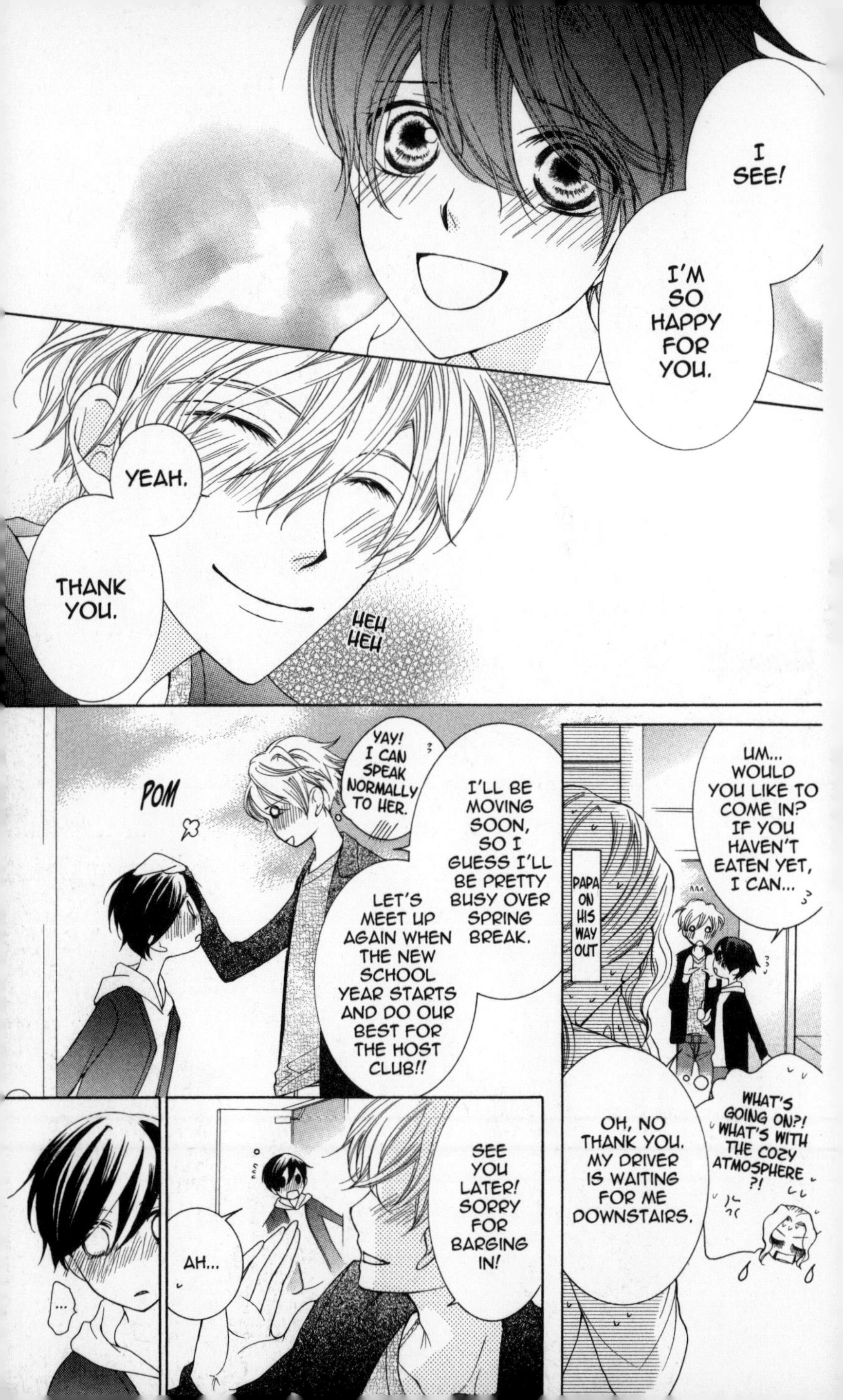
I SEE!
I'M SO HAPPY FOR YOU.
YEAH.
THANK YOU.
HEH HEH
UM... WOULD YOU LIKE TO COME IN? IF YOU HAVEN'T EATEN YET, I CAN...
PAPA ON HIS WAY OUT
YAY! I CAN SPEAK NORMALLY TO HER.
I'LL BE MOVING SOON, SO I GUESS I'LL BE PRETTY BUSY OVER SPRING BREAK.
LET'S MEET UP AGAIN WHEN THE NEW SCHOOL YEAR STARTS AND DO OUR BEST FOR THE HOST CLUB!!
POM
OH, NO THANK YOU. MY DRIVER IS WAITING FOR ME DOWNSTAIRS.
WHAT'S GOING ON?! WHAT'S WITH THE COZY ATMOSPHERE ?!
SEE YOU LATER! SORRY FOR BARGING IN!
AH...
...

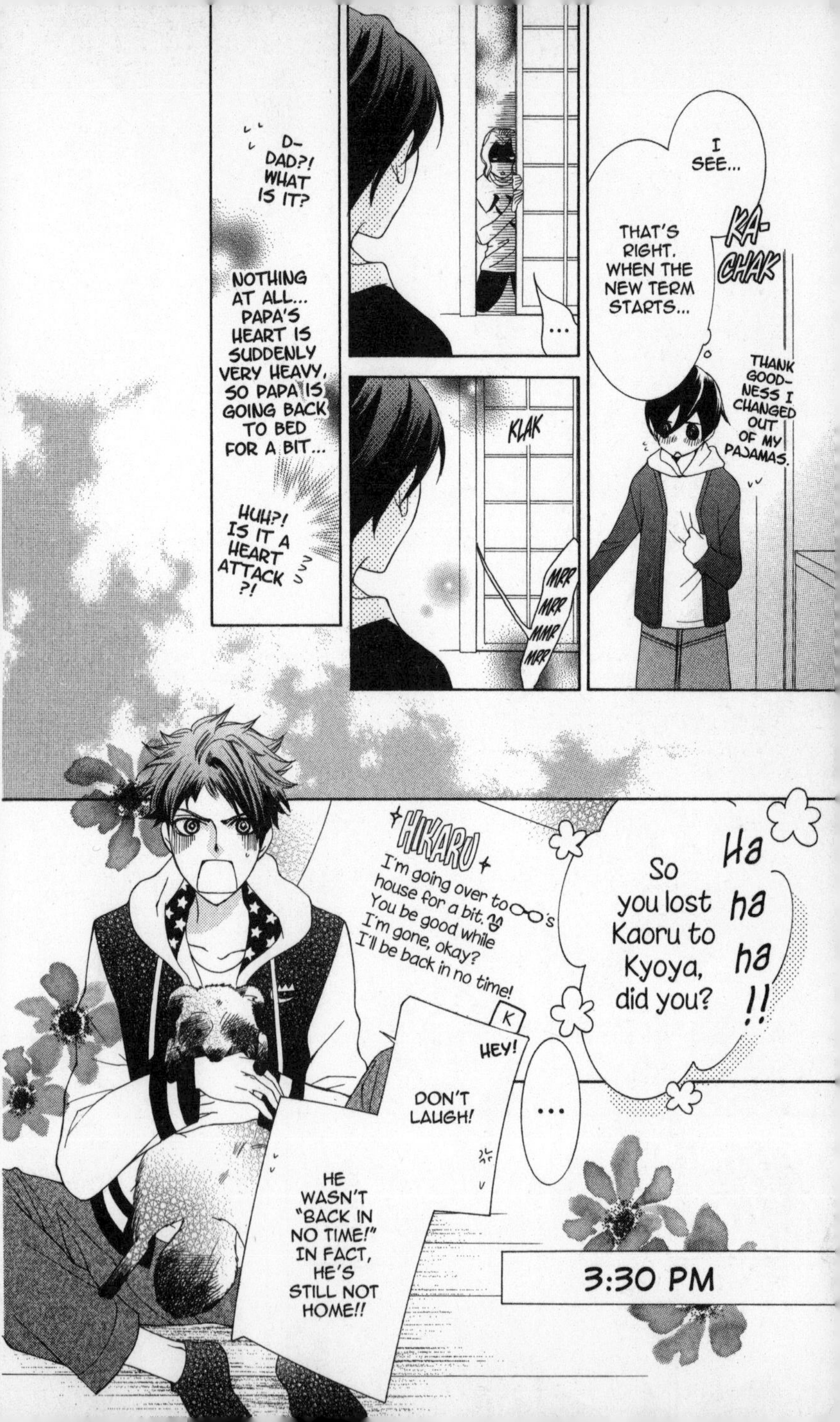
I SEE...
THAT'S RIGHT. WHEN THE NEW TERM STARTS...
KA-CHAK
THANK GOODNESS I CHANGED OUT OF MY PAJAMAS.
...
KLAK
MRR MRR MMR MRR
D-DAD?! WHAT IS IT?
NOTHING AT ALL... PAPA'S HEART IS SUDDENLY VERY HEAVY, SO PAPA IS GOING BACK TO BED FOR A BIT...
HUH?! IS IT A HEART ATTACK ?!
Ha ha ha !!
So you lost Kaoru to Kyoya, did you?
HIKARU
I'm going over to ○○'s house for a bit. You be good while I'm gone, okay? I'll be back in no time!
K
HEY!
DON'T LAUGH!
...
3:30 PM
HE WASN'T "BACK IN NO TIME!" IN FACT, HE'S STILL NOT HOME!!

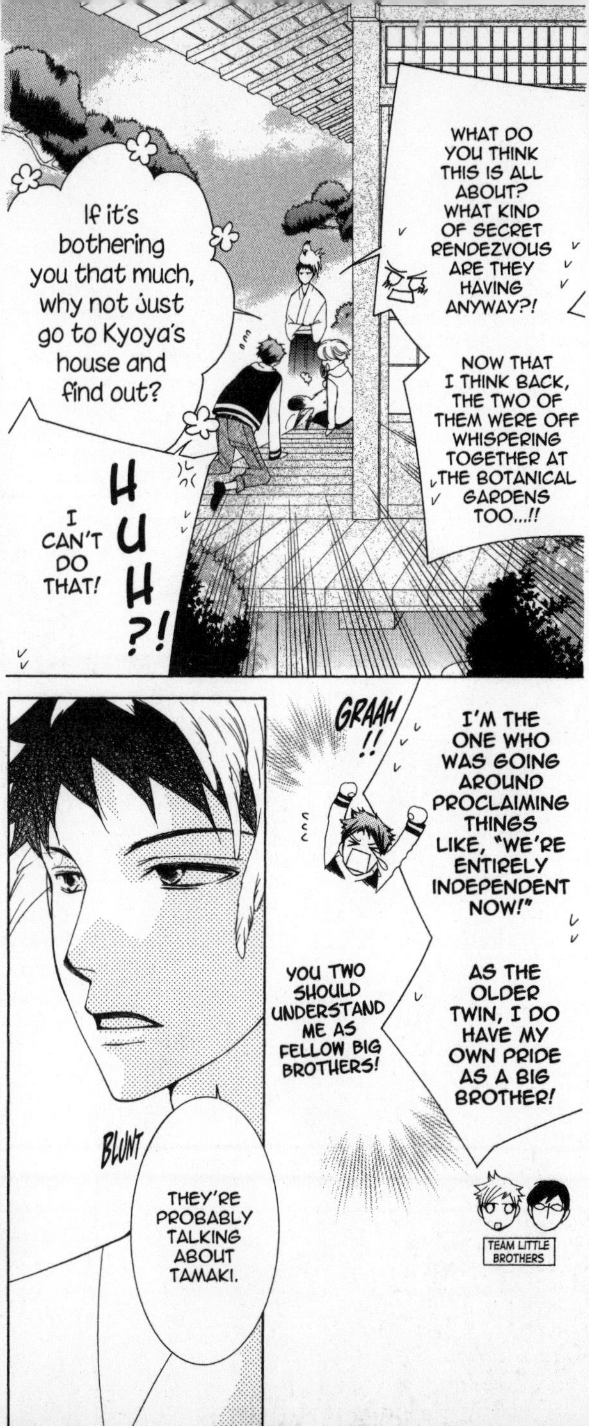
WHAT DO YOU THINK THIS IS ALL ABOUT? WHAT KIND OF SECRET RENDEZVOUS ARE THEY HAVING ANYWAY?!
NOW THAT I THINK BACK, THE TWO OF THEM WERE OFF WHISPERING TOGETHER AT THE BOTANICAL GARDENS TOO...!!
If it's bothering you that much, why not just go to Kyoya's house and find out?
HUH?!
I CAN'T DO THAT!
GRAAH!!
I'M THE ONE WHO WAS GOING AROUND PROCLAIMING THINGS LIKE, "WE'RE ENTIRELY INDEPENDENT NOW!"
AS THE OLDER TWIN, I DO HAVE MY OWN PRIDE AS A BIG BROTHER!
YOU TWO SHOULD UNDERSTAND ME AS FELLOW BIG BROTHERS!
TEAM LITTLE BROTHERS
BLUNT
THEY'RE PROBABLY TALKING ABOUT TAMAKI.

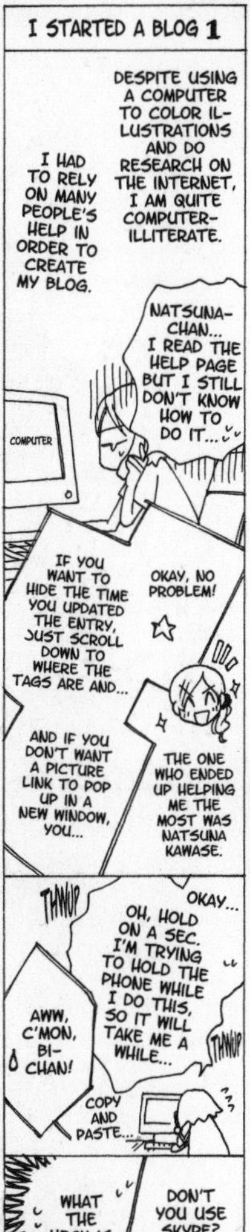
I STARTED A BLOG 1
DESPITE USING A COMPUTER TO COLOR ILLUSTRATIONS AND DO RESEARCH ON THE INTERNET, I AM QUITE COMPUTER-ILLITERATE.
I HAD TO RELY ON MANY PEOPLE'S HELP IN ORDER TO CREATE MY BLOG.
NATSUNA-CHAN... I READ THE HELP PAGE BUT I STILL DON'T KNOW HOW TO DO IT...
COMPUTER
OKAY, NO PROBLEM!
IF YOU WANT TO HIDE THE TIME YOU UPDATED THE ENTRY, JUST SCROLL DOWN TO WHERE THE TAGS ARE AND...
THE ONE WHO ENDED UP HELPING ME THE MOST WAS NATSUNA KAWASE.
AND IF YOU DON'T WANT A PICTURE LINK TO POP UP IN A NEW WINDOW, YOU...
THWUP
OKAY...
OH, HOLD ON A SEC. I'M TRYING TO HOLD THE PHONE WHILE I DO THIS, SO IT WILL TAKE ME A WHILE...
THWUP
AWW, C'MON, BI-CHAN!
COPY AND PASTE...
DON'T YOU USE SKYPE?
THEN YOU CAN TALK WITH BOTH HANDS FREE.
WHAT THE HECK IS SKYPE?!
MYSTERIOUS WORDS FLEW OUT OF HER MOUTH, ONE AFTER THE OTHER...

I HAVE SINCE SIGNED UP FOR SKYPE. IT'S SO HANDY!!

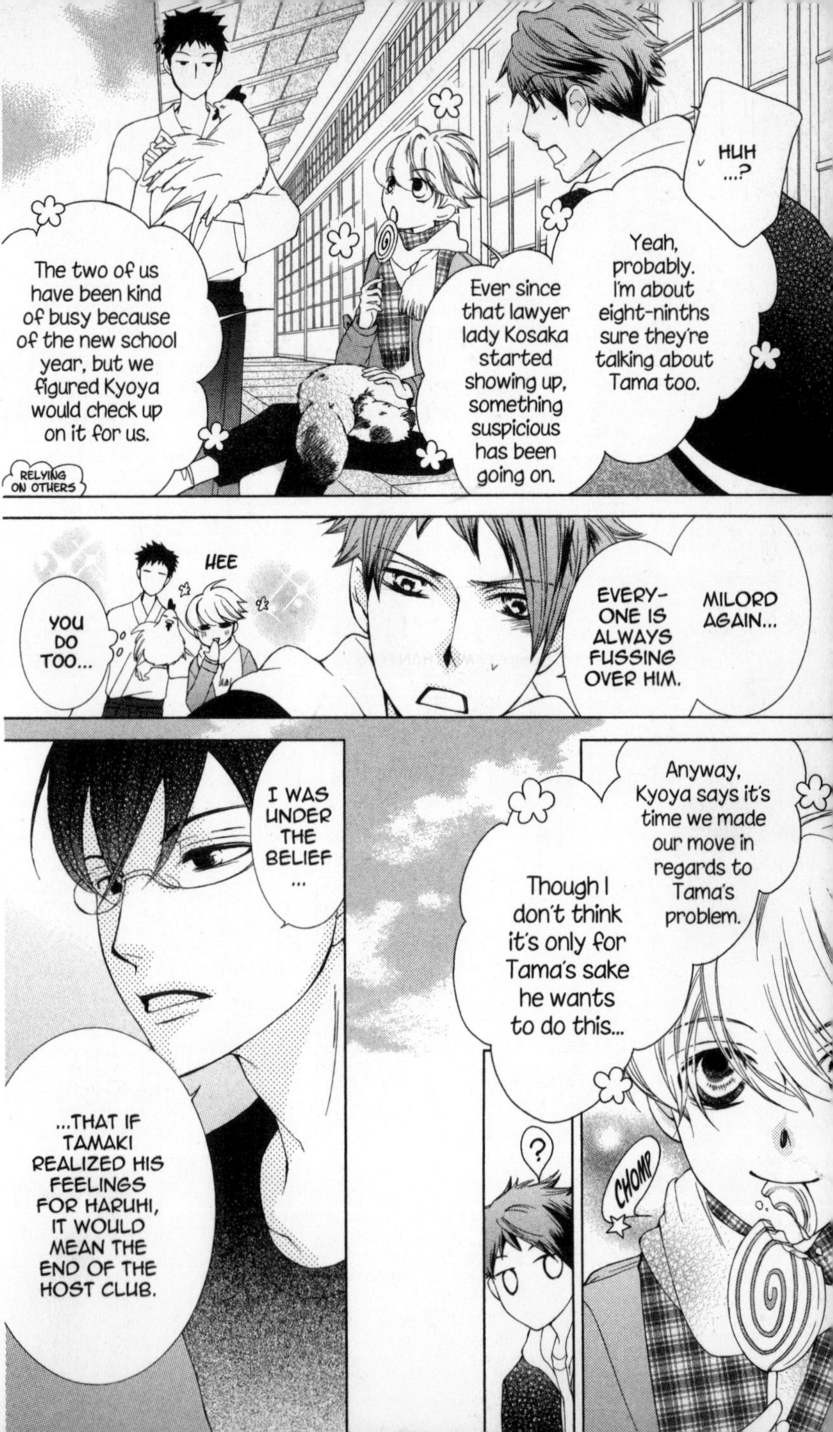
HUH ...?
Yeah, probably. I'm about eight-ninths sure they're talking about Tama too.
Ever since that lawyer lady Kosaka started showing up, something suspicious has been going on.
The two of us have been kind of busy because of the new school year, but we figured Kyoya would check up on it for us.
RELYING ON OTHERS
MILORD AGAIN...
EVERY-ONE IS ALWAYS FUSSING OVER HIM.
HEE
YOU DO TOO...
Anyway, Kyoya says it's time we made our move in regards to Tama's problem.
Though I don't think it's only for Tama's sake he wants to do this...
CHOMP
?
I WAS UNDER THE BELIEF...
...THAT IF TAMAKI REALIZED HIS FEELINGS FOR HARUHI, IT WOULD MEAN THE END OF THE HOST CLUB.

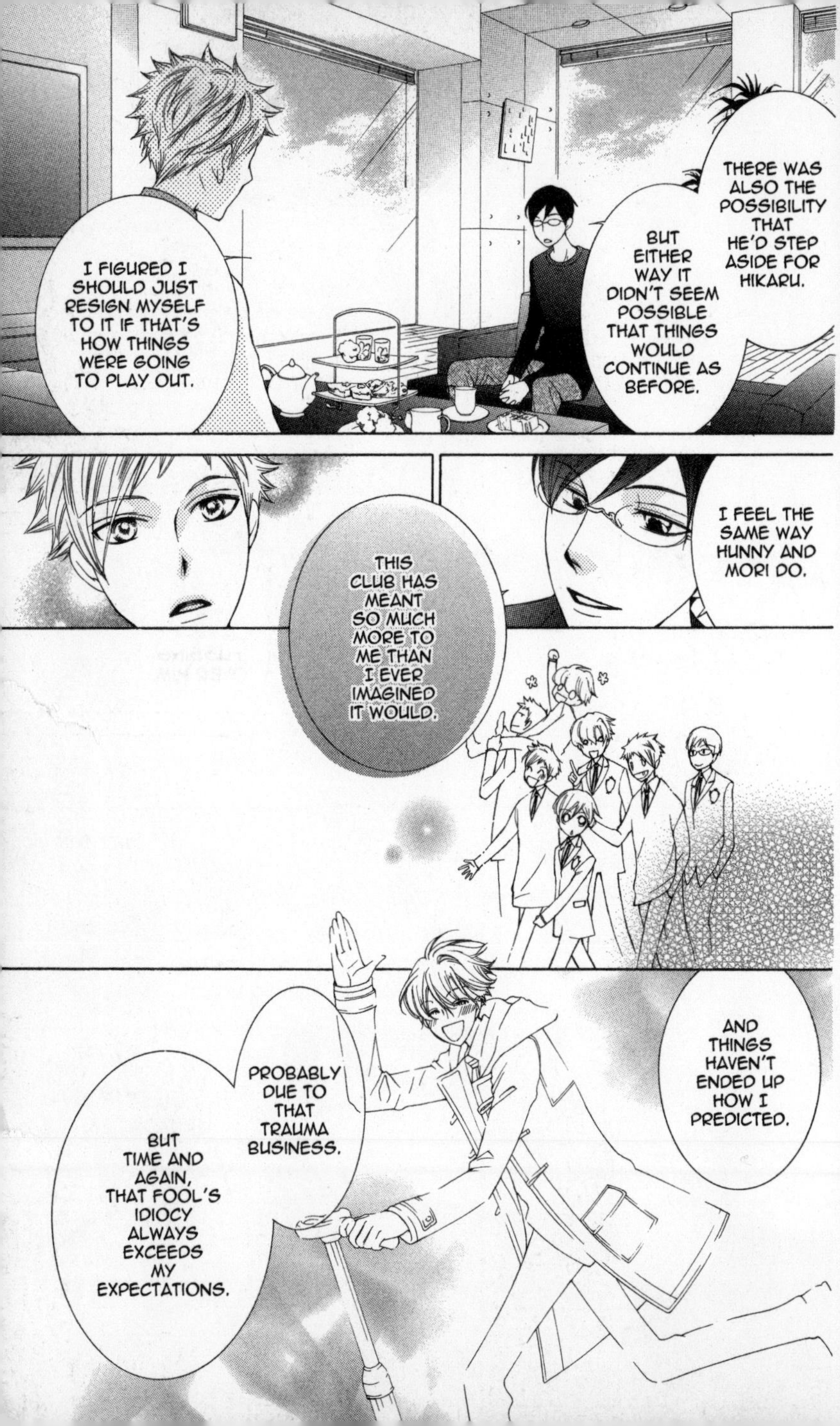
THERE WAS ALSO THE POSSIBILITY THAT HE'D STEP ASIDE FOR HIKARU.
BUT EITHER WAY IT DIDN'T SEEM POSSIBLE THAT THINGS WOULD CONTINUE AS BEFORE.
I FIGURED I SHOULD JUST RESIGN MYSELF TO IT IF THAT'S HOW THINGS WERE GOING TO PLAY OUT.
I FEEL THE SAME WAY HUNNY AND MORI DO.
THIS CLUB HAS MEANT SO MUCH MORE TO ME THAN I EVER IMAGINED IT WOULD.
AND THINGS HAVEN'T ENDED UP HOW I PREDICTED.
PROBABLY DUE TO THAT TRAUMA BUSINESS.
BUT TIME AND AGAIN, THAT FOOL'S IDIOCY ALWAYS EXCEEDS MY EXPECTATIONS.

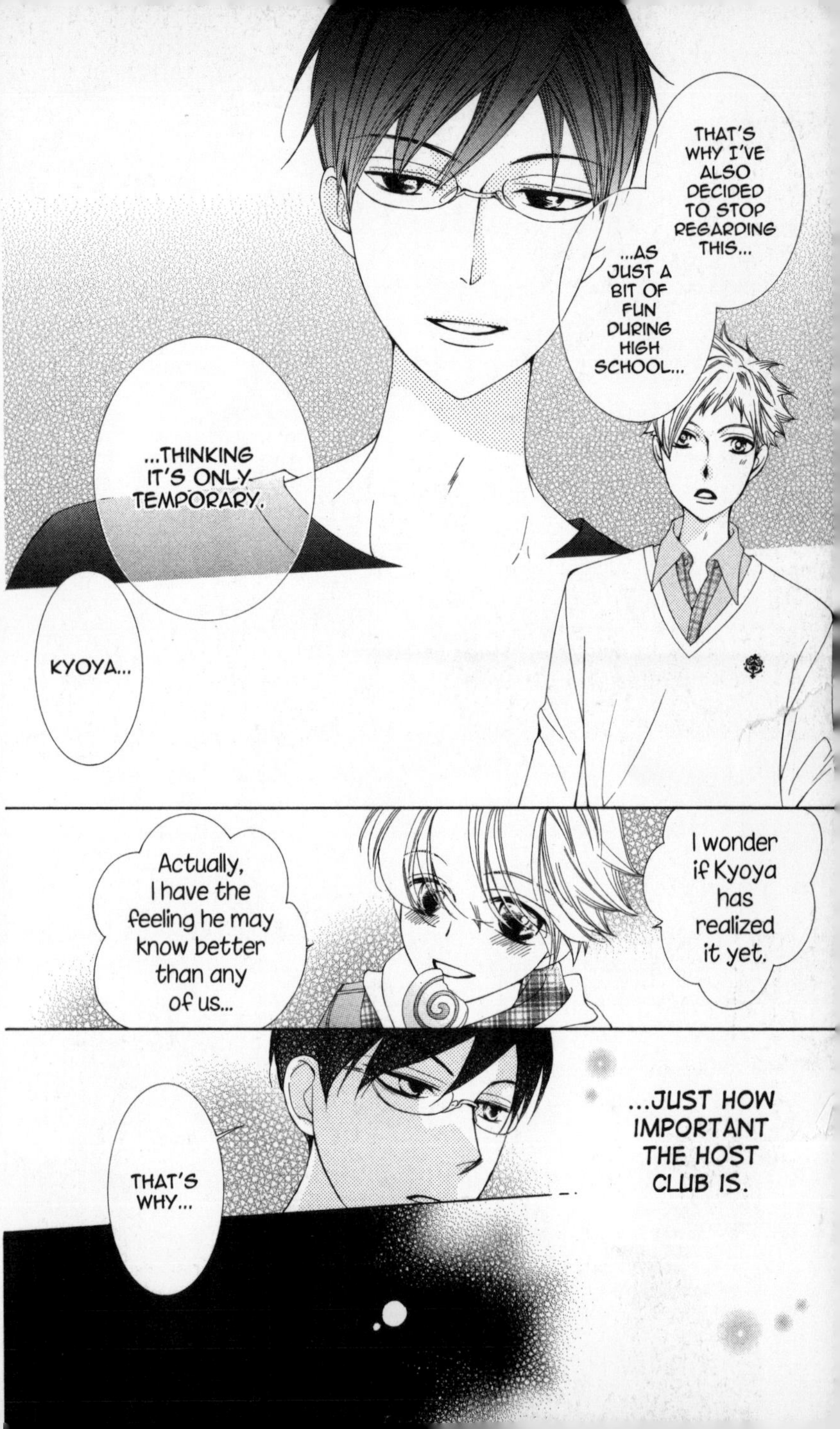
THAT'S WHY I'VE ALSO DECIDED TO STOP REGARDING THIS...
...AS JUST A BIT OF FUN DURING HIGH SCHOOL...
...THINKING IT'S ONLY TEMPORARY.
KYOYA...
I wonder if Kyoya has realized it yet.
Actually, I have the feeling he may know better than any of us...
...JUST HOW IMPORTANT THE HOST CLUB IS.
THAT'S WHY...

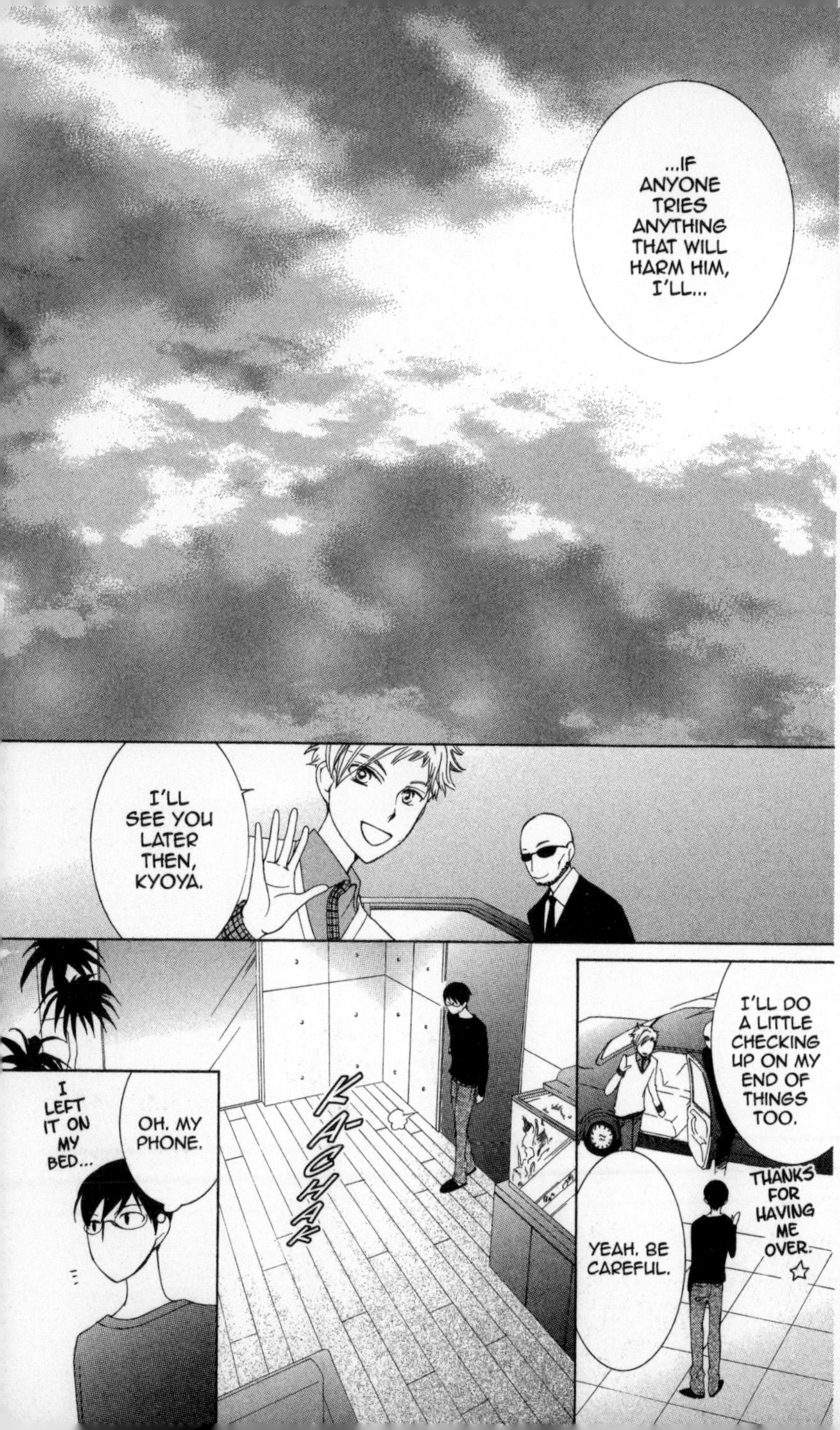
...IF ANYONE TRIES ANYTHING THAT WILL HARM HIM, I'LL...
I'LL SEE YOU LATER THEN, KYOYA.
I'LL DO A LITTLE CHECKING UP ON MY END OF THINGS TOO.
THANKS FOR HAVING ME OVER. ☆
YEAH. BE CAREFUL.
KACHAK
OH. MY PHONE.
I LEFT IT ON MY BED...

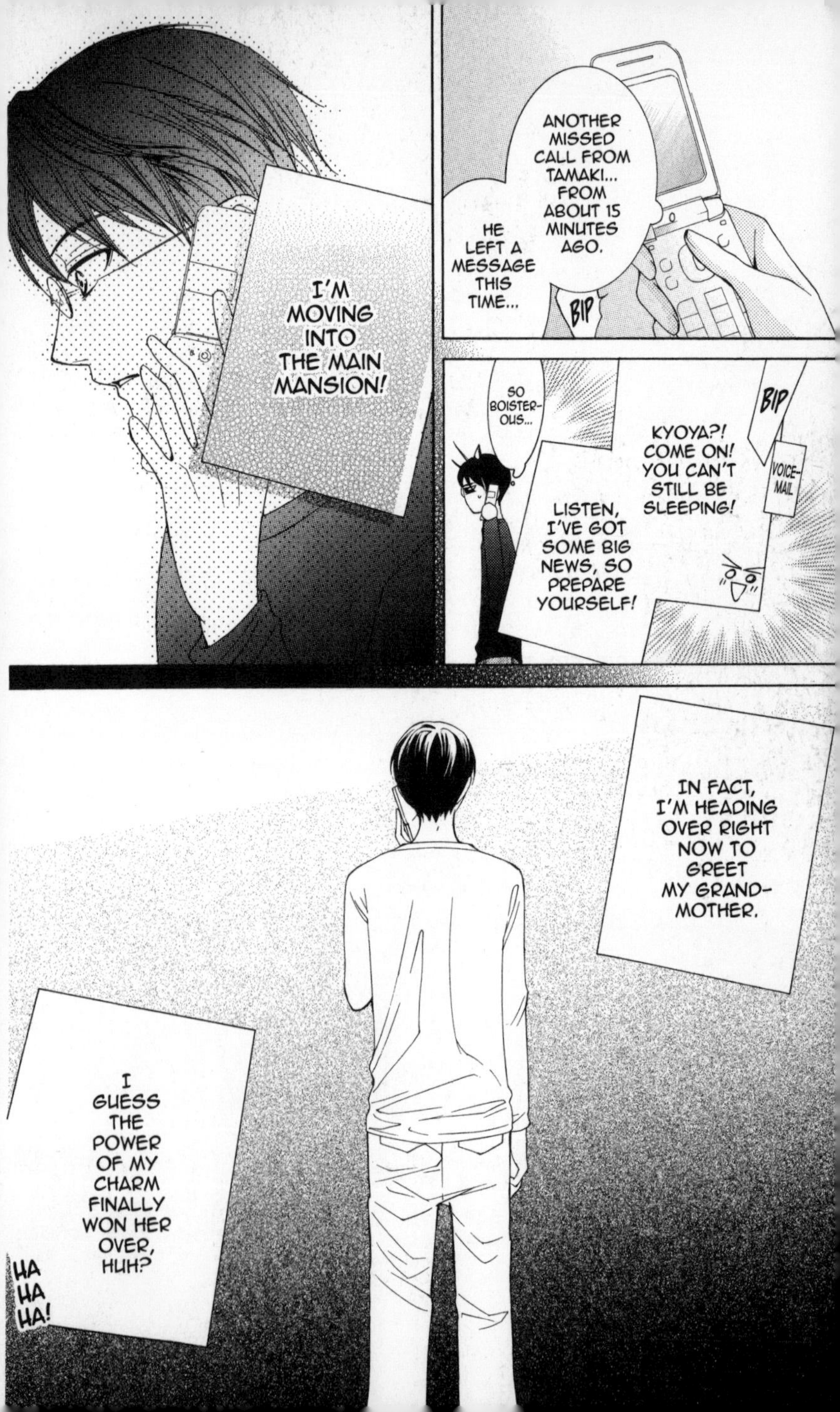
ANOTHER MISSED CALL FROM TAMAKI... FROM ABOUT 15 MINUTES AGO.
HE LEFT A MESSAGE THIS TIME...
BIP
BIP
VOICE-MAIL
KYOYA?! COME ON! YOU CAN'T STILL BE SLEEPING!
LISTEN, I'VE GOT SOME BIG NEWS, SO PREPARE YOURSELF!
SO BOISTER-OUS...
I'M MOVING INTO THE MAIN MANSION!
IN FACT, I'M HEADING OVER RIGHT NOW TO GREET MY GRAND-MOTHER.
I GUESS THE POWER OF MY CHARM FINALLY WON HER OVER, HUH?
HA HA HA!

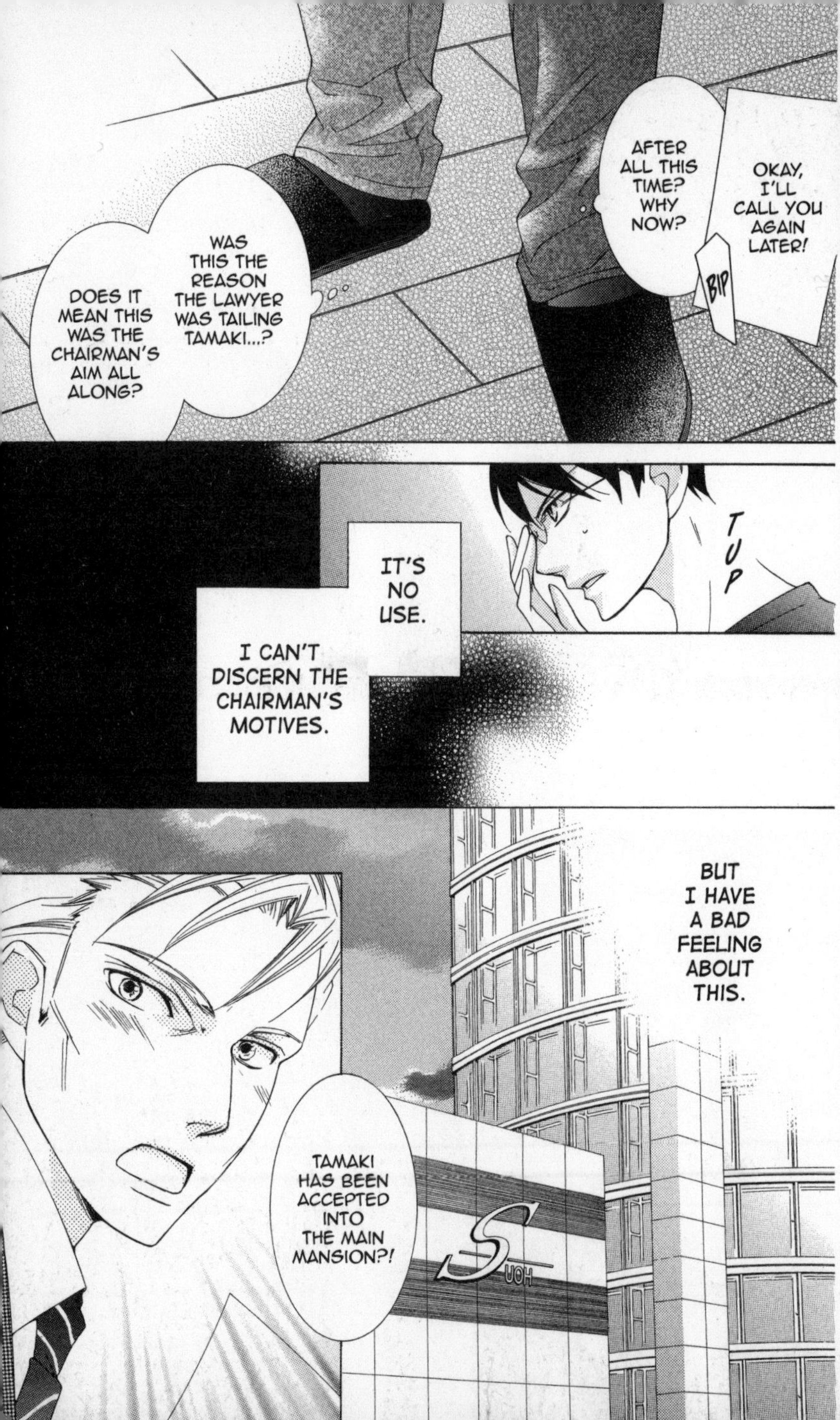
OKAY, I'LL CALL YOU AGAIN LATER!
BIP
AFTER ALL THIS TIME? WHY NOW?
WAS THIS THE REASON THE LAWYER WAS TAILING TAMAKI...?
DOES IT MEAN THIS WAS THE CHAIRMAN'S AIM ALL ALONG?
TUP
IT'S NO USE.
I CAN'T DISCERN THE CHAIRMAN'S MOTIVES.
BUT I HAVE A BAD FEELING ABOUT THIS.
SUOH
TAMAKI HAS BEEN ACCEPTED INTO THE MAIN MANSION?!

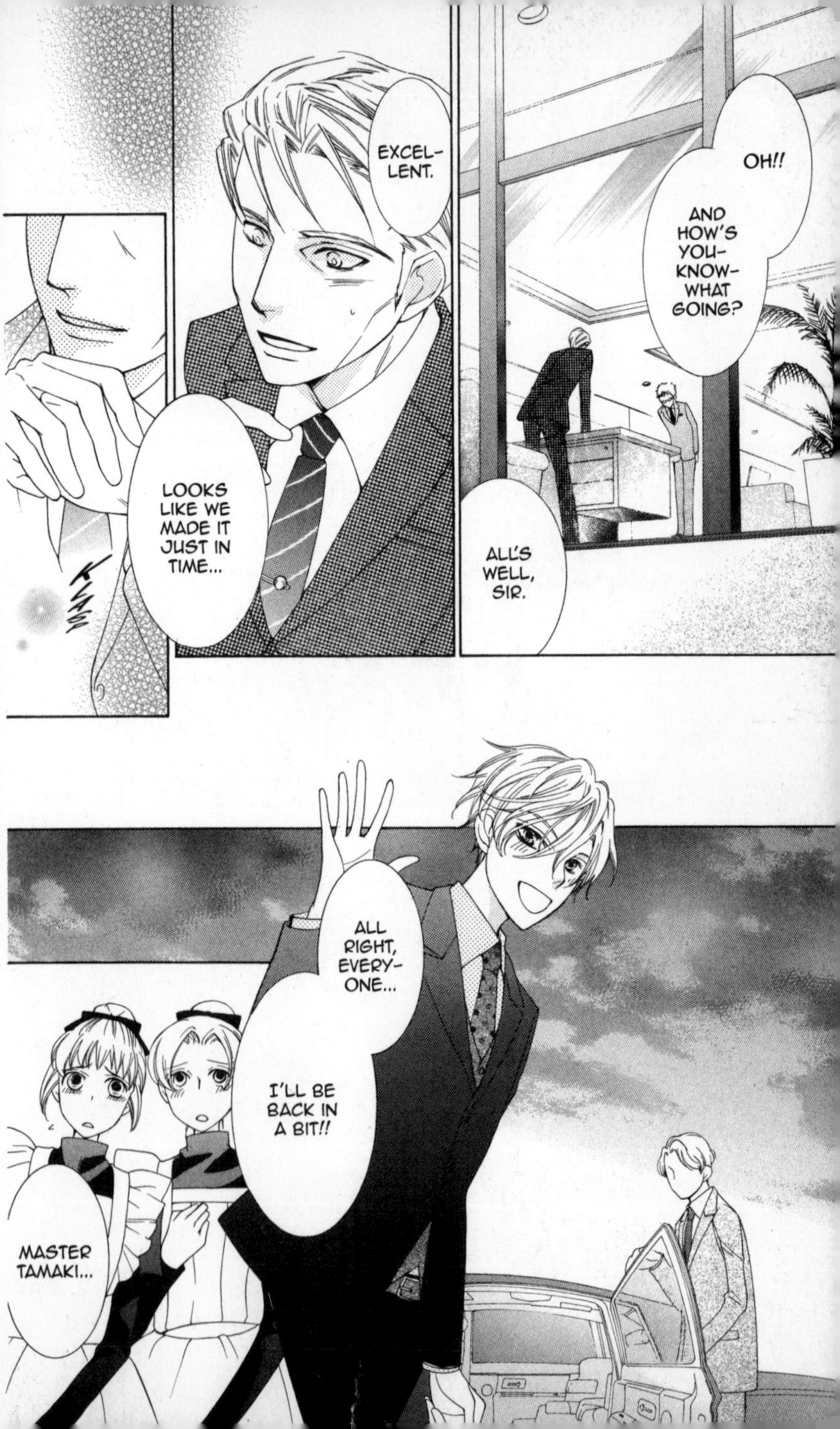
OH!!
AND HOW'S YOU-KNOW-WHAT GOING?
ALL'S WELL, SIR.
EXCEL-LENT.
LOOKS LIKE WE MADE IT JUST IN TIME...
ALL RIGHT, EVERY-ONE...
I'LL BE BACK IN A BIT!!
MASTER TAMAKI...

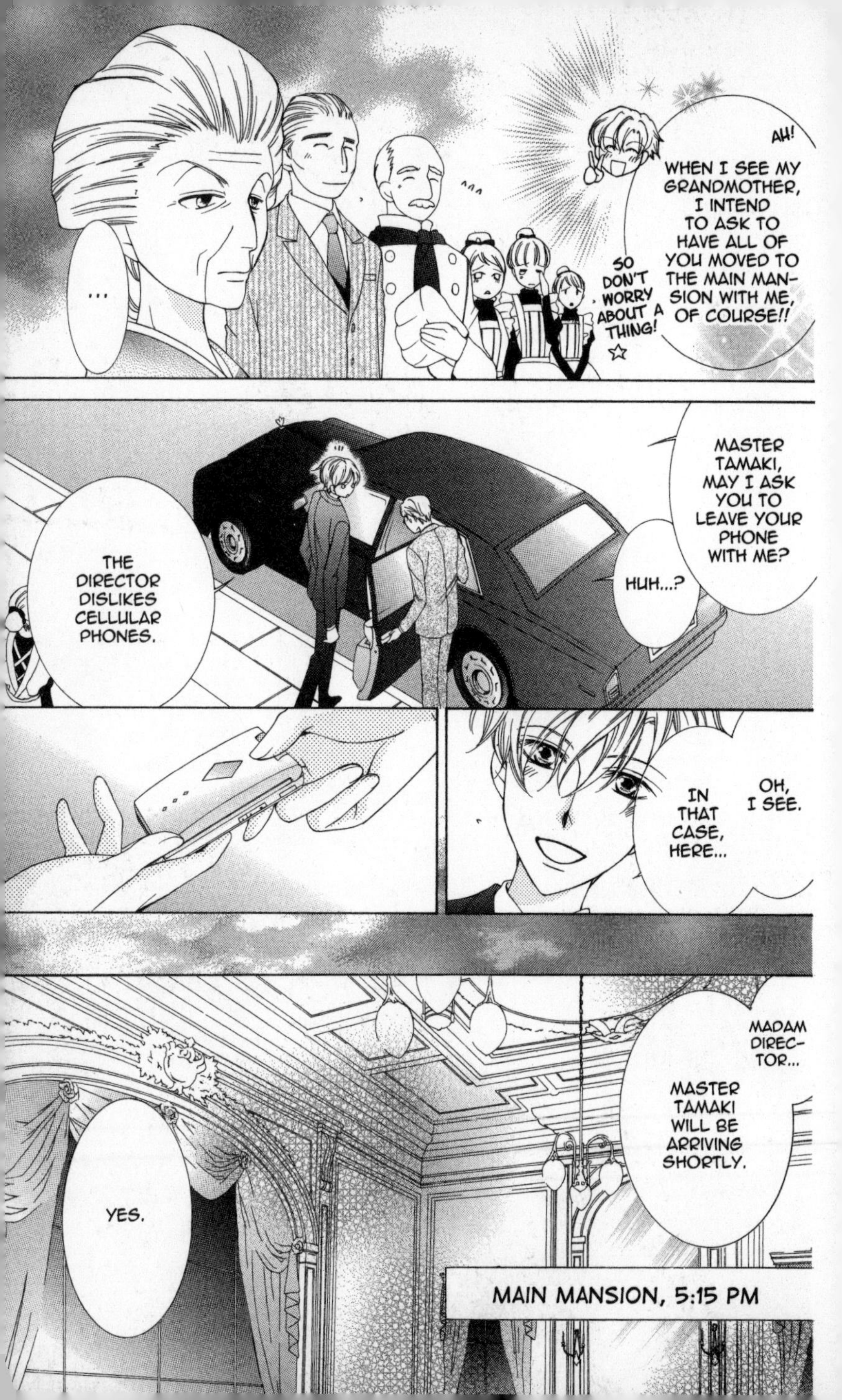
AH!
WHEN I SEE MY GRANDMOTHER, I INTEND TO ASK TO HAVE ALL OF YOU MOVED TO THE MAIN MANSION WITH ME, OF COURSE!!
SO DON'T WORRY ABOUT A THING! ☆
...
MASTER TAMAKI, MAY I ASK YOU TO LEAVE YOUR PHONE WITH ME?
HUH...?
THE DIRECTOR DISLIKES CELLULAR PHONES.
OH, I SEE.
IN THAT CASE, HERE...
MADAM DIRECTOR...
MASTER TAMAKI WILL BE ARRIVING SHORTLY.
YES.
MAIN MANSION, 5:15 PM

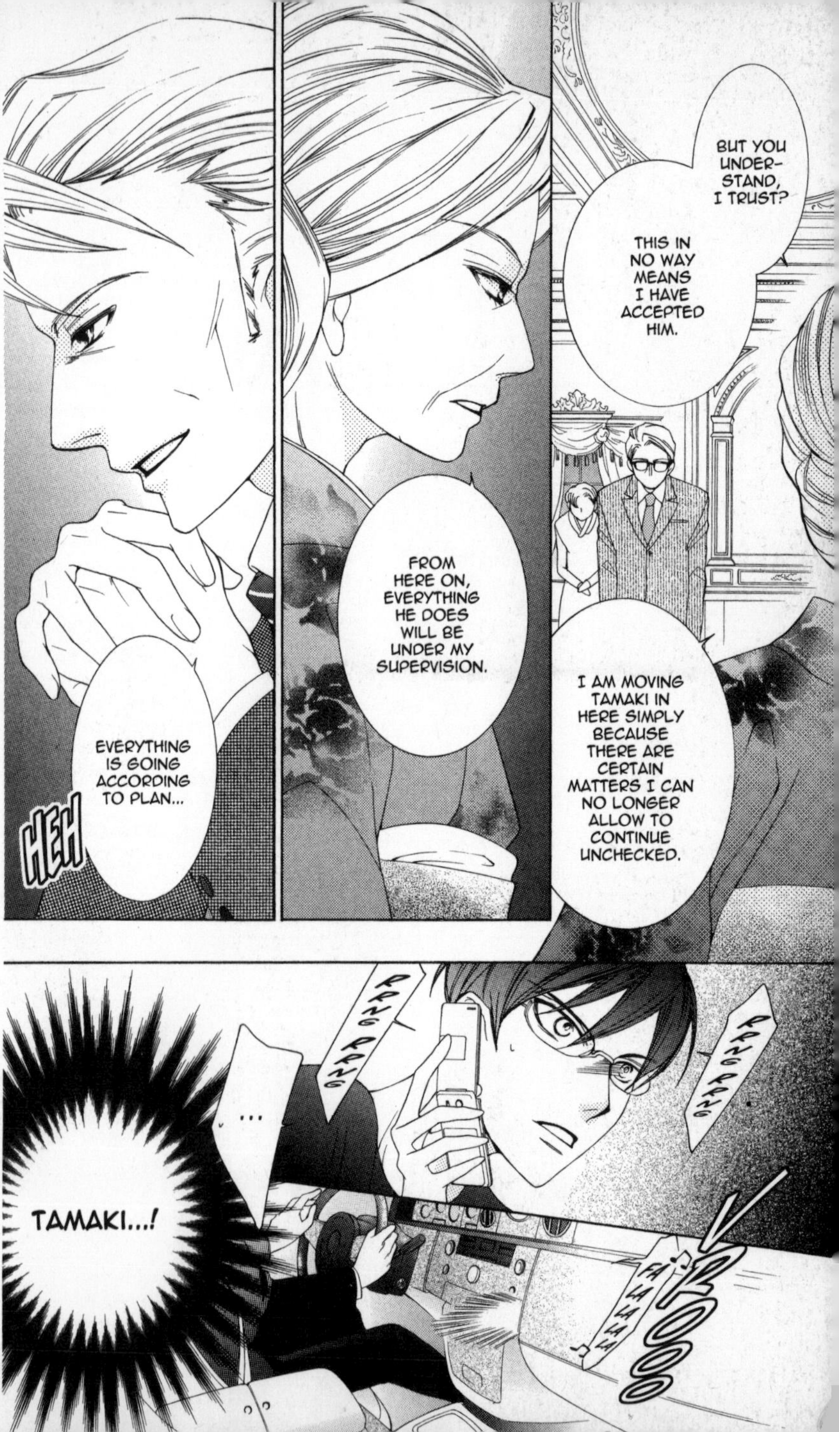
BUT YOU UNDER-STAND, I TRUST?
THIS IN NO WAY MEANS I HAVE ACCEPTED HIM.
I AM MOVING TAMAKI IN HERE SIMPLY BECAUSE THERE ARE CERTAIN MATTERS I CAN NO LONGER ALLOW TO CONTINUE UNCHECKED.
FROM HERE ON, EVERYTHING HE DOES WILL BE UNDER MY SUPERVISION.
EVERYTHING IS GOING ACCORDING TO PLAN...
HEH
RRNG RRNG
VROOOOO
FA LA LA LA
RRNG RRNG
...
TAMAKI...!

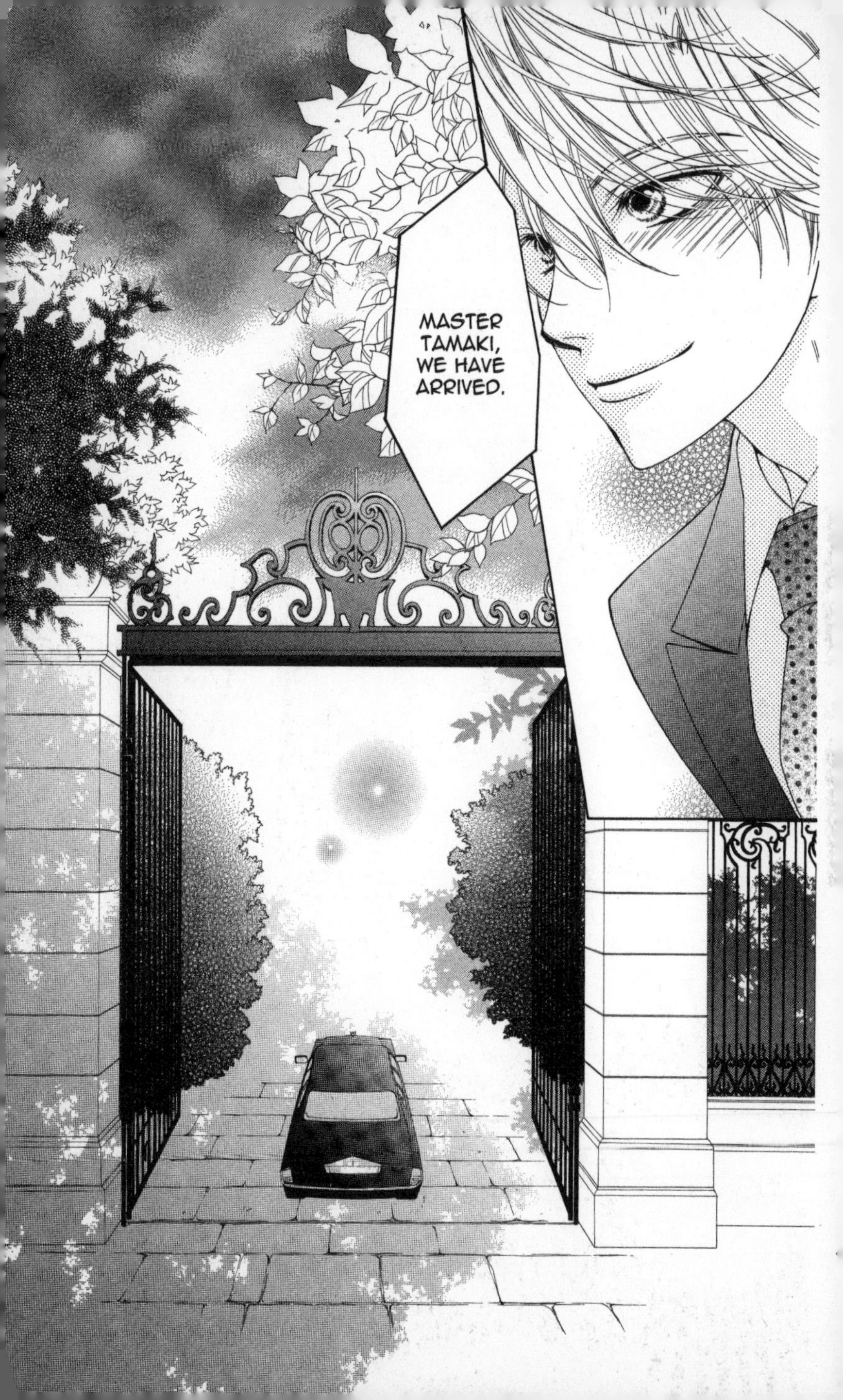
MASTER TAMAKI, WE HAVE ARRIVED.

TEAM☆HATORI'S ROOM

UMEKO

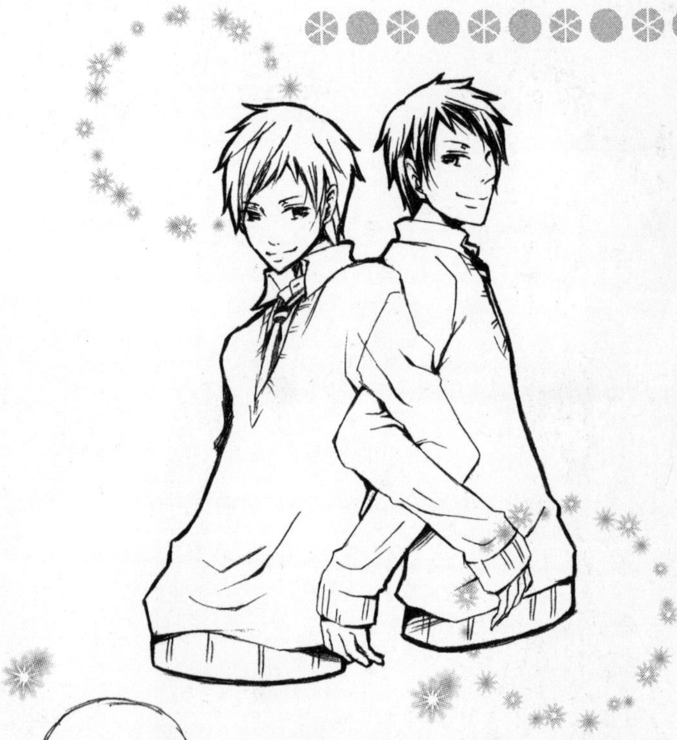

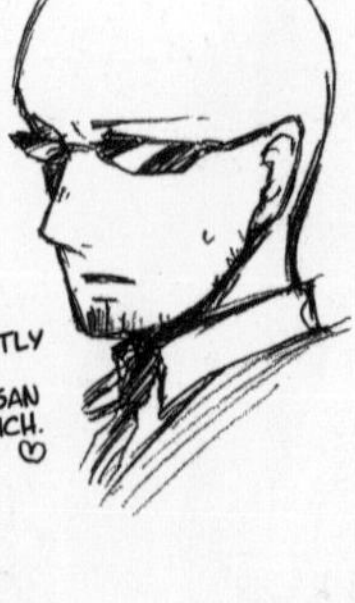
I SECRETLY LIKE HOTTA-SAN VERY MUCH. ♡

OUR NEW STAFF MEMBER, UME-CHAN, DREW PICTURES OF OUR FASHIONABLE TWINS AND HOTTA FOR ME.♡ THEY'RE SO FASHIONABLE... I NEED TO LEARN THIS TOO! UME-CHAN IS ALSO QUITE FASHIONABLE HERSELF: SHE'S AN ADORABLE, PETITE GIRL WHOSE HOBBY IS MAKING SWEETS!☆SHE OFTEN DRESSES LIKE MINNIE MOUSE TOO.

YET SHE'S ALSO A HARDCORE HISTORY BUFF.

WHENEVER WE HAVE FREE TIME, SHE CAN ALWAYS BE FOUND READING SOME HISTORICAL NOVEL OR OTHER. GAP MOE!

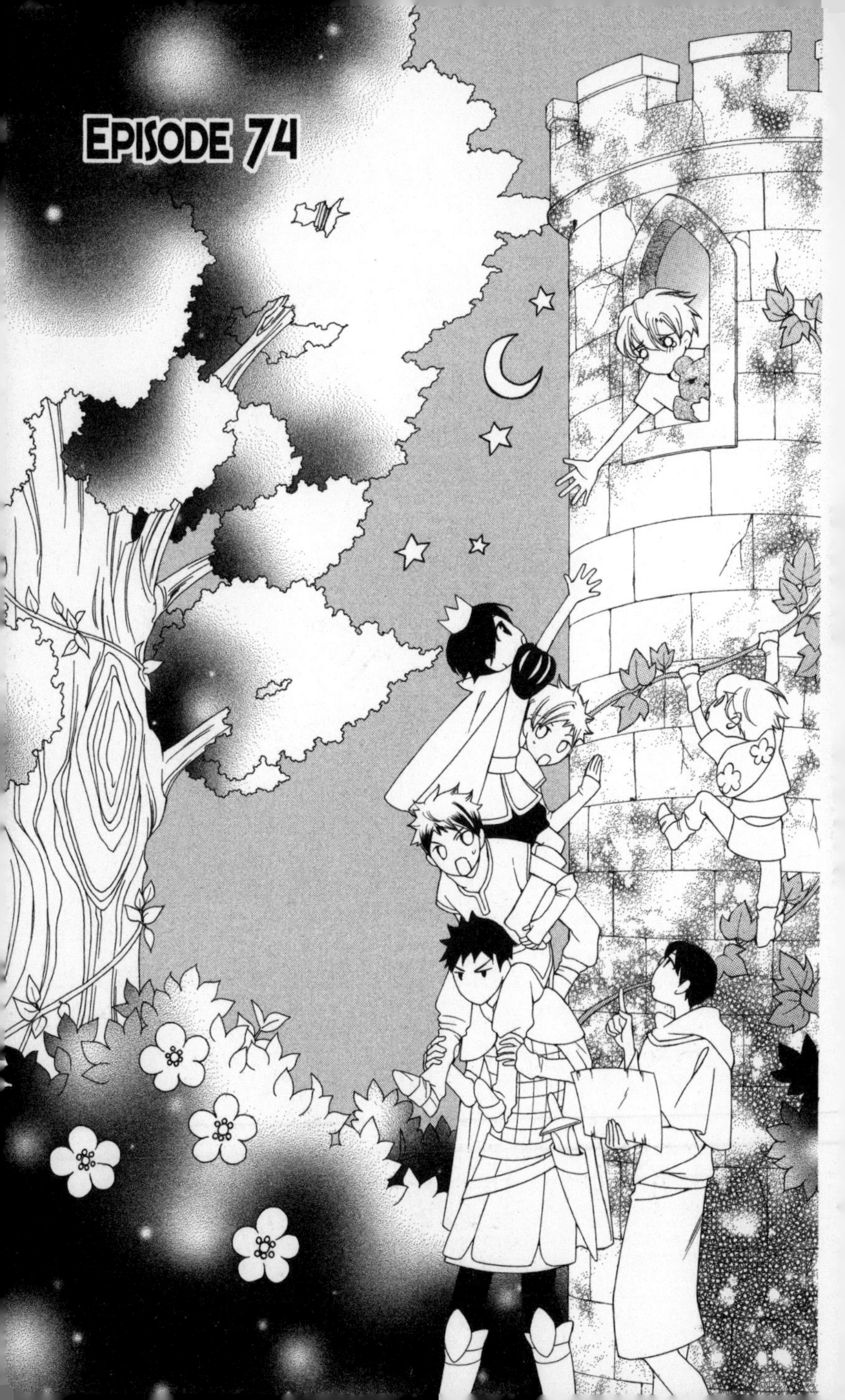
Episode 74

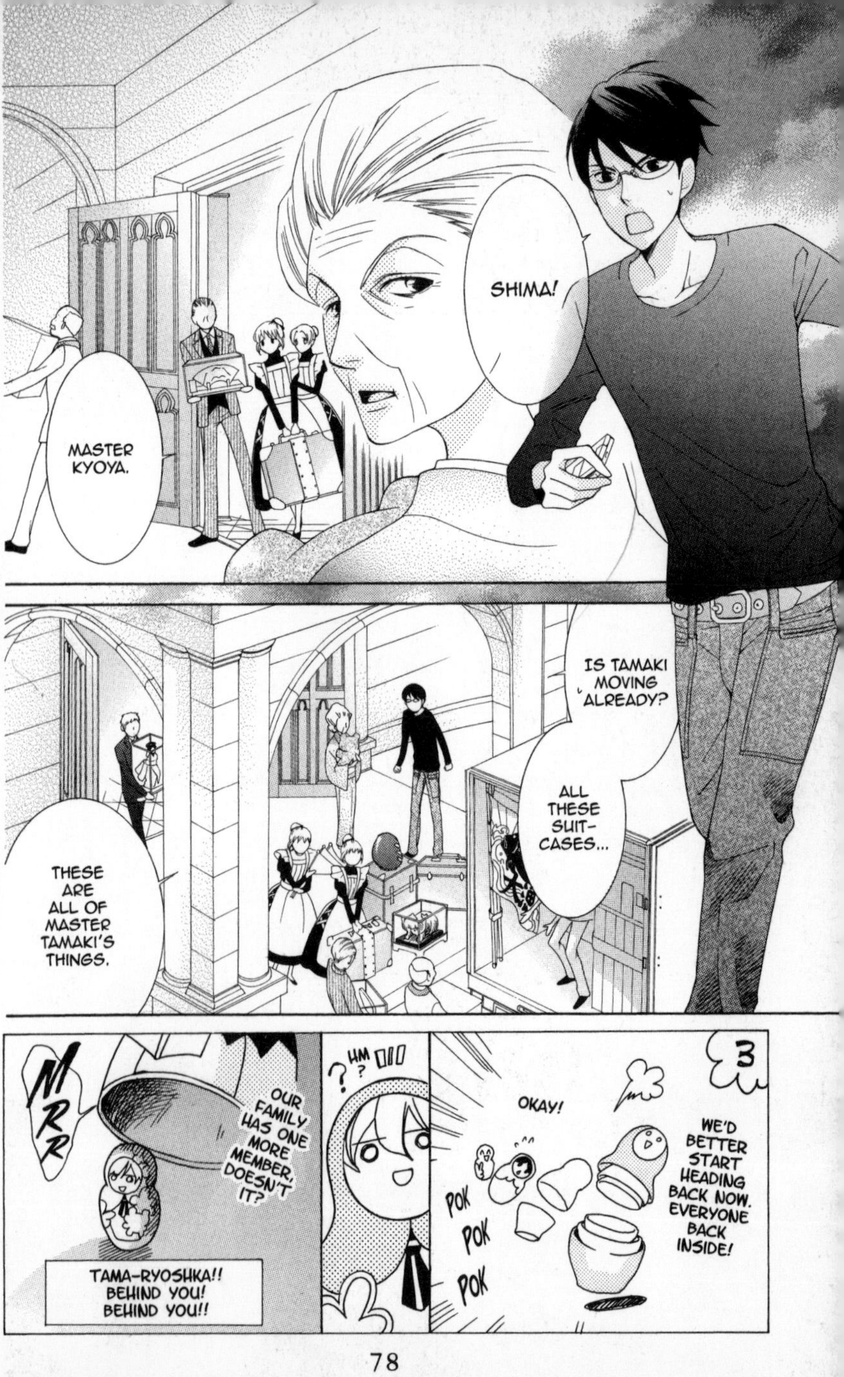
SHIMA!
MASTER KYOYA.
IS TAMAKI MOVING ALREADY?
ALL THESE SUIT-CASES...
THESE ARE ALL OF MASTER TAMAKI'S THINGS.
3
OKAY!
WE'D BETTER START HEADING BACK NOW. EVERYONE BACK INSIDE!
POK
POK
POK
HM ?
OUR FAMILY HAS ONE MORE MEMBER, DOESN'T IT?
MRR
TAMA-RYOSHKA!! BEHIND YOU! BEHIND YOU!!

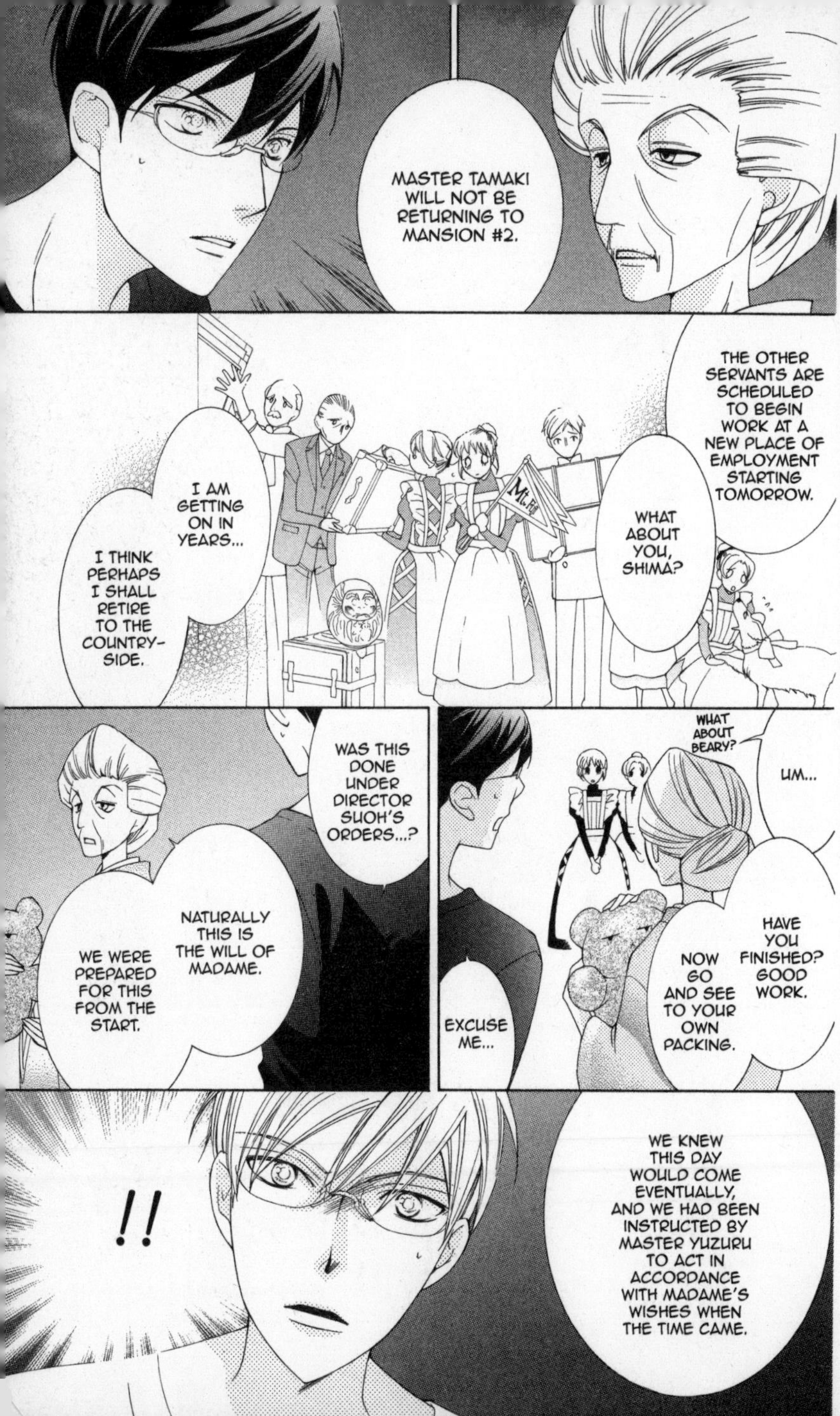
MASTER TAMAKI WILL NOT BE RETURNING TO MANSION #2.
THE OTHER SERVANTS ARE SCHEDULED TO BEGIN WORK AT A NEW PLACE OF EMPLOYMENT STARTING TOMORROW.
WHAT ABOUT YOU, SHIMA?
I AM GETTING ON IN YEARS...
I THINK PERHAPS I SHALL RETIRE TO THE COUNTRY-SIDE.
UM...
WHAT ABOUT BEARY?
HAVE YOU FINISHED? GOOD WORK.
NOW GO AND SEE TO YOUR OWN PACKING.
EXCUSE ME...
WAS THIS DONE UNDER DIRECTOR SUOH'S ORDERS...?
NATURALLY THIS IS THE WILL OF MADAME.
WE WERE PREPARED FOR THIS FROM THE START.
WE KNEW THIS DAY WOULD COME EVENTUALLY, AND WE HAD BEEN INSTRUCTED BY MASTER YUZURU TO ACT IN ACCORDANCE WITH MADAME'S WISHES WHEN THE TIME CAME.
!!

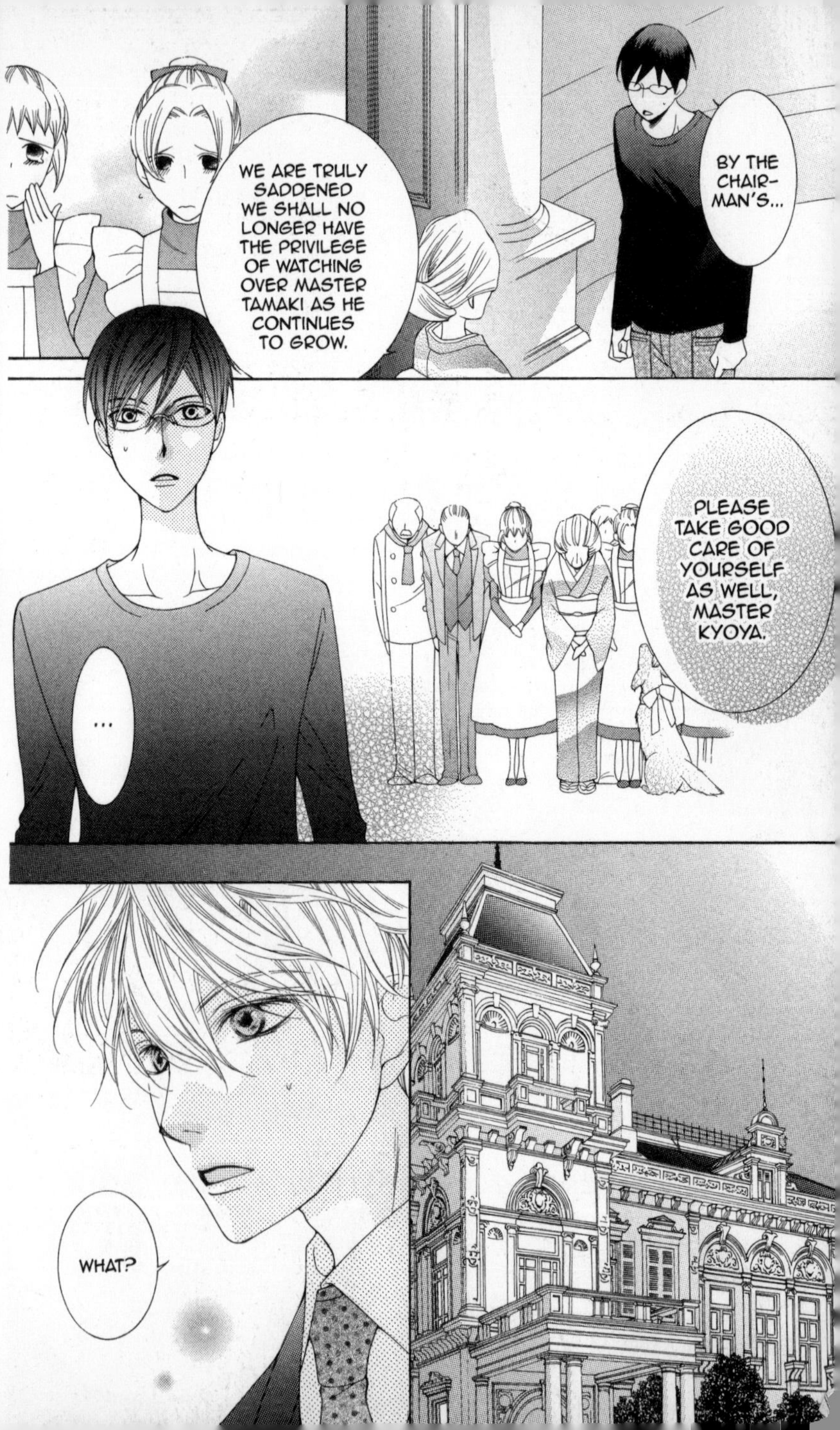
BY THE CHAIR-MAN'S...
WE ARE TRULY SADDENED WE SHALL NO LONGER HAVE THE PRIVILEGE OF WATCHING OVER MASTER TAMAKI AS HE CONTINUES TO GROW.
PLEASE TAKE GOOD CARE OF YOURSELF AS WELL, MASTER KYOYA.
...
WHAT?

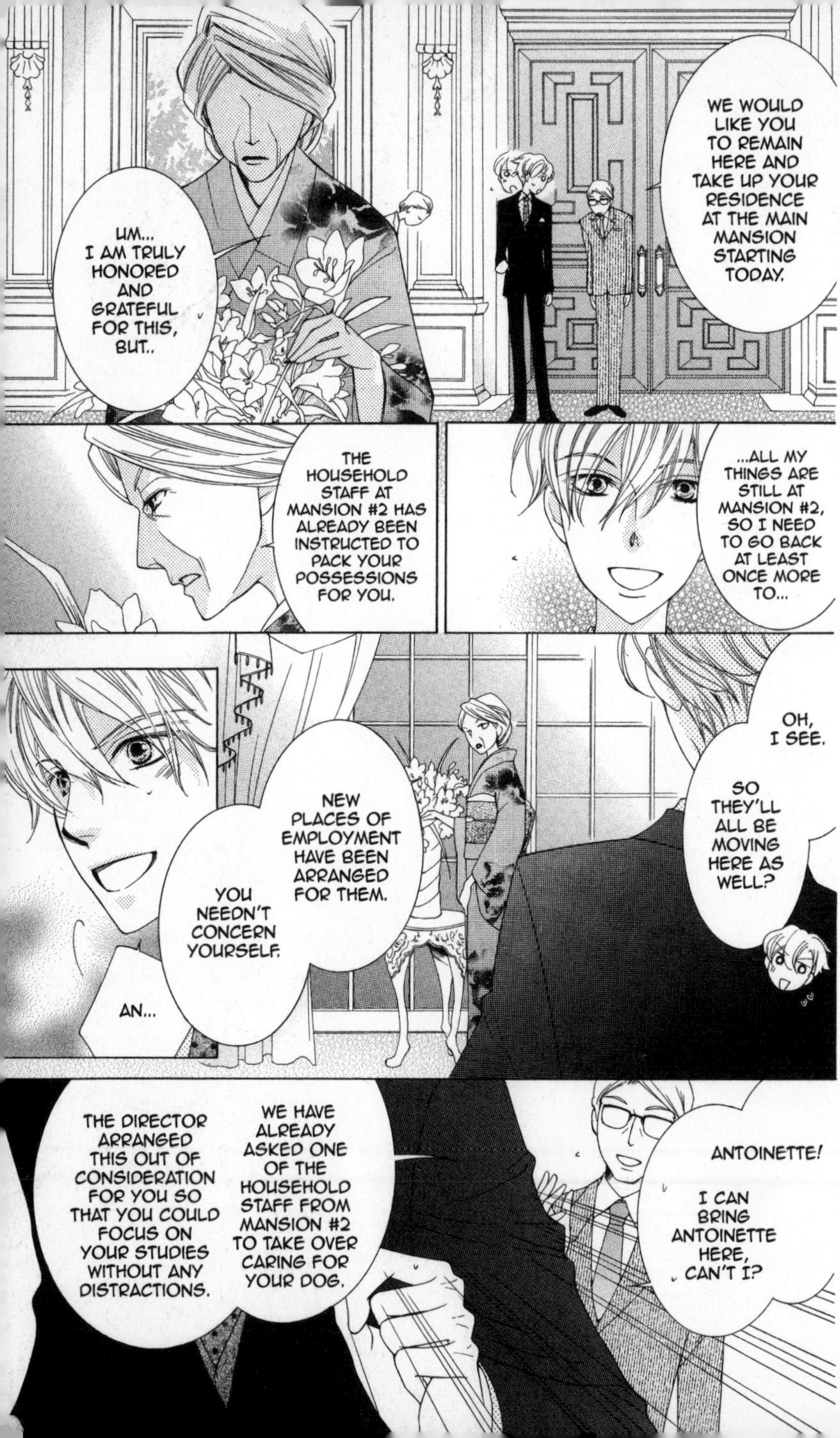
WE WOULD LIKE YOU TO REMAIN HERE AND TAKE UP YOUR RESIDENCE AT THE MAIN MANSION STARTING TODAY.
UM... I AM TRULY HONORED AND GRATEFUL FOR THIS, BUT..
...ALL MY THINGS ARE STILL AT MANSION #2, SO I NEED TO GO BACK AT LEAST ONCE MORE TO...
THE HOUSEHOLD STAFF AT MANSION #2 HAS ALREADY BEEN INSTRUCTED TO PACK YOUR POSSESSIONS FOR YOU.
OH, I SEE.
SO THEY'LL ALL BE MOVING HERE AS WELL?
NEW PLACES OF EMPLOYMENT HAVE BEEN ARRANGED FOR THEM.
YOU NEEDN'T CONCERN YOURSELF.
AN...
ANTOINETTE!
I CAN BRING ANTOINETTE HERE, CAN'T I?
WE HAVE ALREADY ASKED ONE OF THE HOUSEHOLD STAFF FROM MANSION #2 TO TAKE OVER CARING FOR YOUR DOG.
THE DIRECTOR ARRANGED THIS OUT OF CONSIDERATION FOR YOU SO THAT YOU COULD FOCUS ON YOUR STUDIES WITHOUT ANY DISTRACTIONS.

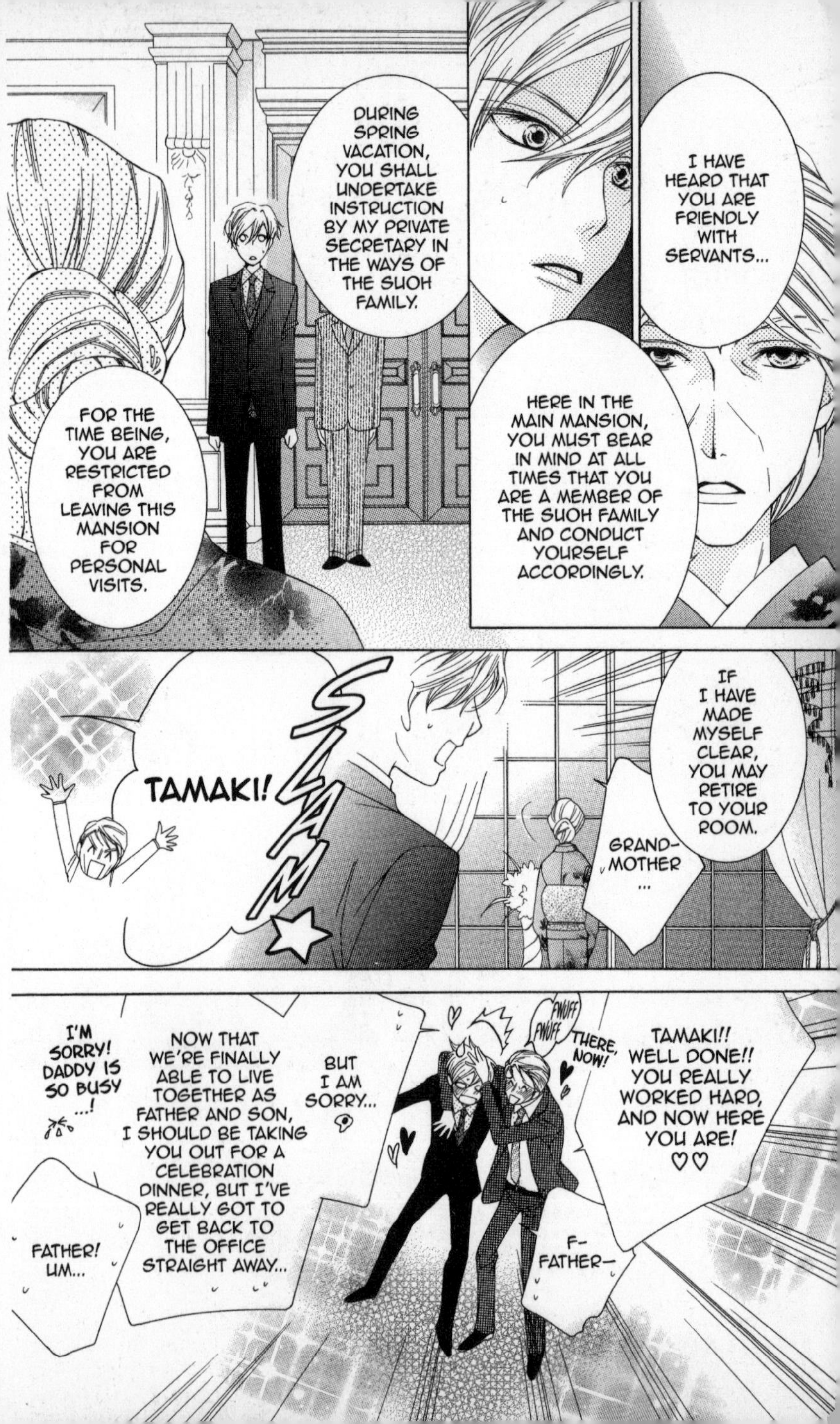
I HAVE HEARD THAT YOU ARE FRIENDLY WITH SERVANTS...
HERE IN THE MAIN MANSION, YOU MUST BEAR IN MIND AT ALL TIMES THAT YOU ARE A MEMBER OF THE SUOH FAMILY AND CONDUCT YOURSELF ACCORDINGLY.
DURING SPRING VACATION, YOU SHALL UNDERTAKE INSTRUCTION BY MY PRIVATE SECRETARY IN THE WAYS OF THE SUOH FAMILY.
FOR THE TIME BEING, YOU ARE RESTRICTED FROM LEAVING THIS MANSION FOR PERSONAL VISITS.
IF I HAVE MADE MYSELF CLEAR, YOU MAY RETIRE TO YOUR ROOM.
GRAND-MOTHER...
SLAM
TAMAKI!
TAMAKI!! WELL DONE!! YOU REALLY WORKED HARD, AND NOW HERE YOU ARE! ♡♡
FWUFF FWUFF
THERE, NOW!
F-FATHER—
BUT I AM SORRY...
NOW THAT WE'RE FINALLY ABLE TO LIVE TOGETHER AS FATHER AND SON, I SHOULD BE TAKING YOU OUT FOR A CELEBRATION DINNER, BUT I'VE REALLY GOT TO GET BACK TO THE OFFICE STRAIGHT AWAY...
I'M SORRY! DADDY IS SO BUSY...!
FATHER! UM...

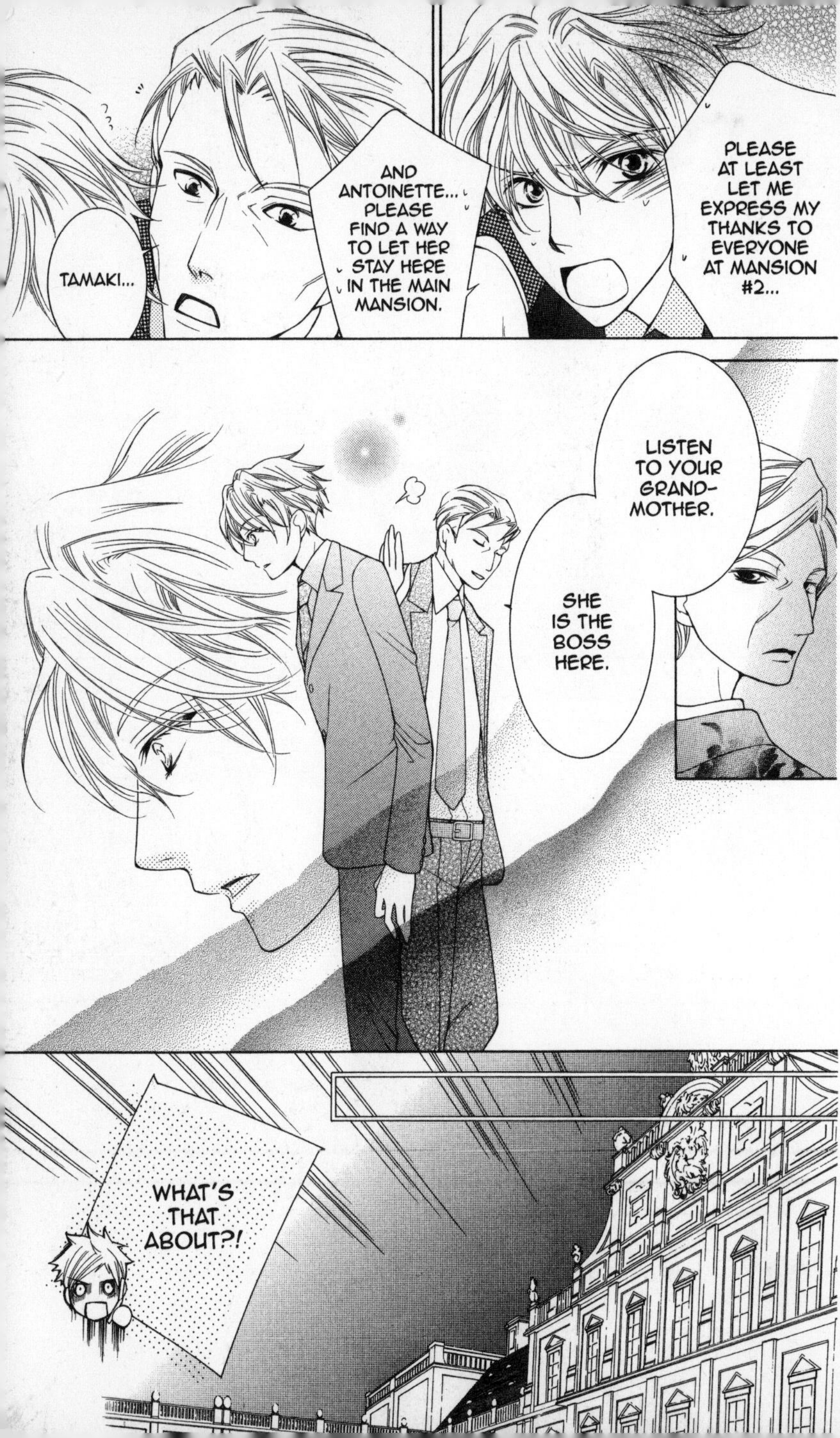
PLEASE AT LEAST LET ME EXPRESS MY THANKS TO EVERYONE AT MANSION #2...
AND ANTOINETTE... PLEASE FIND A WAY TO LET HER STAY HERE IN THE MAIN MANSION.
TAMAKI...
LISTEN TO YOUR GRAND-MOTHER.
SHE IS THE BOSS HERE.
WHAT'S THAT ABOUT?!

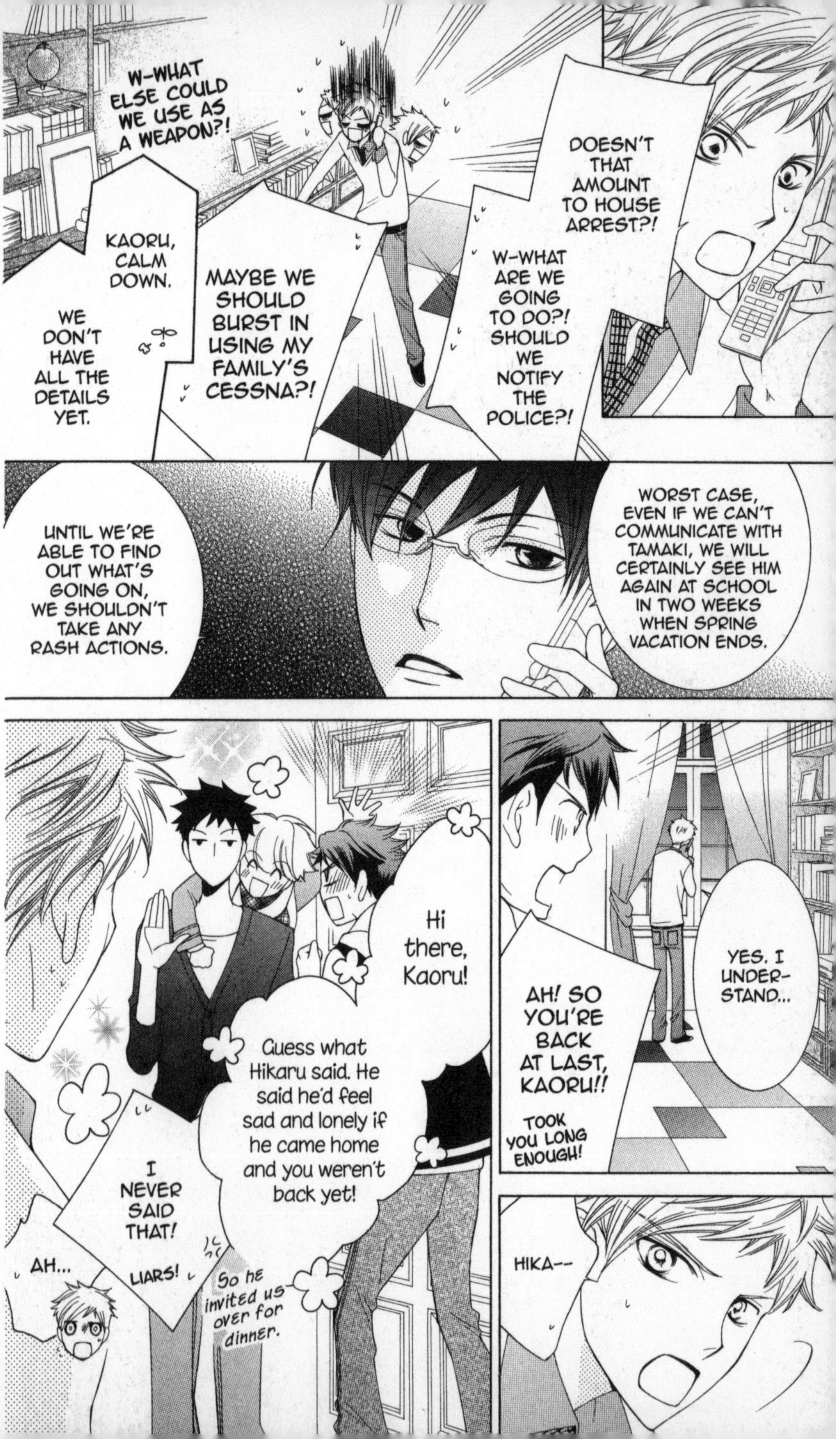
DOESN'T THAT AMOUNT TO HOUSE ARREST?!
W-WHAT ARE WE GOING TO DO?! SHOULD WE NOTIFY THE POLICE?!
MAYBE WE SHOULD BURST IN USING MY FAMILY'S CESSNA?!
W-WHAT ELSE COULD WE USE AS A WEAPON?!
KAORU, CALM DOWN.
WE DON'T HAVE ALL THE DETAILS YET.
WORST CASE, EVEN IF WE CAN'T COMMUNICATE WITH TAMAKI, WE WILL CERTAINLY SEE HIM AGAIN AT SCHOOL IN TWO WEEKS WHEN SPRING VACATION ENDS.
UNTIL WE'RE ABLE TO FIND OUT WHAT'S GOING ON, WE SHOULDN'T TAKE ANY RASH ACTIONS.
YES. I UNDER-STAND...
AH! SO YOU'RE BACK AT LAST, KAORU!!
TOOK YOU LONG ENOUGH!
HIKA--
Hi there, Kaoru!
Guess what Hikaru said. He said he'd feel sad and lonely if he came home and you weren't back yet!
I NEVER SAID THAT!
LIARS!
AH...
So he invited us over for dinner.

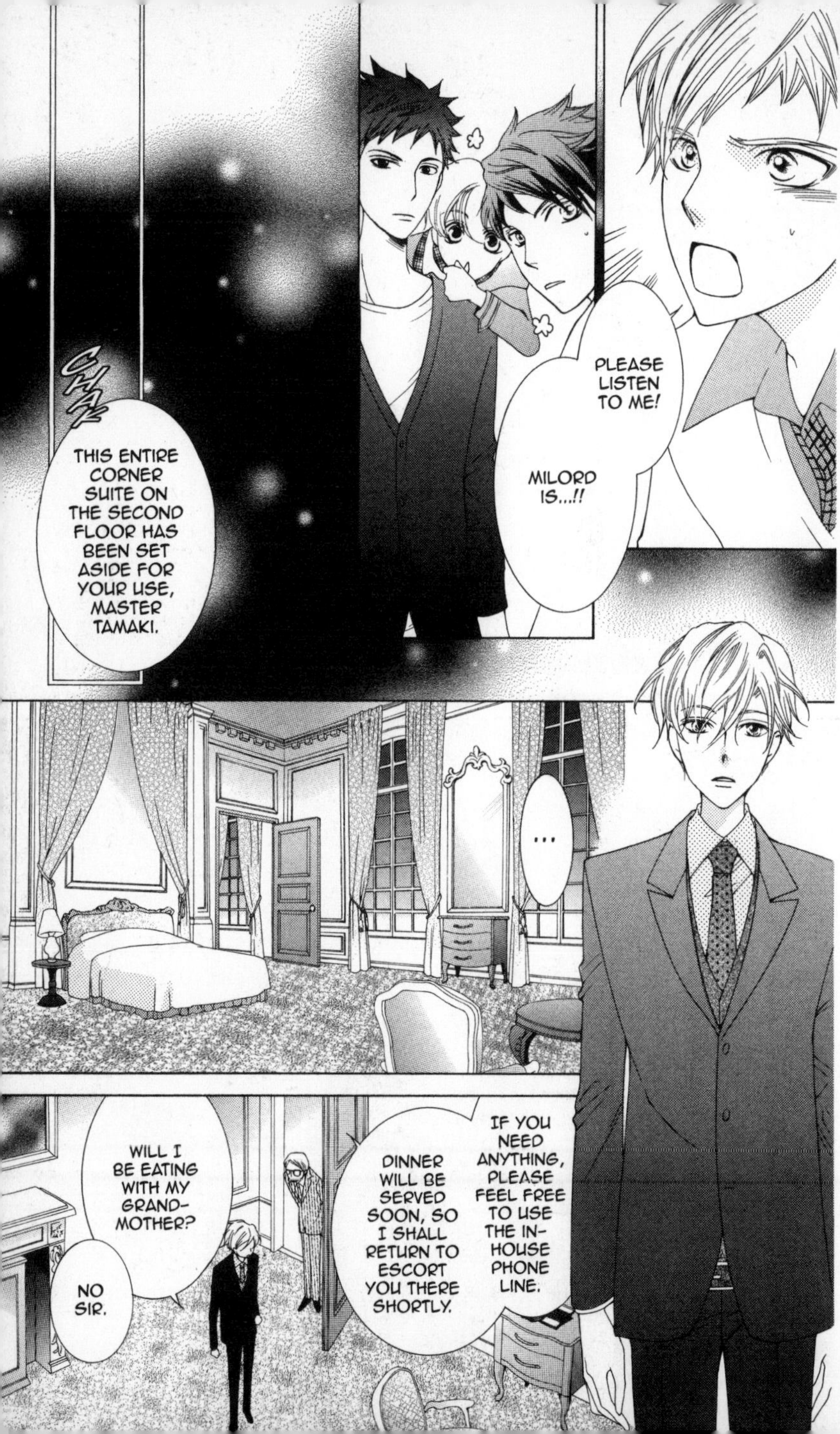
PLEASE LISTEN TO ME!
MILORD IS...!!
CHAK
THIS ENTIRE CORNER SUITE ON THE SECOND FLOOR HAS BEEN SET ASIDE FOR YOUR USE, MASTER TAMAKI.
...
IF YOU NEED ANYTHING, PLEASE FEEL FREE TO USE THE IN-HOUSE PHONE LINE.
DINNER WILL BE SERVED SOON, SO I SHALL RETURN TO ESCORT YOU THERE SHORTLY.
WILL I BE EATING WITH MY GRAND-MOTHER?
NO SIR.

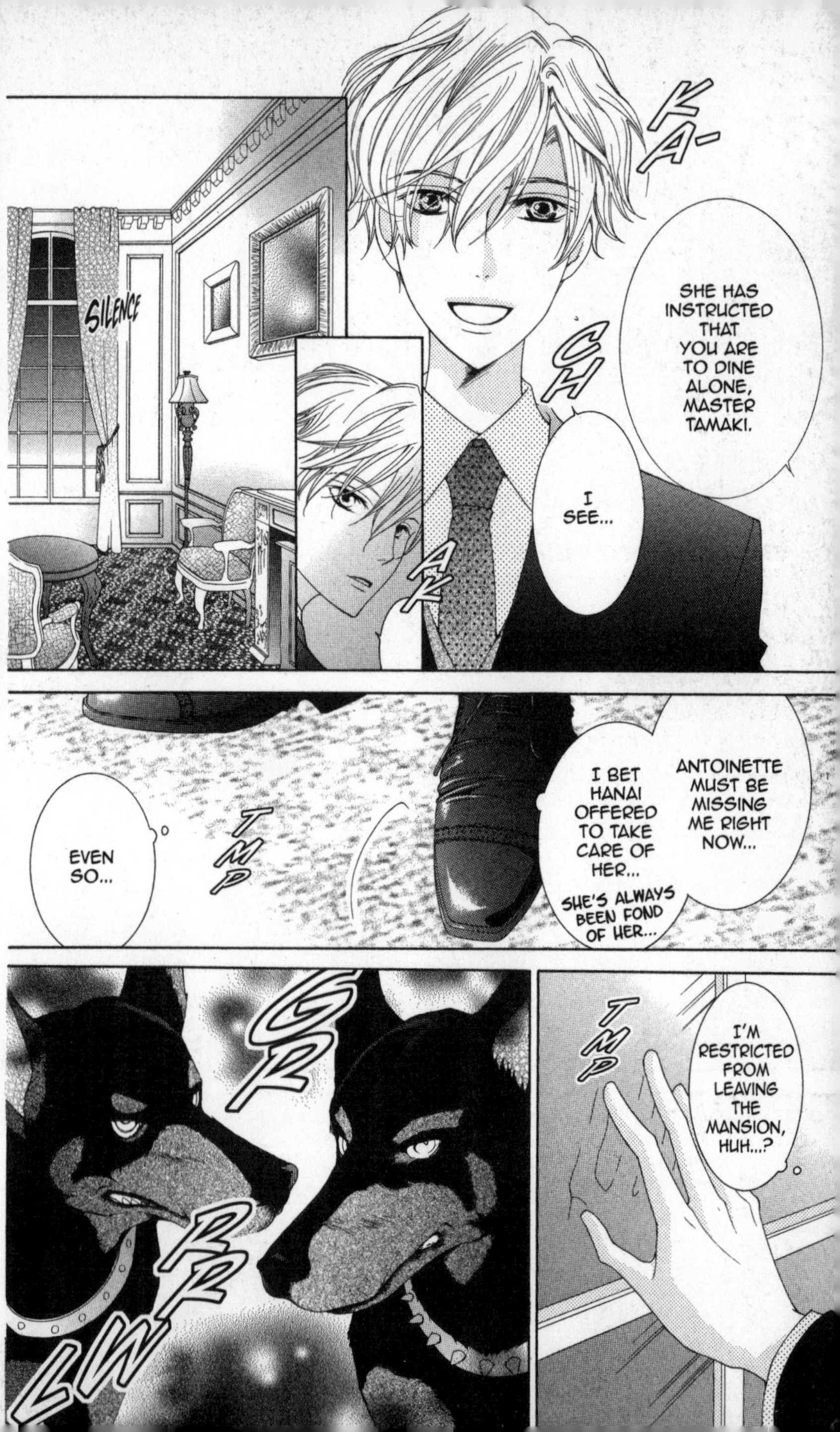
KA-CHAK
SHE HAS INSTRUCTED THAT YOU ARE TO DINE ALONE, MASTER TAMAKI.
I SEE...
SILENCE
ANTOINETTE MUST BE MISSING ME RIGHT NOW...
I BET HANAI OFFERED TO TAKE CARE OF HER...
SHE'S ALWAYS BEEN FOND OF HER...
TMP
EVEN SO...
TMP
I'M RESTRICTED FROM LEAVING THE MANSION, HUH...?
GRRRLW

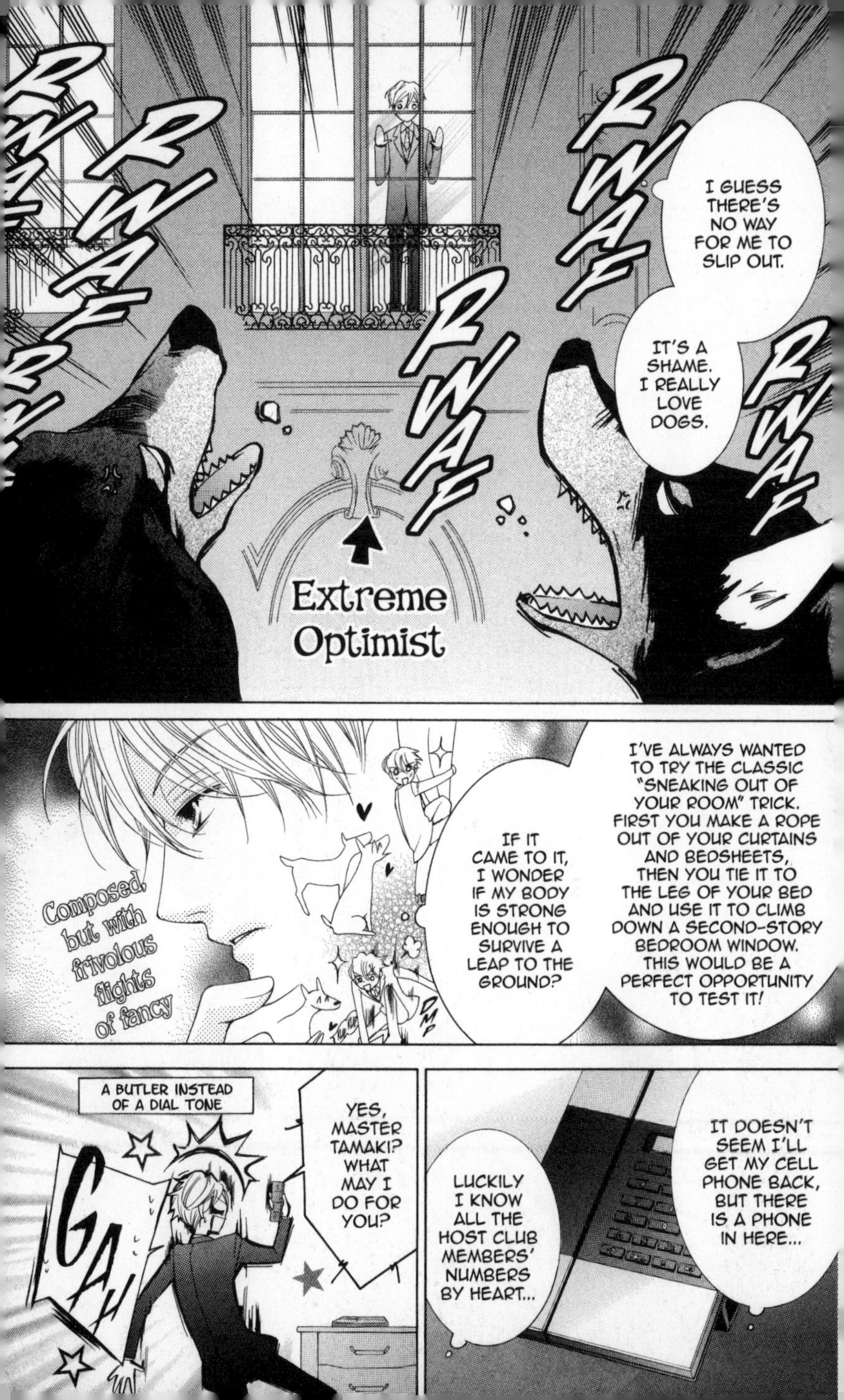
RWAF RWAF
I GUESS THERE'S NO WAY FOR ME TO SLIP OUT.
IT'S A SHAME. I REALLY LOVE DOGS.
RWAF RWAF
RWAF RWAF
Extreme Optimist
I'VE ALWAYS WANTED TO TRY THE CLASSIC "SNEAKING OUT OF YOUR ROOM" TRICK. FIRST YOU MAKE A ROPE OUT OF YOUR CURTAINS AND BEDSHEETS, THEN YOU TIE IT TO THE LEG OF YOUR BED AND USE IT TO CLIMB DOWN A SECOND-STORY BEDROOM WINDOW. THIS WOULD BE A PERFECT OPPORTUNITY TO TEST IT!
IF IT CAME TO IT, I WONDER IF MY BODY IS STRONG ENOUGH TO SURVIVE A LEAP TO THE GROUND?
Composed, but with frivolous flights of fancy
IT DOESN'T SEEM I'LL GET MY CELL PHONE BACK, BUT THERE IS A PHONE IN HERE...
LUCKILY I KNOW ALL THE HOST CLUB MEMBERS' NUMBERS BY HEART...
A BUTLER INSTEAD OF A DIAL TONE
YES, MASTER TAMAKI? WHAT MAY I DO FOR YOU?
GAH

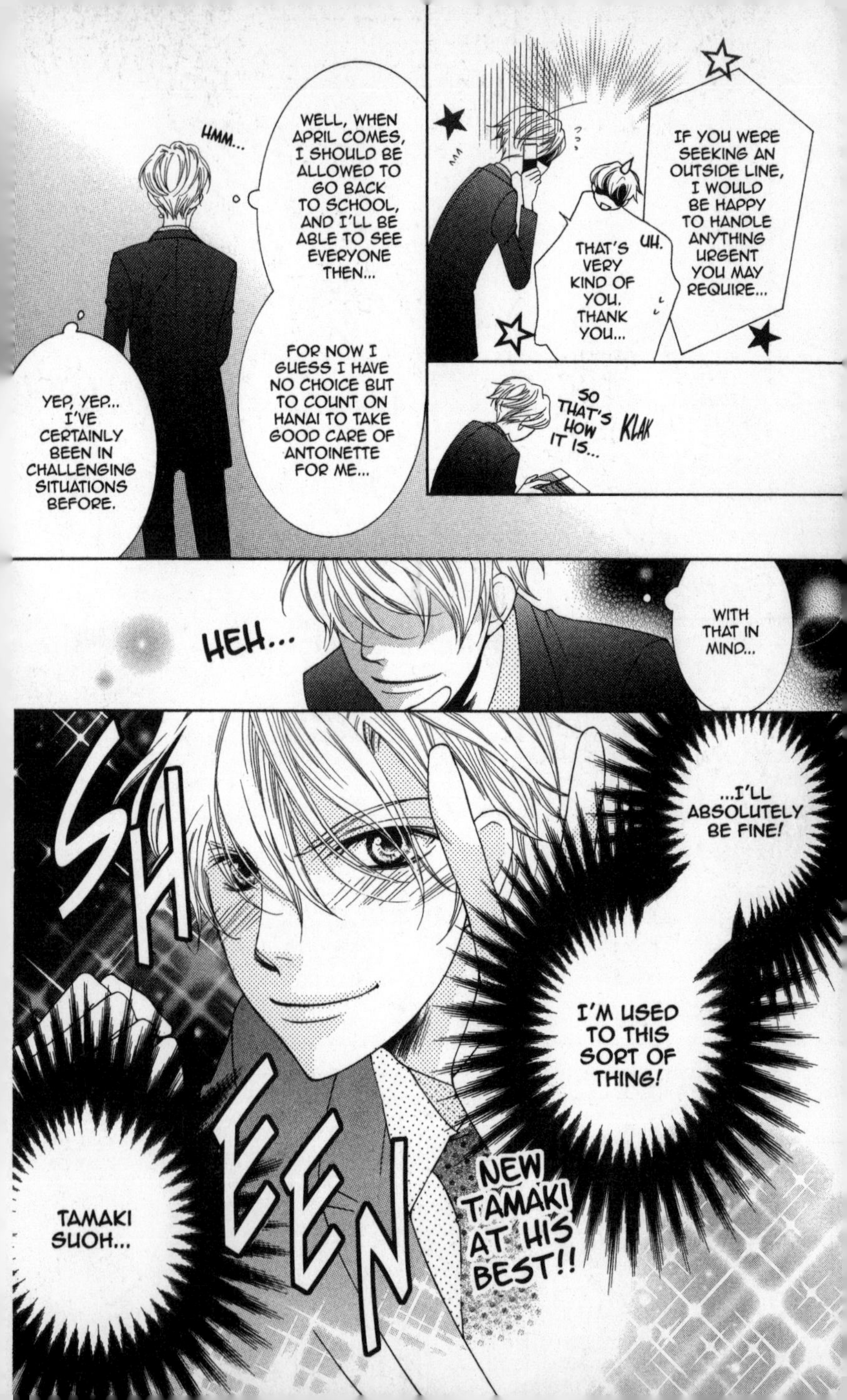
IF YOU WERE SEEKING AN OUTSIDE LINE, I WOULD BE HAPPY TO HANDLE ANYTHING URGENT YOU MAY REQUIRE...
UH.
THAT'S VERY KIND OF YOU. THANK YOU...
KLAK
SO THAT'S HOW IT IS...
WELL, WHEN APRIL COMES, I SHOULD BE ALLOWED TO GO BACK TO SCHOOL, AND I'LL BE ABLE TO SEE EVERYONE THEN...
HMM...
FOR NOW I GUESS I HAVE NO CHOICE BUT TO COUNT ON HANAI TO TAKE GOOD CARE OF ANTOINETTE FOR ME...
YEP, YEP... I'VE CERTAINLY BEEN IN CHALLENGING SITUATIONS BEFORE.
WITH THAT IN MIND...
HEH...
...I'LL ABSOLUTELY BE FINE!
SHEEN
I'M USED TO THIS SORT OF THING!
NEW TAMAKI AT HIS BEST!!
TAMAKI SUOH...

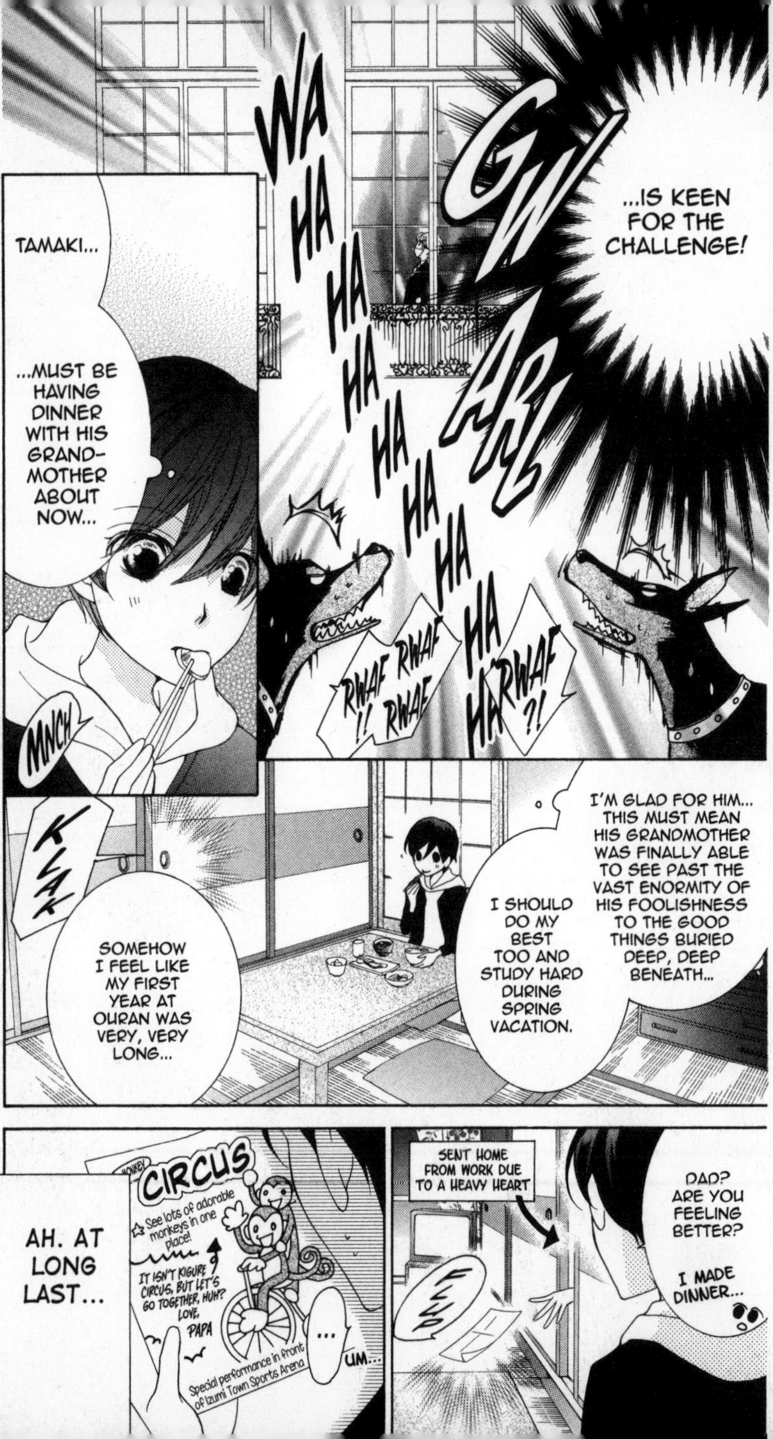
...IS KEEN FOR THE CHALLENGE!
GWARR
WA HA HA HA HA HA HA HA HA HA HA
RWAF RWAF RWAF !!
RWAF ?!
TAMAKI...
...MUST BE HAVING DINNER WITH HIS GRANDMOTHER ABOUT NOW...
MNCH
I'M GLAD FOR HIM... THIS MUST MEAN HIS GRANDMOTHER WAS FINALLY ABLE TO SEE PAST THE VAST ENORMITY OF HIS FOOLISHNESS TO THE GOOD THINGS BURIED DEEP, DEEP BENEATH...
I SHOULD DO MY BEST TOO AND STUDY HARD DURING SPRING VACATION.
SOMEHOW I FEEL LIKE MY FIRST YEAR AT OURAN WAS VERY, VERY LONG...
KLAK
DAD? ARE YOU FEELING BETTER?
I MADE DINNER...
SENT HOME FROM WORK DUE TO A HEAVY HEART
FLUP
UM...
...
CIRCUS
MONKEY
See lots of adorable monkeys in one place!
IT ISN'T KIGURE CIRCUS, BUT LET'S GO TOGETHER, HUH? LOVE, PAPA
Special performance in front of Izumi Town Sports Arena
AH. AT LONG LAST...

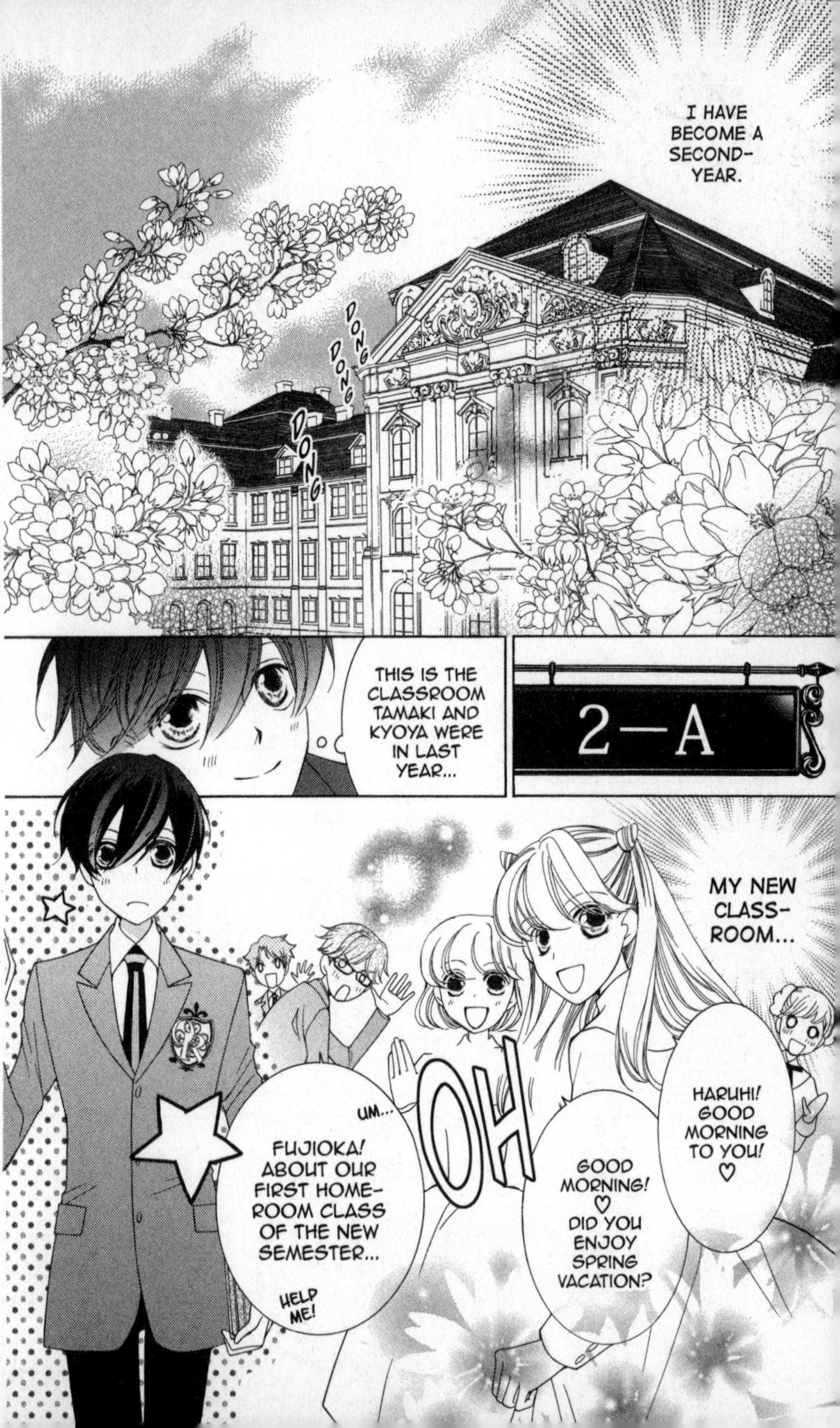
I HAVE BECOME A SECOND-YEAR.
DONG DONG
DONG DONG
2—A
THIS IS THE CLASSROOM TAMAKI AND KYOYA WERE IN LAST YEAR...
MY NEW CLASSROOM...
HARUHI! GOOD MORNING TO YOU! ♡
GOOD MORNING! ♡ DID YOU ENJOY SPRING VACATION?
OH
UM...
FUJIOKA! ABOUT OUR FIRST HOMEROOM CLASS OF THE NEW SEMESTER...
HELP ME!

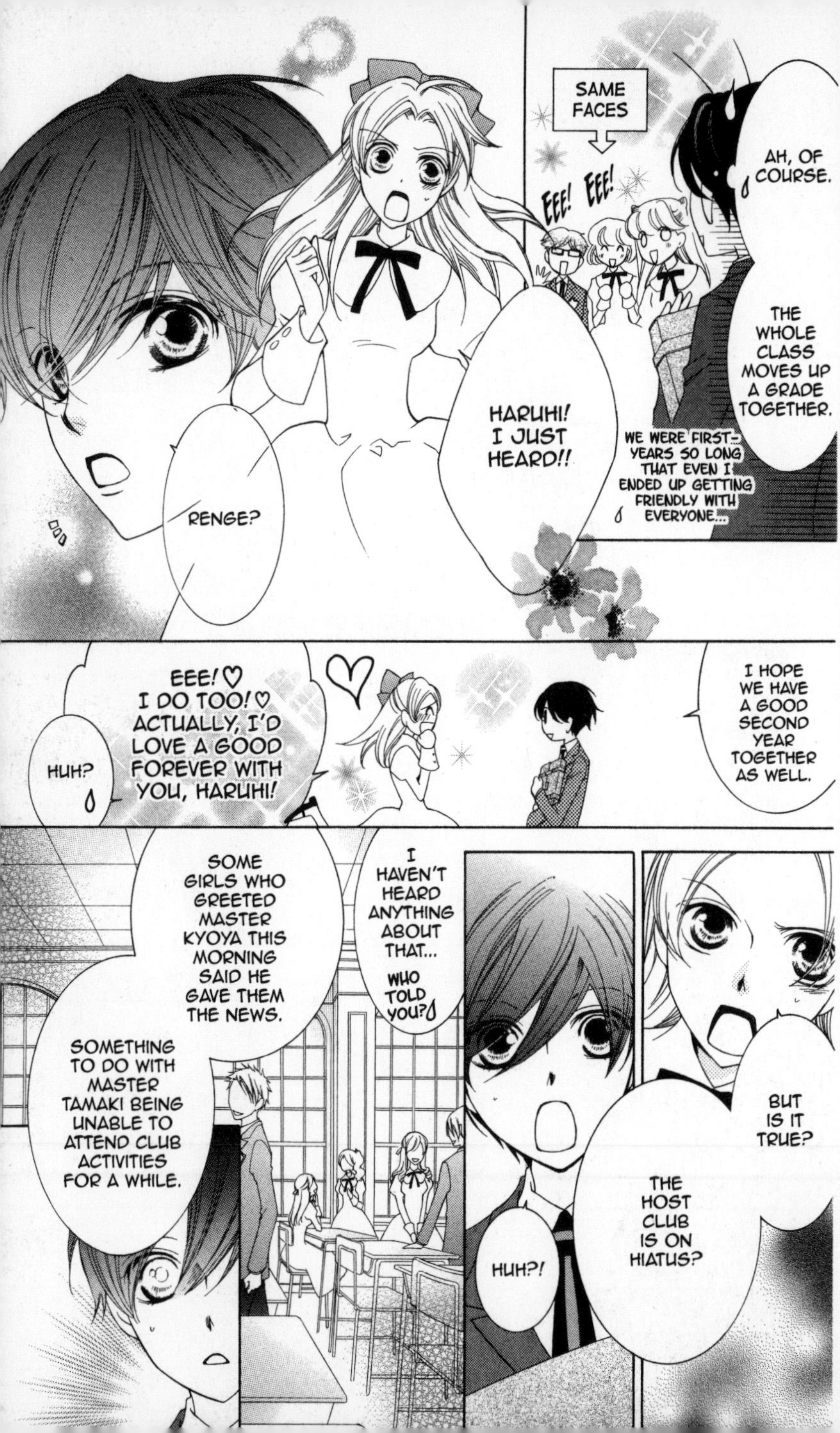
AH, OF COURSE.
THE WHOLE CLASS MOVES UP A GRADE TOGETHER.
SAME FACES
EEE! EEE!
WE WERE FIRST-YEARS SO LONG THAT EVEN I ENDED UP GETTING FRIENDLY WITH EVERYONE...
HARUHI! I JUST HEARD!!
RENGE?
I HOPE WE HAVE A GOOD SECOND YEAR TOGETHER AS WELL.
EEE! ♡ I DO TOO! ♡ ACTUALLY, I'D LOVE A GOOD FOREVER WITH YOU, HARUHI!
HUH?
BUT IS IT TRUE?
THE HOST CLUB IS ON HIATUS?
HUH?!
I HAVEN'T HEARD ANYTHING ABOUT THAT...
WHO TOLD YOU?
SOME GIRLS WHO GREETED MASTER KYOYA THIS MORNING SAID HE GAVE THEM THE NEWS.
SOMETHING TO DO WITH MASTER TAMAKI BEING UNABLE TO ATTEND CLUB ACTIVITIES FOR A WHILE.

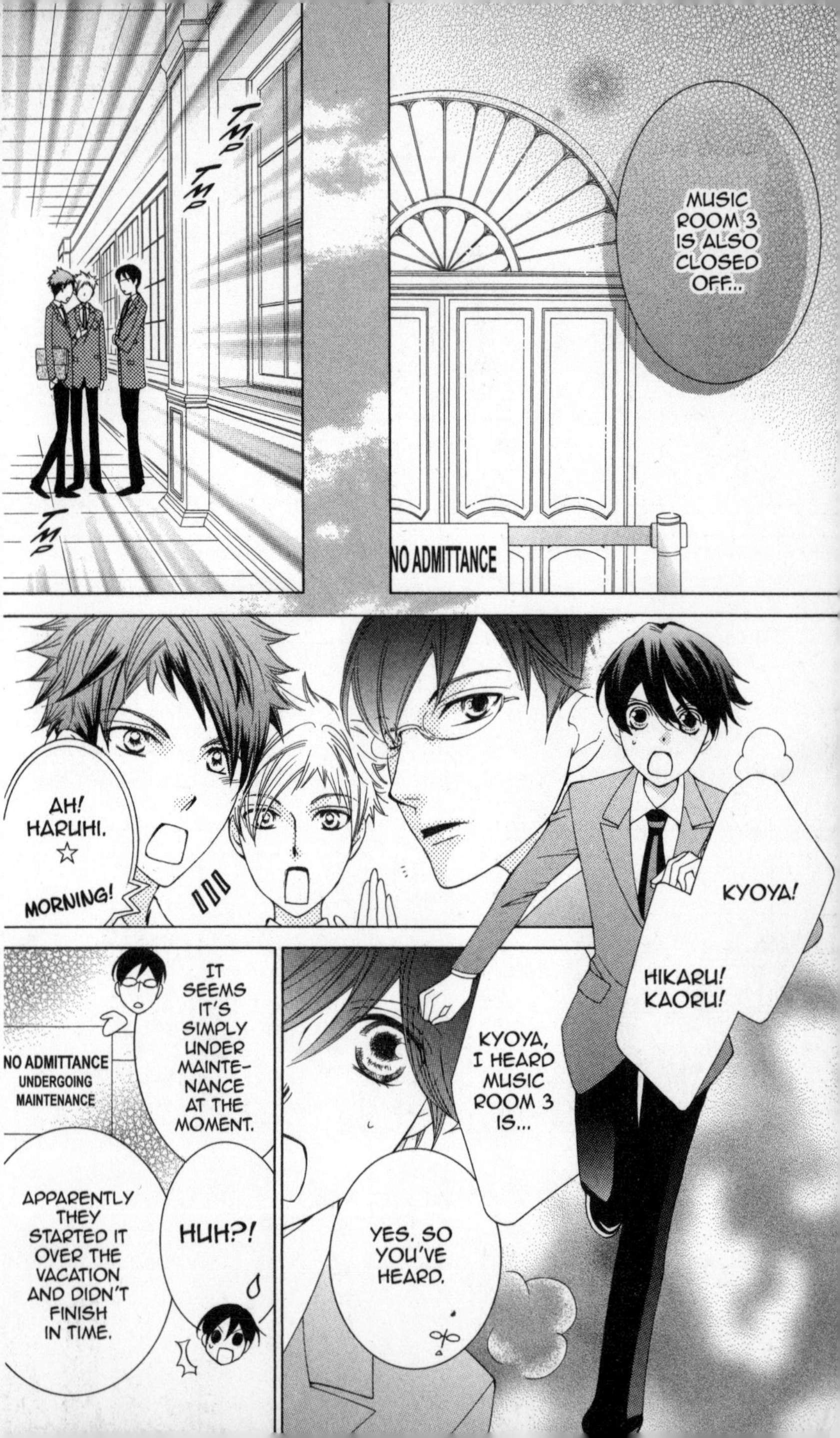
MUSIC ROOM 3 IS ALSO CLOSED OFF...
NO ADMITTANCE
TMP TMP
TMP TMP
TMP
KYOYA!
HIKARU! KAORU!
AH! HARUHI. ☆
MORNING!
KYOYA, I HEARD MUSIC ROOM 3 IS...
YES. SO YOU'VE HEARD.
NO ADMITTANCE
UNDERGOING MAINTENANCE
IT SEEMS IT'S SIMPLY UNDER MAINTE-NANCE AT THE MOMENT.
HUH?!
APPARENTLY THEY STARTED IT OVER THE VACATION AND DIDN'T FINISH IN TIME.

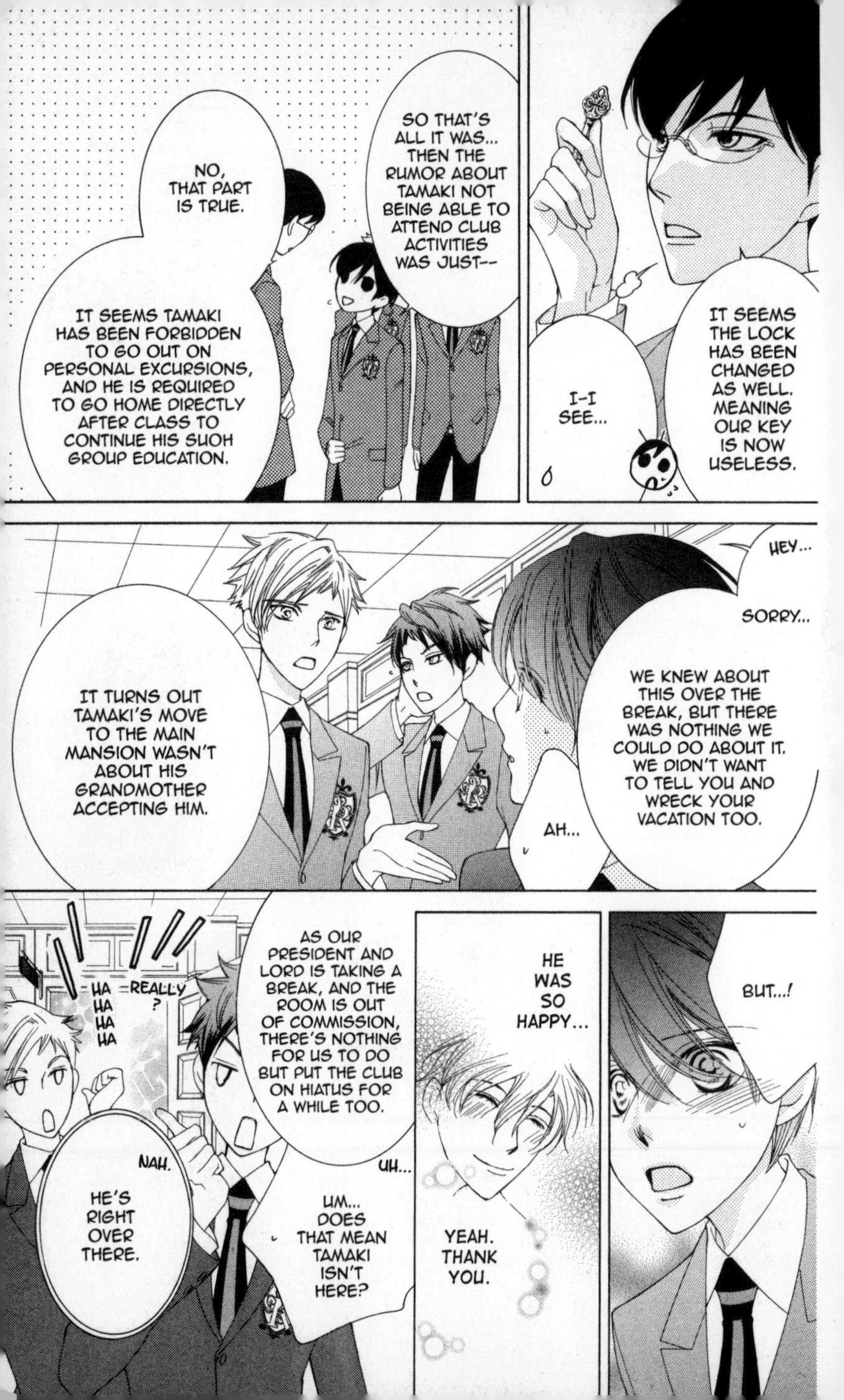
IT SEEMS THE LOCK HAS BEEN CHANGED AS WELL. MEANING OUR KEY IS NOW USELESS.
I-I SEE...
SO THAT'S ALL IT WAS... THEN THE RUMOR ABOUT TAMAKI NOT BEING ABLE TO ATTEND CLUB ACTIVITIES WAS JUST--
NO, THAT PART IS TRUE.
IT SEEMS TAMAKI HAS BEEN FORBIDDEN TO GO OUT ON PERSONAL EXCURSIONS, AND HE IS REQUIRED TO GO HOME DIRECTLY AFTER CLASS TO CONTINUE HIS SUOH GROUP EDUCATION.
HEY...
SORRY...
WE KNEW ABOUT THIS OVER THE BREAK, BUT THERE WAS NOTHING WE COULD DO ABOUT IT. WE DIDN'T WANT TO TELL YOU AND WRECK YOUR VACATION TOO.
AH...
IT TURNS OUT TAMAKI'S MOVE TO THE MAIN MANSION WASN'T ABOUT HIS GRANDMOTHER ACCEPTING HIM.
BUT...!
HE WAS SO HAPPY...
YEAH. THANK YOU.
AS OUR PRESIDENT AND LORD IS TAKING A BREAK, AND THE ROOM IS OUT OF COMMISSION, THERE'S NOTHING FOR US TO DO BUT PUT THE CLUB ON HIATUS FOR A WHILE TOO.
UH...
UM... DOES THAT MEAN TAMAKI ISN'T HERE?
REALLY?
HA HA HA HA
NAH.
HE'S RIGHT OVER THERE.

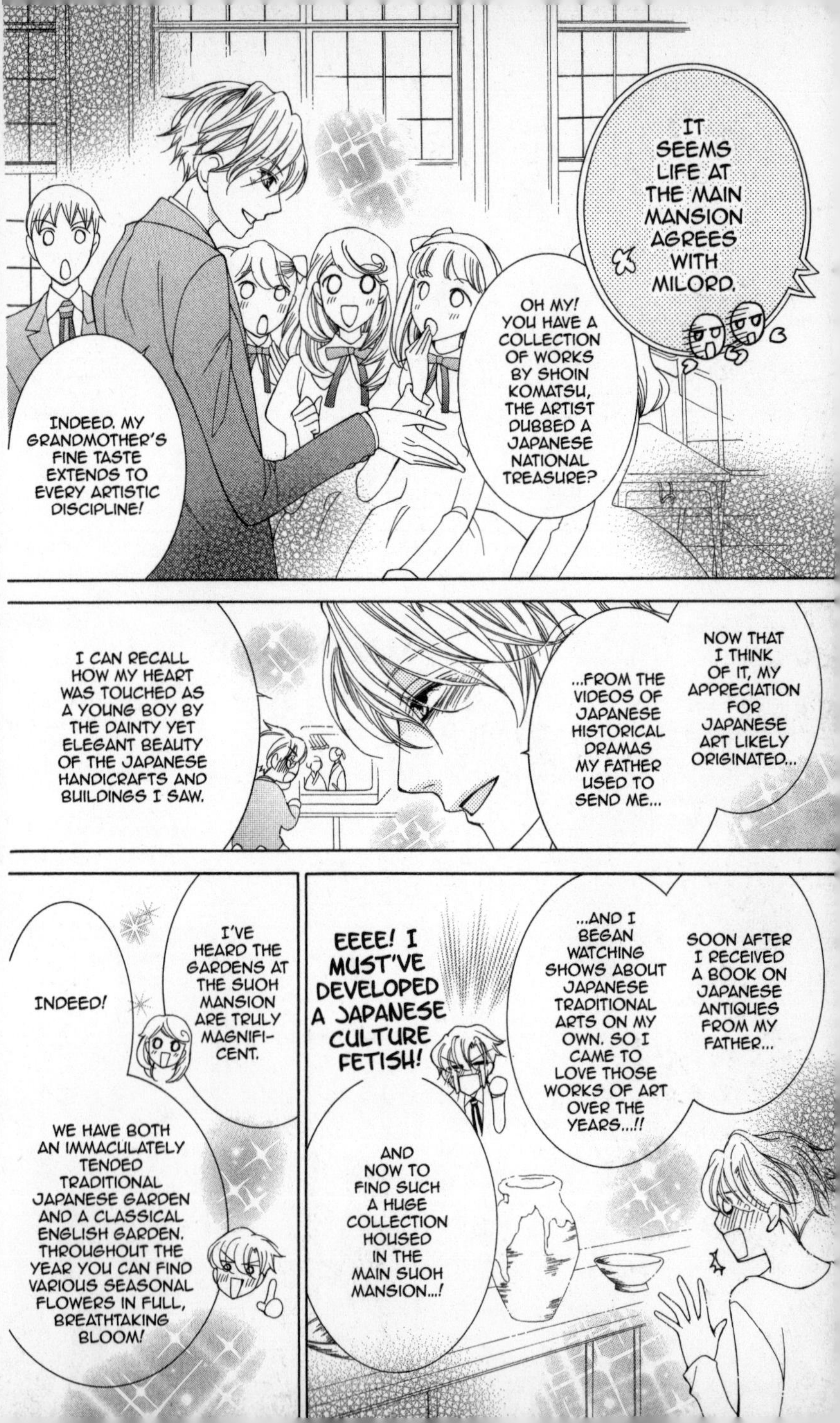
IT SEEMS LIFE AT THE MAIN MANSION AGREES WITH MILORD.
OH MY! YOU HAVE A COLLECTION OF WORKS BY SHOIN KOMATSU, THE ARTIST DUBBED A JAPANESE NATIONAL TREASURE?
INDEED. MY GRANDMOTHER'S FINE TASTE EXTENDS TO EVERY ARTISTIC DISCIPLINE!
NOW THAT I THINK OF IT, MY APPRECIATION FOR JAPANESE ART LIKELY ORIGINATED...
...FROM THE VIDEOS OF JAPANESE HISTORICAL DRAMAS MY FATHER USED TO SEND ME...
I CAN RECALL HOW MY HEART WAS TOUCHED AS A YOUNG BOY BY THE DAINTY YET ELEGANT BEAUTY OF THE JAPANESE HANDICRAFTS AND BUILDINGS I SAW.
SOON AFTER I RECEIVED A BOOK ON JAPANESE ANTIQUES FROM MY FATHER...
...AND I BEGAN WATCHING SHOWS ABOUT JAPANESE TRADITIONAL ARTS ON MY OWN. SO I CAME TO LOVE THOSE WORKS OF ART OVER THE YEARS...!!
EEEE! I MUST'VE DEVELOPED A JAPANESE CULTURE FETISH!
AND NOW TO FIND SUCH A HUGE COLLECTION HOUSED IN THE MAIN SUOH MANSION...!
I'VE HEARD THE GARDENS AT THE SUOH MANSION ARE TRULY MAGNIFI-CENT.
INDEED!
WE HAVE BOTH AN IMMACULATELY TENDED TRADITIONAL JAPANESE GARDEN AND A CLASSICAL ENGLISH GARDEN. THROUGHOUT THE YEAR YOU CAN FIND VARIOUS SEASONAL FLOWERS IN FULL, BREATHTAKING BLOOM!

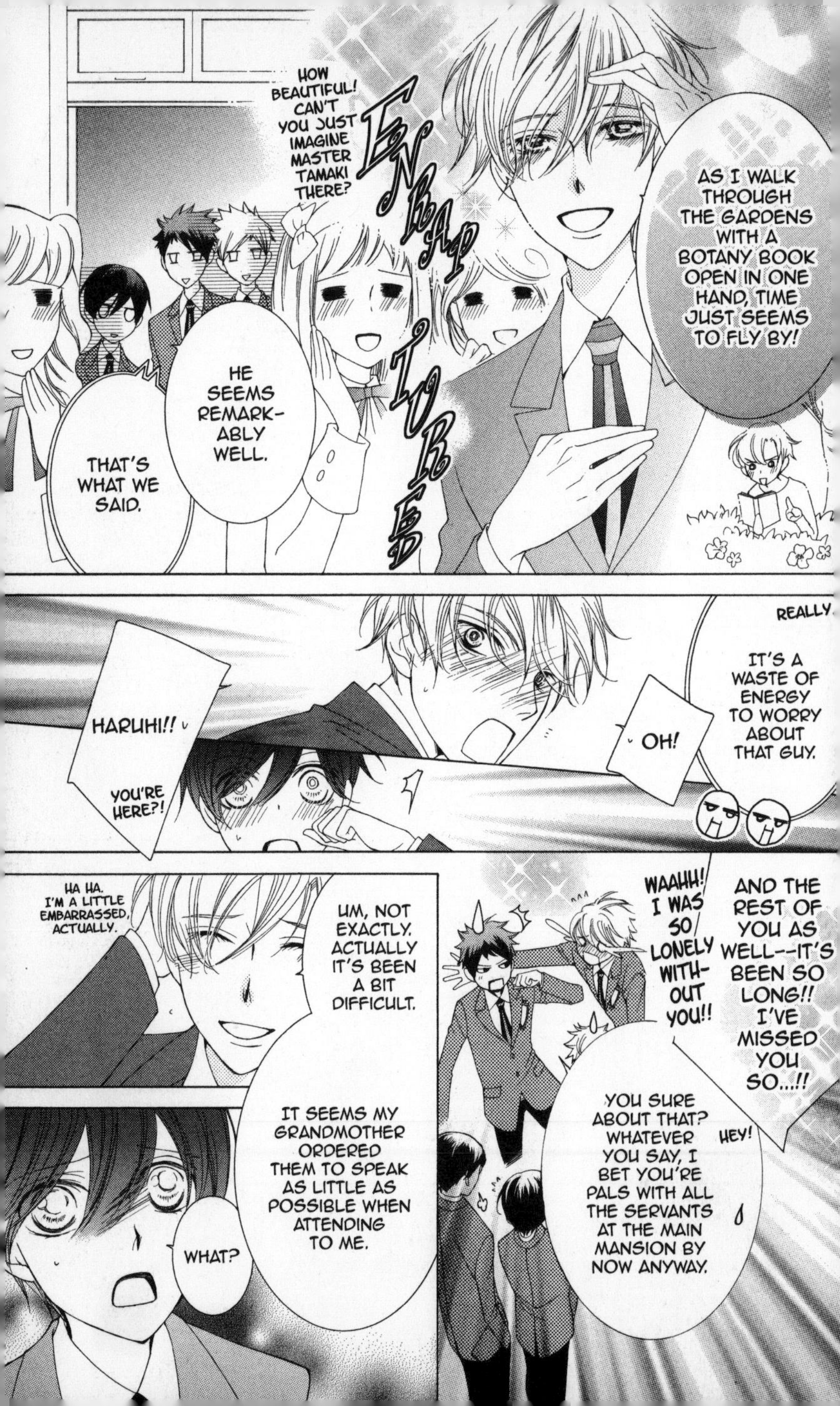
AS I WALK THROUGH THE GARDENS WITH A BOTANY BOOK OPEN IN ONE HAND, TIME JUST SEEMS TO FLY BY!
ENRAPTURED
HOW BEAUTIFUL! CAN'T YOU JUST IMAGINE MASTER TAMAKI THERE?
HE SEEMS REMARKABLY WELL.
THAT'S WHAT WE SAID.
REALLY.
IT'S A WASTE OF ENERGY TO WORRY ABOUT THAT GUY.
OH!
HARUHI!!
YOU'RE HERE?!
AND THE REST OF YOU AS WELL--IT'S BEEN SO LONG!! I'VE MISSED YOU SO...!!
WAAHH! I WAS SO LONELY WITHOUT YOU!!
HEY!
YOU SURE ABOUT THAT? WHATEVER YOU SAY, I BET YOU'RE PALS WITH ALL THE SERVANTS AT THE MAIN MANSION BY NOW ANYWAY.
UM, NOT EXACTLY. ACTUALLY IT'S BEEN A BIT DIFFICULT.
HA HA. I'M A LITTLE EMBARRASSED, ACTUALLY.
IT SEEMS MY GRANDMOTHER ORDERED THEM TO SPEAK AS LITTLE AS POSSIBLE WHEN ATTENDING TO ME.
WHAT?

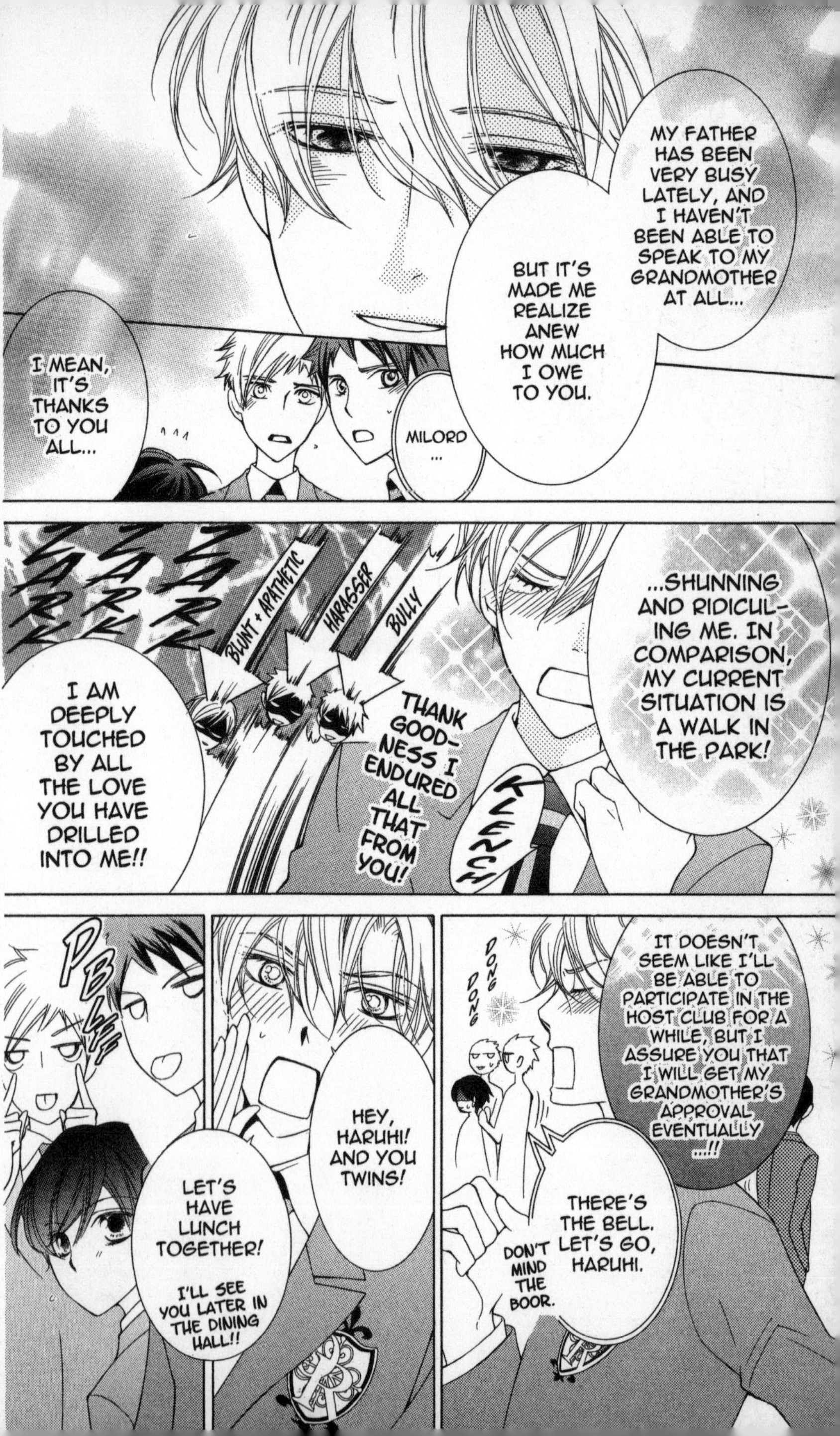
MY FATHER HAS BEEN VERY BUSY LATELY, AND I HAVEN'T BEEN ABLE TO SPEAK TO MY GRANDMOTHER AT ALL...
BUT IT'S MADE ME REALIZE ANEW HOW MUCH I OWE TO YOU.
MILORD ...
I MEAN, IT'S THANKS TO YOU ALL...
...SHUNNING AND RIDICUL-ING ME. IN COMPARISON, MY CURRENT SITUATION IS A WALK IN THE PARK!
KLENCH
THANK GOOD-NESS I ENDURED ALL THAT FROM YOU!
BULLY
HARASSER
BLUNT + APATHETIC
ZSARK
ZSARK
I AM DEEPLY TOUCHED BY ALL THE LOVE YOU HAVE DRILLED INTO ME!!
IT DOESN'T SEEM LIKE I'LL BE ABLE TO PARTICIPATE IN THE HOST CLUB FOR A WHILE, BUT I ASSURE YOU THAT I WILL GET MY GRANDMOTHER'S APPROVAL EVENTUALLY ...!!
DONG DONG
THERE'S THE BELL. LET'S GO, HARUHI.
DON'T MIND THE BOOR.
HEY, HARUHI! AND YOU TWINS!
LET'S HAVE LUNCH TOGETHER!
I'LL SEE YOU LATER IN THE DINING HALL!!
PBLEH

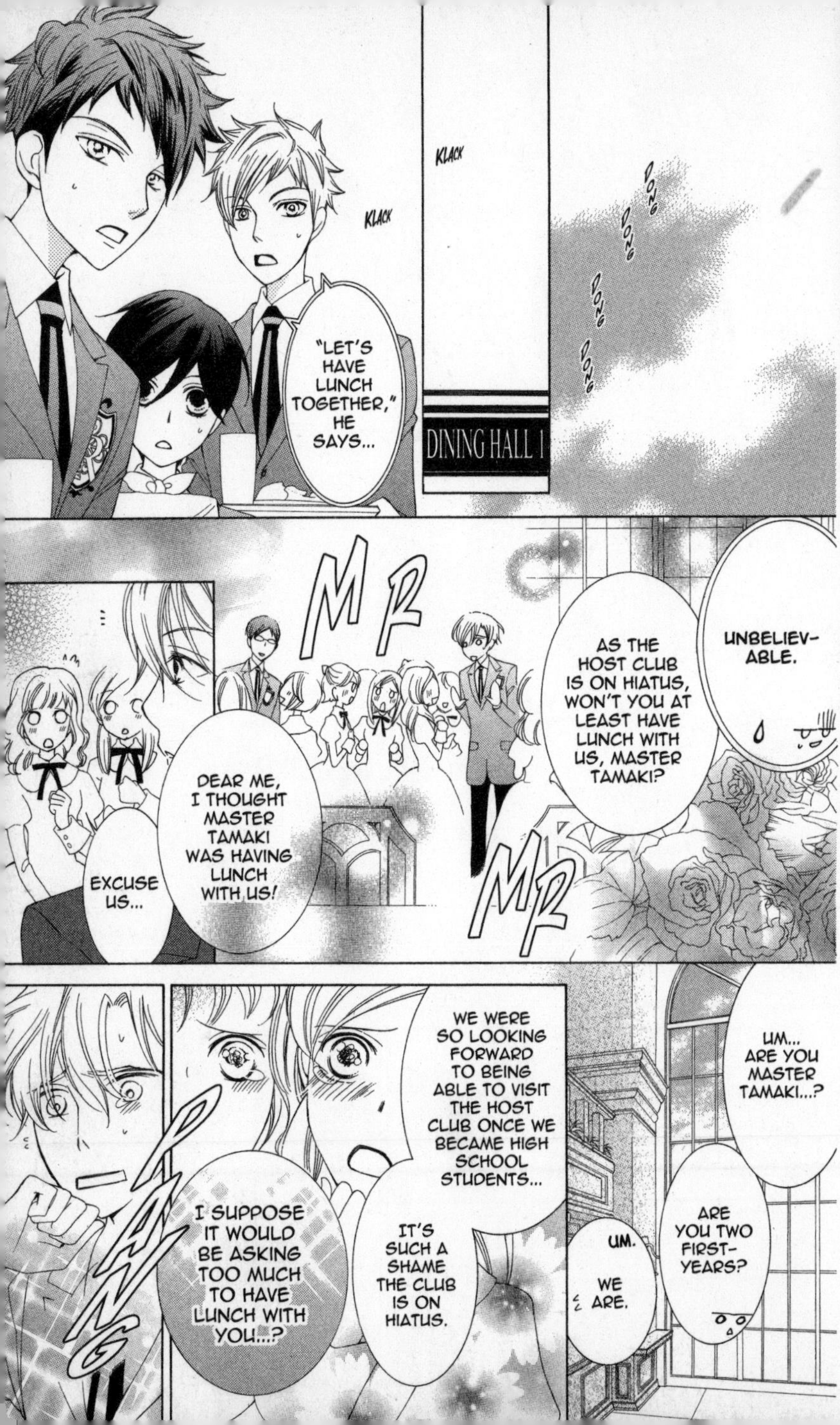
DONG
DONG
DONG
DONG
DINING HALL 1
KLACK
KLACK
"LET'S HAVE LUNCH TOGETHER," HE SAYS...
UNBELIEV-ABLE.
AS THE HOST CLUB IS ON HIATUS, WON'T YOU AT LEAST HAVE LUNCH WITH US, MASTER TAMAKI?
MR
MR
DEAR ME, I THOUGHT MASTER TAMAKI WAS HAVING LUNCH WITH US!
EXCUSE US...
UM... ARE YOU MASTER TAMAKI...?
ARE YOU TWO FIRST-YEARS?
UM.
WE ARE.
WE WERE SO LOOKING FORWARD TO BEING ABLE TO VISIT THE HOST CLUB ONCE WE BECAME HIGH SCHOOL STUDENTS...
IT'S SUCH A SHAME THE CLUB IS ON HIATUS.
I SUPPOSE IT WOULD BE ASKING TOO MUCH TO HAVE LUNCH WITH YOU...?

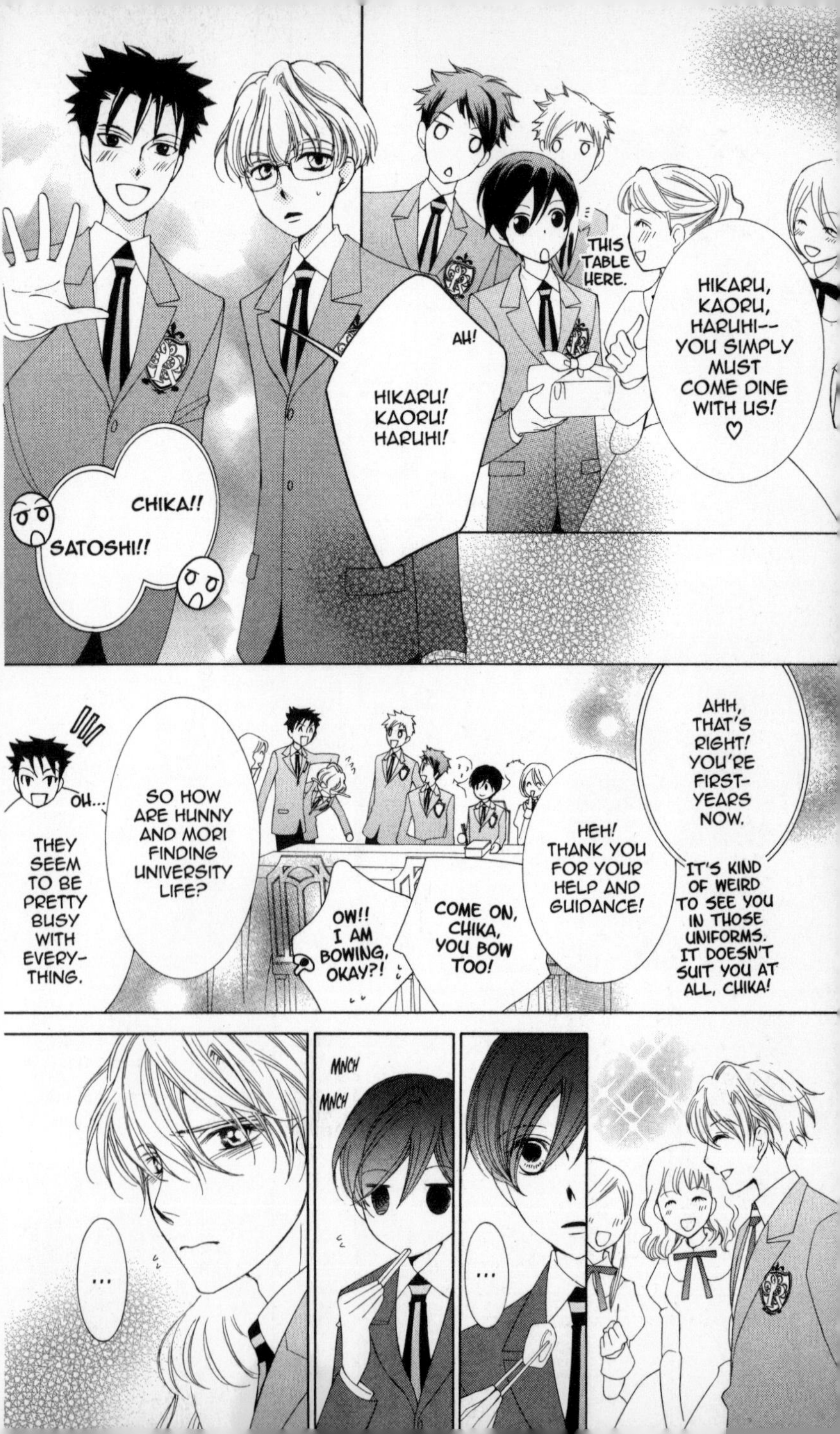
HIKARU, KAORU, HARUHI-- YOU SIMPLY MUST COME DINE WITH US! ♡
THIS TABLE HERE.
AH!
HIKARU! KAORU! HARUHI!
CHIKA!!
SATOSHI!!
AHH, THAT'S RIGHT! YOU'RE FIRST-YEARS NOW.
IT'S KIND OF WEIRD TO SEE YOU IN THOSE UNIFORMS. IT DOESN'T SUIT YOU AT ALL, CHIKA!
HEH! THANK YOU FOR YOUR HELP AND GUIDANCE!
COME ON, CHIKA, YOU BOW TOO!
OW!! I AM BOWING, OKAY?!
SO HOW ARE HUNNY AND MORI FINDING UNIVERSITY LIFE?
OH...
THEY SEEM TO BE PRETTY BUSY WITH EVERY-THING.
...
MNCH
MNCH
...

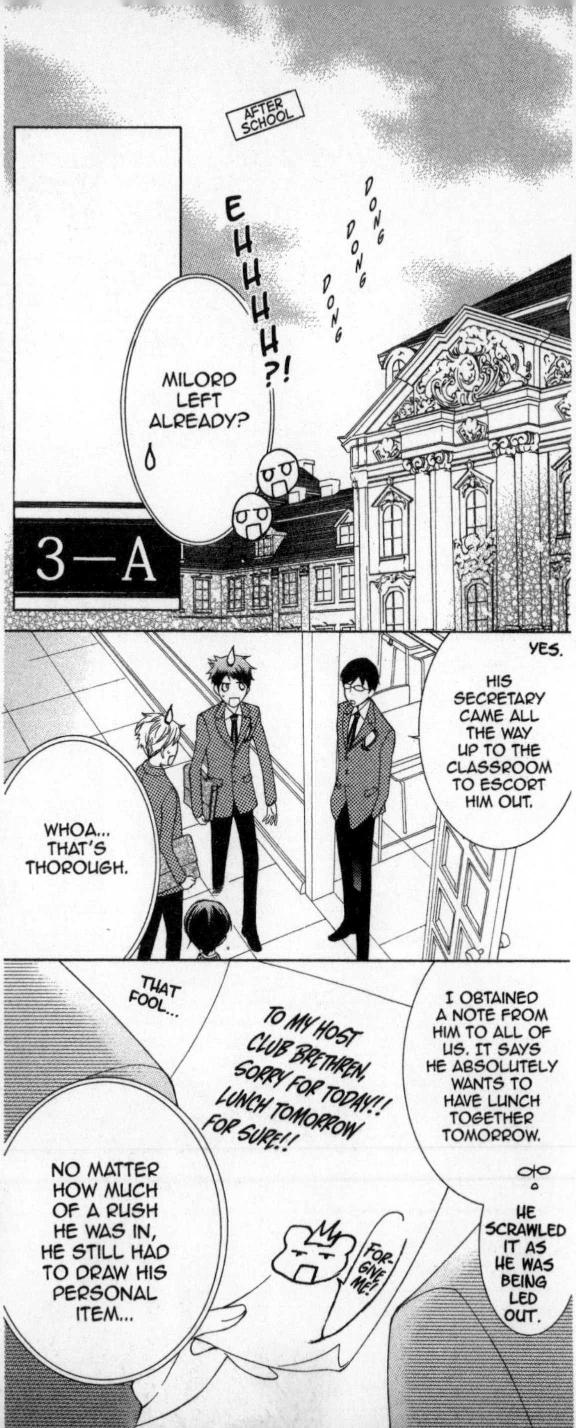
AFTER SCHOOL
DONG DONG DONG
EHHHHH?!
MILORD LEFT ALREADY?
3—A
YES.
HIS SECRETARY CAME ALL THE WAY UP TO THE CLASSROOM TO ESCORT HIM OUT.
WHOA... THAT'S THOROUGH.
I OBTAINED A NOTE FROM HIM TO ALL OF US. IT SAYS HE ABSOLUTELY WANTS TO HAVE LUNCH TOGETHER TOMORROW.
TO MY HOST CLUB BRETHREN, SORRY FOR TODAY!! LUNCH TOMORROW FOR SURE!!
THAT FOOL...
HE SCRAWLED IT AS HE WAS BEING LED OUT.
FOR-GIVE ME!
NO MATTER HOW MUCH OF A RUSH HE WAS IN, HE STILL HAD TO DRAW HIS PERSONAL ITEM...

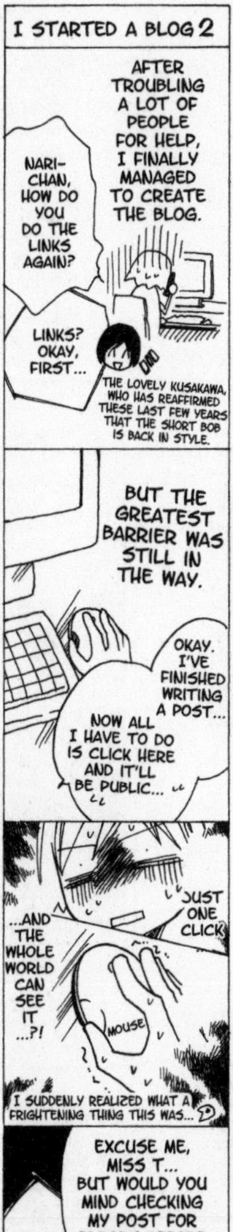
I STARTED A BLOG 2
AFTER TROUBLING A LOT OF PEOPLE FOR HELP, I FINALLY MANAGED TO CREATE THE BLOG.
NARI-CHAN, HOW DO YOU DO THE LINKS AGAIN?
LINKS? OKAY, FIRST...
THE LOVELY KUSAKAWA, WHO HAS REAFFIRMED THESE LAST FEW YEARS THAT THE SHORT BOB IS BACK IN STYLE.
BUT THE GREATEST BARRIER WAS STILL IN THE WAY.
OKAY. I'VE FINISHED WRITING A POST...
NOW ALL I HAVE TO DO IS CLICK HERE AND IT'LL BE PUBLIC...
JUST ONE CLICK
...AND THE WHOLE WORLD CAN SEE IT ...?!
MOUSE
I SUDDENLY REALIZED WHAT A FRIGHTENING THING THIS WAS...
EXCUSE ME, MISS T... BUT WOULD YOU MIND CHECKING MY POST FOR ERRORS BEFORE I PUBLISH IT?
THAT'S SIMPLE ENOUGH.
LILY-LIVERED HATORI
BOTHERING PEOPLE AGAIN...

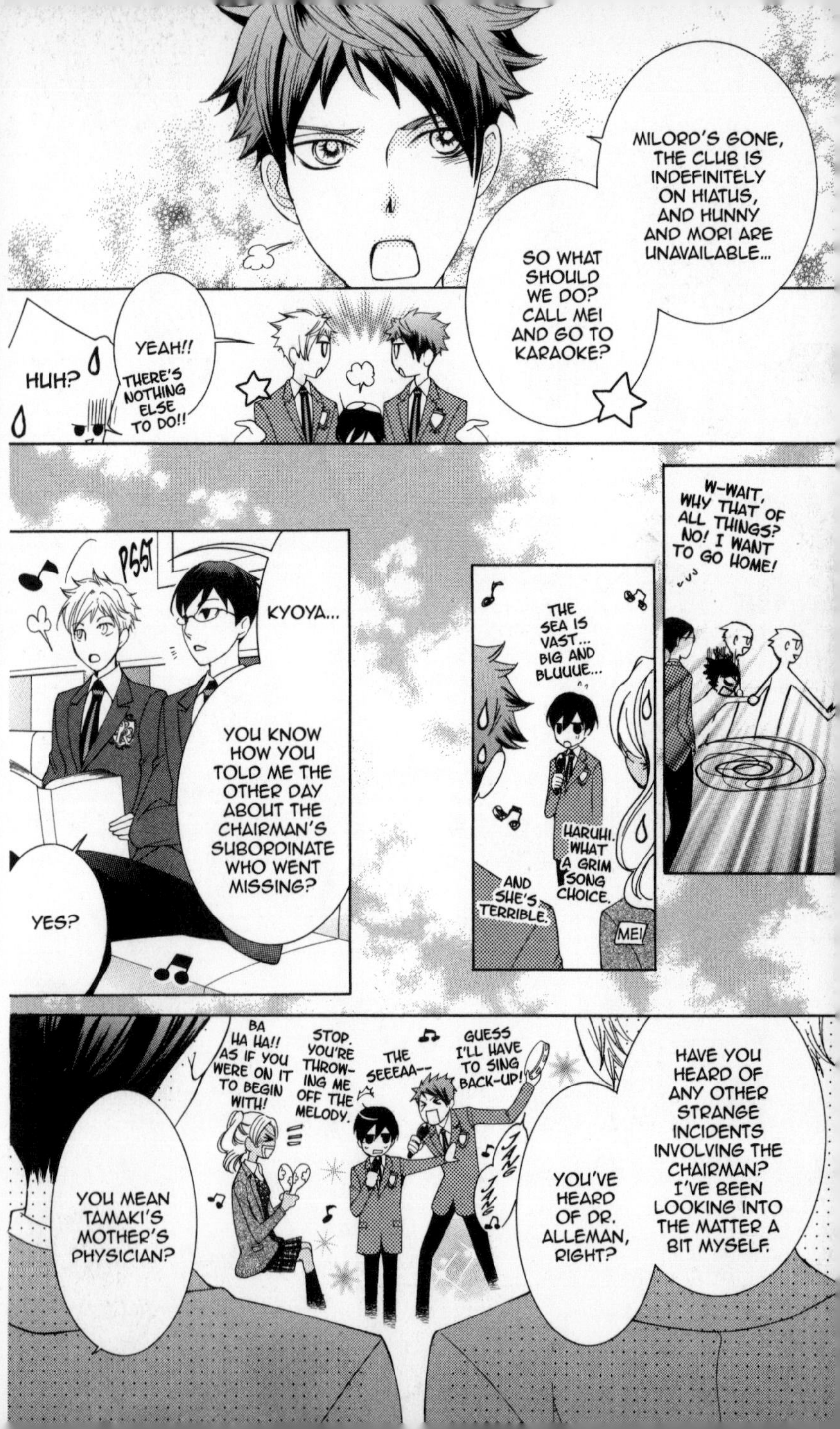
MILORD'S GONE, THE CLUB IS INDEFINITELY ON HIATUS, AND HUNNY AND MORI ARE UNAVAILABLE...
SO WHAT SHOULD WE DO? CALL MEI AND GO TO KARAOKE?
YEAH!! THERE'S NOTHING ELSE TO DO!!
HUH?
W-WAIT, WHY THAT OF ALL THINGS? NO! I WANT TO GO HOME!
THE SEA IS VAST... BIG AND BLUUUE...
HARUHI. WHAT A GRIM SONG CHOICE.
AND SHE'S TERRIBLE.
MEI
PSST
KYOYA...
YOU KNOW HOW YOU TOLD ME THE OTHER DAY ABOUT THE CHAIRMAN'S SUBORDINATE WHO WENT MISSING?
YES?
HAVE YOU HEARD OF ANY OTHER STRANGE INCIDENTS INVOLVING THE CHAIRMAN? I'VE BEEN LOOKING INTO THE MATTER A BIT MYSELF.
YOU'VE HEARD OF DR. ALLEMAN, RIGHT?
GUESS I'LL HAVE TO SING BACK-UP!
THE SEEEAA--
STOP. YOU'RE THROWING ME OFF THE MELODY.
BA HA HA!! AS IF YOU WERE ON IT TO BEGIN WITH!
JANG JANG
YOU MEAN TAMAKI'S MOTHER'S PHYSICIAN?

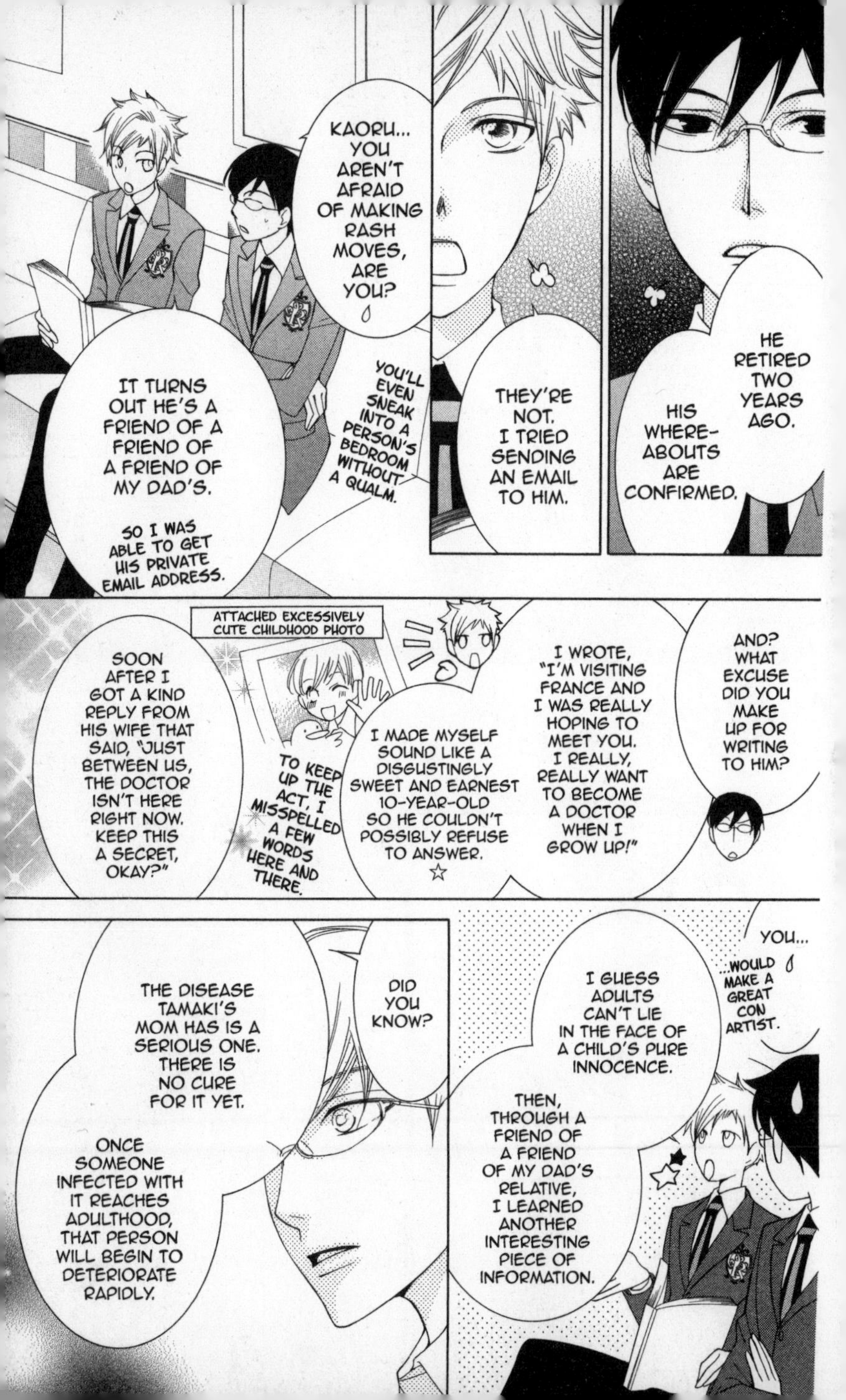
HE RETIRED TWO YEARS AGO.
HIS WHEREABOUTS ARE CONFIRMED.
THEY'RE NOT. I TRIED SENDING AN EMAIL TO HIM.
KAORU... YOU AREN'T AFRAID OF MAKING RASH MOVES, ARE YOU?
YOU'LL EVEN SNEAK INTO A PERSON'S BEDROOM WITHOUT A QUALM.
IT TURNS OUT HE'S A FRIEND OF A FRIEND OF A FRIEND OF MY DAD'S.
SO I WAS ABLE TO GET HIS PRIVATE EMAIL ADDRESS.
AND? WHAT EXCUSE DID YOU MAKE UP FOR WRITING TO HIM?
I WROTE, "I'M VISITING FRANCE AND I WAS REALLY HOPING TO MEET YOU. I REALLY, REALLY WANT TO BECOME A DOCTOR WHEN I GROW UP!"
I MADE MYSELF SOUND LIKE A DISGUSTINGLY SWEET AND EARNEST 10-YEAR-OLD SO HE COULDN'T POSSIBLY REFUSE TO ANSWER. ☆
TO KEEP UP THE ACT, I MISSPELLED A FEW WORDS HERE AND THERE.
ATTACHED EXCESSIVELY CUTE CHILDHOOD PHOTO
SOON AFTER I GOT A KIND REPLY FROM HIS WIFE THAT SAID, "JUST BETWEEN US, THE DOCTOR ISN'T HERE RIGHT NOW. KEEP THIS A SECRET, OKAY?"
YOU...
...WOULD MAKE A GREAT CON ARTIST.
I GUESS ADULTS CAN'T LIE IN THE FACE OF A CHILD'S PURE INNOCENCE.
THEN, THROUGH A FRIEND OF A FRIEND OF MY DAD'S RELATIVE, I LEARNED ANOTHER INTERESTING PIECE OF INFORMATION.
DID YOU KNOW?
THE DISEASE TAMAKI'S MOM HAS IS A SERIOUS ONE. THERE IS NO CURE FOR IT YET.
ONCE SOMEONE INFECTED WITH IT REACHES ADULTHOOD, THAT PERSON WILL BEGIN TO DETERIORATE RAPIDLY.

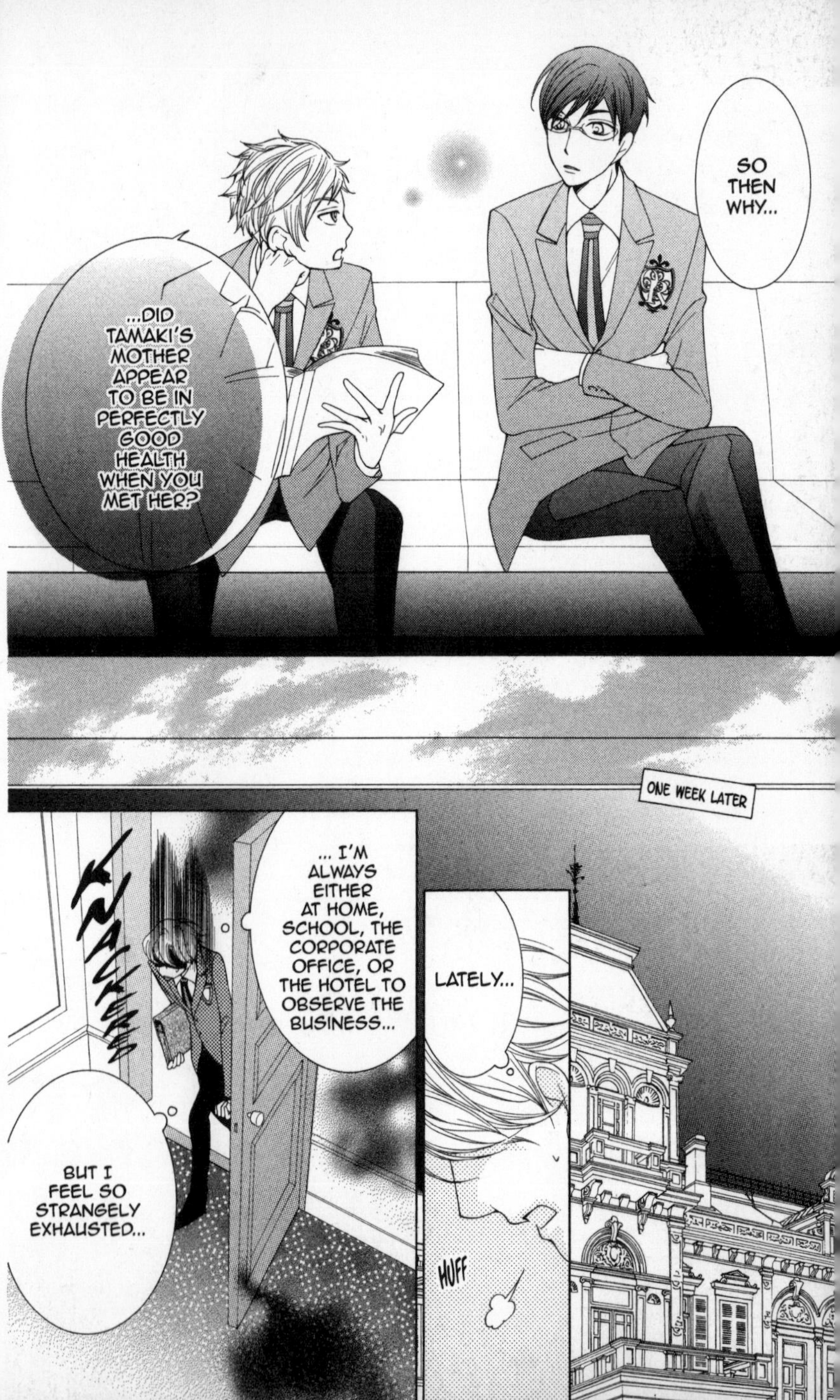
SO THEN WHY...
...DID TAMAKI'S MOTHER APPEAR TO BE IN PERFECTLY GOOD HEALTH WHEN YOU MET HER?
ONE WEEK LATER
LATELY...
HUFF
... I'M ALWAYS EITHER AT HOME, SCHOOL, THE CORPORATE OFFICE, OR THE HOTEL TO OBSERVE THE BUSINESS...
BUT I FEEL SO STRANGELY EXHAUSTED...

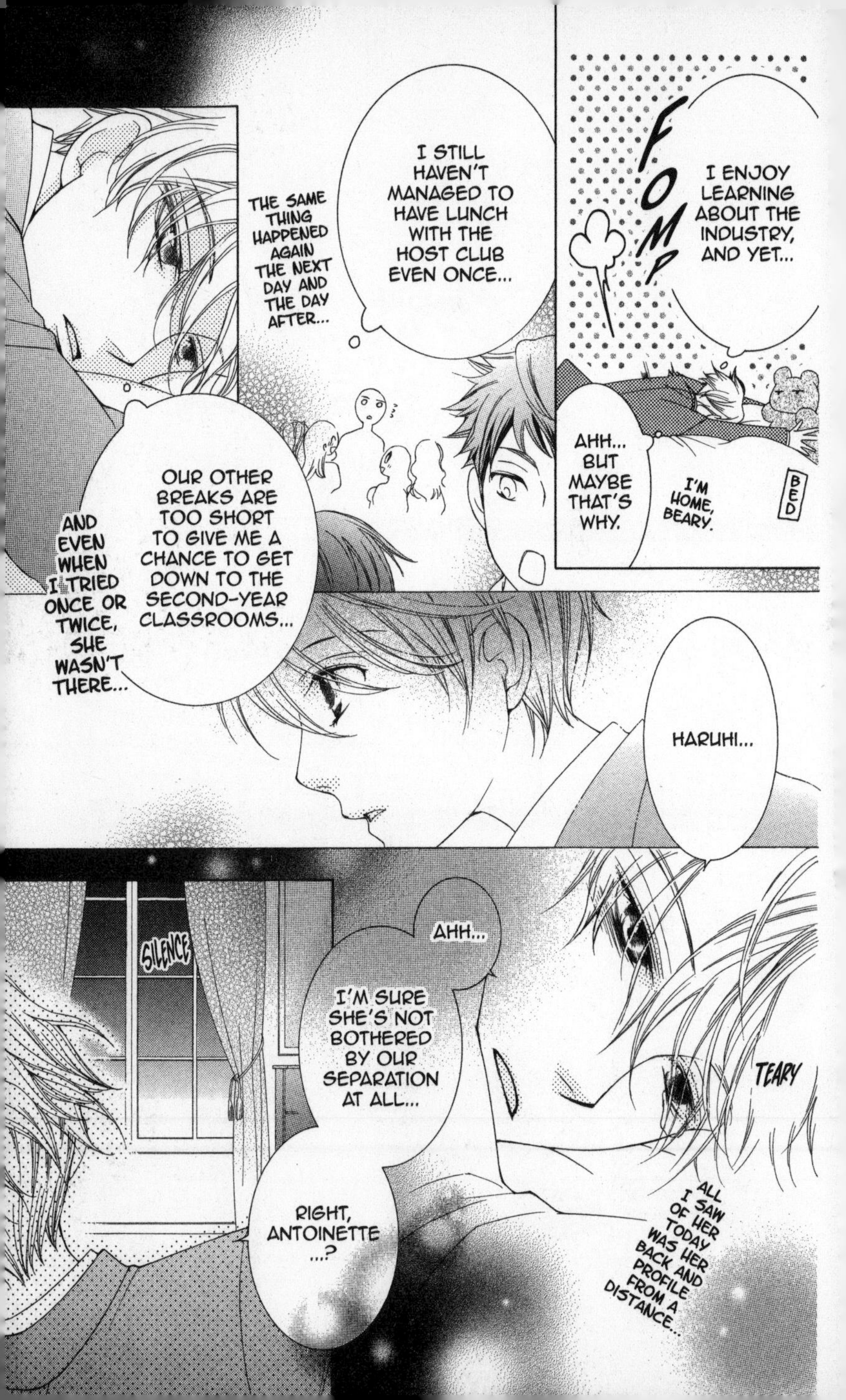
I ENJOY LEARNING ABOUT THE INDUSTRY, AND YET...
FOMP
BED
I'M HOME, BEARY.
AHH... BUT MAYBE THAT'S WHY.
I STILL HAVEN'T MANAGED TO HAVE LUNCH WITH THE HOST CLUB EVEN ONCE...
THE SAME THING HAPPENED AGAIN THE NEXT DAY AND THE DAY AFTER...
OUR OTHER BREAKS ARE TOO SHORT TO GIVE ME A CHANCE TO GET DOWN TO THE SECOND-YEAR CLASSROOMS...
AND EVEN WHEN I TRIED ONCE OR TWICE, SHE WASN'T THERE...
HARUHI...
ALL I SAW OF HER TODAY WAS HER BACK AND PROFILE FROM A DISTANCE...
TEARY
AHH...
I'M SURE SHE'S NOT BOTHERED BY OUR SEPARATION AT ALL...
RIGHT, ANTOINETTE ...?
SILENCE

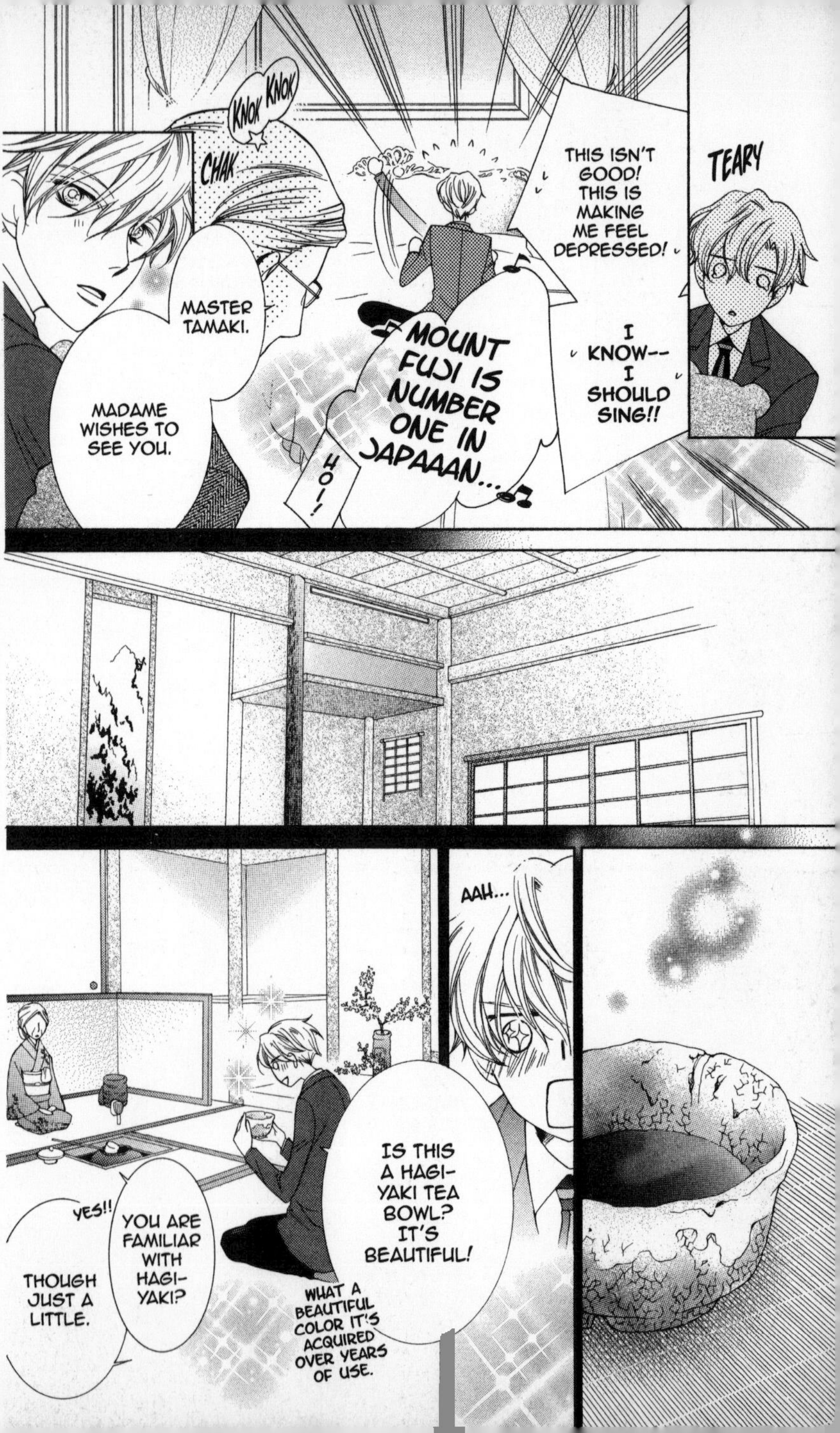
TEARY
THIS ISN'T GOOD! THIS IS MAKING ME FEEL DEPRESSED!
I KNOW-- I SHOULD SING!!
MOUNT FUJI IS NUMBER ONE IN JAPAAAN...
HOI!
KNOK KNOK
CHAK
MASTER TAMAKI.
MADAME WISHES TO SEE YOU.
AAH...
IS THIS A HAGI-YAKI TEA BOWL? IT'S BEAUTIFUL!
WHAT A BEAUTIFUL COLOR IT'S ACQUIRED OVER YEARS OF USE.
YOU ARE FAMILIAR WITH HAGI-YAKI?
YES!!
THOUGH JUST A LITTLE.

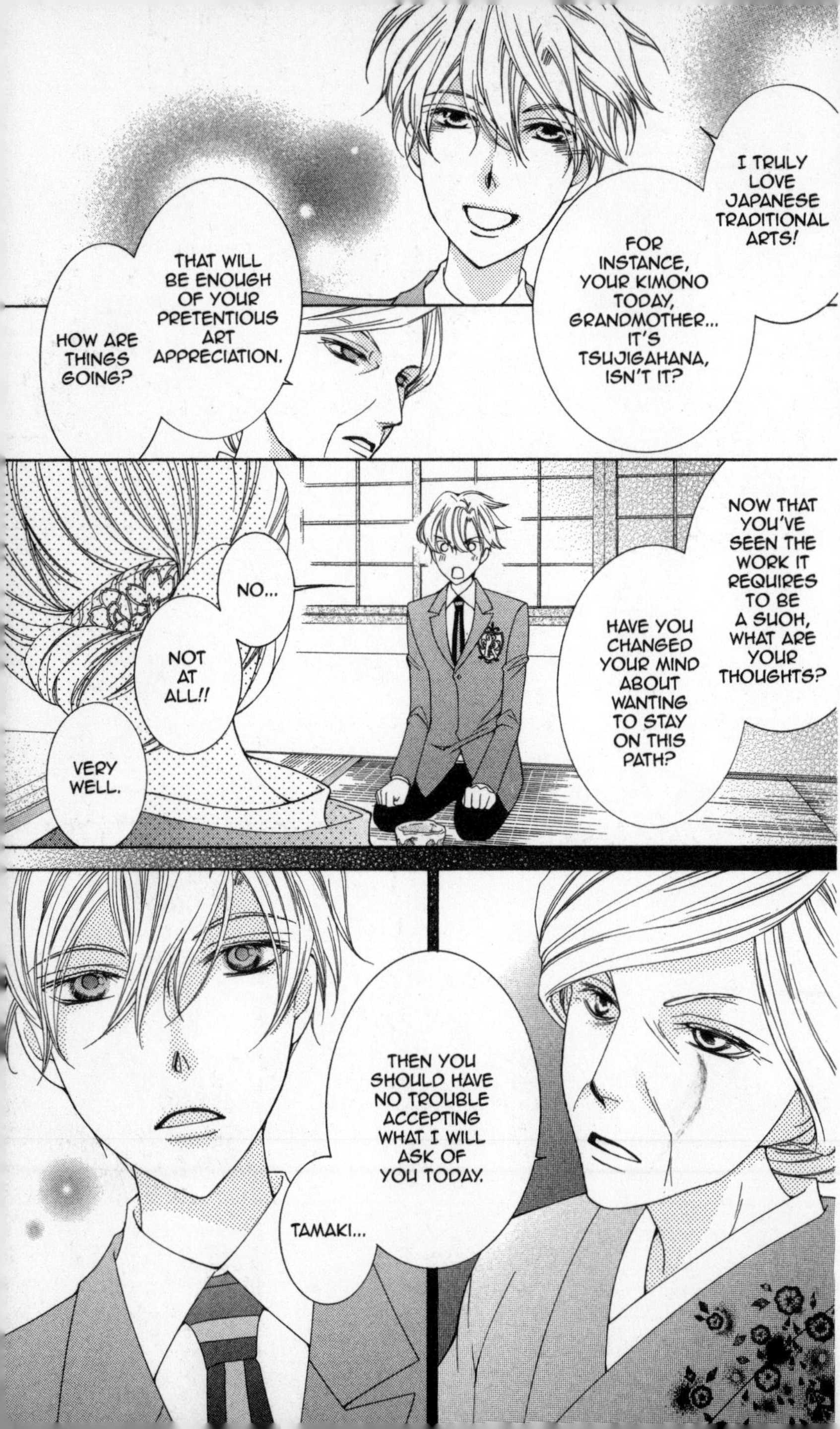
I TRULY LOVE JAPANESE TRADITIONAL ARTS!
FOR INSTANCE, YOUR KIMONO TODAY, GRANDMOTHER... IT'S TSUJIGAHANA, ISN'T IT?
THAT WILL BE ENOUGH OF YOUR PRETENTIOUS ART APPRECIATION.
HOW ARE THINGS GOING?
NOW THAT YOU'VE SEEN THE WORK IT REQUIRES TO BE A SUOH, WHAT ARE YOUR THOUGHTS?
HAVE YOU CHANGED YOUR MIND ABOUT WANTING TO STAY ON THIS PATH?
NO...
NOT AT ALL!!
VERY WELL.
THEN YOU SHOULD HAVE NO TROUBLE ACCEPTING WHAT I WILL ASK OF YOU TODAY.
TAMAKI...

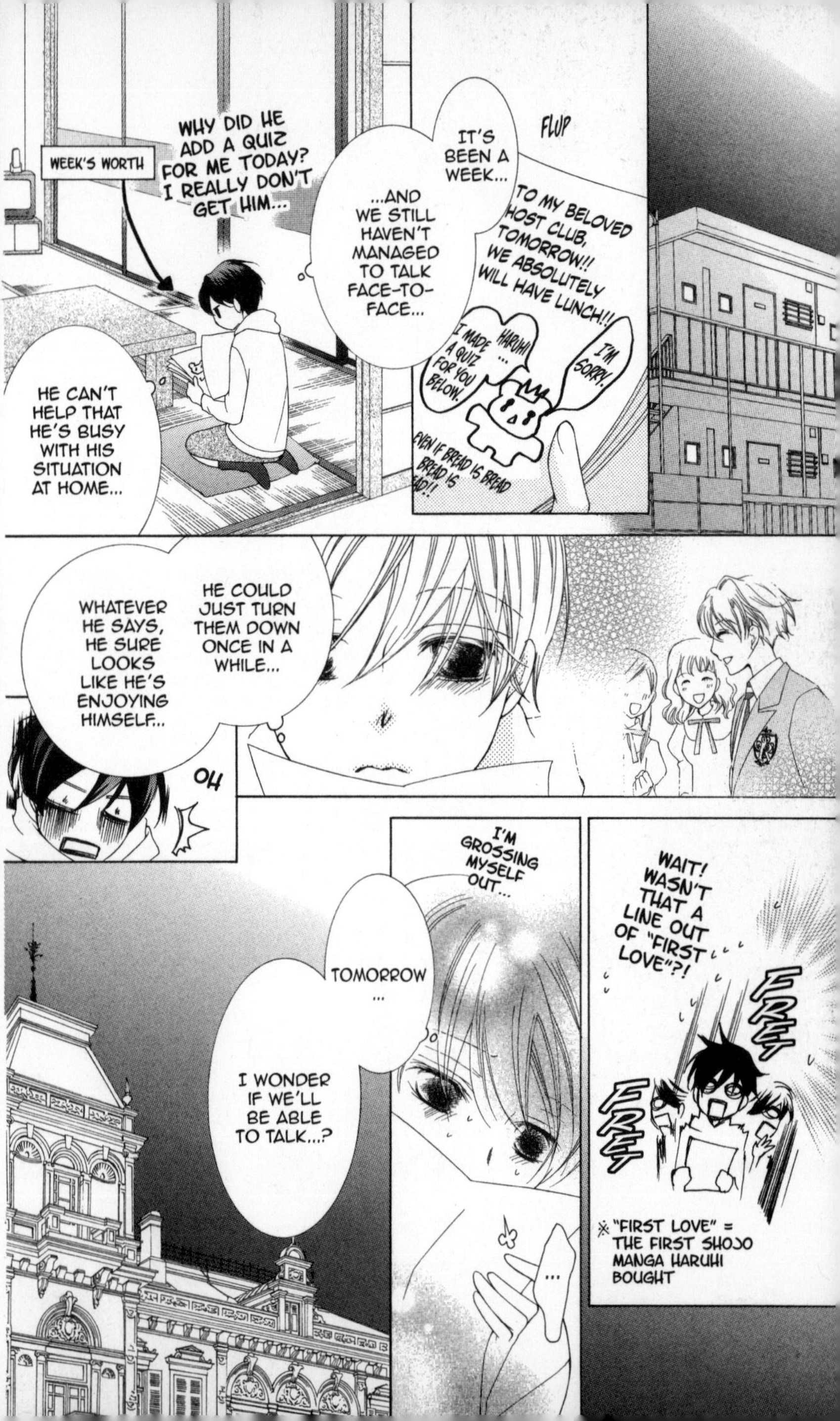
FLUP
IT'S BEEN A WEEK...
...AND WE STILL HAVEN'T MANAGED TO TALK FACE-TO-FACE...
TO MY BELOVED HOST CLUB, TOMORROW!! WE ABSOLUTELY WILL HAVE LUNCH!!
I'M SORRY.
HARUHI ...
I MADE A QUIZ FOR YOU BELOW.
EVEN IF BREAD IS BREAD BREAD IS
WHY DID HE ADD A QUIZ FOR ME TODAY? I REALLY DON'T GET HIM...
WEEK'S WORTH
HE CAN'T HELP THAT HE'S BUSY WITH HIS SITUATION AT HOME...
HE COULD JUST TURN THEM DOWN ONCE IN A WHILE...
WHATEVER HE SAYS, HE SURE LOOKS LIKE HE'S ENJOYING HIMSELF...
OH
WAIT! WASN'T THAT A LINE OUT OF "FIRST LOVE"?!
FREAK
FREAK
※ "FIRST LOVE" = THE FIRST SHOJO MANGA HARUHI BOUGHT
I'M GROSSING MYSELF OUT...
TOMORROW ...
I WONDER IF WE'LL BE ABLE TO TALK...?
...

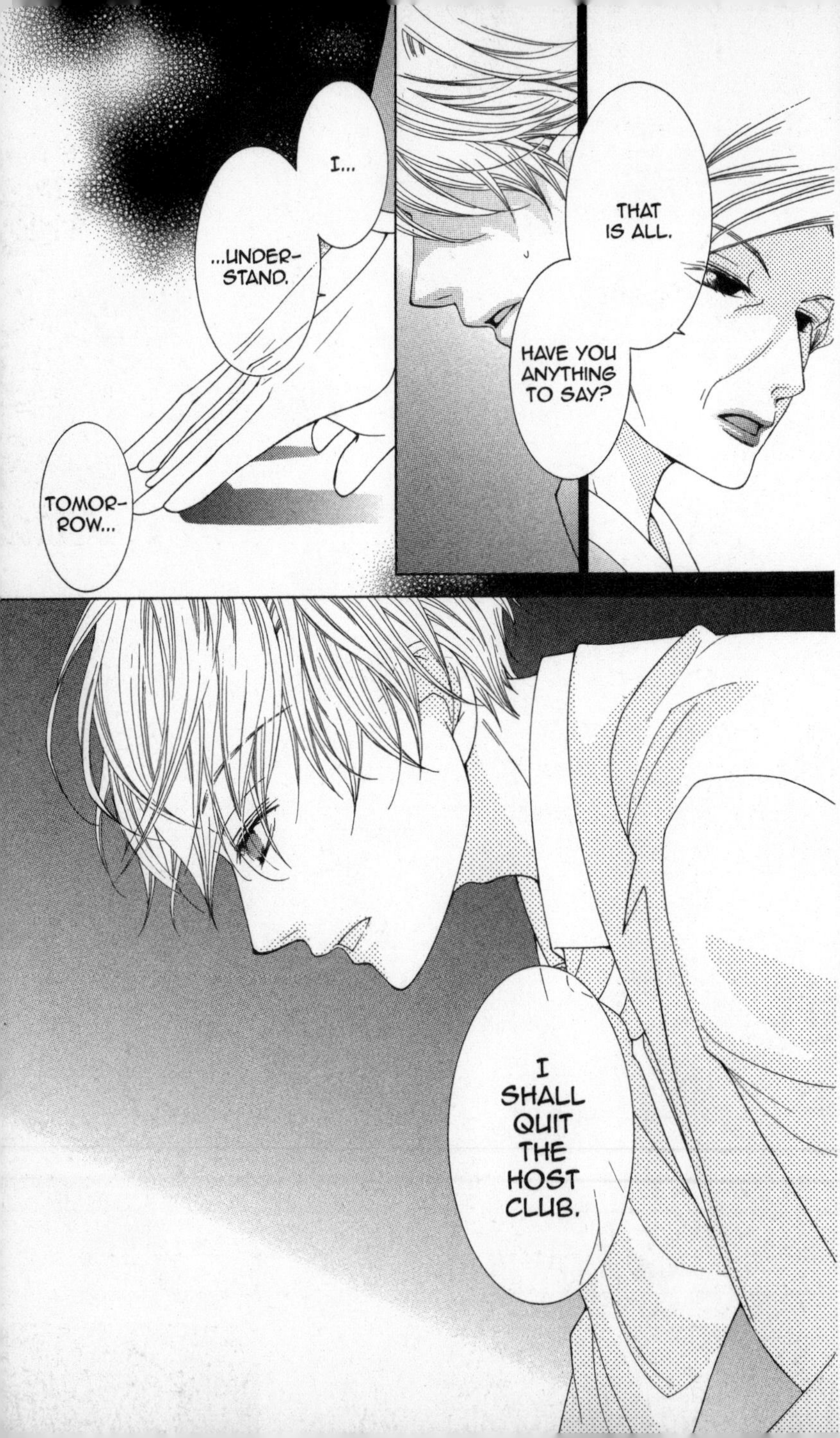
THAT IS ALL.
HAVE YOU ANYTHING TO SAY?
I...
...UNDERSTAND.
TOMORROW...
I SHALL QUIT THE HOST CLUB.

EPISODE 75

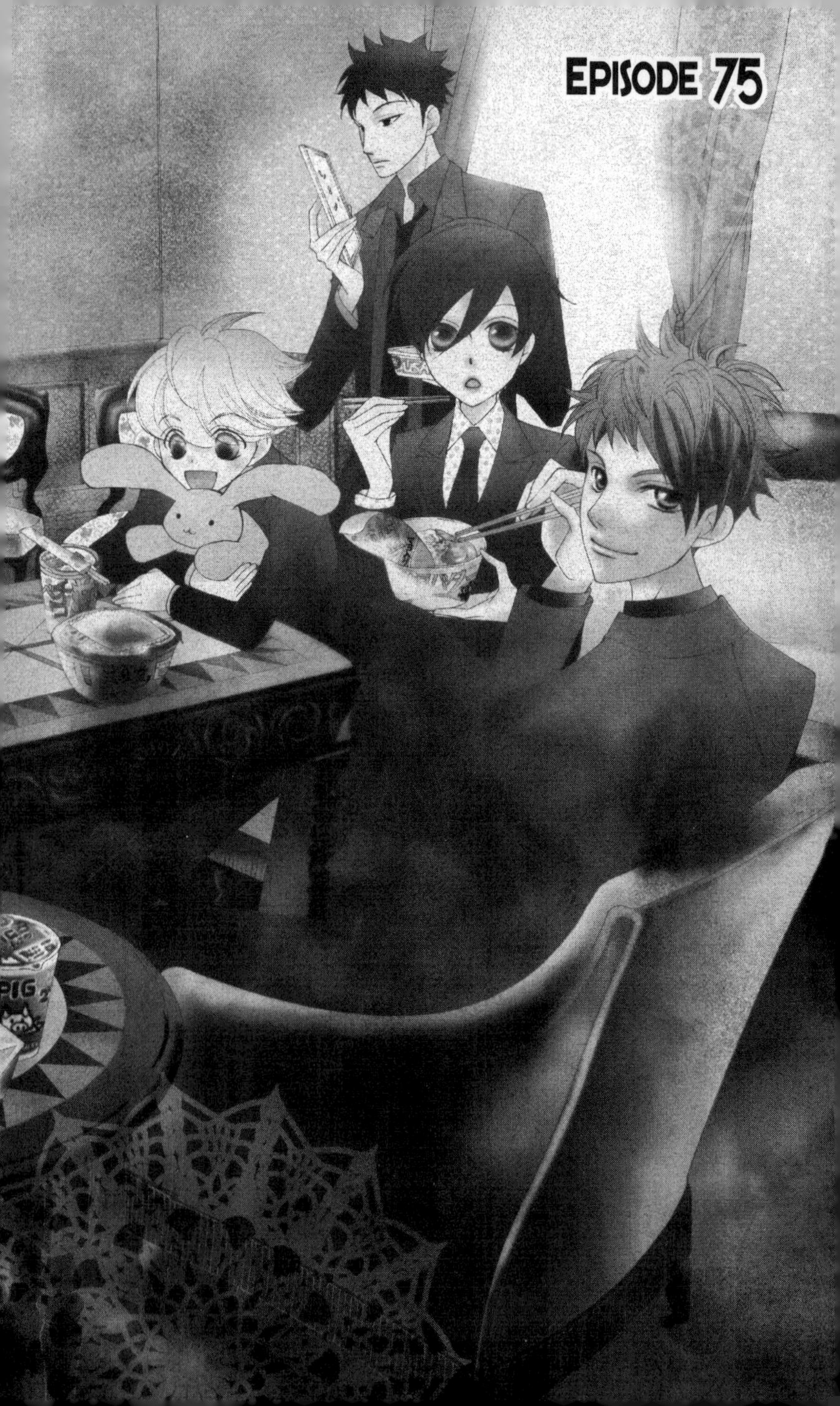
PIG

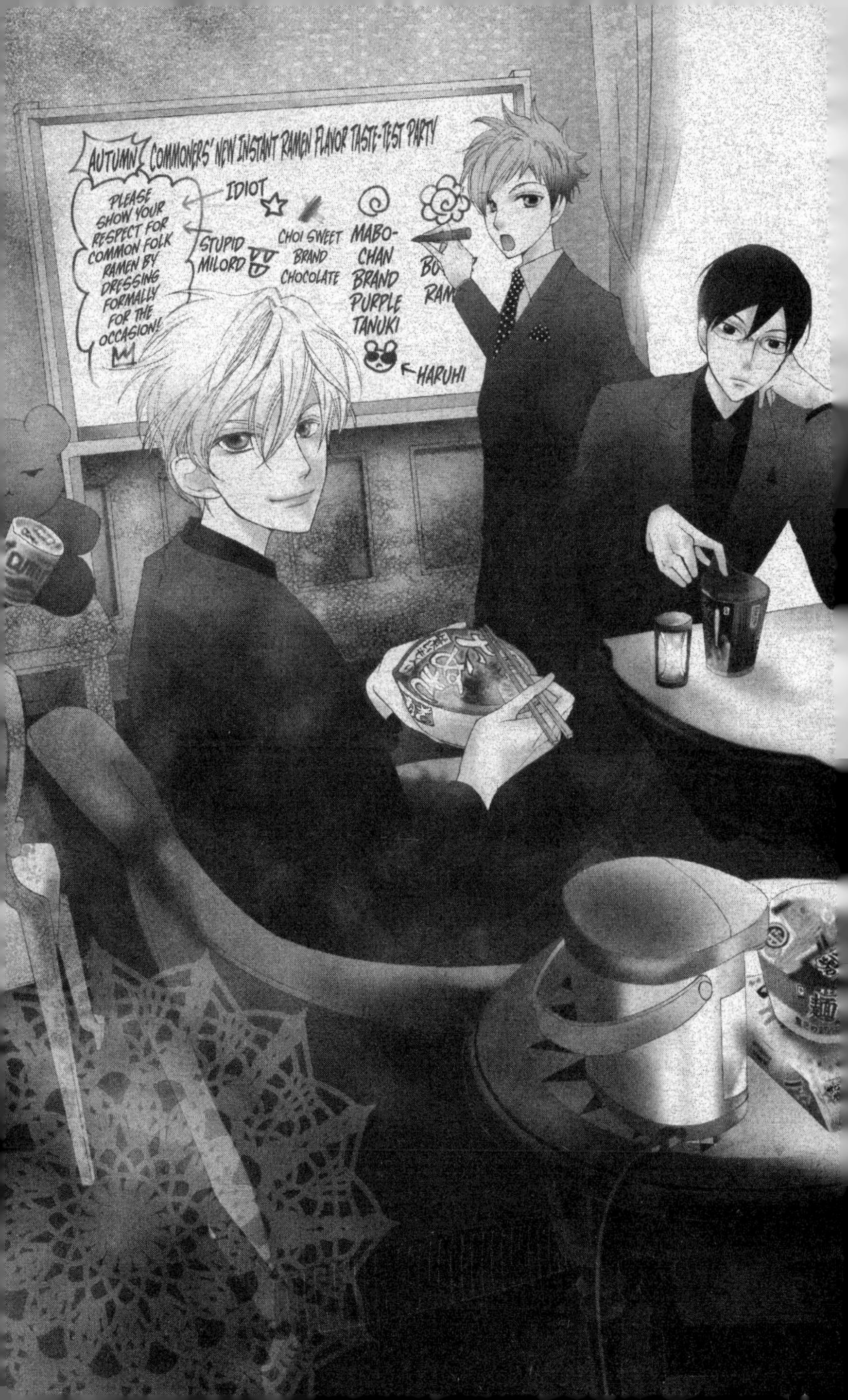
AUTUMN COMMONERS' NEW INSTANT RAMEN FLAVOR TASTE-TEST PARTY
PLEASE SHOW YOUR RESPECT FOR COMMON FOLK RAMEN BY DRESSING FORMALLY FOR THE OCCASION!
IDIOT
STUPID MILORD
CHOI SWEET BRAND CHOCOLATE
MABO-CHAN BRAND PURPLE TANUKI
HARUHI

CHIYUKI FROM
MILLENNIUM SNOW

SORRY I'M
STILL DRAWING
CHARACTERS
FROM ANOTHER
MANGA LIKE
I DID IN THE
LAST VOLUME.

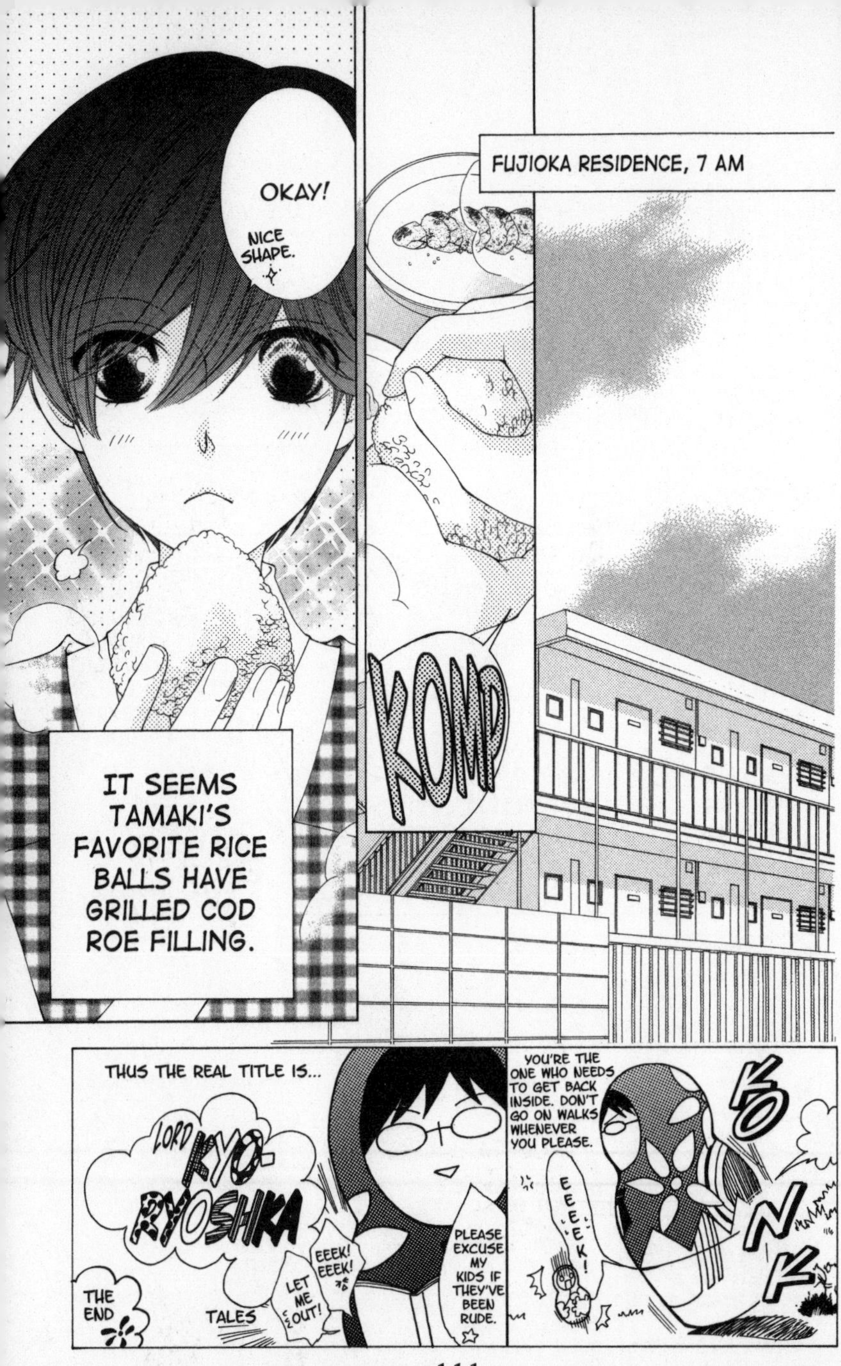
FUJIOKA RESIDENCE, 7 AM
KOMP
OKAY!
NICE SHAPE.
IT SEEMS TAMAKI'S FAVORITE RICE BALLS HAVE GRILLED COD ROE FILLING.
YOU'RE THE ONE WHO NEEDS TO GET BACK INSIDE. DON'T GO ON WALKS WHENEVER YOU PLEASE.
KONK
EEEEK!
THUS THE REAL TITLE IS...
LORD KYO-RYOSHKA TALES
PLEASE EXCUSE MY KIDS IF THEY'VE BEEN RUDE.
EEEK! EEEK!
LET ME OUT!
THE END

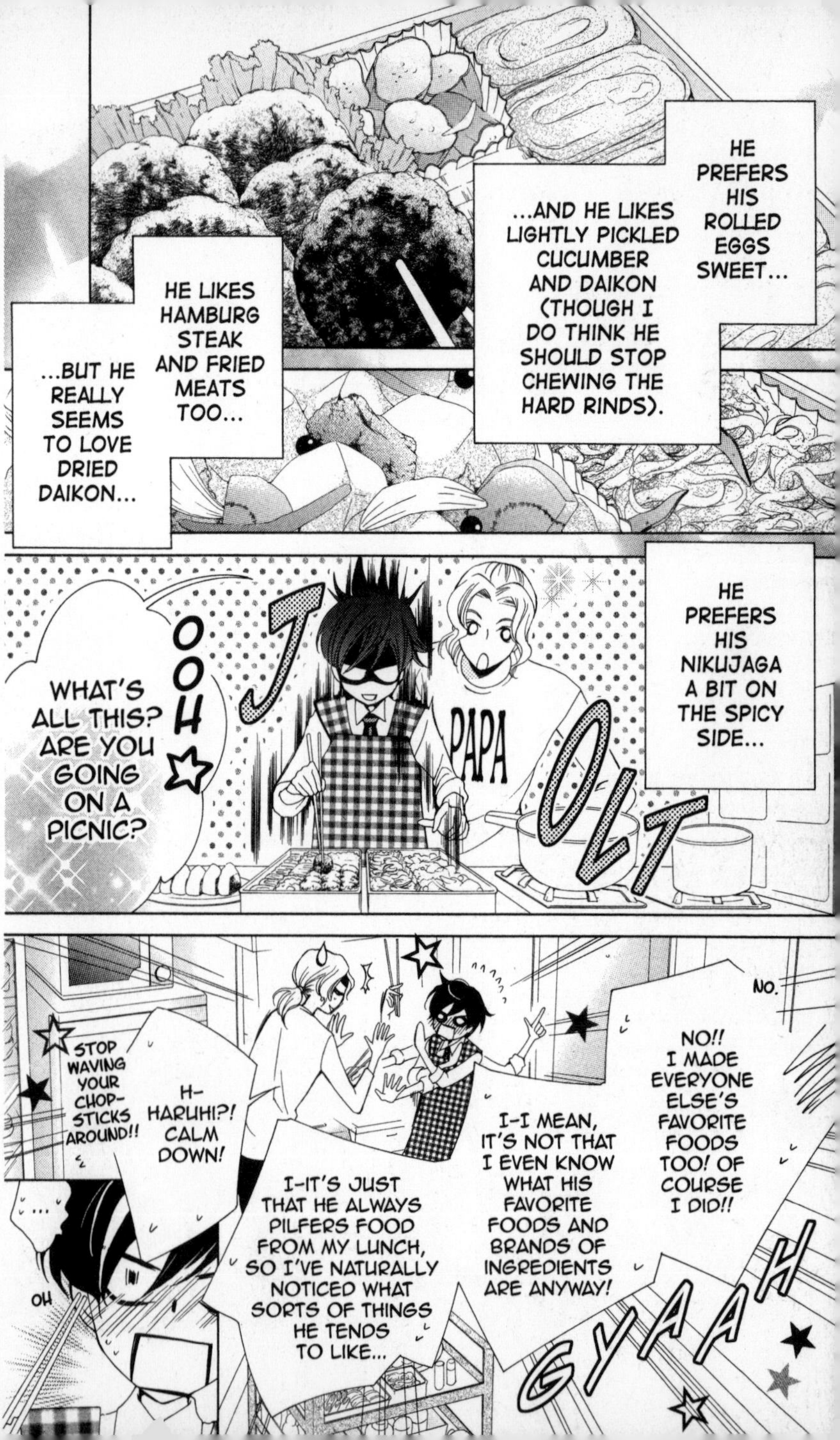
HE PREFERS HIS ROLLED EGGS SWEET...
...AND HE LIKES LIGHTLY PICKLED CUCUMBER AND DAIKON (THOUGH I DO THINK HE SHOULD STOP CHEWING THE HARD RINDS).
HE LIKES HAMBURG STEAK AND FRIED MEATS TOO...
...BUT HE REALLY SEEMS TO LOVE DRIED DAIKON...
HE PREFERS HIS NIKUJAGA A BIT ON THE SPICY SIDE...
JOLT
PAPA
OOH☆
WHAT'S ALL THIS? ARE YOU GOING ON A PICNIC?
NO.
NO!! I MADE EVERYONE ELSE'S FAVORITE FOODS TOO! OF COURSE I DID!!
I-I MEAN, IT'S NOT THAT I EVEN KNOW WHAT HIS FAVORITE FOODS AND BRANDS OF INGREDIENTS ARE ANYWAY!
GYAAH
I-IT'S JUST THAT HE ALWAYS PILFERS FOOD FROM MY LUNCH, SO I'VE NATURALLY NOTICED WHAT SORTS OF THINGS HE TENDS TO LIKE...
H-HARUHI?! CALM DOWN!
STOP WAVING YOUR CHOP-STICKS AROUND!!
...
OH

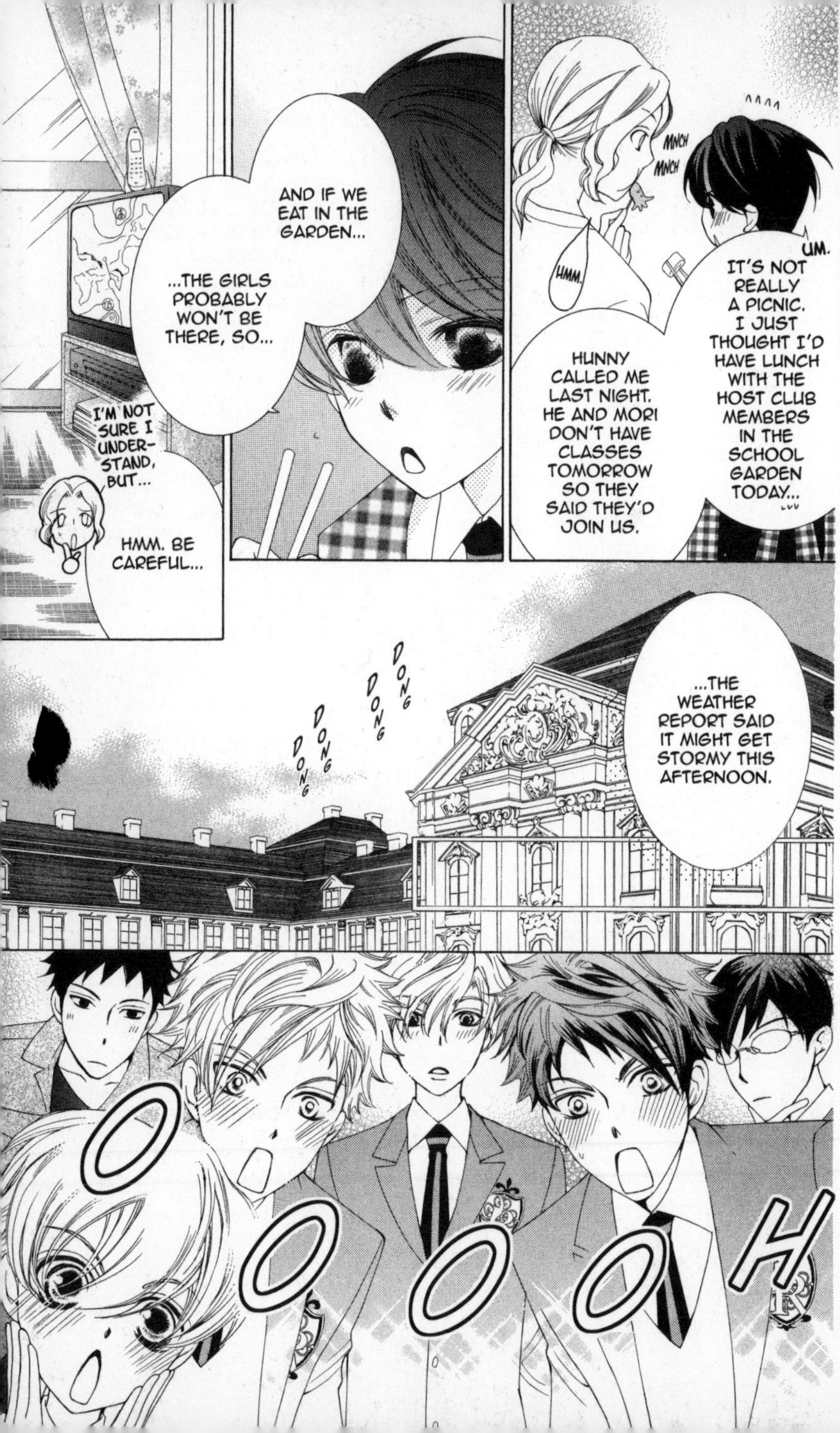
MNCH
MNCH
UM.
IT'S NOT REALLY A PICNIC. I JUST THOUGHT I'D HAVE LUNCH WITH THE HOST CLUB MEMBERS IN THE SCHOOL GARDEN TODAY...
HMM.
HUNNY CALLED ME LAST NIGHT. HE AND MORI DON'T HAVE CLASSES TOMORROW SO THEY SAID THEY'D JOIN US.
AND IF WE EAT IN THE GARDEN...
...THE GIRLS PROBABLY WON'T BE THERE, SO...
I'M NOT SURE I UNDERSTAND, BUT...
HMM. BE CAREFUL...
...THE WEATHER REPORT SAID IT MIGHT GET STORMY THIS AFTERNOON.
DONG
DONG
DONG
DONG
OOOOOH

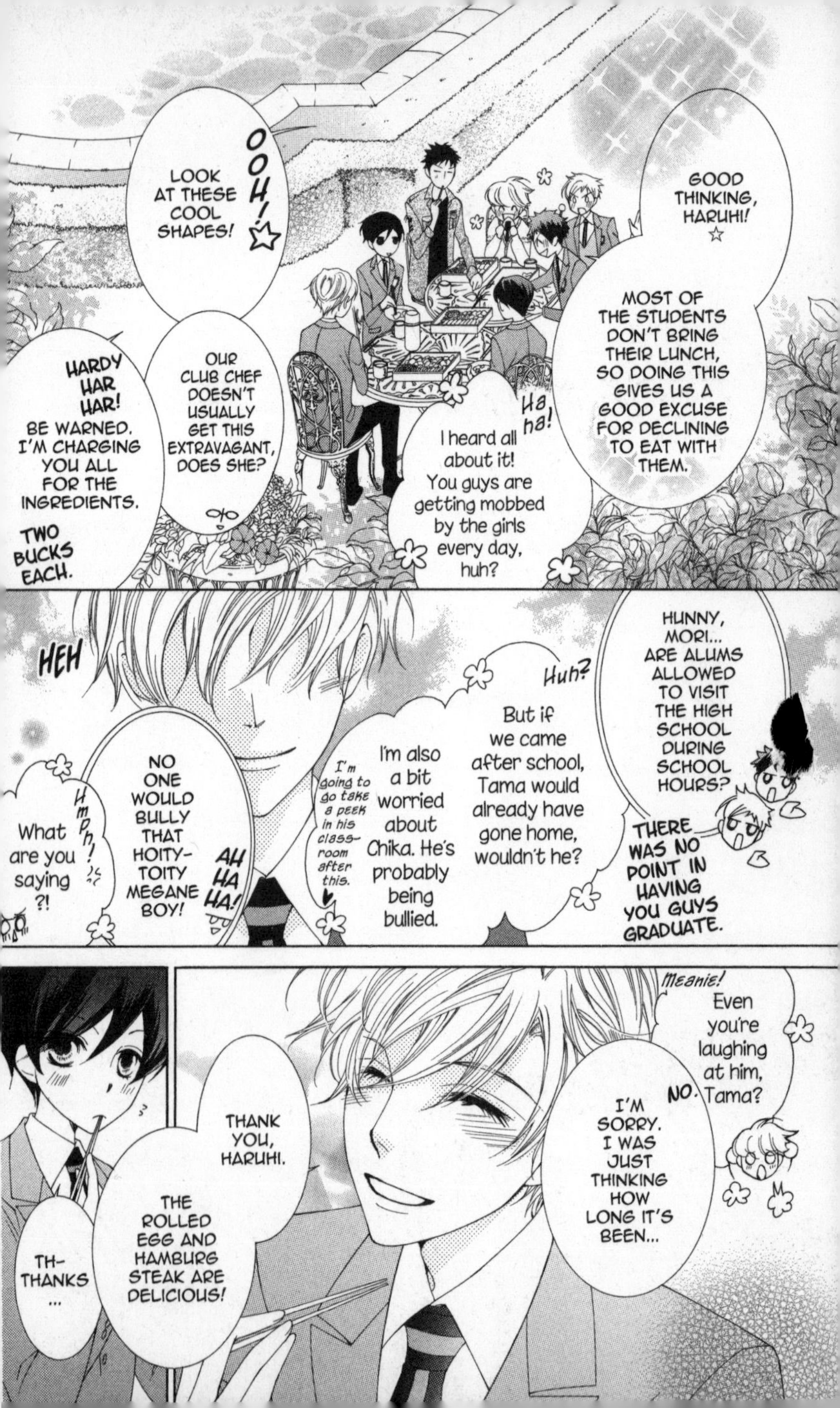
GOOD THINKING, HARUHI! ☆
OOH! ☆
LOOK AT THESE COOL SHAPES!
MOST OF THE STUDENTS DON'T BRING THEIR LUNCH, SO DOING THIS GIVES US A GOOD EXCUSE FOR DECLINING TO EAT WITH THEM.
Ha ha!
I heard all about it! You guys are getting mobbed by the girls every day, huh?
OUR CLUB CHEF DOESN'T USUALLY GET THIS EXTRAVAGANT, DOES SHE?
HARDY HAR HAR! BE WARNED. I'M CHARGING YOU ALL FOR THE INGREDIENTS.
TWO BUCKS EACH.
HUNNY, MORI... ARE ALUMS ALLOWED TO VISIT THE HIGH SCHOOL DURING SCHOOL HOURS?
THERE WAS NO POINT IN HAVING YOU GUYS GRADUATE.
Huh?
But if we came after school, Tama would already have gone home, wouldn't he?
I'm also a bit worried about Chika. He's probably being bullied.
I'm going to go take a peek in his class-room after this.
HEH
AH HA HA!
NO ONE WOULD BULLY THAT HOITY-TOITY MEGANE BOY!
Hmph!
What are you saying?!
Meanie!
Even you're laughing at him, Tama?
NO.
I'M SORRY. I WAS JUST THINKING HOW LONG IT'S BEEN...
THANK YOU, HARUHI.
THE ROLLED EGG AND HAMBURG STEAK ARE DELICIOUS!
TH-THANKS...

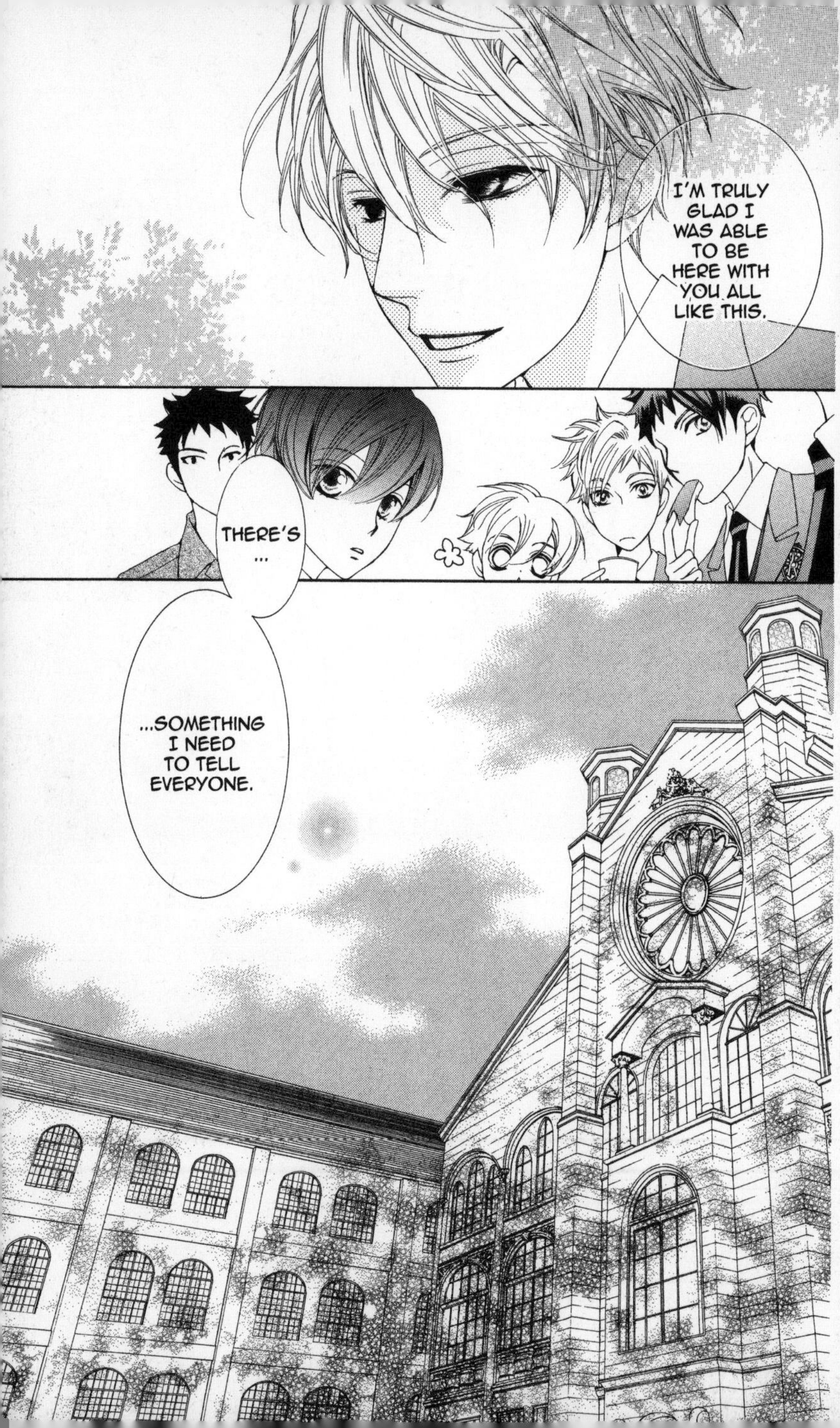
I'M TRULY GLAD I WAS ABLE TO BE HERE WITH YOU ALL LIKE THIS.
THERE'S ...
...SOMETHING I NEED TO TELL EVERYONE.

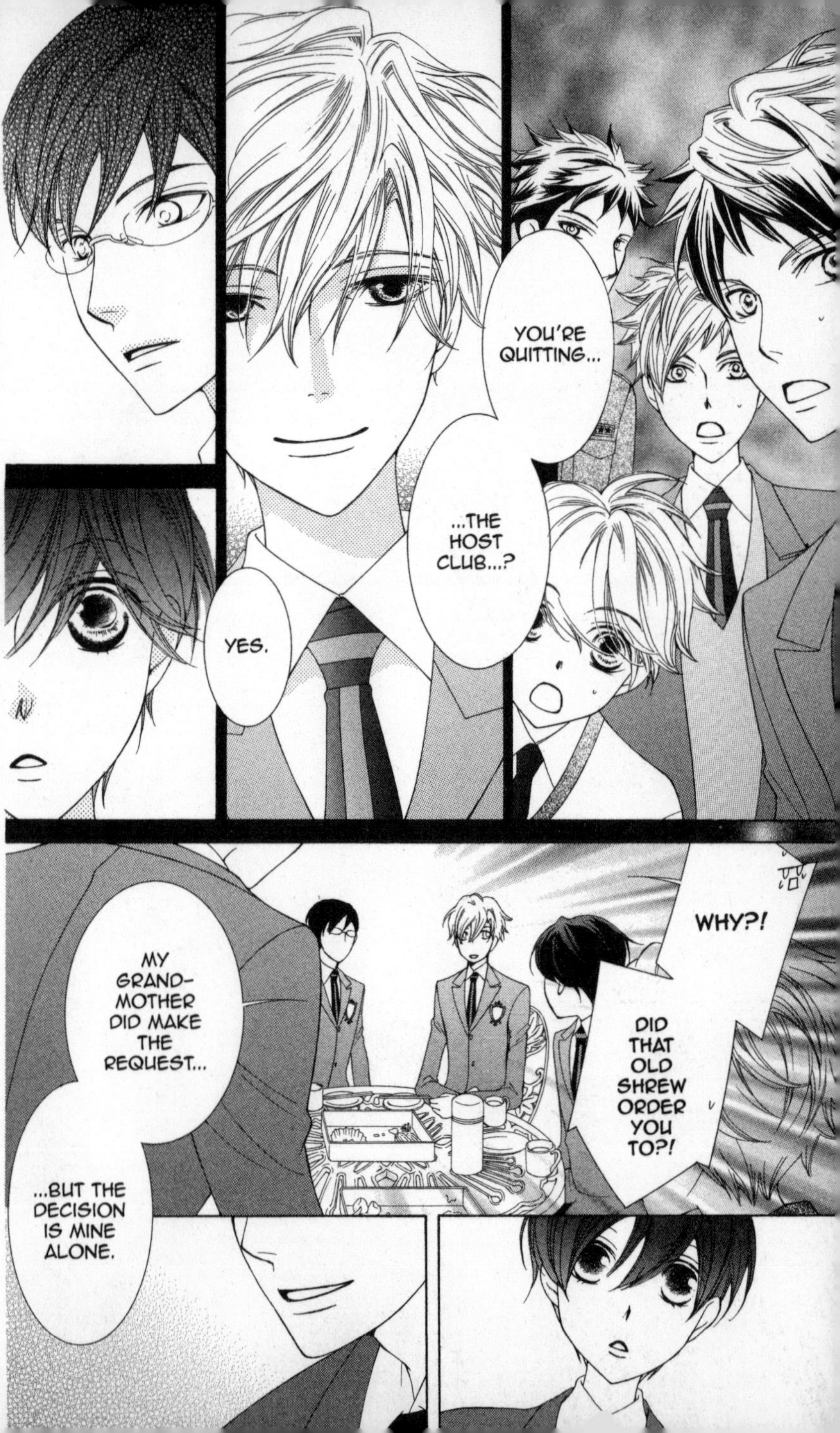
YOU'RE QUITTING...
...THE HOST CLUB...?
YES.
WHY?!
DID THAT OLD SHREW ORDER YOU TO?!
MY GRAND-MOTHER DID MAKE THE REQUEST...
...BUT THE DECISION IS MINE ALONE.

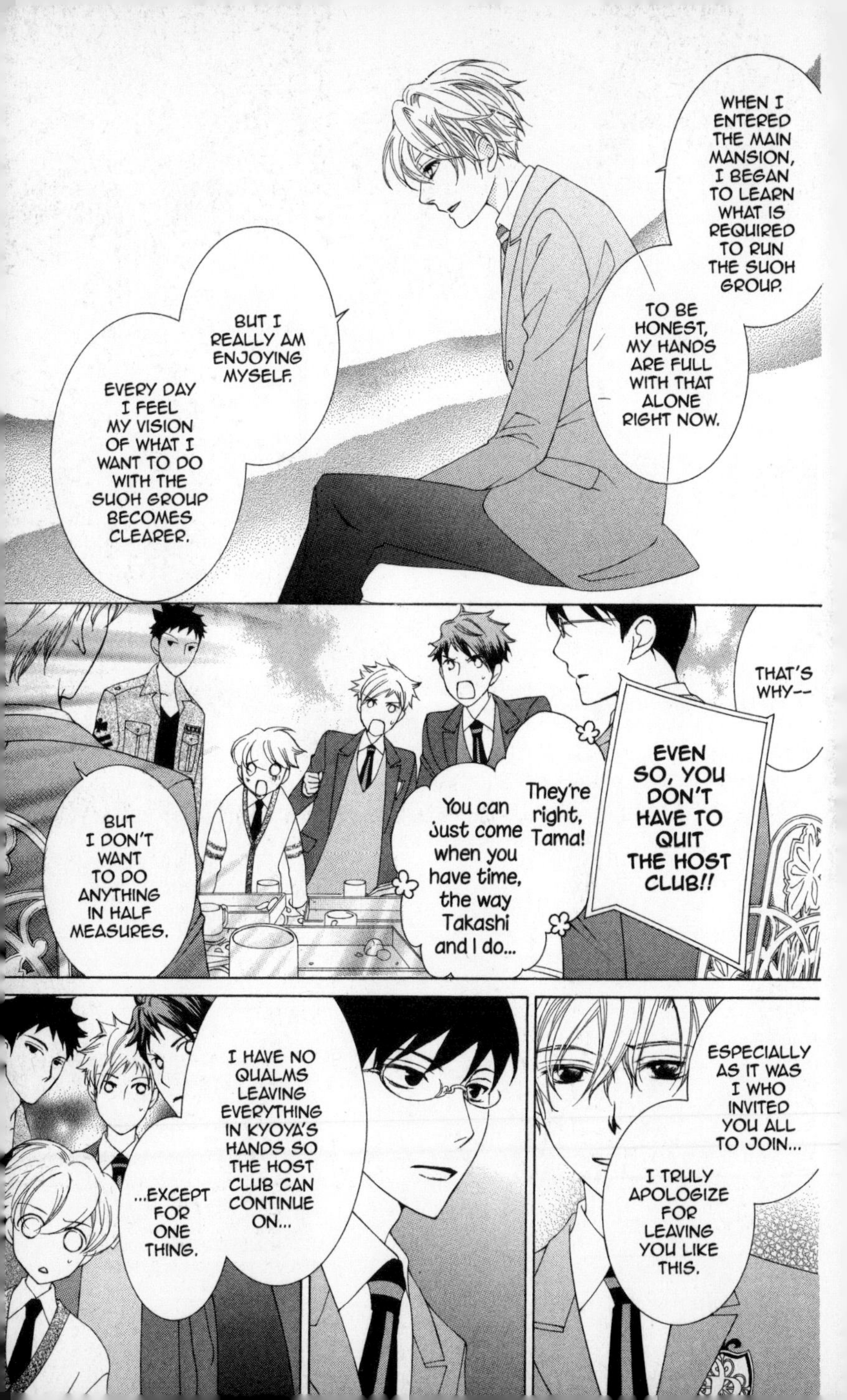
WHEN I ENTERED THE MAIN MANSION, I BEGAN TO LEARN WHAT IS REQUIRED TO RUN THE SUOH GROUP.
TO BE HONEST, MY HANDS ARE FULL WITH THAT ALONE RIGHT NOW.
BUT I REALLY AM ENJOYING MYSELF.
EVERY DAY I FEEL MY VISION OF WHAT I WANT TO DO WITH THE SUOH GROUP BECOMES CLEARER.
THAT'S WHY--
EVEN SO, YOU DON'T HAVE TO QUIT THE HOST CLUB!!
They're right, Tama!
You can just come when you have time, the way Takashi and I do...
BUT I DON'T WANT TO DO ANYTHING IN HALF MEASURES.
ESPECIALLY AS IT WAS I WHO INVITED YOU ALL TO JOIN...
I TRULY APOLOGIZE FOR LEAVING YOU LIKE THIS.
I HAVE NO QUALMS LEAVING EVERYTHING IN KYOYA'S HANDS SO THE HOST CLUB CAN CONTINUE ON...
...EXCEPT FOR ONE THING.

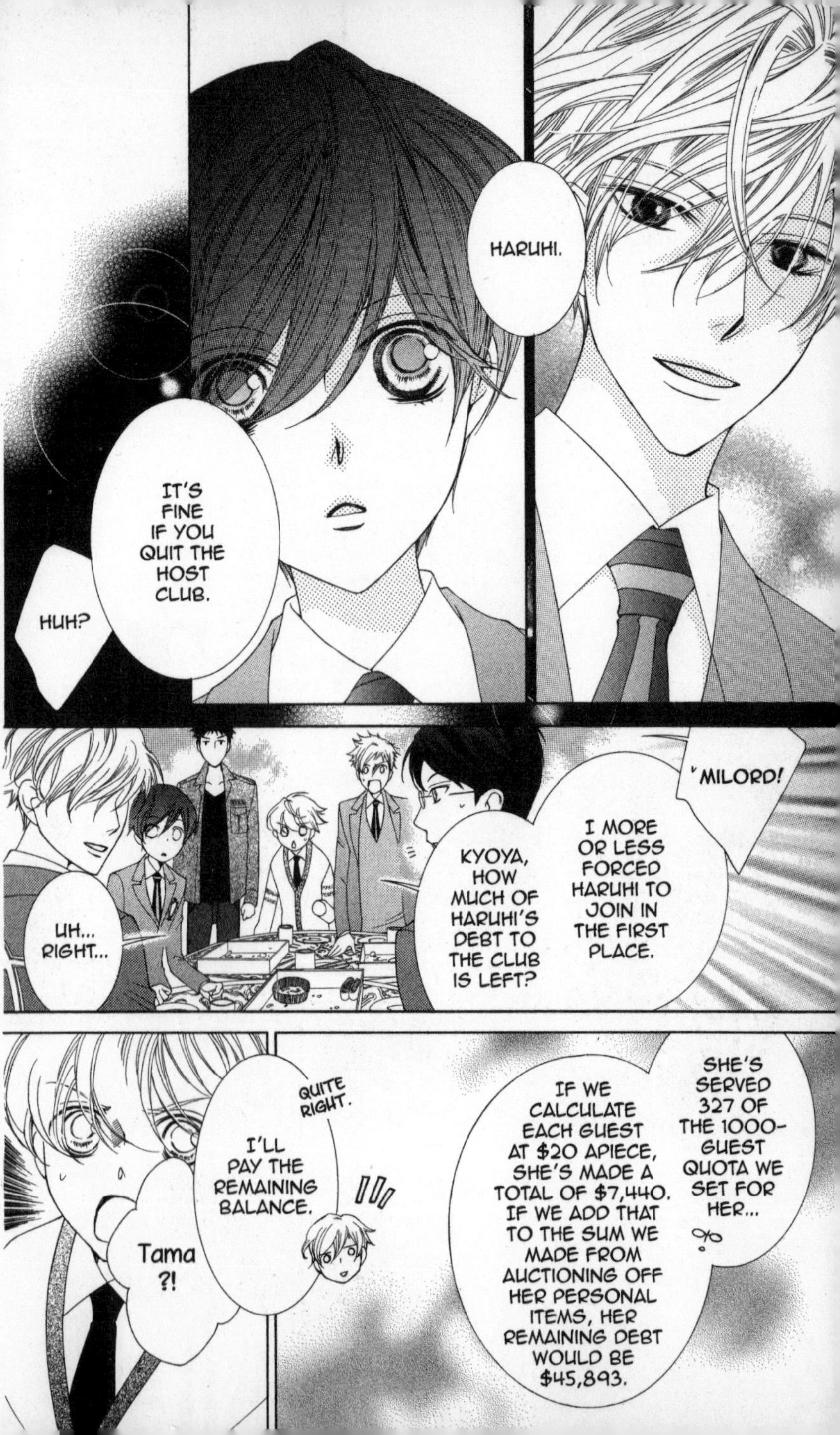
HARUHI.
IT'S FINE IF YOU QUIT THE HOST CLUB.
HUH?
MILORD!
I MORE OR LESS FORCED HARUHI TO JOIN IN THE FIRST PLACE.
KYOYA, HOW MUCH OF HARUHI'S DEBT TO THE CLUB IS LEFT?
UH... RIGHT...
SHE'S SERVED 327 OF THE 1000-GUEST QUOTA WE SET FOR HER...
IF WE CALCULATE EACH GUEST AT $20 APIECE, SHE'S MADE A TOTAL OF $7,440. IF WE ADD THAT TO THE SUM WE MADE FROM AUCTIONING OFF HER PERSONAL ITEMS, HER REMAINING DEBT WOULD BE $45,893.
QUITE RIGHT.
I'LL PAY THE REMAINING BALANCE.
Tama ?!

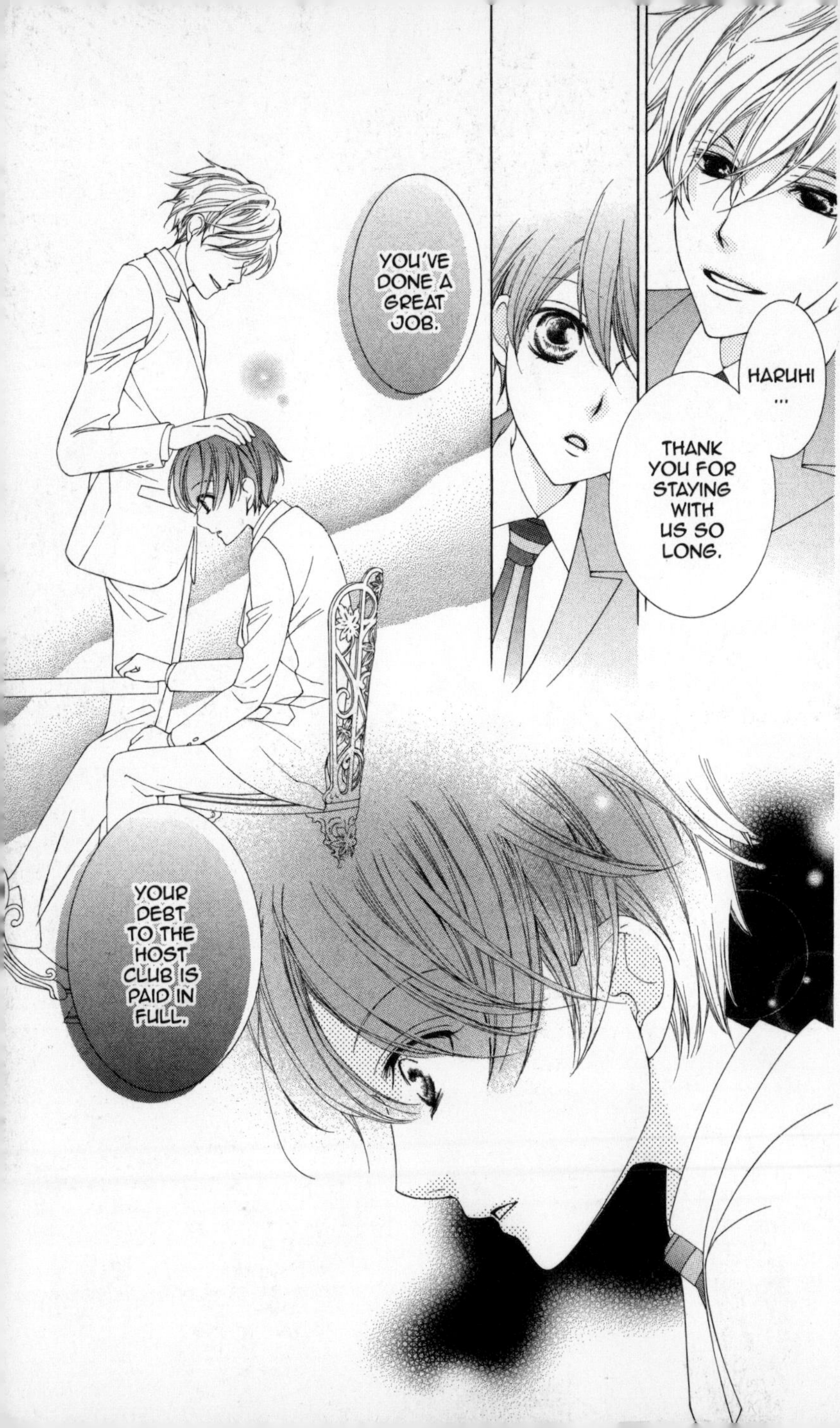
HARUHI ...
THANK YOU FOR STAYING WITH US SO LONG.
YOU'VE DONE A GREAT JOB.
YOUR DEBT TO THE HOST CLUB IS PAID IN FULL.

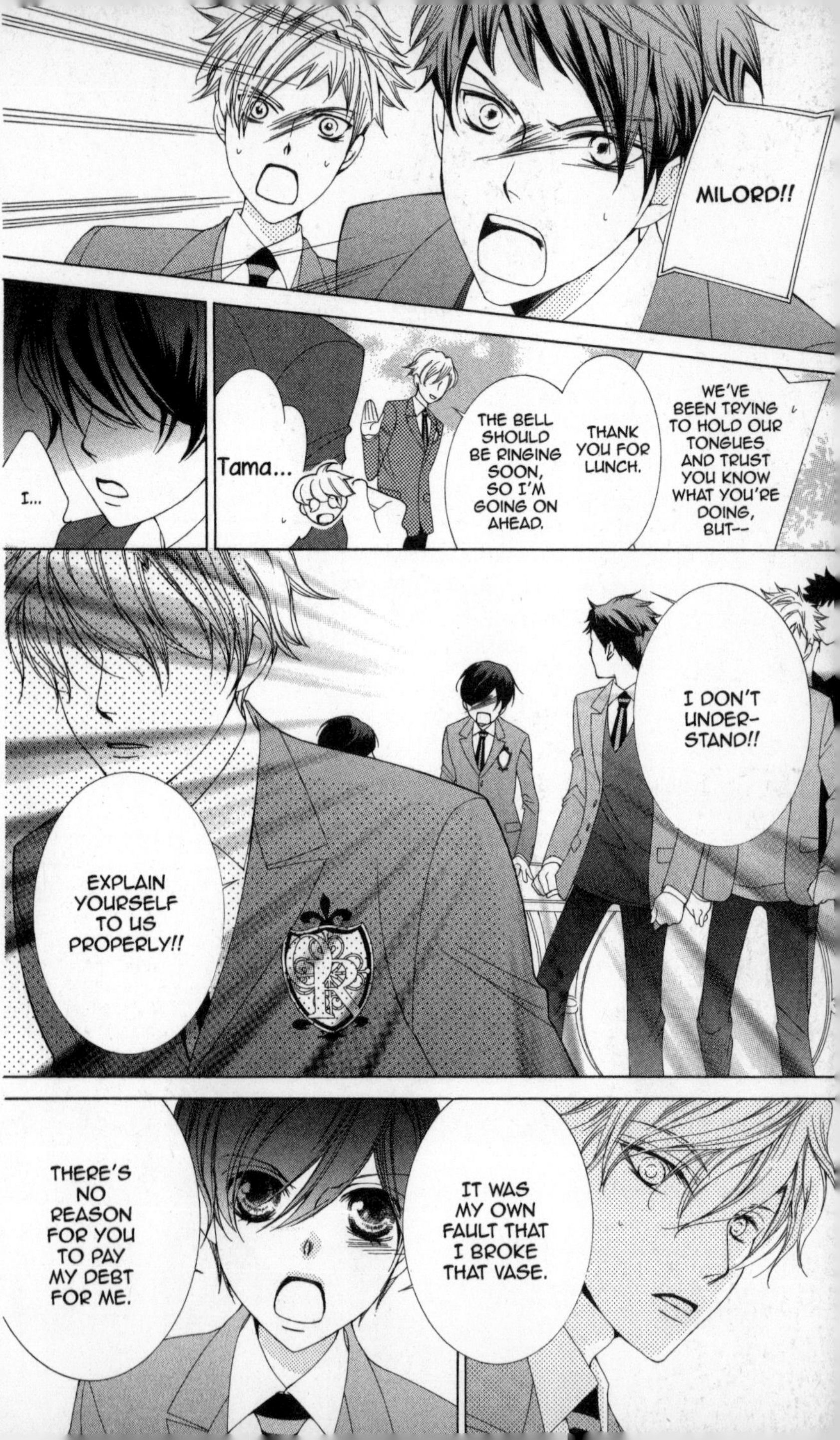
MILORD!!
WE'VE BEEN TRYING TO HOLD OUR TONGUES AND TRUST YOU KNOW WHAT YOU'RE DOING, BUT--
THANK YOU FOR LUNCH.
THE BELL SHOULD BE RINGING SOON, SO I'M GOING ON AHEAD.
Tama...
I...
I DON'T UNDER-STAND!!
EXPLAIN YOURSELF TO US PROPERLY!!
IT WAS MY OWN FAULT THAT I BROKE THAT VASE.
THERE'S NO REASON FOR YOU TO PAY MY DEBT FOR ME.

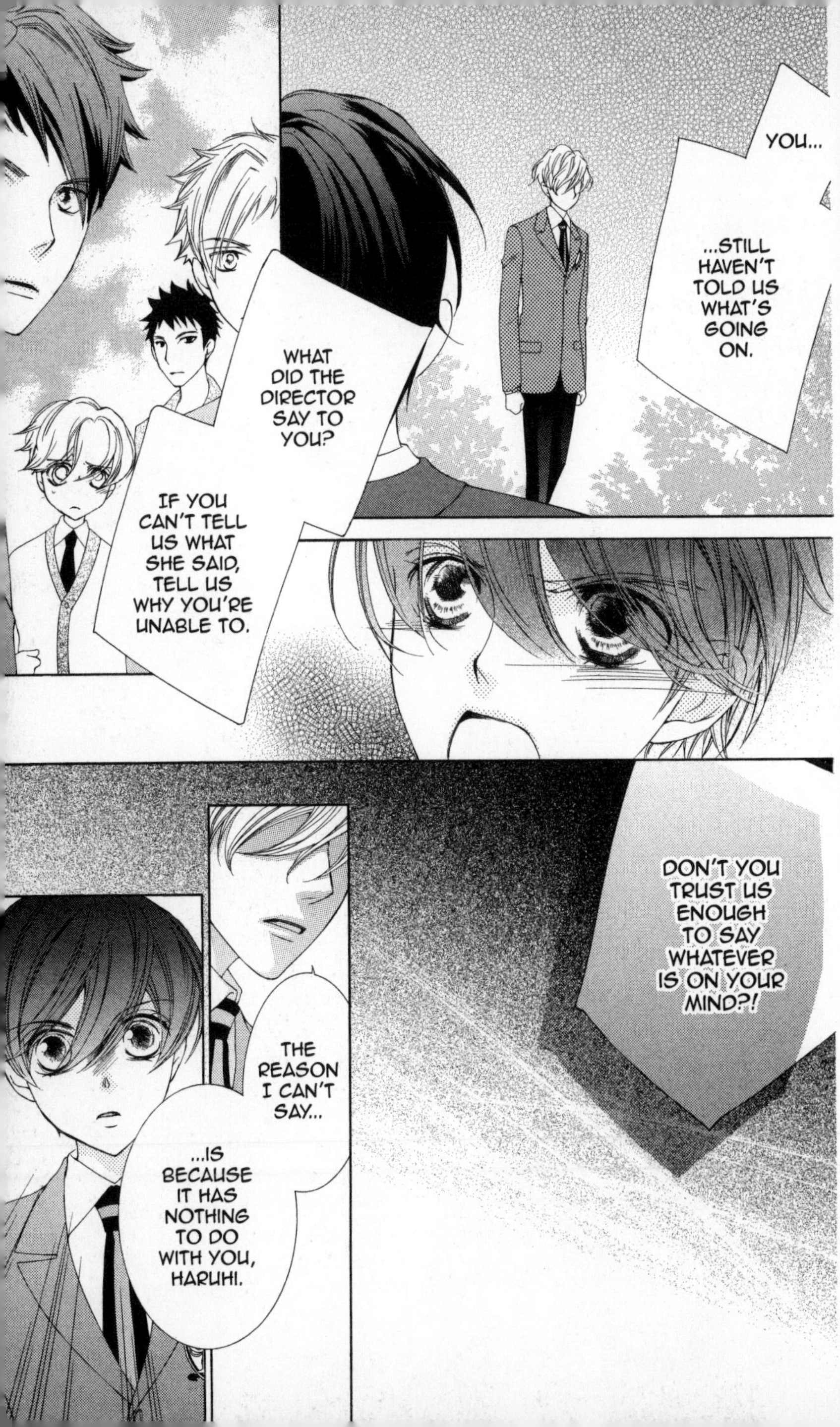
YOU...
...STILL HAVEN'T TOLD US WHAT'S GOING ON.
WHAT DID THE DIRECTOR SAY TO YOU?
IF YOU CAN'T TELL US WHAT SHE SAID, TELL US WHY YOU'RE UNABLE TO.
DON'T YOU TRUST US ENOUGH TO SAY WHATEVER IS ON YOUR MIND?!
THE REASON I CAN'T SAY...
...IS BECAUSE IT HAS NOTHING TO DO WITH YOU, HARUHI.

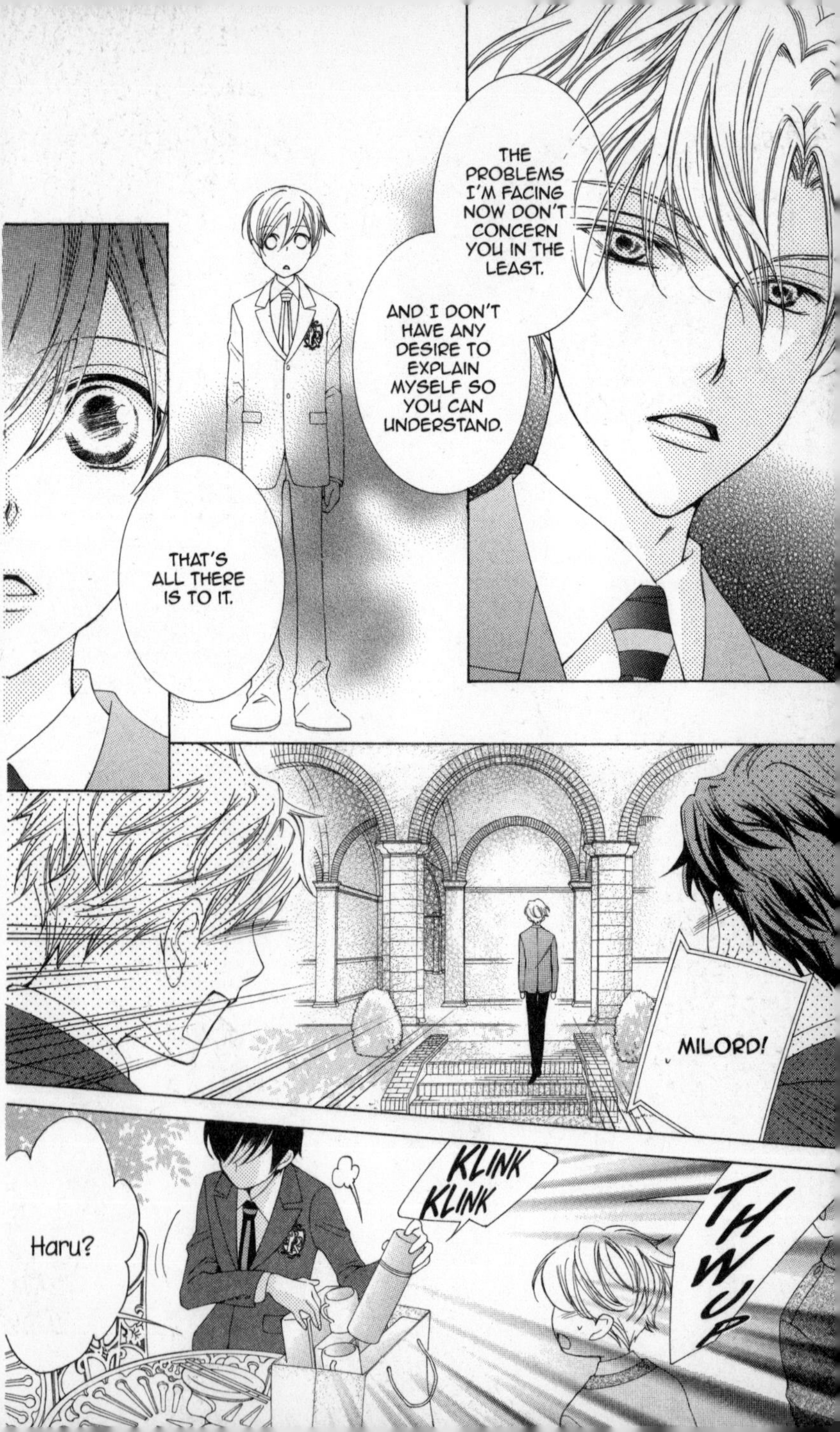
THE PROBLEMS I'M FACING NOW DON'T CONCERN YOU IN THE LEAST.
AND I DON'T HAVE ANY DESIRE TO EXPLAIN MYSELF SO YOU CAN UNDERSTAND.
THAT'S ALL THERE IS TO IT.
MILORD!
THWUP
KLINK KLINK
Haru?

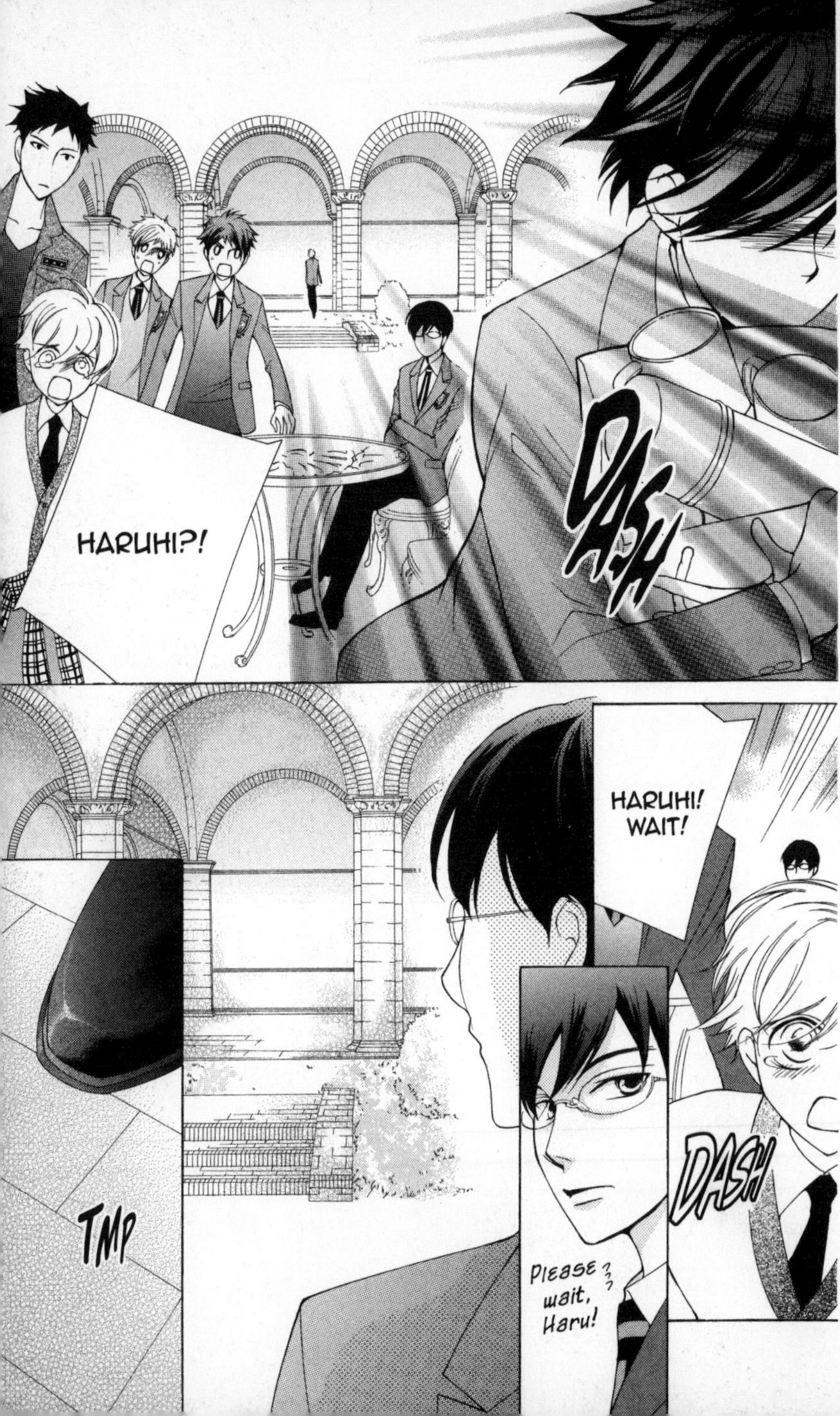
DASH
HARUHI?!
HARUHI! WAIT!
DASH
Please wait, Haru!
TMP

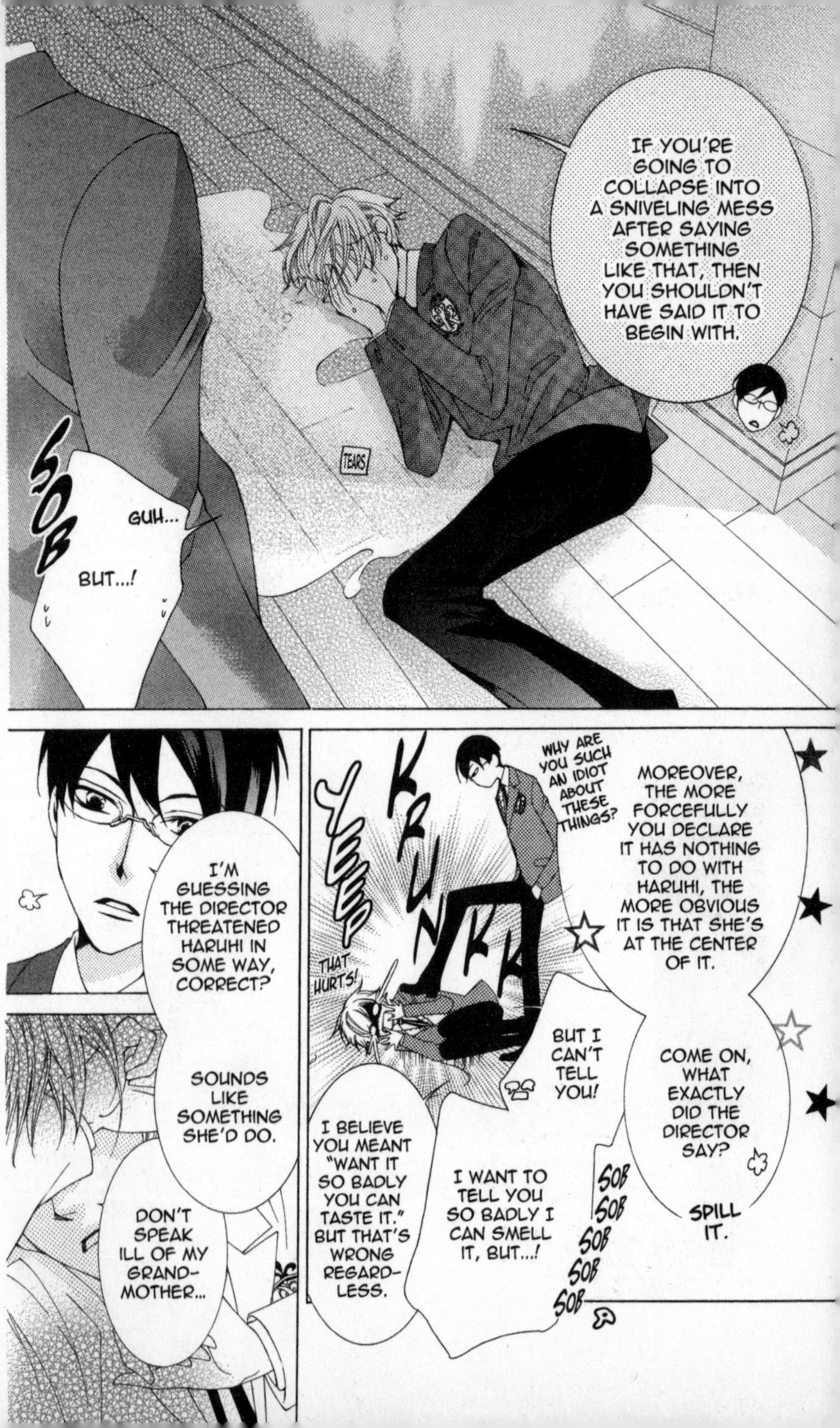
IF YOU'RE GOING TO COLLAPSE INTO A SNIVELING MESS AFTER SAYING SOMETHING LIKE THAT, THEN YOU SHOULDN'T HAVE SAID IT TO BEGIN WITH.
TEARS
SOB
GUH...
BUT...!
MOREOVER, THE MORE FORCEFULLY YOU DECLARE IT HAS NOTHING TO DO WITH HARUHI, THE MORE OBVIOUS IT IS THAT SHE'S AT THE CENTER OF IT.
WHY ARE YOU SUCH AN IDIOT ABOUT THESE THINGS?
KRUNK
THAT HURTS!
COME ON, WHAT EXACTLY DID THE DIRECTOR SAY?
SPILL IT.
BUT I CAN'T TELL YOU!
I WANT TO TELL YOU SO BADLY I CAN SMELL IT, BUT...!
SOB SOB SOB SOB SOB
I BELIEVE YOU MEANT "WANT IT SO BADLY YOU CAN TASTE IT." BUT THAT'S WRONG REGARDLESS.
I'M GUESSING THE DIRECTOR THREATENED HARUHI IN SOME WAY, CORRECT?
SOUNDS LIKE SOMETHING SHE'D DO.
DON'T SPEAK ILL OF MY GRANDMOTHER...

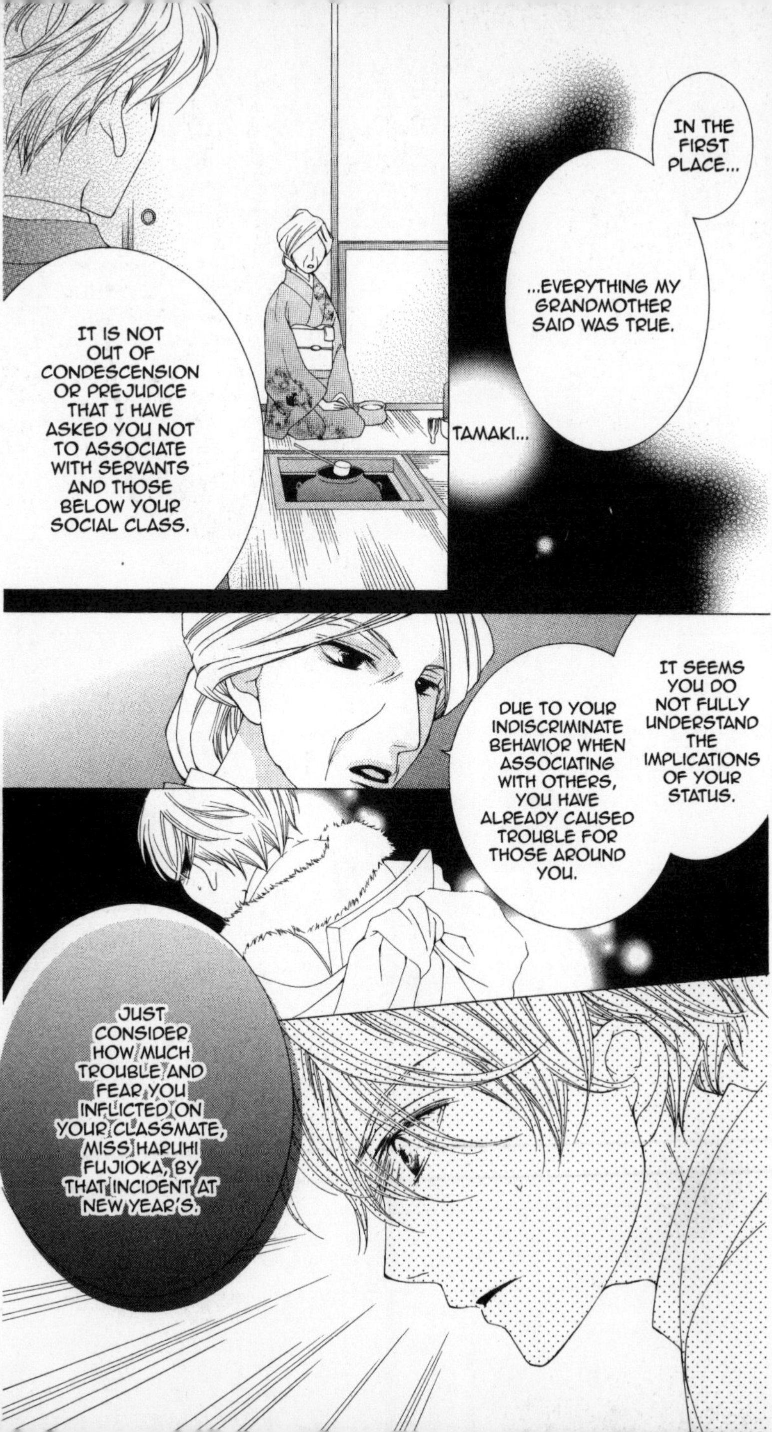
IN THE FIRST PLACE...
...EVERYTHING MY GRANDMOTHER SAID WAS TRUE.
TAMAKI...
IT IS NOT OUT OF CONDESCENSION OR PREJUDICE THAT I HAVE ASKED YOU NOT TO ASSOCIATE WITH SERVANTS AND THOSE BELOW YOUR SOCIAL CLASS.
IT SEEMS YOU DO NOT FULLY UNDERSTAND THE IMPLICATIONS OF YOUR STATUS.
DUE TO YOUR INDISCRIMINATE BEHAVIOR WHEN ASSOCIATING WITH OTHERS, YOU HAVE ALREADY CAUSED TROUBLE FOR THOSE AROUND YOU.
JUST CONSIDER HOW MUCH TROUBLE AND FEAR YOU INFLICTED ON YOUR CLASSMATE, MISS HARUHI FUJIOKA, BY THAT INCIDENT AT NEW YEAR'S.

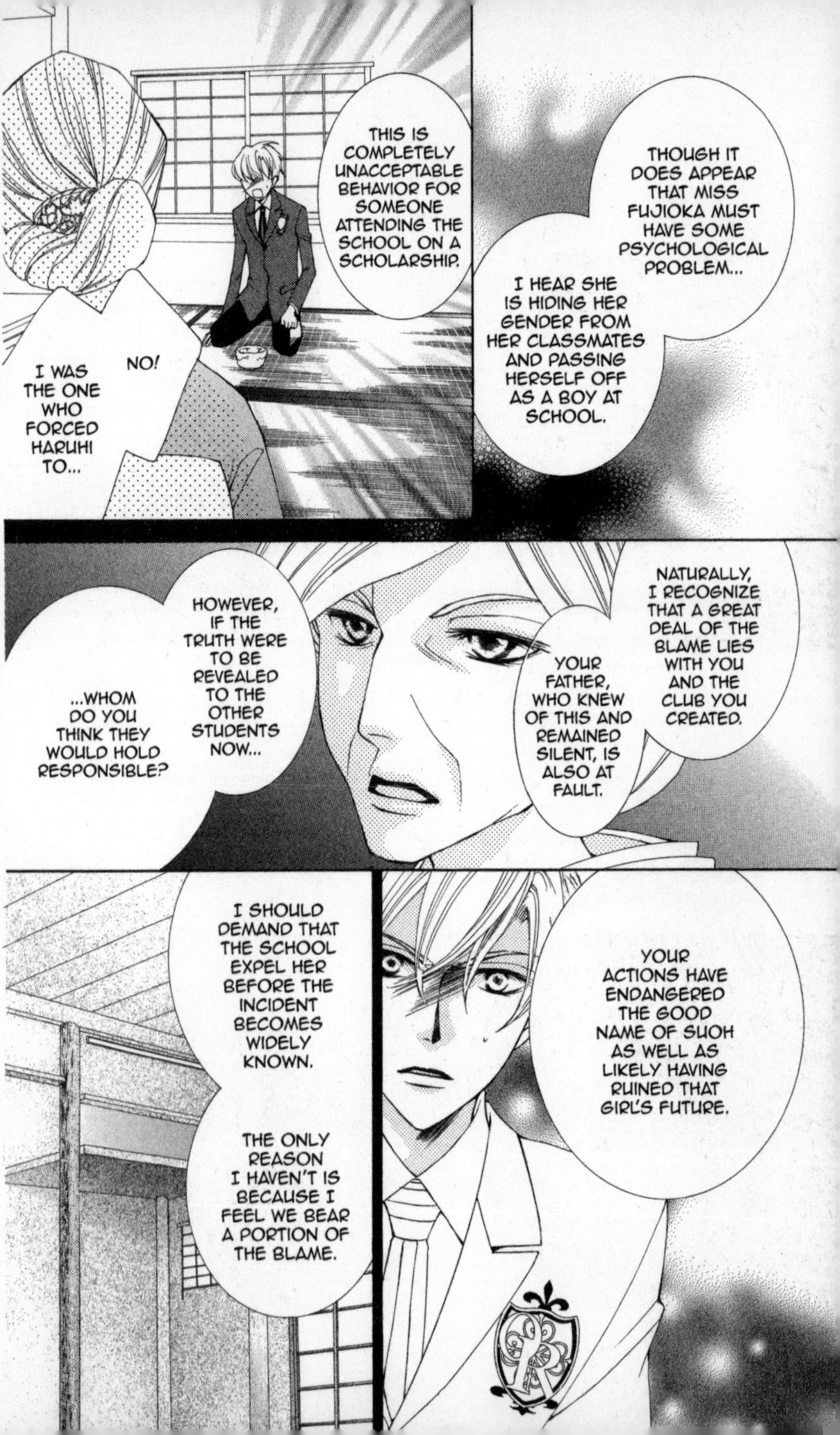
THOUGH IT DOES APPEAR THAT MISS FUJIOKA MUST HAVE SOME PSYCHOLOGICAL PROBLEM...
I HEAR SHE IS HIDING HER GENDER FROM HER CLASSMATES AND PASSING HERSELF OFF AS A BOY AT SCHOOL.
THIS IS COMPLETELY UNACCEPTABLE BEHAVIOR FOR SOMEONE ATTENDING THE SCHOOL ON A SCHOLARSHIP.
NO!
I WAS THE ONE WHO FORCED HARUHI TO...
NATURALLY, I RECOGNIZE THAT A GREAT DEAL OF THE BLAME LIES WITH YOU AND THE CLUB YOU CREATED.
YOUR FATHER, WHO KNEW OF THIS AND REMAINED SILENT, IS ALSO AT FAULT.
HOWEVER, IF THE TRUTH WERE TO BE REVEALED TO THE OTHER STUDENTS NOW...
...WHOM DO YOU THINK THEY WOULD HOLD RESPONSIBLE?
YOUR ACTIONS HAVE ENDANGERED THE GOOD NAME OF SUOH AS WELL AS LIKELY HAVING RUINED THAT GIRL'S FUTURE.
I SHOULD DEMAND THAT THE SCHOOL EXPEL HER BEFORE THE INCIDENT BECOMES WIDELY KNOWN.
THE ONLY REASON I HAVEN'T IS BECAUSE I FEEL WE BEAR A PORTION OF THE BLAME.

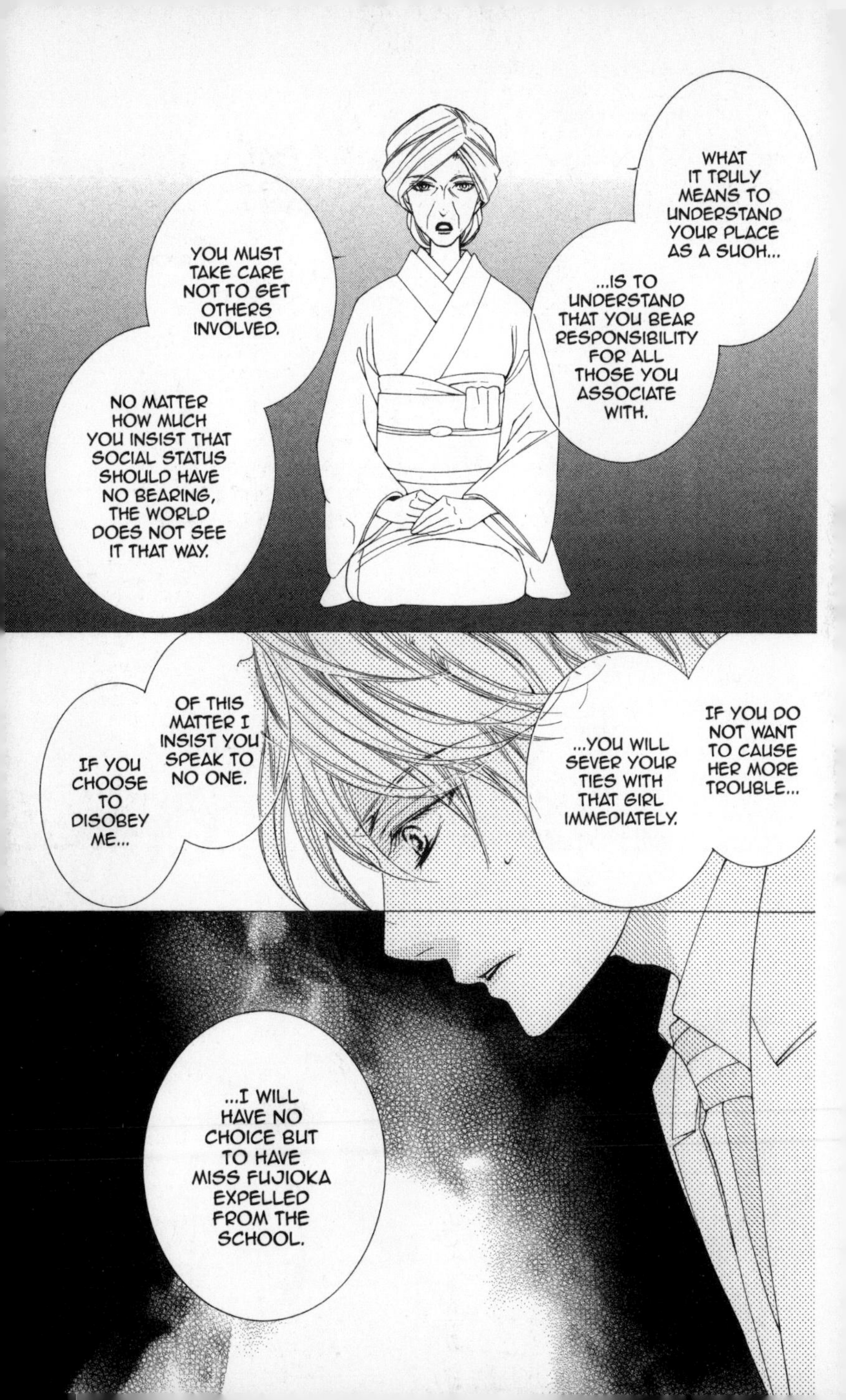
WHAT IT TRULY MEANS TO UNDERSTAND YOUR PLACE AS A SUOH...
...IS TO UNDERSTAND THAT YOU BEAR RESPONSIBILITY FOR ALL THOSE YOU ASSOCIATE WITH.
YOU MUST TAKE CARE NOT TO GET OTHERS INVOLVED.
NO MATTER HOW MUCH YOU INSIST THAT SOCIAL STATUS SHOULD HAVE NO BEARING, THE WORLD DOES NOT SEE IT THAT WAY.
IF YOU DO NOT WANT TO CAUSE HER MORE TROUBLE...
...YOU WILL SEVER YOUR TIES WITH THAT GIRL IMMEDIATELY.
OF THIS MATTER I INSIST YOU SPEAK TO NO ONE.
IF YOU CHOOSE TO DISOBEY ME...
...I WILL HAVE NO CHOICE BUT TO HAVE MISS FUJIOKA EXPELLED FROM THE SCHOOL.

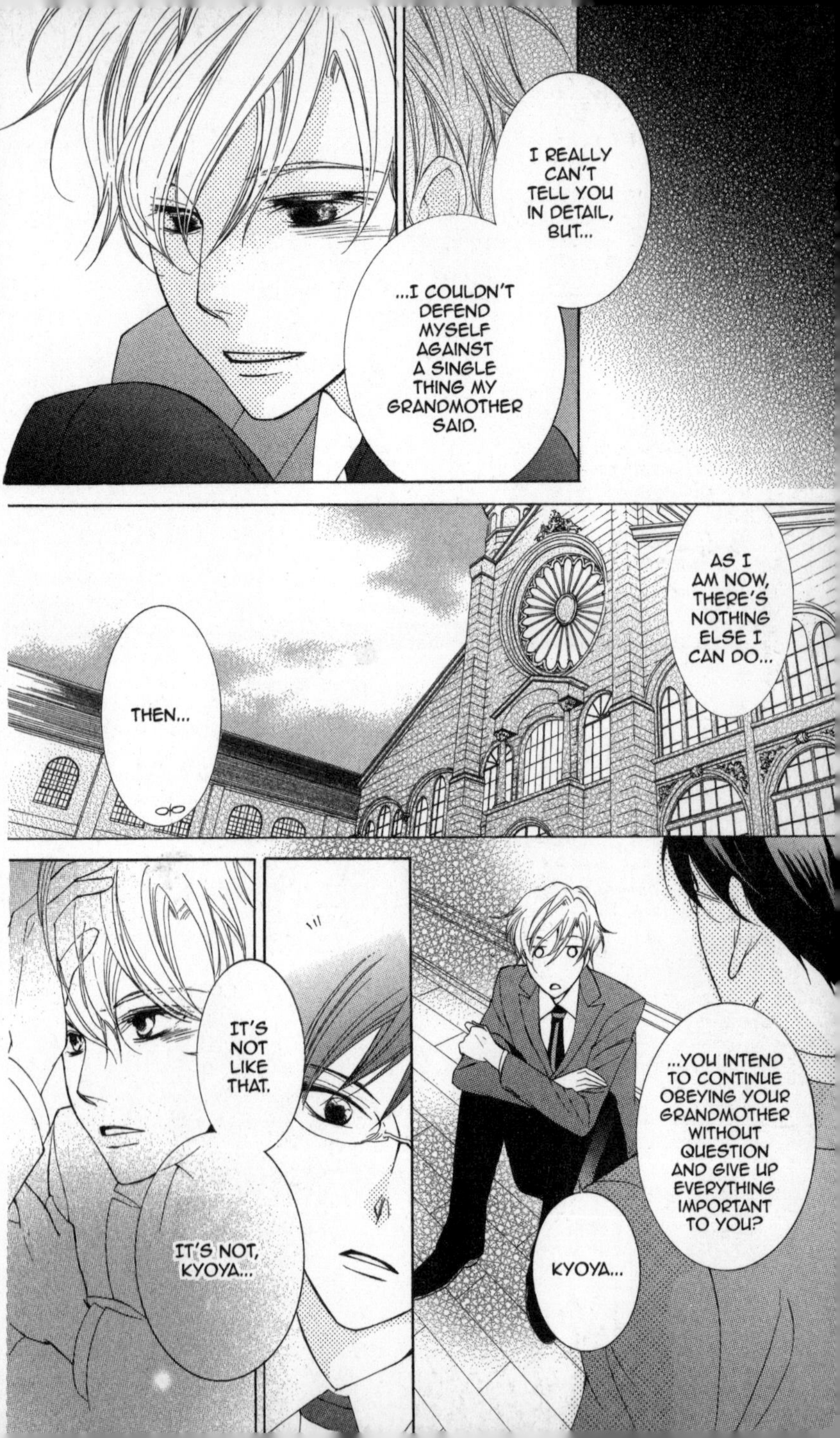
I REALLY CAN'T TELL YOU IN DETAIL, BUT...
...I COULDN'T DEFEND MYSELF AGAINST A SINGLE THING MY GRANDMOTHER SAID.
AS I AM NOW, THERE'S NOTHING ELSE I CAN DO...
THEN...
...YOU INTEND TO CONTINUE OBEYING YOUR GRANDMOTHER WITHOUT QUESTION AND GIVE UP EVERYTHING IMPORTANT TO YOU?
KYOYA...
IT'S NOT LIKE THAT.
IT'S NOT, KYOYA...

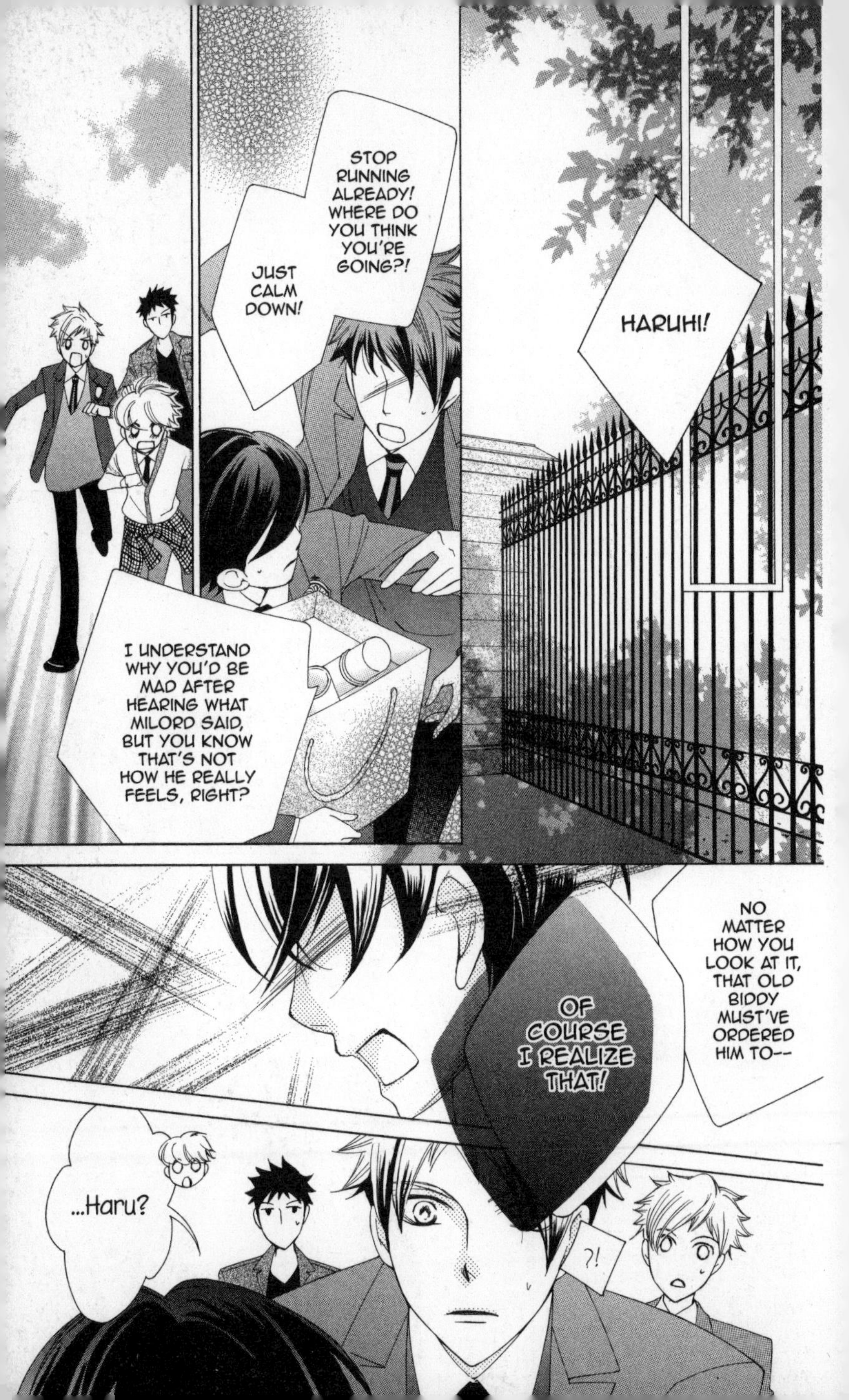
HARUHI!
STOP RUNNING ALREADY! WHERE DO YOU THINK YOU'RE GOING?!
JUST CALM DOWN!
I UNDERSTAND WHY YOU'D BE MAD AFTER HEARING WHAT MILORD SAID, BUT YOU KNOW THAT'S NOT HOW HE REALLY FEELS, RIGHT?
NO MATTER HOW YOU LOOK AT IT, THAT OLD BIDDY MUST'VE ORDERED HIM TO--
OF COURSE I REALIZE THAT!
?!
...Haru?

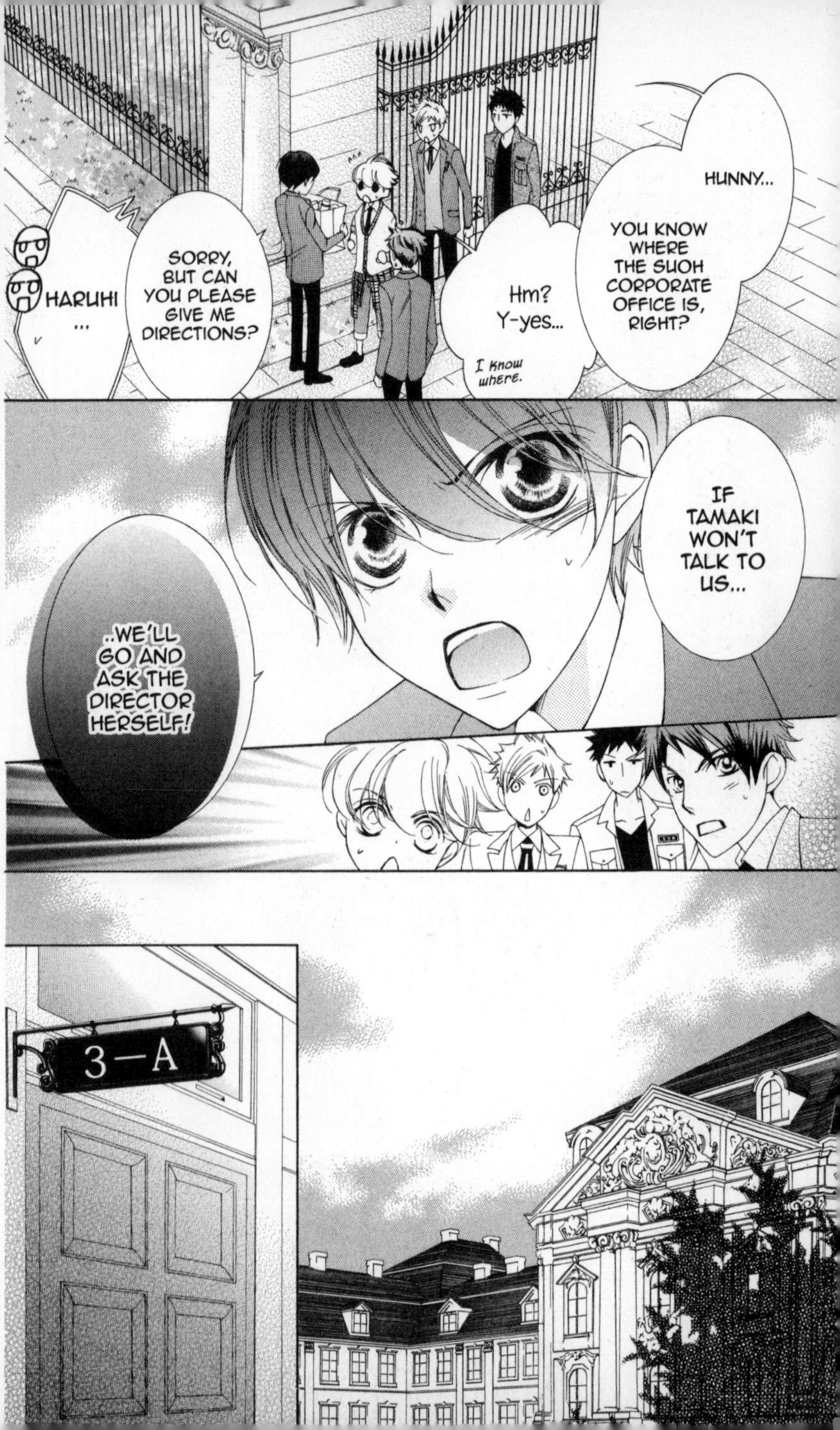
HUNNY...
YOU KNOW WHERE THE SUOH CORPORATE OFFICE IS, RIGHT?
Hm? Y-yes...
I know where.
SORRY, BUT CAN YOU PLEASE GIVE ME DIRECTIONS?
HARUHI ...
IF TAMAKI WON'T TALK TO US...
..WE'LL GO AND ASK THE DIRECTOR HERSELF!
3—A

I STARTED A BLOG 3

SO IF YOU'RE WONDERING WHY I WOULD EVEN CREATE A BLOG DESPITE ALL THIS...

INCIDENTALLY, I STILL DON'T KNOW HOW TO ADD EMOTICONS...

(; ;) (^ ^;) ← I CAN PAINSTAKINGLY DO THESE. I'M REALLY TRYING, YOU KNOW... YOU'RE LAUGHING, AREN'T YOU?

IT'S BECAUSE THE READERS--ESPECIALLY THE TANKOUBON READERS (WHO DON'T READ IT IN *LALA* MAGAZINE)--OFTEN SEND ME LETTERS LIKE THIS...

OH...

THE DRAMA CD IS SOLD OUT ALREADY. (CRIES)

I WANTED THE SPECIAL INSERT ITEM TOO!

EVEN THOUGH IT'S A BLOG MEANT TO BE VIEWED ON A PC, YOU CAN VIEW IT FROM YOUR PHONE TOO. PLEASE DO COME VISIT IF YOU'D LIKE! ☆

BY THE WAY, MY BLOG TITLE IS KIND OF LONG, ISN'T IT?

I KIND OF REGRET IT NOW.

BUT IN ANY CASE, HERE'S MY ANNOUNCEMENT!

PLEASE BE SURE TO TAKE A LOOK AT *LALA* 2010 MAGAZINE ISSUE 8 OR 9, OKAY?

THAT CONCLUDES MY ANNOUNCEMENT. ★

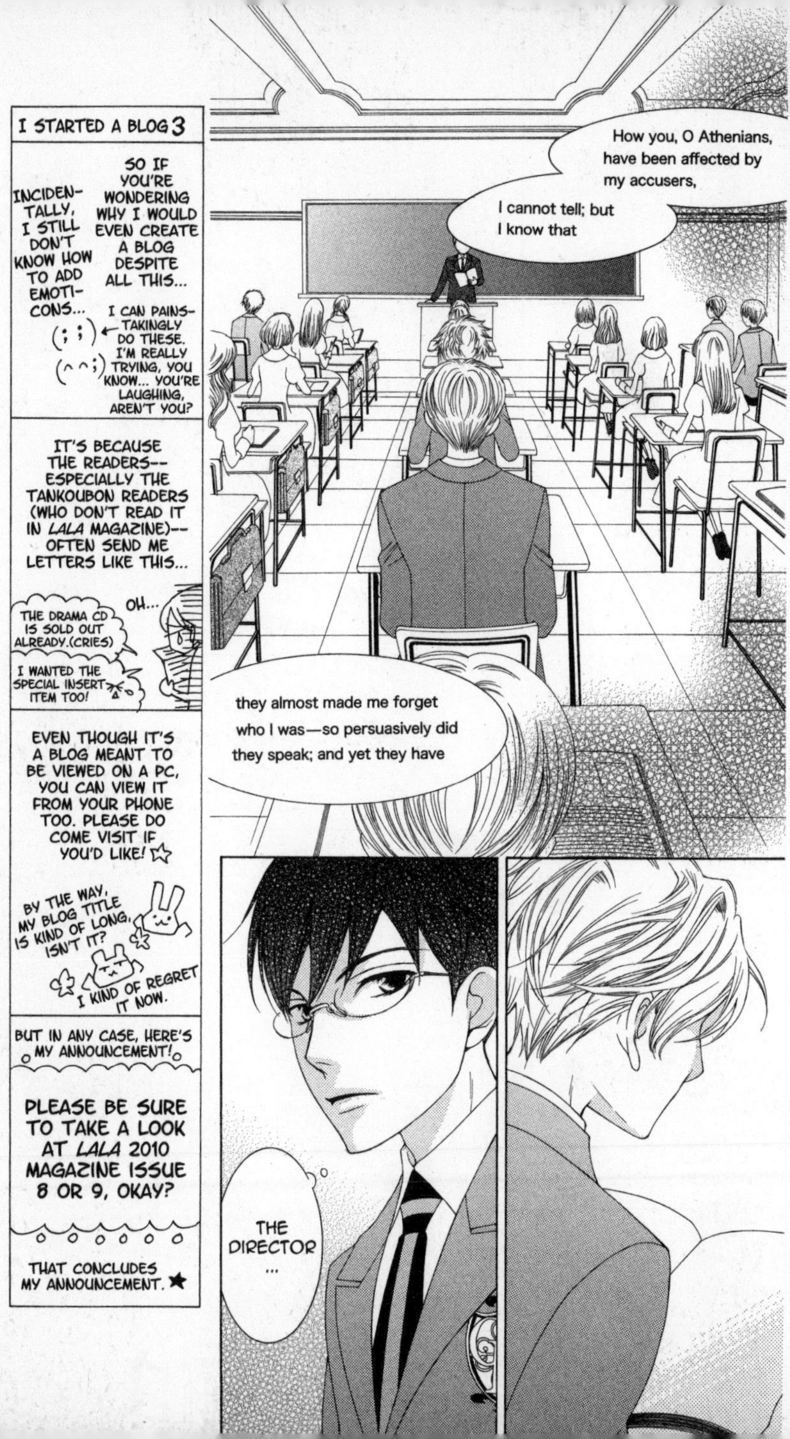
How you, O Athenians, have been affected by my accusers,
I cannot tell; but I know that
they almost made me forget who I was—so persuasively did they speak; and yet they have
THE DIRECTOR ...

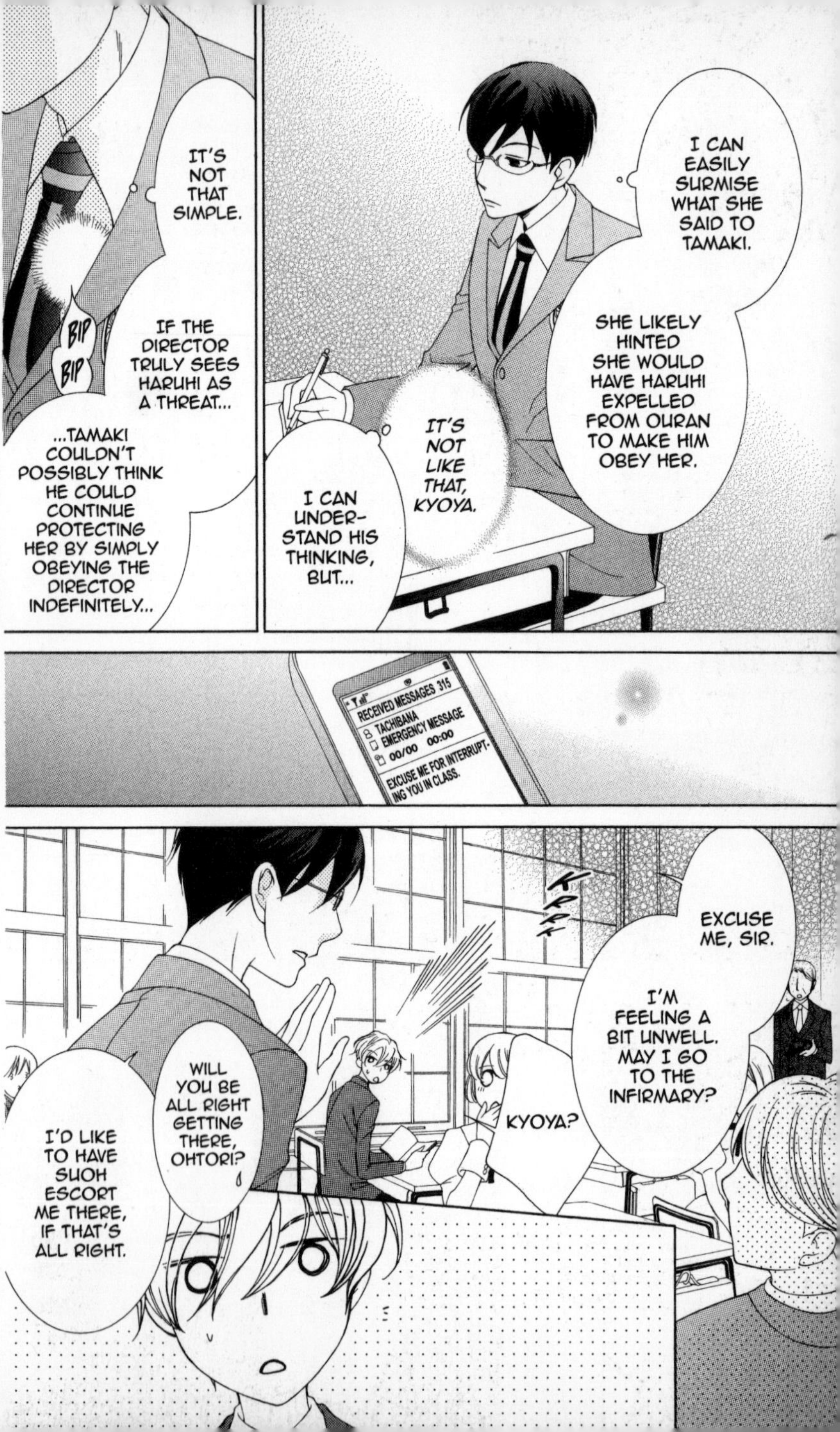
I CAN EASILY SURMISE WHAT SHE SAID TO TAMAKI.
SHE LIKELY HINTED SHE WOULD HAVE HARUHI EXPELLED FROM OURAN TO MAKE HIM OBEY HER.
IT'S NOT LIKE THAT, KYOYA.
I CAN UNDER-STAND HIS THINKING, BUT...
IT'S NOT THAT SIMPLE.
BIP BIP
IF THE DIRECTOR TRULY SEES HARUHI AS A THREAT...
...TAMAKI COULDN'T POSSIBLY THINK HE COULD CONTINUE PROTECTING HER BY SIMPLY OBEYING THE DIRECTOR INDEFINITELY...
RECEIVED MESSAGES 315
TACHIBANA
EMERGENCY MESSAGE
00/00 00:00
EXCUSE ME FOR INTERRUPT-ING YOU IN CLASS.
KRRR
EXCUSE ME, SIR.
I'M FEELING A BIT UNWELL. MAY I GO TO THE INFIRMARY?
KYOYA?
WILL YOU BE ALL RIGHT GETTING THERE, OHTORI?
I'D LIKE TO HAVE SUOH ESCORT ME THERE, IF THAT'S ALL RIGHT.

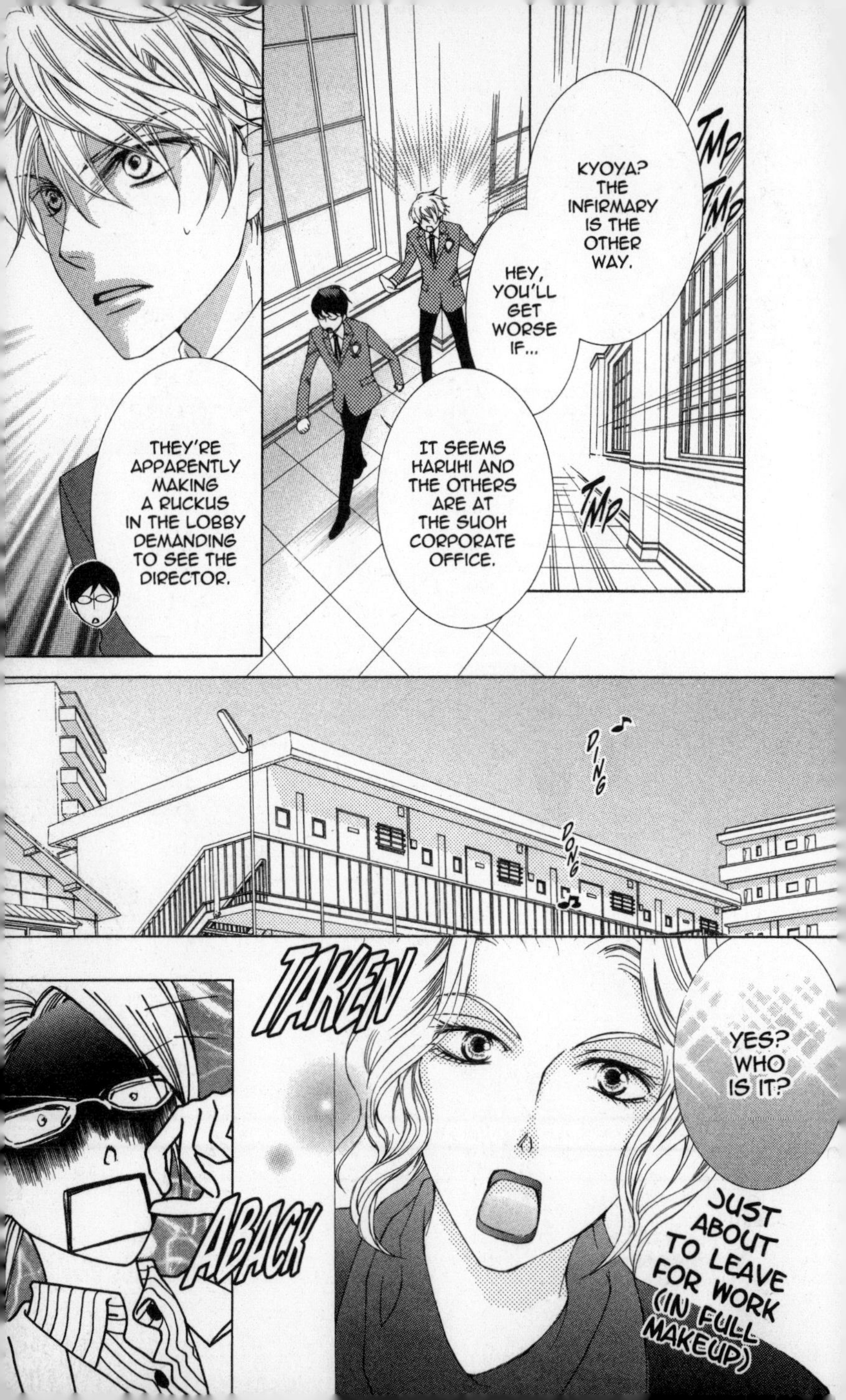
KYOYA? THE INFIRMARY IS THE OTHER WAY.
TMP TMP
HEY, YOU'LL GET WORSE IF...
IT SEEMS HARUHI AND THE OTHERS ARE AT THE SUOH CORPORATE OFFICE.
TMP
THEY'RE APPARENTLY MAKING A RUCKUS IN THE LOBBY DEMANDING TO SEE THE DIRECTOR.
DING
DONG
YES? WHO IS IT?
JUST ABOUT TO LEAVE FOR WORK (IN FULL MAKEUP)
TAKEN
ABACK

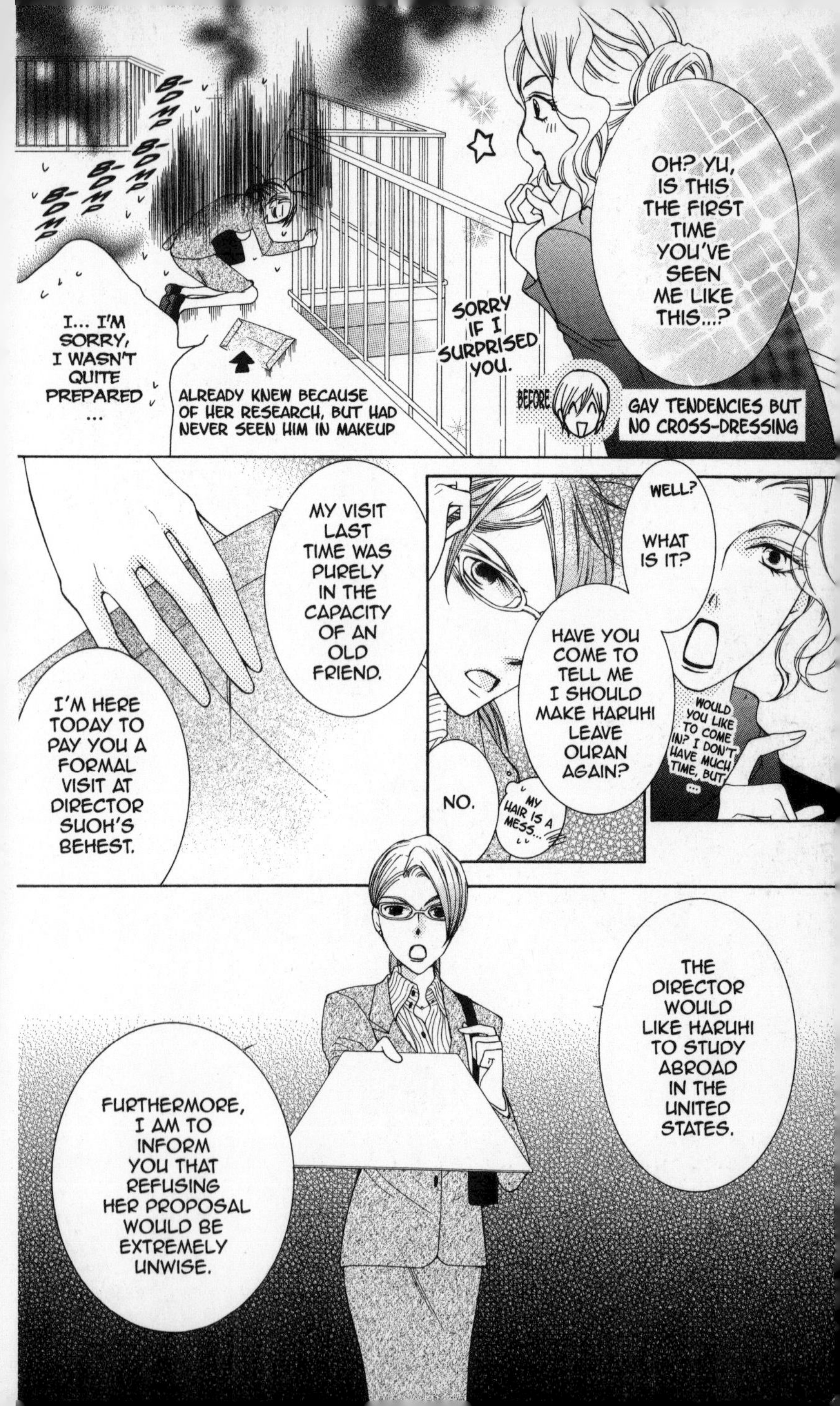

OH? YU, IS THIS THE FIRST TIME YOU'VE SEEN ME LIKE THIS...?
BEFORE
GAY TENDENCIES BUT NO CROSS-DRESSING
SORRY IF I SURPRISED YOU.
B-DOMP B-DOMP B-DOMP B-DOMP
I... I'M SORRY, I WASN'T QUITE PREPARED ...
ALREADY KNEW BECAUSE OF HER RESEARCH, BUT HAD NEVER SEEN HIM IN MAKEUP
WELL?
WHAT IS IT?
WOULD YOU LIKE TO COME IN? I DON'T HAVE MUCH TIME, BUT...
HAVE YOU COME TO TELL ME I SHOULD MAKE HARUHI LEAVE OURAN AGAIN?
MY HAIR IS A MESS...
NO.
MY VISIT LAST TIME WAS PURELY IN THE CAPACITY OF AN OLD FRIEND.
I'M HERE TODAY TO PAY YOU A FORMAL VISIT AT DIRECTOR SUOH'S BEHEST.
THE DIRECTOR WOULD LIKE HARUHI TO STUDY ABROAD IN THE UNITED STATES.
FURTHERMORE, I AM TO INFORM YOU THAT REFUSING HER PROPOSAL WOULD BE EXTREMELY UNWISE.

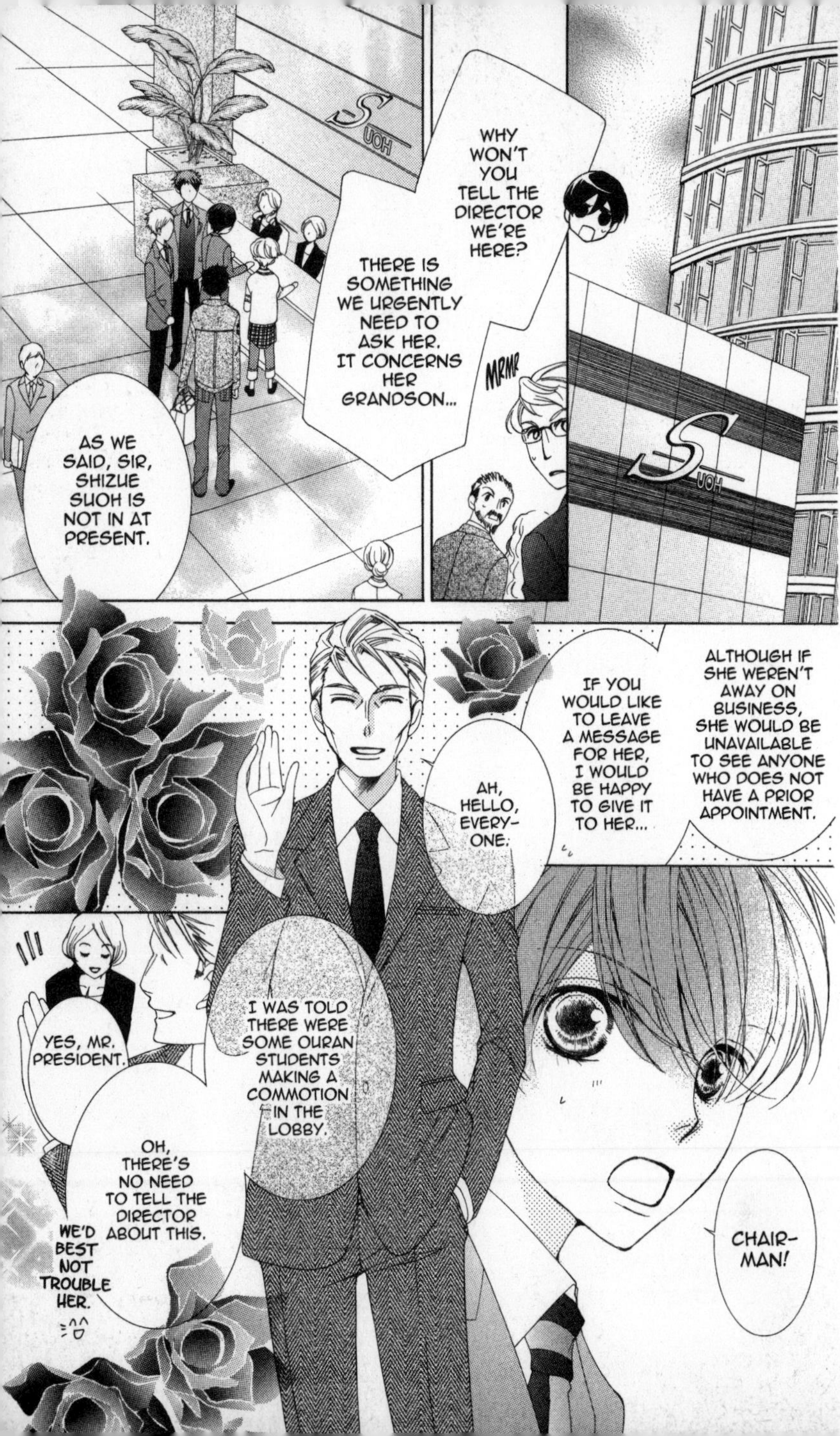
WHY WON'T YOU TELL THE DIRECTOR WE'RE HERE?
THERE IS SOMETHING WE URGENTLY NEED TO ASK HER. IT CONCERNS HER GRANDSON...
MRMR
AS WE SAID, SIR, SHIZUE SUOH IS NOT IN AT PRESENT.
ALTHOUGH IF SHE WEREN'T AWAY ON BUSINESS, SHE WOULD BE UNAVAILABLE TO SEE ANYONE WHO DOES NOT HAVE A PRIOR APPOINTMENT.
IF YOU WOULD LIKE TO LEAVE A MESSAGE FOR HER, I WOULD BE HAPPY TO GIVE IT TO HER...
AH, HELLO, EVERY-ONE.
CHAIR-MAN!
I WAS TOLD THERE WERE SOME OURAN STUDENTS MAKING A COMMOTION IN THE LOBBY.
YES, MR. PRESIDENT.
OH, THERE'S NO NEED TO TELL THE DIRECTOR ABOUT THIS.
WE'D BEST NOT TROUBLE HER.

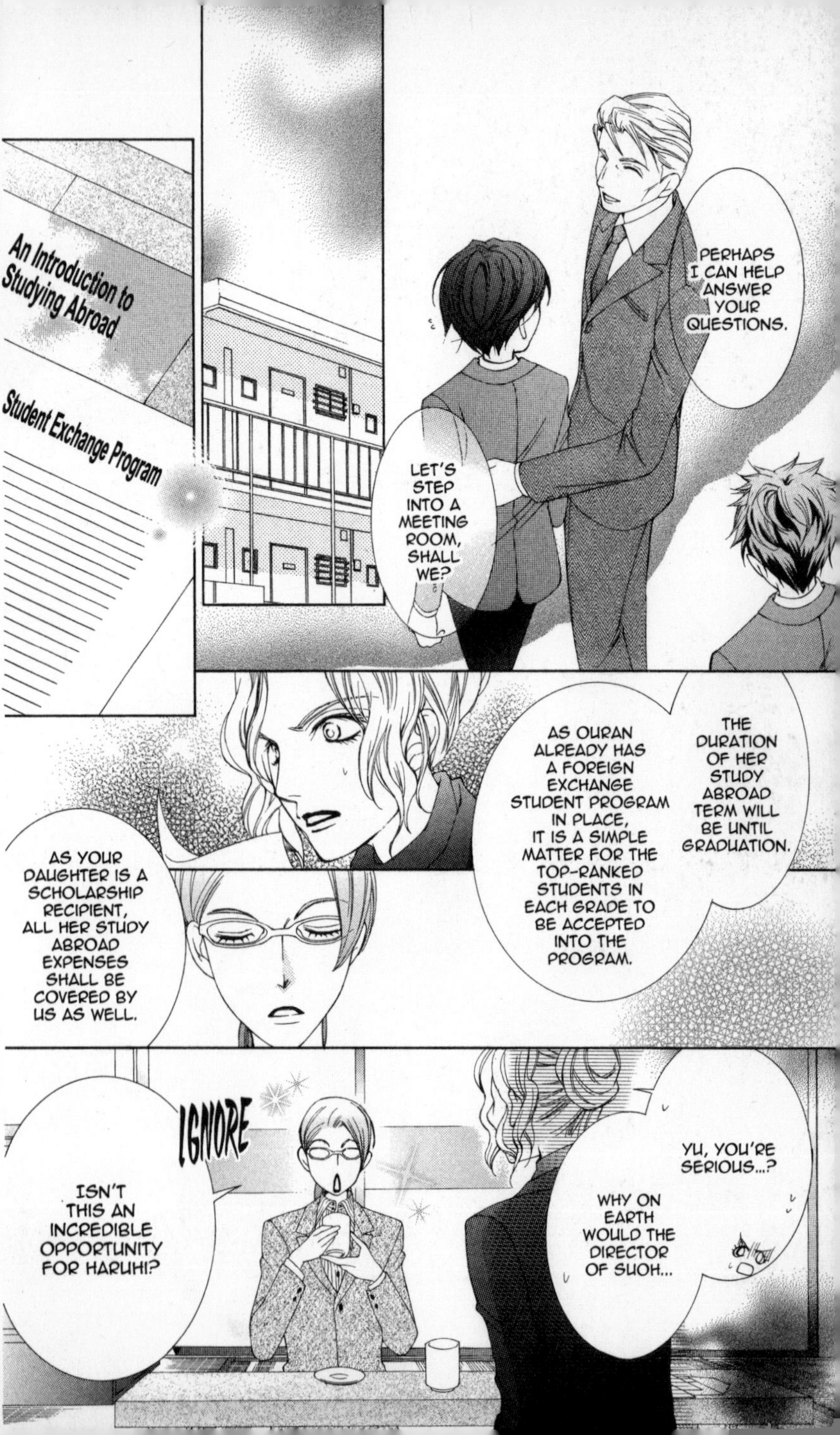
PERHAPS I CAN HELP ANSWER YOUR QUESTIONS.
LET'S STEP INTO A MEETING ROOM, SHALL WE?
An Introduction to Studying Abroad
Student Exchange Program
THE DURATION OF HER STUDY ABROAD TERM WILL BE UNTIL GRADUATION.
AS OURAN ALREADY HAS A FOREIGN EXCHANGE STUDENT PROGRAM IN PLACE, IT IS A SIMPLE MATTER FOR THE TOP-RANKED STUDENTS IN EACH GRADE TO BE ACCEPTED INTO THE PROGRAM.
AS YOUR DAUGHTER IS A SCHOLARSHIP RECIPIENT, ALL HER STUDY ABROAD EXPENSES SHALL BE COVERED BY US AS WELL.
YU, YOU'RE SERIOUS...?
WHY ON EARTH WOULD THE DIRECTOR OF SUOH...
IGNORE
ISN'T THIS AN INCREDIBLE OPPORTUNITY FOR HARUHI?

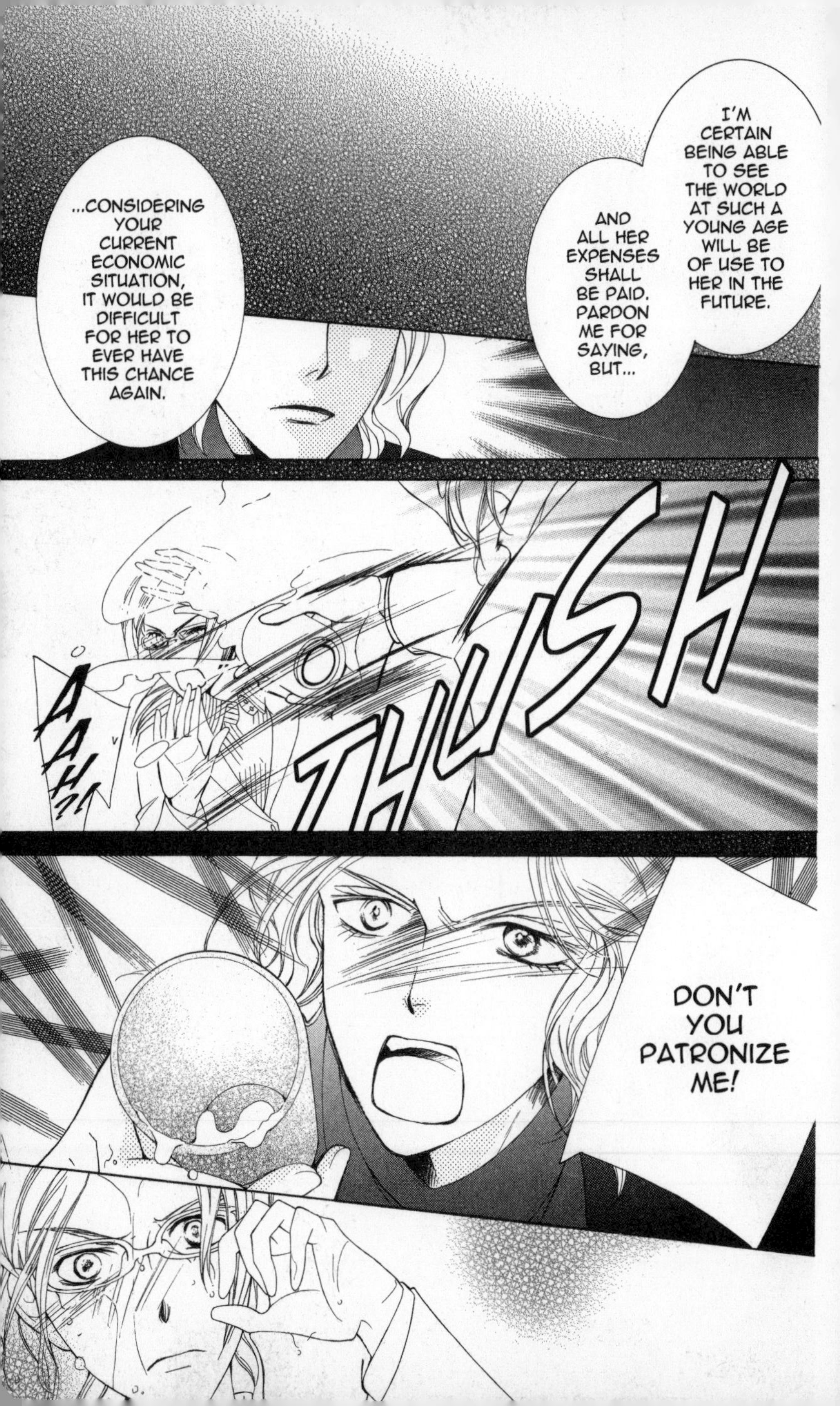
I'M CERTAIN BEING ABLE TO SEE THE WORLD AT SUCH A YOUNG AGE WILL BE OF USE TO HER IN THE FUTURE.
AND ALL HER EXPENSES SHALL BE PAID. PARDON ME FOR SAYING, BUT...
...CONSIDERING YOUR CURRENT ECONOMIC SITUATION, IT WOULD BE DIFFICULT FOR HER TO EVER HAVE THIS CHANCE AGAIN.
THUSH
AAH!?
DON'T YOU PATRONIZE ME!

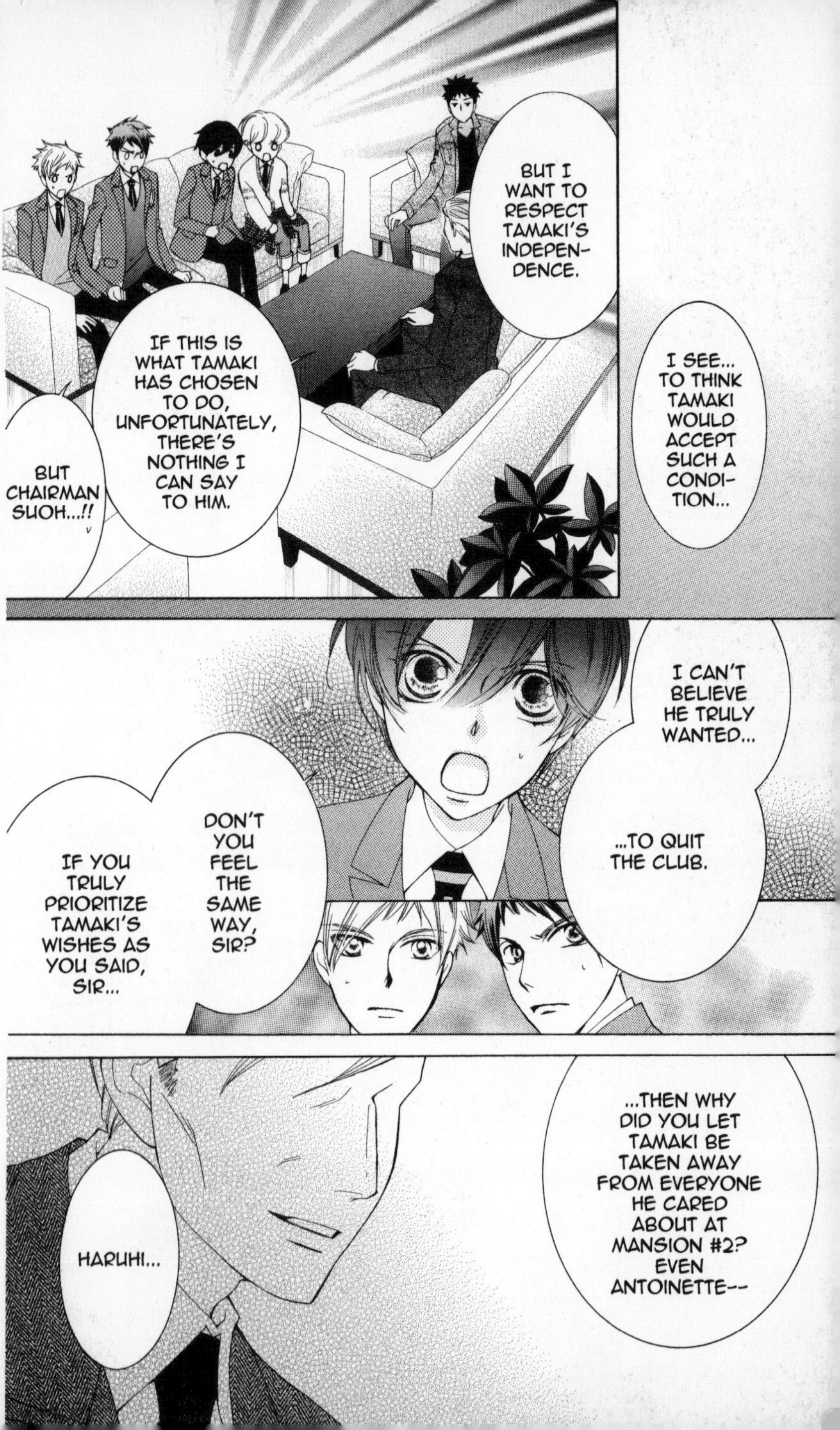
I SEE... TO THINK TAMAKI WOULD ACCEPT SUCH A CONDITION...
BUT I WANT TO RESPECT TAMAKI'S INDEPENDENCE.
IF THIS IS WHAT TAMAKI HAS CHOSEN TO DO, UNFORTUNATELY, THERE'S NOTHING I CAN SAY TO HIM.
BUT CHAIRMAN SUOH...!!
I CAN'T BELIEVE HE TRULY WANTED...
...TO QUIT THE CLUB.
DON'T YOU FEEL THE SAME WAY, SIR?
IF YOU TRULY PRIORITIZE TAMAKI'S WISHES AS YOU SAID, SIR...
...THEN WHY DID YOU LET TAMAKI BE TAKEN AWAY FROM EVERYONE HE CARED ABOUT AT MANSION #2? EVEN ANTOINETTE--
HARUHI...

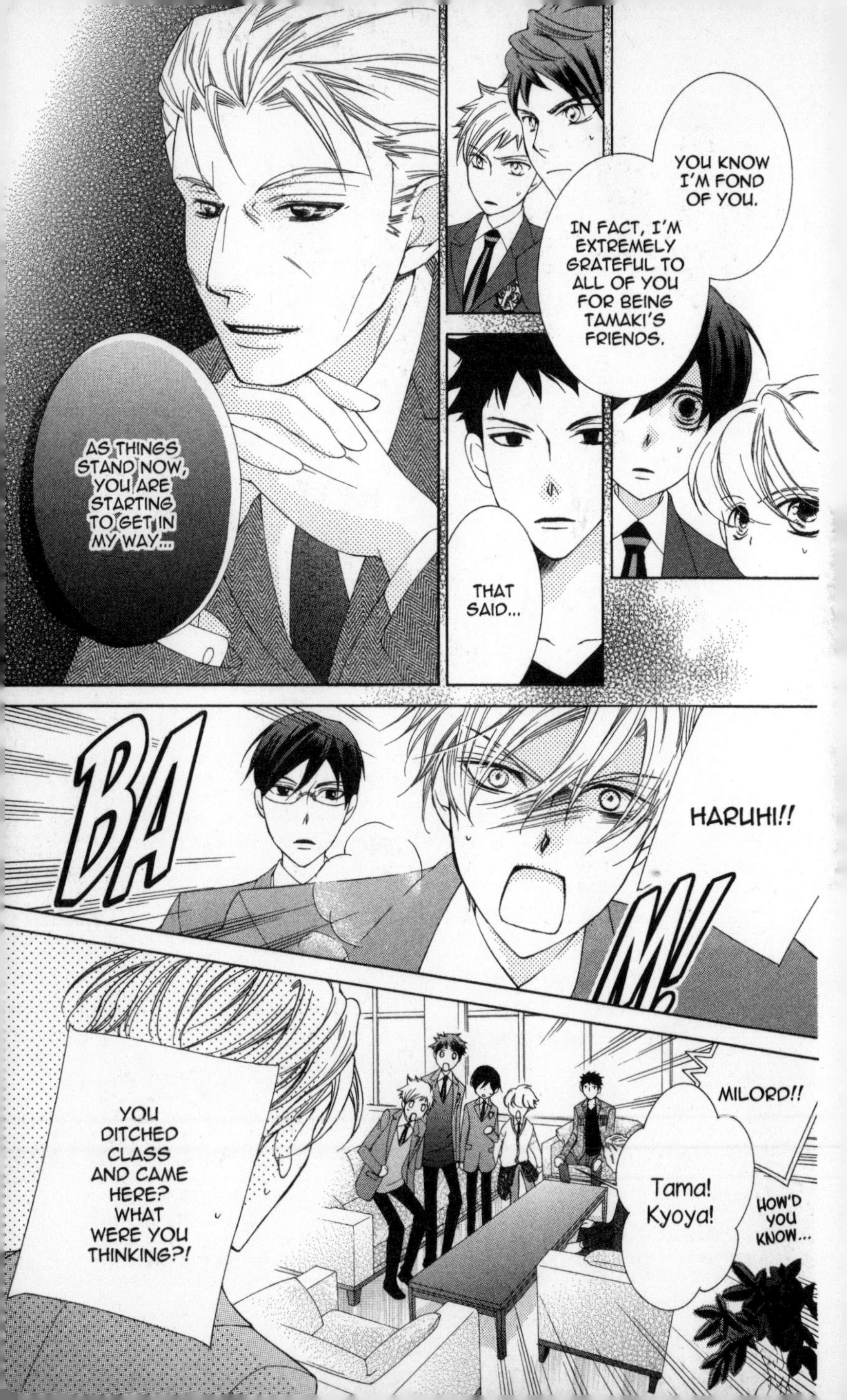
YOU KNOW I'M FOND OF YOU.
IN FACT, I'M EXTREMELY GRATEFUL TO ALL OF YOU FOR BEING TAMAKI'S FRIENDS.
THAT SAID...
AS THINGS STAND NOW, YOU ARE STARTING TO GET IN MY WAY...
HARUHI!!
BAM!
MILORD!!
Tama! Kyoya!
HOW'D YOU KNOW...
YOU DITCHED CLASS AND CAME HERE? WHAT WERE YOU THINKING?!

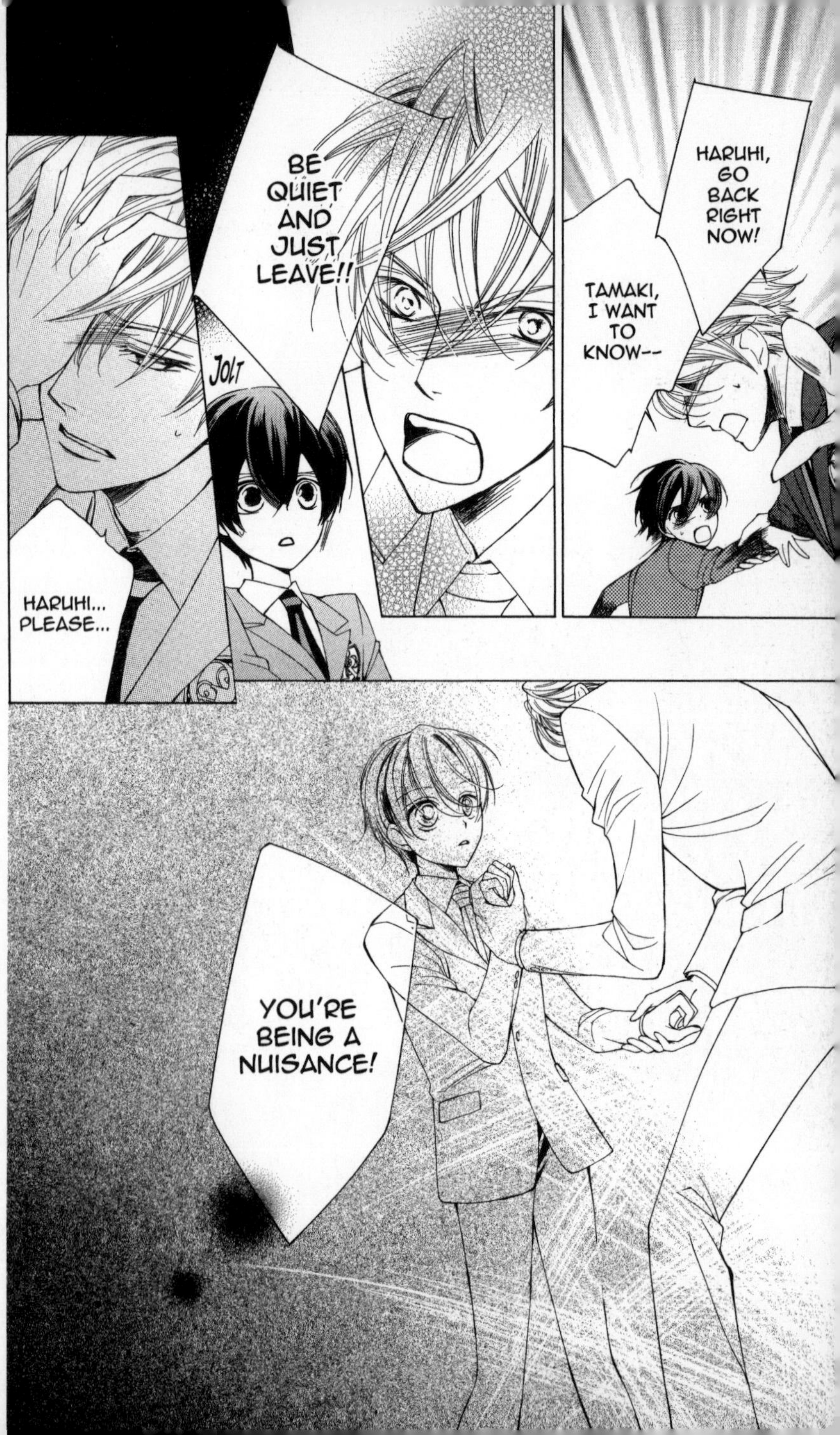
HARUHI, GO BACK RIGHT NOW!
TAMAKI, I WANT TO KNOW--
BE QUIET AND JUST LEAVE!!
JOLT
HARUHI... PLEASE...
YOU'RE BEING A NUISANCE!

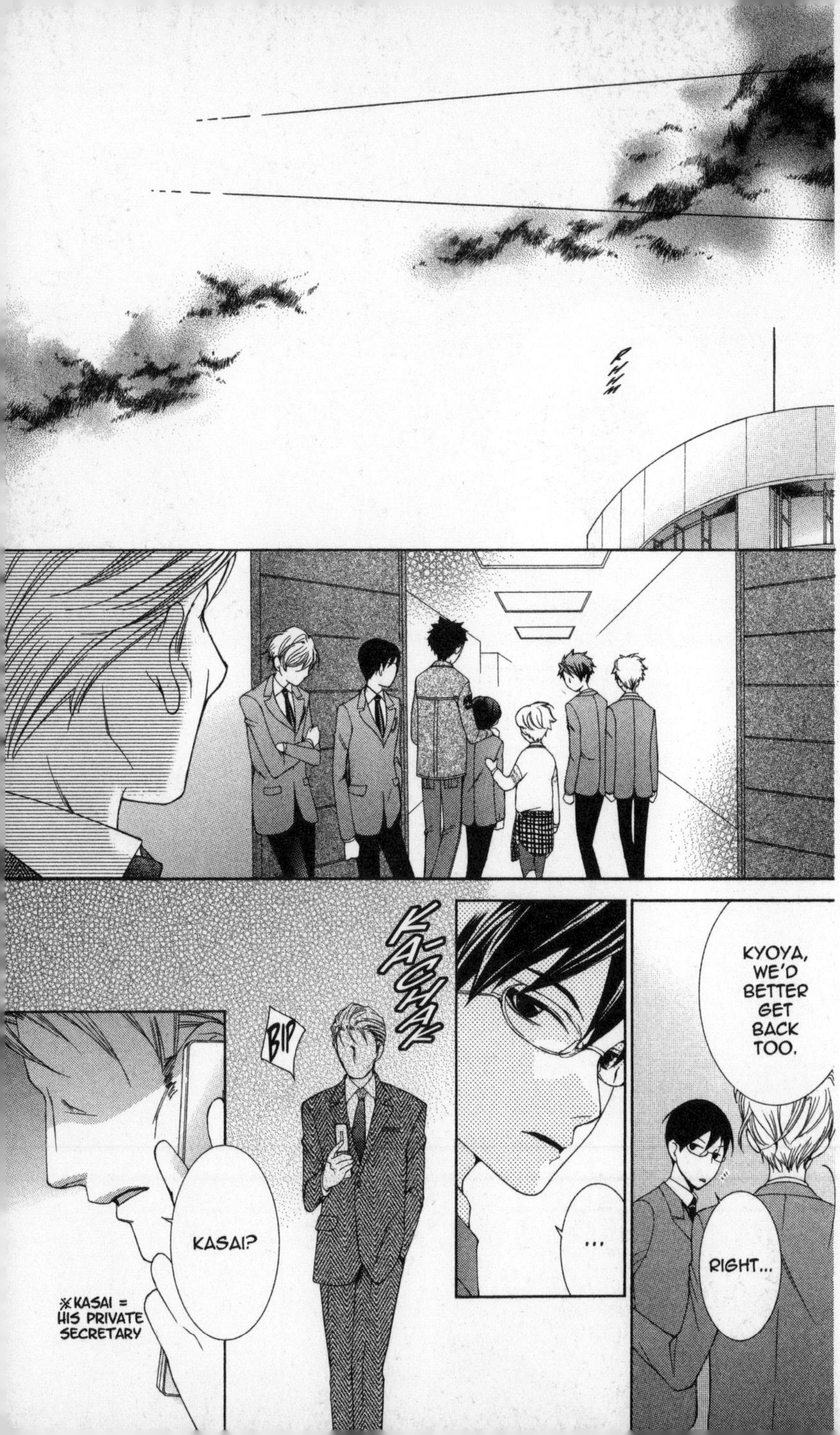
KYOYA, WE'D BETTER GET BACK TOO.
RIGHT...
...
KA-CHAK
BIP
KASAI?
※KASAI = HIS PRIVATE SECRETARY

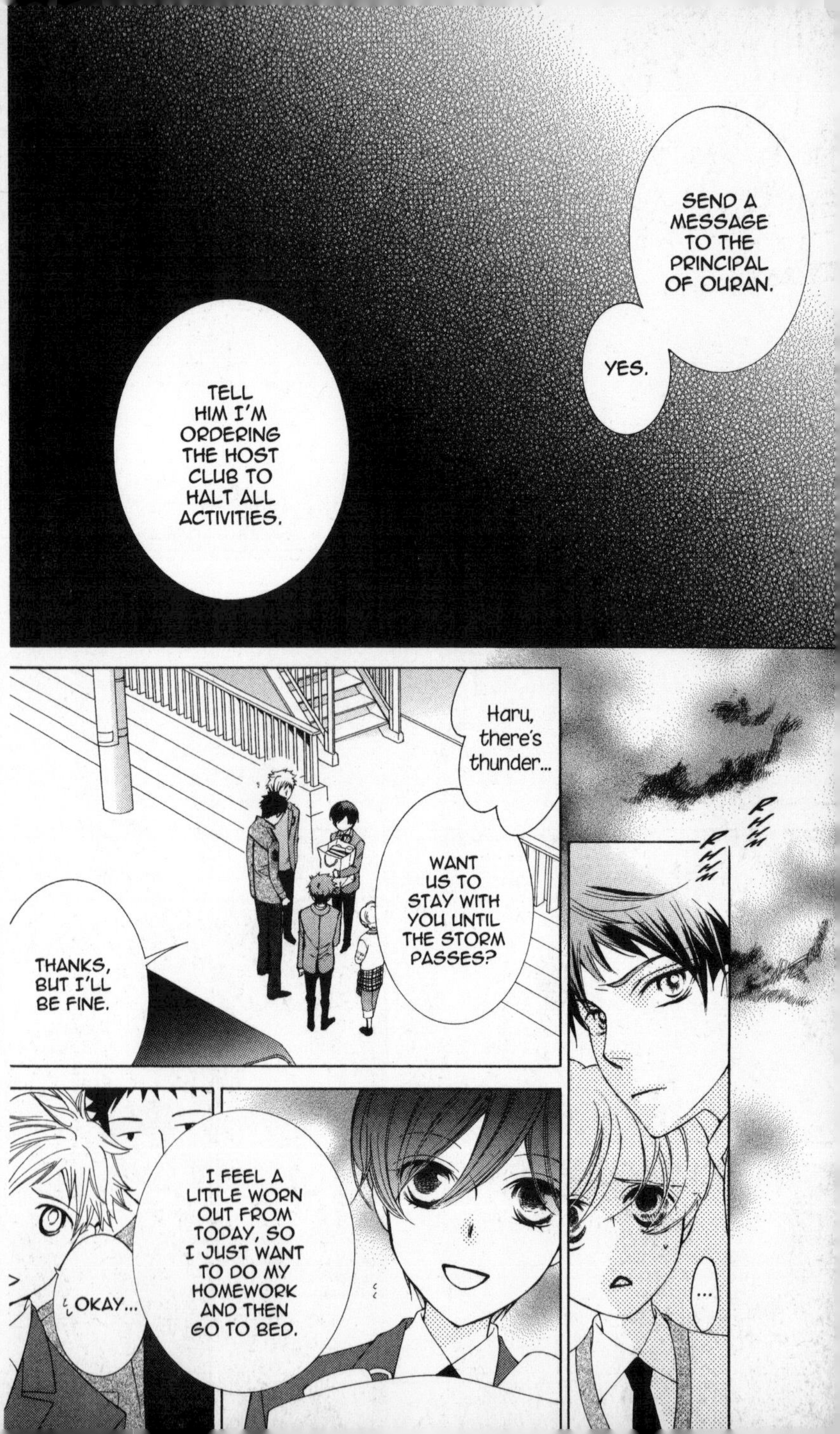
SEND A MESSAGE TO THE PRINCIPAL OF OURAN.
YES.
TELL HIM I'M ORDERING THE HOST CLUB TO HALT ALL ACTIVITIES.
Haru, there's thunder...
WANT US TO STAY WITH YOU UNTIL THE STORM PASSES?
RHHH
RHHH
THANKS, BUT I'LL BE FINE.
I FEEL A LITTLE WORN OUT FROM TODAY, SO I JUST WANT TO DO MY HOMEWORK AND THEN GO TO BED.
OKAY...
...

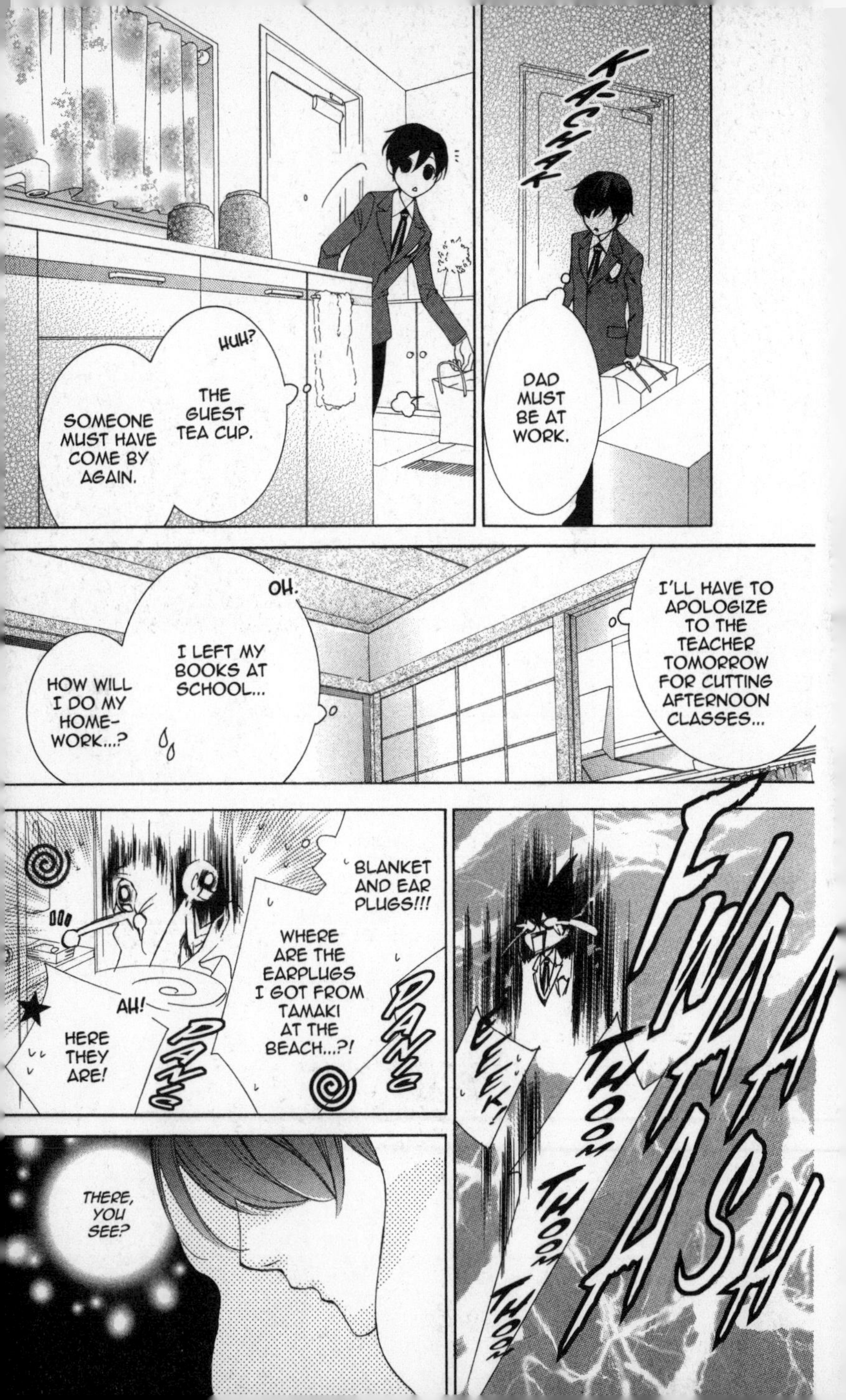
KA-CHAK
DAD MUST BE AT WORK.
HUH?
THE GUEST TEA CUP.
SOMEONE MUST HAVE COME BY AGAIN.
I'LL HAVE TO APOLOGIZE TO THE TEACHER TOMORROW FOR CUTTING AFTERNOON CLASSES...
OH.
I LEFT MY BOOKS AT SCHOOL...
HOW WILL I DO MY HOME-WORK...?
FWAAASH
THOOM THOOM THOOM THOOM
EEEEK!
BLANKET AND EAR PLUGS!!!
WHERE ARE THE EARPLUGS I GOT FROM TAMAKI AT THE BEACH...?!
PANG
PANG
AH!
HERE THEY ARE!
THERE, YOU SEE?

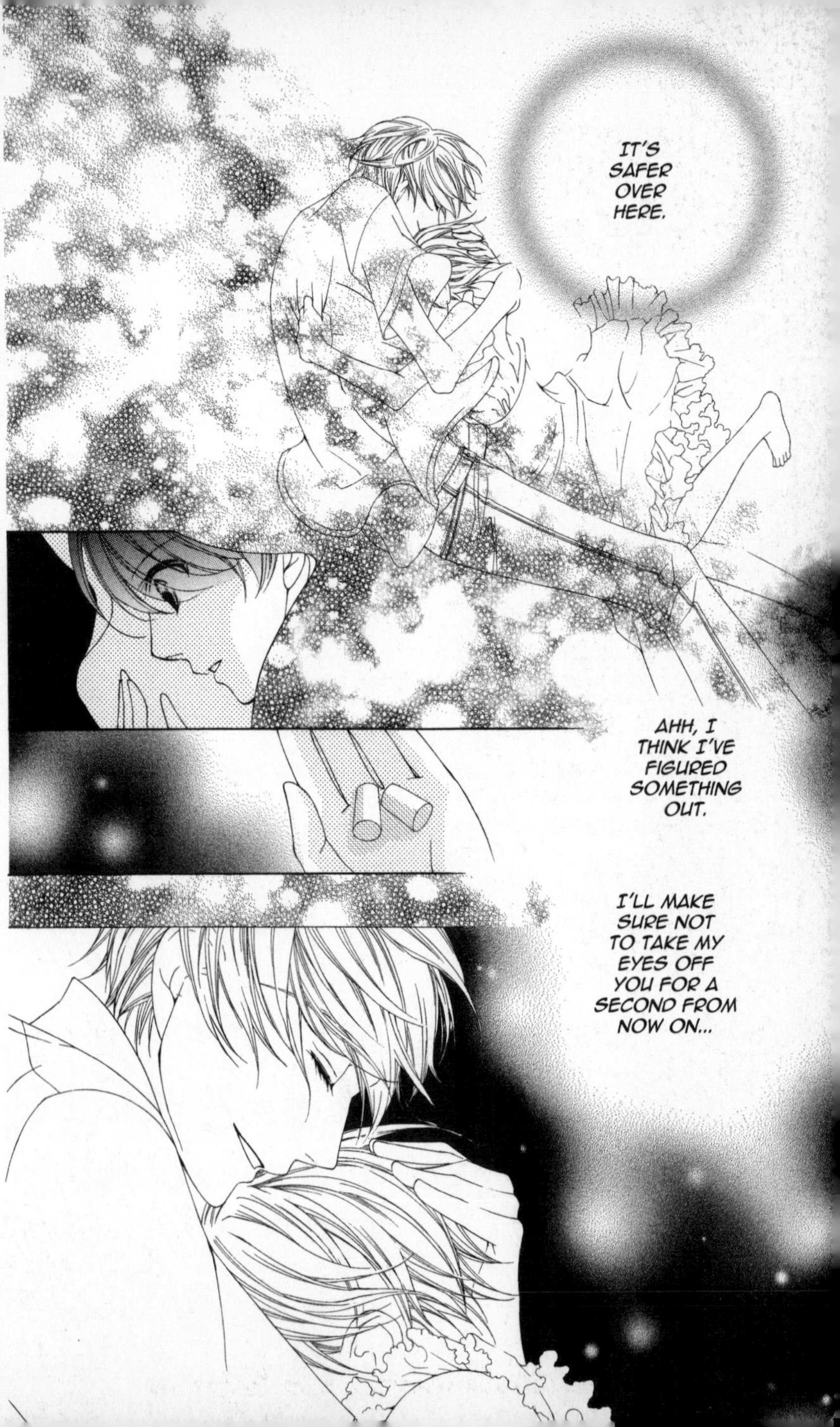
IT'S SAFER OVER HERE.
AHH, I THINK I'VE FIGURED SOMETHING OUT.
I'LL MAKE SURE NOT TO TAKE MY EYES OFF YOU FOR A SECOND FROM NOW ON...

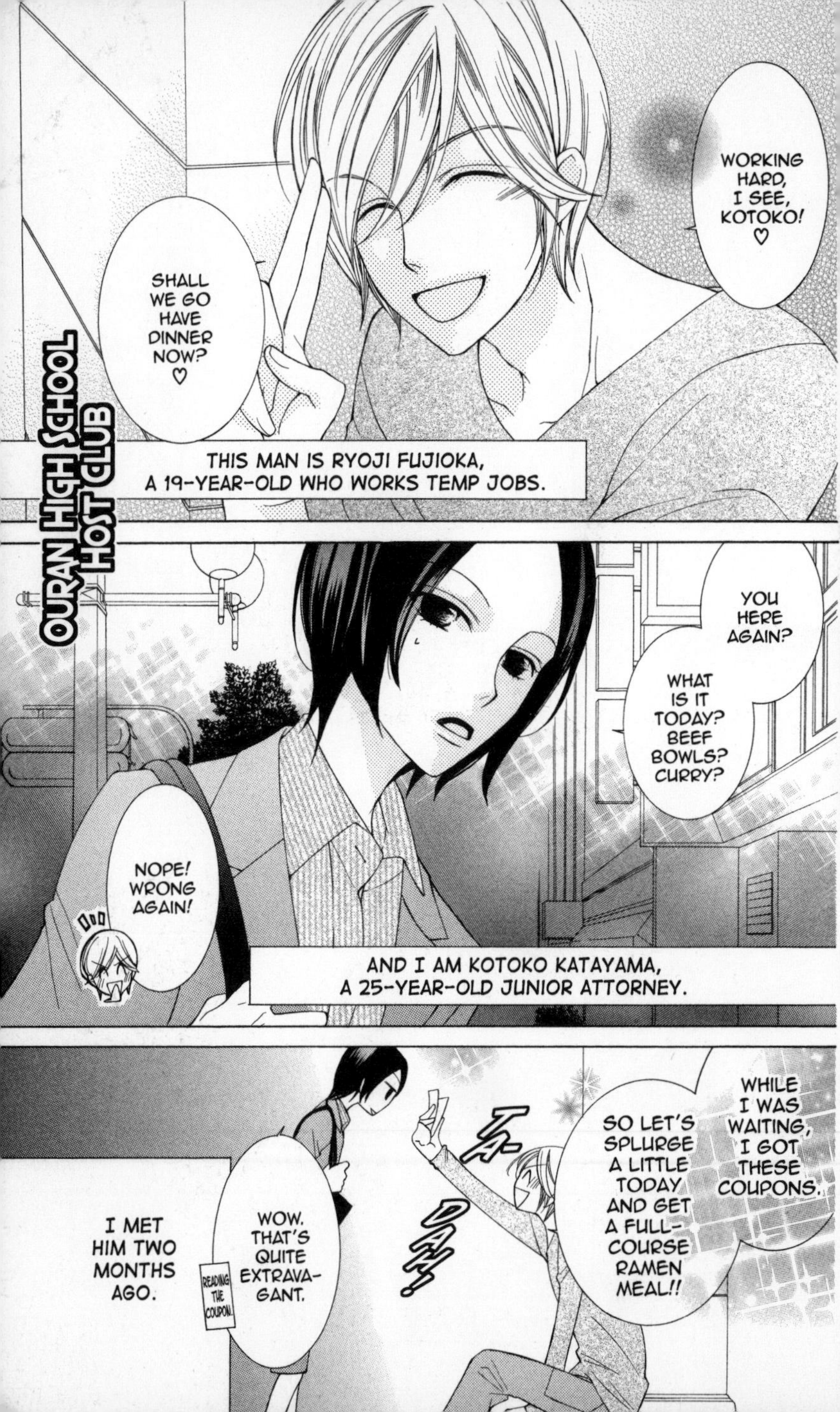
WORKING HARD, I SEE, KOTOKO! ♡
SHALL WE GO HAVE DINNER NOW? ♡
THIS MAN IS RYOJI FUJIOKA, A 19-YEAR-OLD WHO WORKS TEMP JOBS.
YOU HERE AGAIN?
WHAT IS IT TODAY? BEEF BOWLS? CURRY?
NOPE! WRONG AGAIN!
AND I AM KOTOKO KATAYAMA, A 25-YEAR-OLD JUNIOR ATTORNEY.
WHILE I WAS WAITING, I GOT THESE COUPONS.
SO LET'S SPLURGE A LITTLE TODAY AND GET A FULL-COURSE RAMEN MEAL!!
TA-DAH!!
WOW. THAT'S QUITE EXTRAVA-GANT.
READING THE COUPON.
I MET HIM TWO MONTHS AGO.

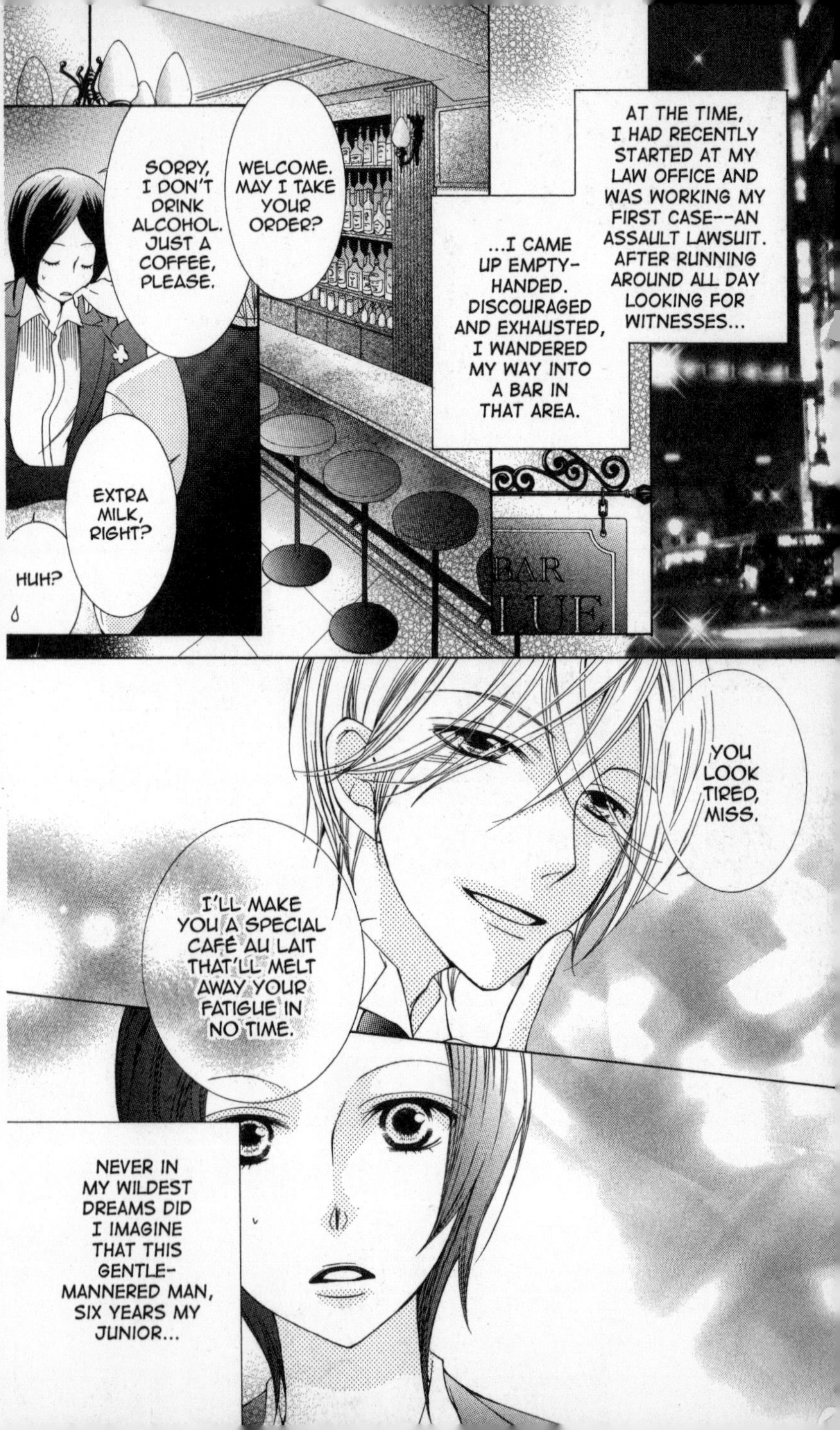
AT THE TIME, I HAD RECENTLY STARTED AT MY LAW OFFICE AND WAS WORKING MY FIRST CASE--AN ASSAULT LAWSUIT. AFTER RUNNING AROUND ALL DAY LOOKING FOR WITNESSES...
...I CAME UP EMPTY-HANDED. DISCOURAGED AND EXHAUSTED, I WANDERED MY WAY INTO A BAR IN THAT AREA.
BAR
WELCOME. MAY I TAKE YOUR ORDER?
SORRY, I DON'T DRINK ALCOHOL. JUST A COFFEE, PLEASE.
EXTRA MILK, RIGHT?
HUH?
YOU LOOK TIRED, MISS.
I'LL MAKE YOU A SPECIAL CAFÉ AU LAIT THAT'LL MELT AWAY YOUR FATIGUE IN NO TIME.
NEVER IN MY WILDEST DREAMS DID I IMAGINE THAT THIS GENTLE-MANNERED MAN, SIX YEARS MY JUNIOR...

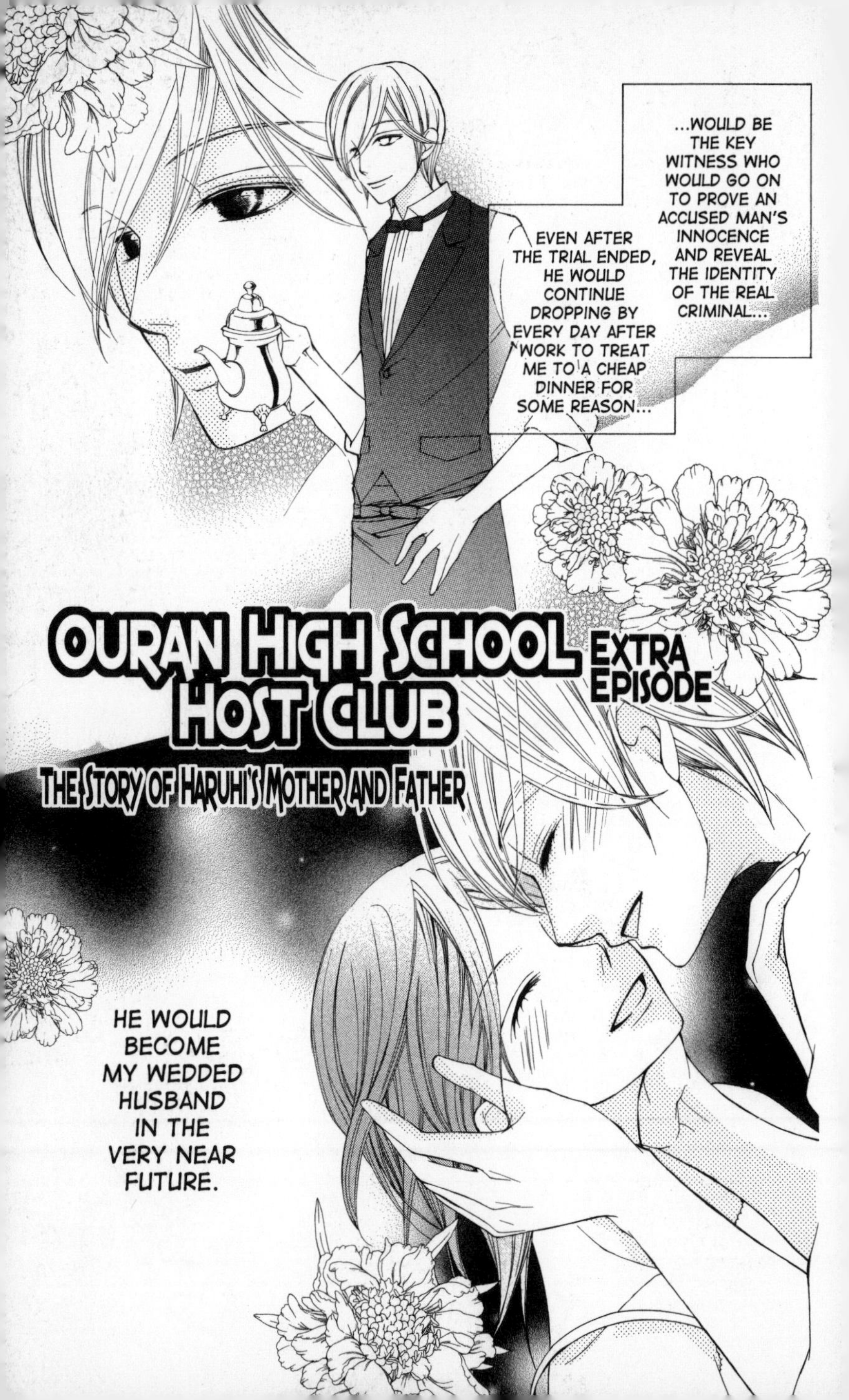
...WOULD BE THE KEY WITNESS WHO WOULD GO ON TO PROVE AN ACCUSED MAN'S INNOCENCE AND REVEAL THE IDENTITY OF THE REAL CRIMINAL...
EVEN AFTER THE TRIAL ENDED, HE WOULD CONTINUE DROPPING BY EVERY DAY AFTER WORK TO TREAT ME TO A CHEAP DINNER FOR SOME REASON...
OURAN HIGH SCHOOL HOST CLUB
EXTRA EPISODE
THE STORY OF HARUHI'S MOTHER AND FATHER
HE WOULD BECOME MY WEDDED HUSBAND IN THE VERY NEAR FUTURE.

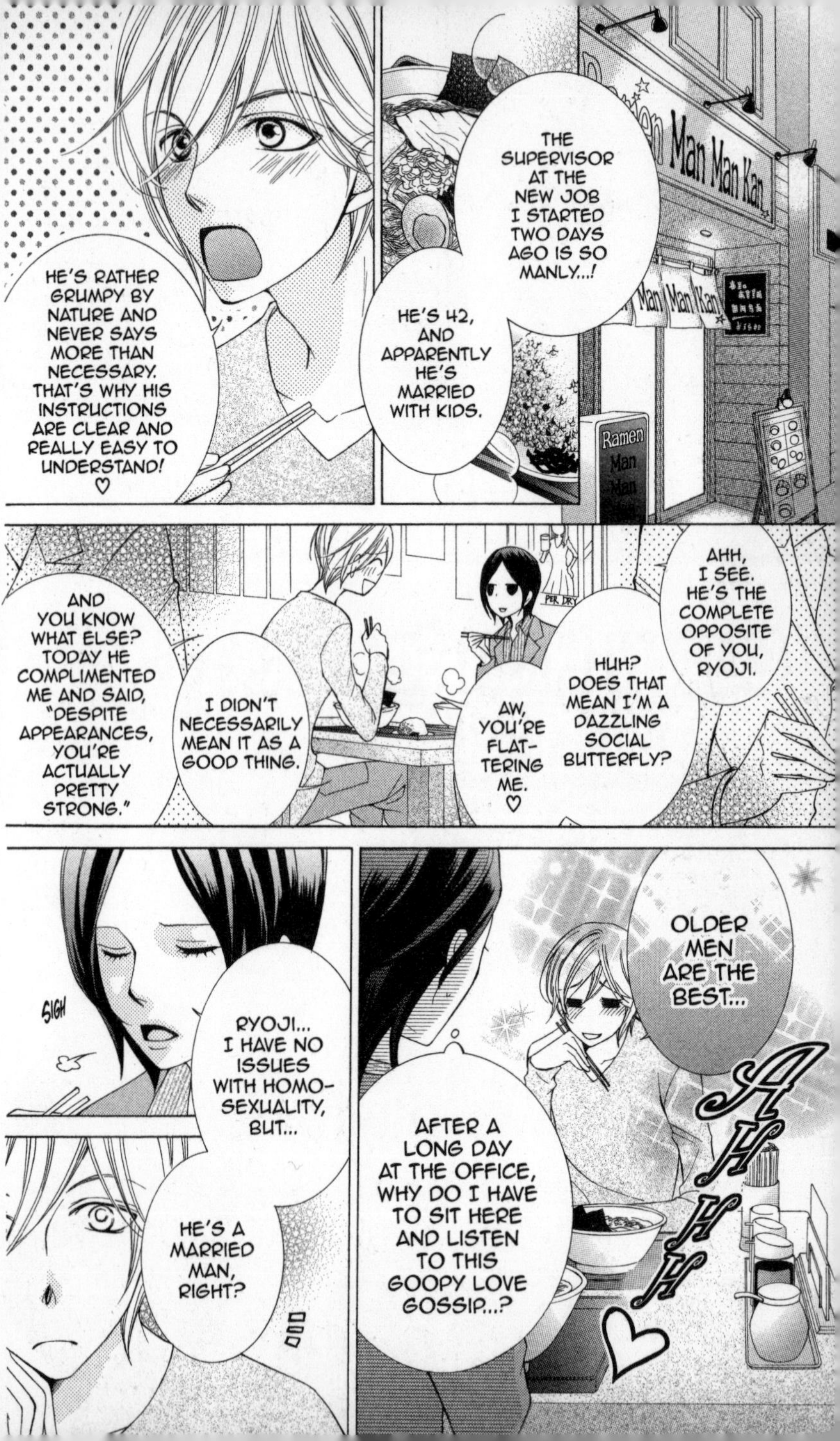
Man Man Kan
THE SUPERVISOR AT THE NEW JOB I STARTED TWO DAYS AGO IS SO MANLY...!
HE'S 42, AND APPARENTLY HE'S MARRIED WITH KIDS.
Ramen Man Man
HE'S RATHER GRUMPY BY NATURE AND NEVER SAYS MORE THAN NECESSARY. THAT'S WHY HIS INSTRUCTIONS ARE CLEAR AND REALLY EASY TO UNDERSTAND! ♡
AHH, I SEE. HE'S THE COMPLETE OPPOSITE OF YOU, RYOJI.
HUH? DOES THAT MEAN I'M A DAZZLING SOCIAL BUTTERFLY?
AW, YOU'RE FLATTERING ME. ♡
I DIDN'T NECESSARILY MEAN IT AS A GOOD THING.
AND YOU KNOW WHAT ELSE? TODAY HE COMPLIMENTED ME AND SAID, "DESPITE APPEARANCES, YOU'RE ACTUALLY PRETTY STRONG."
OLDER MEN ARE THE BEST...
AHHHH ♡
AFTER A LONG DAY AT THE OFFICE, WHY DO I HAVE TO SIT HERE AND LISTEN TO THIS GOOPY LOVE GOSSIP...?
SIGH
RYOJI... I HAVE NO ISSUES WITH HOMO-SEXUALITY, BUT...
HE'S A MARRIED MAN, RIGHT?

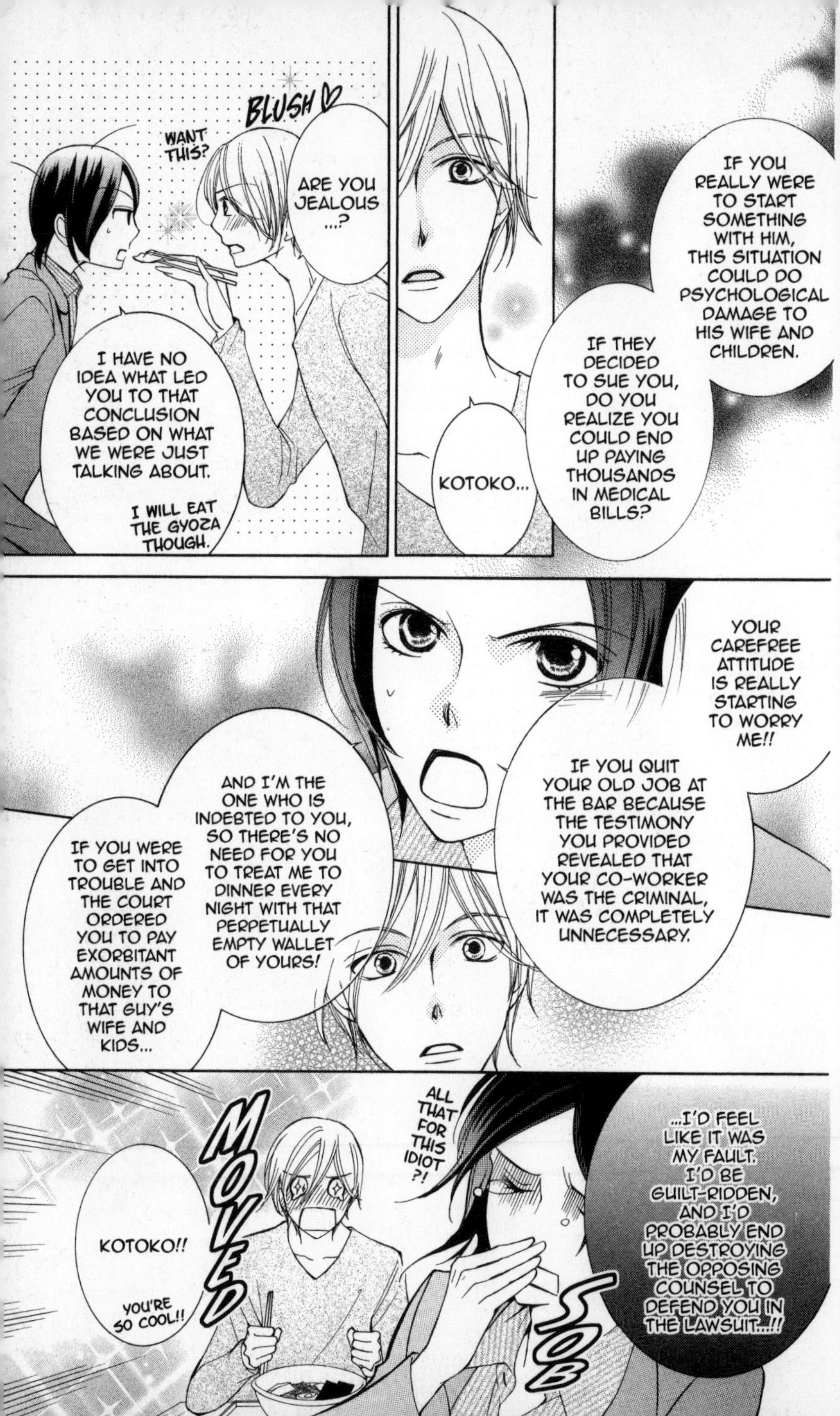
IF YOU REALLY WERE TO START SOMETHING WITH HIM, THIS SITUATION COULD DO PSYCHOLOGICAL DAMAGE TO HIS WIFE AND CHILDREN.
IF THEY DECIDED TO SUE YOU, DO YOU REALIZE YOU COULD END UP PAYING THOUSANDS IN MEDICAL BILLS?
KOTOKO...
BLUSH
ARE YOU JEALOUS ...?
WANT THIS?
I HAVE NO IDEA WHAT LED YOU TO THAT CONCLUSION BASED ON WHAT WE WERE JUST TALKING ABOUT.
I WILL EAT THE GYOZA THOUGH.
YOUR CAREFREE ATTITUDE IS REALLY STARTING TO WORRY ME!!
IF YOU QUIT YOUR OLD JOB AT THE BAR BECAUSE THE TESTIMONY YOU PROVIDED REVEALED THAT YOUR CO-WORKER WAS THE CRIMINAL, IT WAS COMPLETELY UNNECESSARY.
AND I'M THE ONE WHO IS INDEBTED TO YOU, SO THERE'S NO NEED FOR YOU TO TREAT ME TO DINNER EVERY NIGHT WITH THAT PERPETUALLY EMPTY WALLET OF YOURS!
IF YOU WERE TO GET INTO TROUBLE AND THE COURT ORDERED YOU TO PAY EXORBITANT AMOUNTS OF MONEY TO THAT GUY'S WIFE AND KIDS...
...I'D FEEL LIKE IT WAS MY FAULT. I'D BE GUILT-RIDDEN, AND I'D PROBABLY END UP DESTROYING THE OPPOSING COUNSEL TO DEFEND YOU IN THE LAWSUIT...!!
SOB
ALL THAT FOR THIS IDIOT ?!
MOVED
KOTOKO!!
YOU'RE SO COOL!!

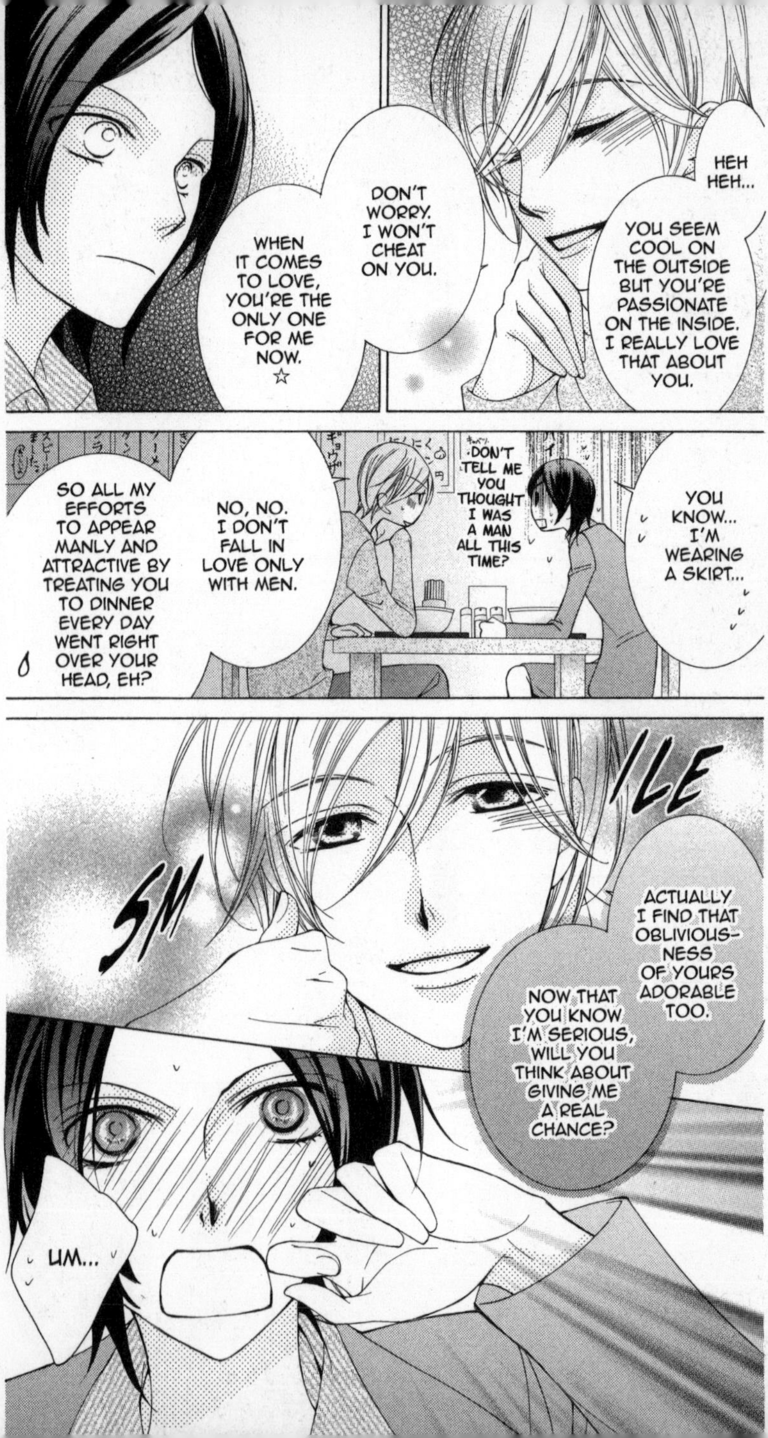
HEH HEH...
YOU SEEM COOL ON THE OUTSIDE BUT YOU'RE PASSIONATE ON THE INSIDE. I REALLY LOVE THAT ABOUT YOU.
DON'T WORRY. I WON'T CHEAT ON YOU.
WHEN IT COMES TO LOVE, YOU'RE THE ONLY ONE FOR ME NOW. ☆
YOU KNOW... I'M WEARING A SKIRT...
DON'T TELL ME YOU THOUGHT I WAS A MAN ALL THIS TIME?
NO, NO. I DON'T FALL IN LOVE ONLY WITH MEN.
SO ALL MY EFFORTS TO APPEAR MANLY AND ATTRACTIVE BY TREATING YOU TO DINNER EVERY DAY WENT RIGHT OVER YOUR HEAD, EH?
SM ILE
ACTUALLY I FIND THAT OBLIVIOUS-NESS OF YOURS ADORABLE TOO.
NOW THAT YOU KNOW I'M SERIOUS, WILL YOU THINK ABOUT GIVING ME A REAL CHANCE?
UM...

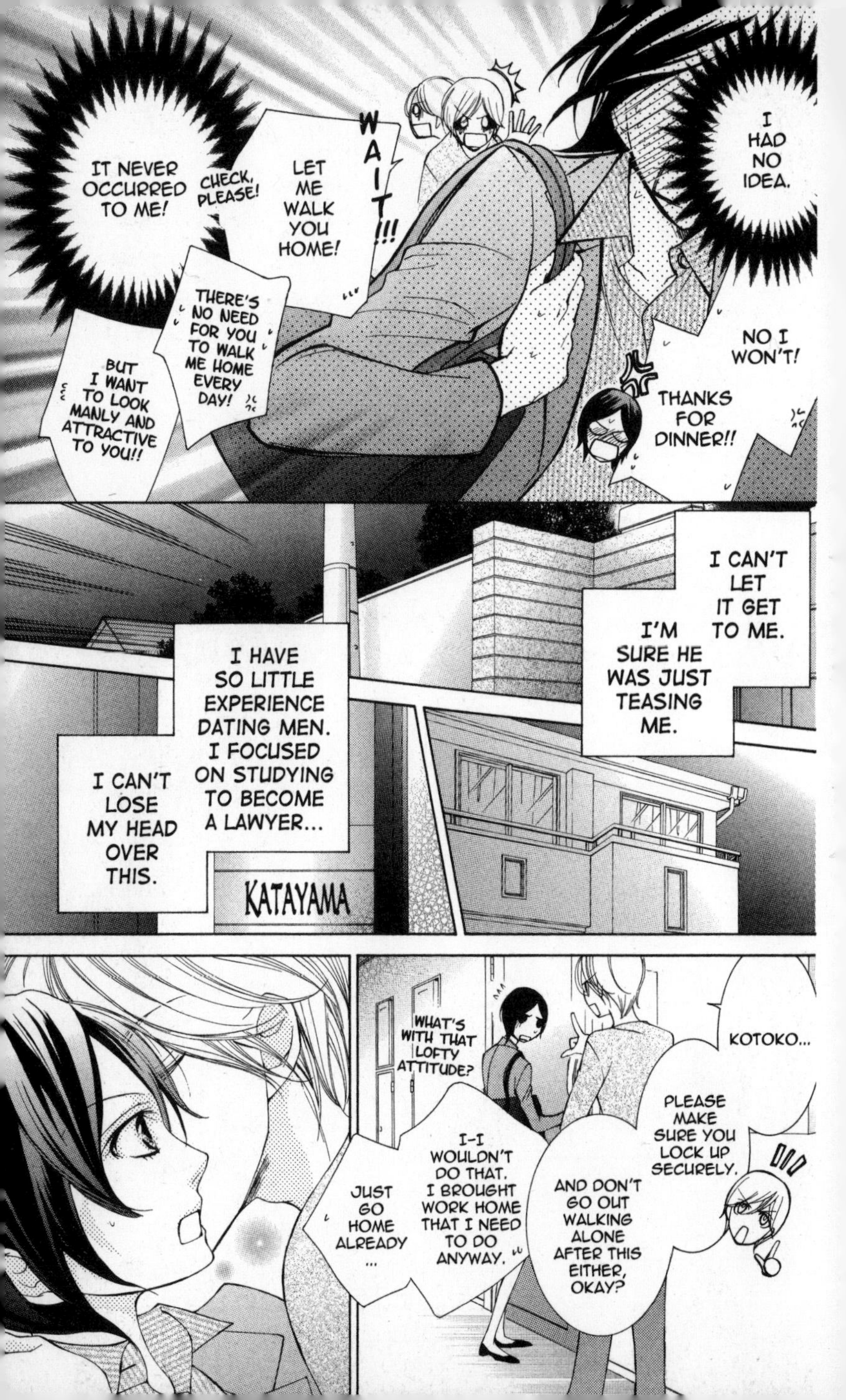
I HAD NO IDEA.
WAIT!!!
LET ME WALK YOU HOME!
CHECK, PLEASE!
IT NEVER OCCURRED TO ME!
NO I WON'T!
THANKS FOR DINNER!!
THERE'S NO NEED FOR YOU TO WALK ME HOME EVERY DAY!
BUT I WANT TO LOOK MANLY AND ATTRACTIVE TO YOU!!
I CAN'T LET IT GET TO ME.
I'M SURE HE WAS JUST TEASING ME.
I HAVE SO LITTLE EXPERIENCE DATING MEN. I FOCUSED ON STUDYING TO BECOME A LAWYER...
I CAN'T LOSE MY HEAD OVER THIS.
KATAYAMA
KOTOKO...
PLEASE MAKE SURE YOU LOCK UP SECURELY.
AND DON'T GO OUT WALKING ALONE AFTER THIS EITHER, OKAY?
WHAT'S WITH THAT LOFTY ATTITUDE?
I-I WOULDN'T DO THAT. I BROUGHT WORK HOME THAT I NEED TO DO ANYWAY.
JUST GO HOME ALREADY ...

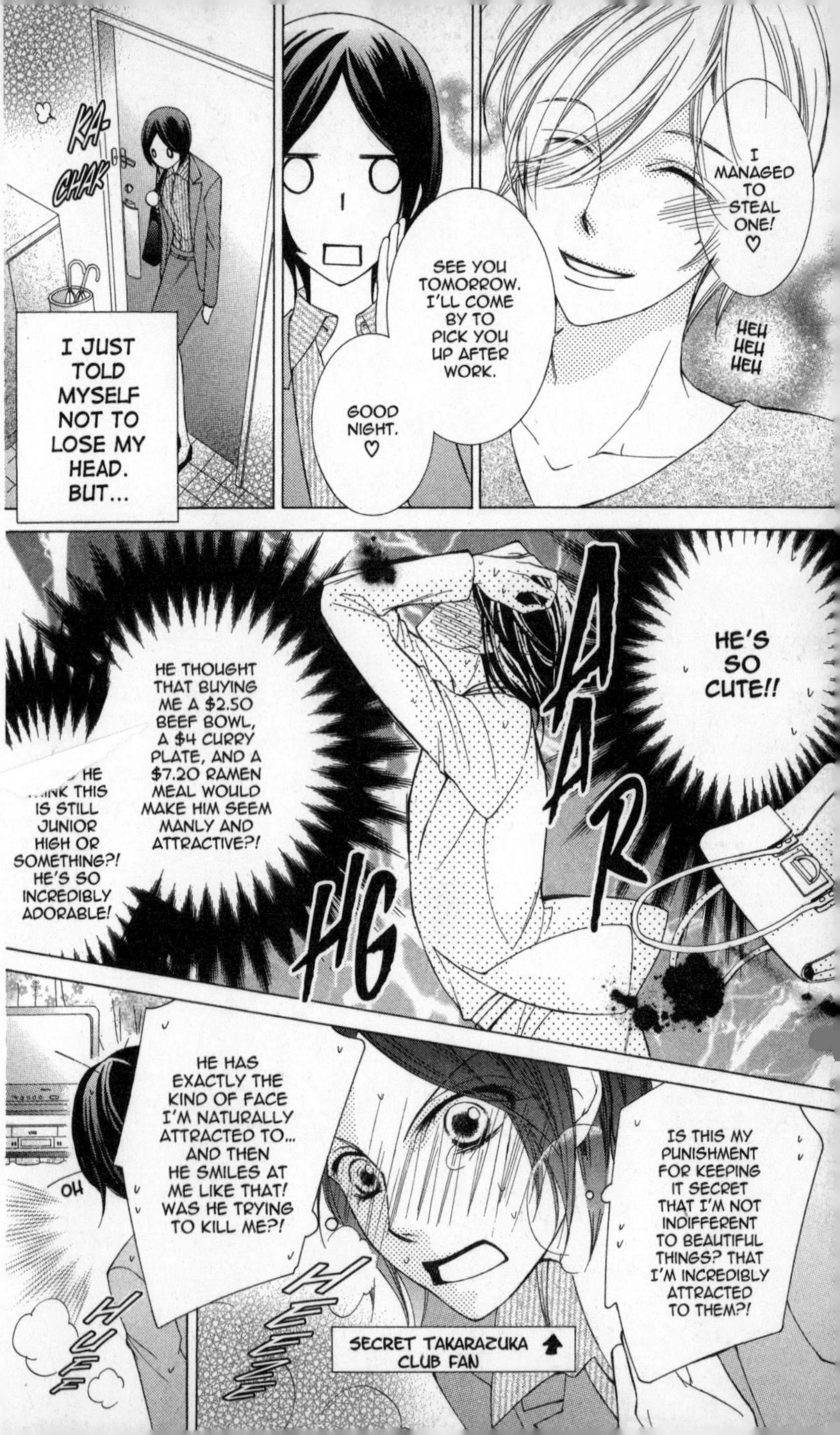
I MANAGED TO STEAL ONE! ♥
HEH HEH HEH
SEE YOU TOMORROW. I'LL COME BY TO PICK YOU UP AFTER WORK.
GOOD NIGHT. ♥
KA-CHAK
I JUST TOLD MYSELF NOT TO LOSE MY HEAD. BUT...
HE'S SO CUTE!!
AAAR
HG
HE THOUGHT THAT BUYING ME A $2.50 BEEF BOWL, A $4 CURRY PLATE, AND A $7.20 RAMEN MEAL WOULD MAKE HIM SEEM MANLY AND ATTRACTIVE?!
D HE INK THIS IS STILL JUNIOR HIGH OR SOMETHING?! HE'S SO INCREDIBLY ADORABLE!
IS THIS MY PUNISHMENT FOR KEEPING IT SECRET THAT I'M NOT INDIFFERENT TO BEAUTIFUL THINGS? THAT I'M INCREDIBLY ATTRACTED TO THEM?!
HE HAS EXACTLY THE KIND OF FACE I'M NATURALLY ATTRACTED TO... AND THEN HE SMILES AT ME LIKE THAT! WAS HE TRYING TO KILL ME?!
HEEEEE
SECRET TAKARAZUKA CLUB FAN
OH
HUFF

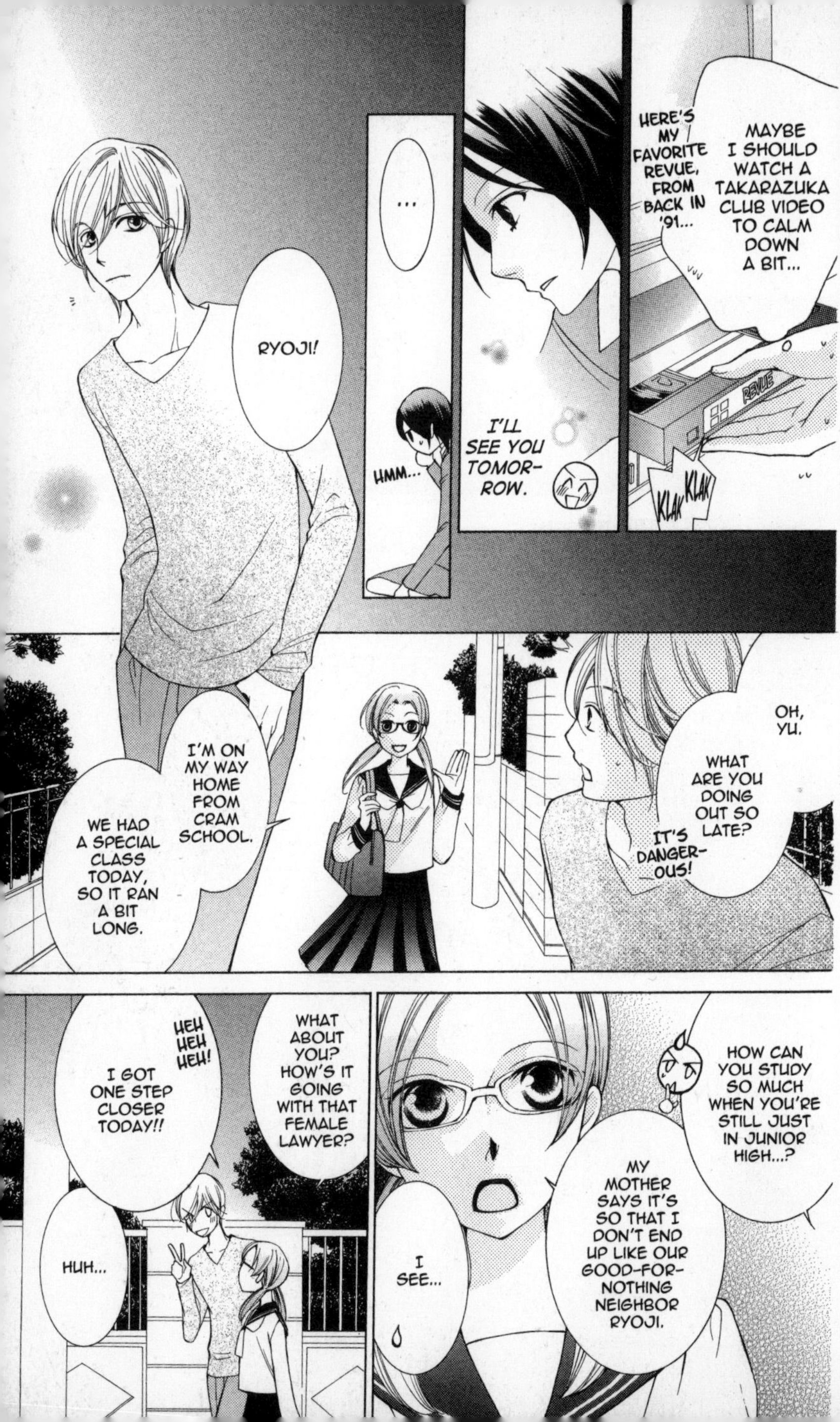
MAYBE I SHOULD WATCH A TAKARAZUKA CLUB VIDEO TO CALM DOWN A BIT...
HERE'S MY FAVORITE REVUE, FROM BACK IN '91...
REVUE
KLAK
KLAK
I'LL SEE YOU TOMORROW.
...
HMM...
RYOJI!
OH, YU.
WHAT ARE YOU DOING OUT SO LATE?
IT'S DANGEROUS!
I'M ON MY WAY HOME FROM CRAM SCHOOL.
WE HAD A SPECIAL CLASS TODAY, SO IT RAN A BIT LONG.
HOW CAN YOU STUDY SO MUCH WHEN YOU'RE STILL JUST IN JUNIOR HIGH...?
MY MOTHER SAYS IT'S SO THAT I DON'T END UP LIKE OUR GOOD-FOR-NOTHING NEIGHBOR RYOJI.
I SEE...
WHAT ABOUT YOU? HOW'S IT GOING WITH THAT FEMALE LAWYER?
HEH HEH HEH!
I GOT ONE STEP CLOSER TODAY!!
HUH...

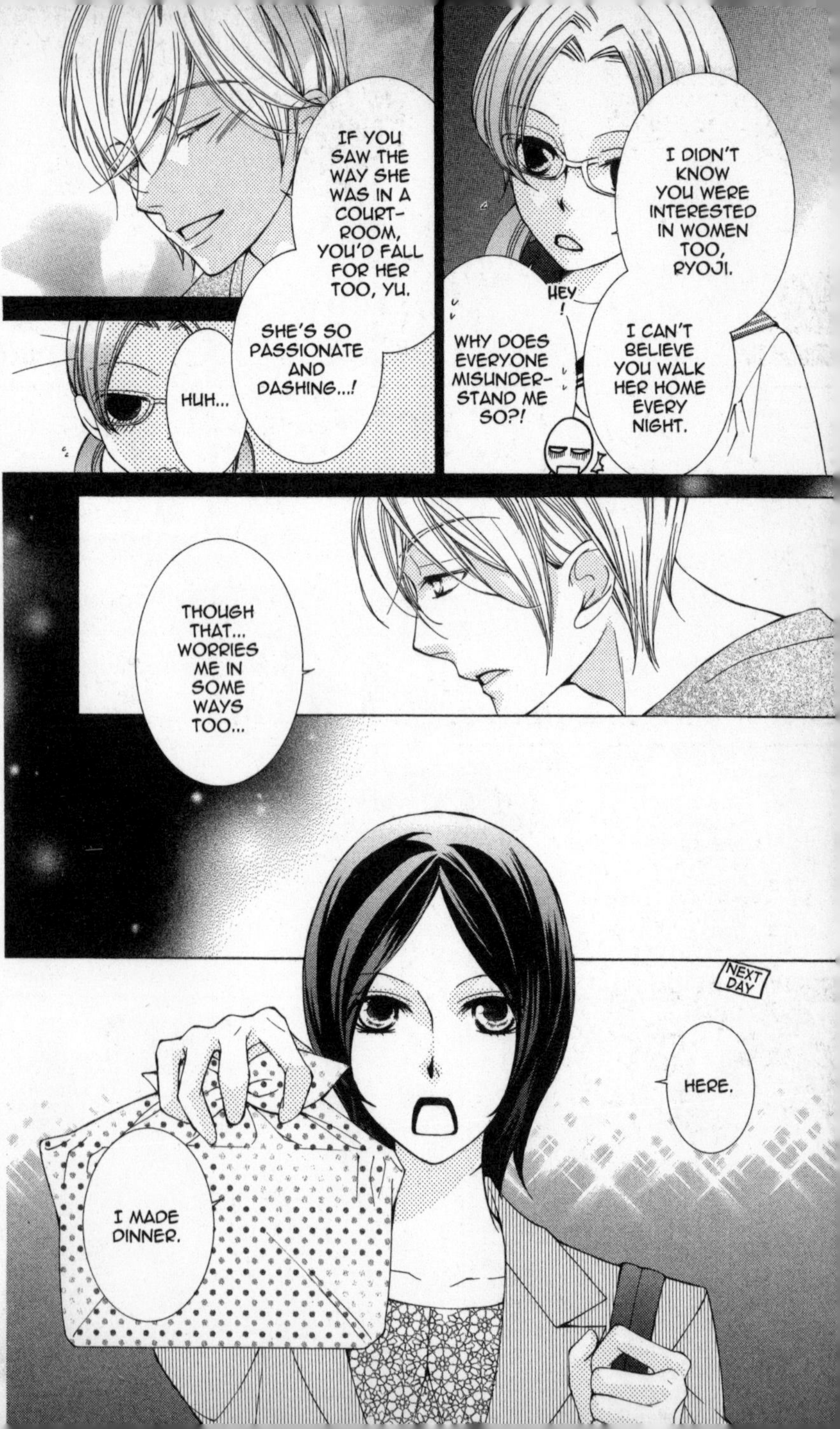
I DIDN'T KNOW YOU WERE INTERESTED IN WOMEN TOO, RYOJI.
I CAN'T BELIEVE YOU WALK HER HOME EVERY NIGHT.
HEY!
WHY DOES EVERYONE MISUNDERSTAND ME SO?!
IF YOU SAW THE WAY SHE WAS IN A COURT-ROOM, YOU'D FALL FOR HER TOO, YU.
SHE'S SO PASSIONATE AND DASHING...!
HUH...
THOUGH THAT... WORRIES ME IN SOME WAYS TOO...
NEXT DAY
HERE.
I MADE DINNER.

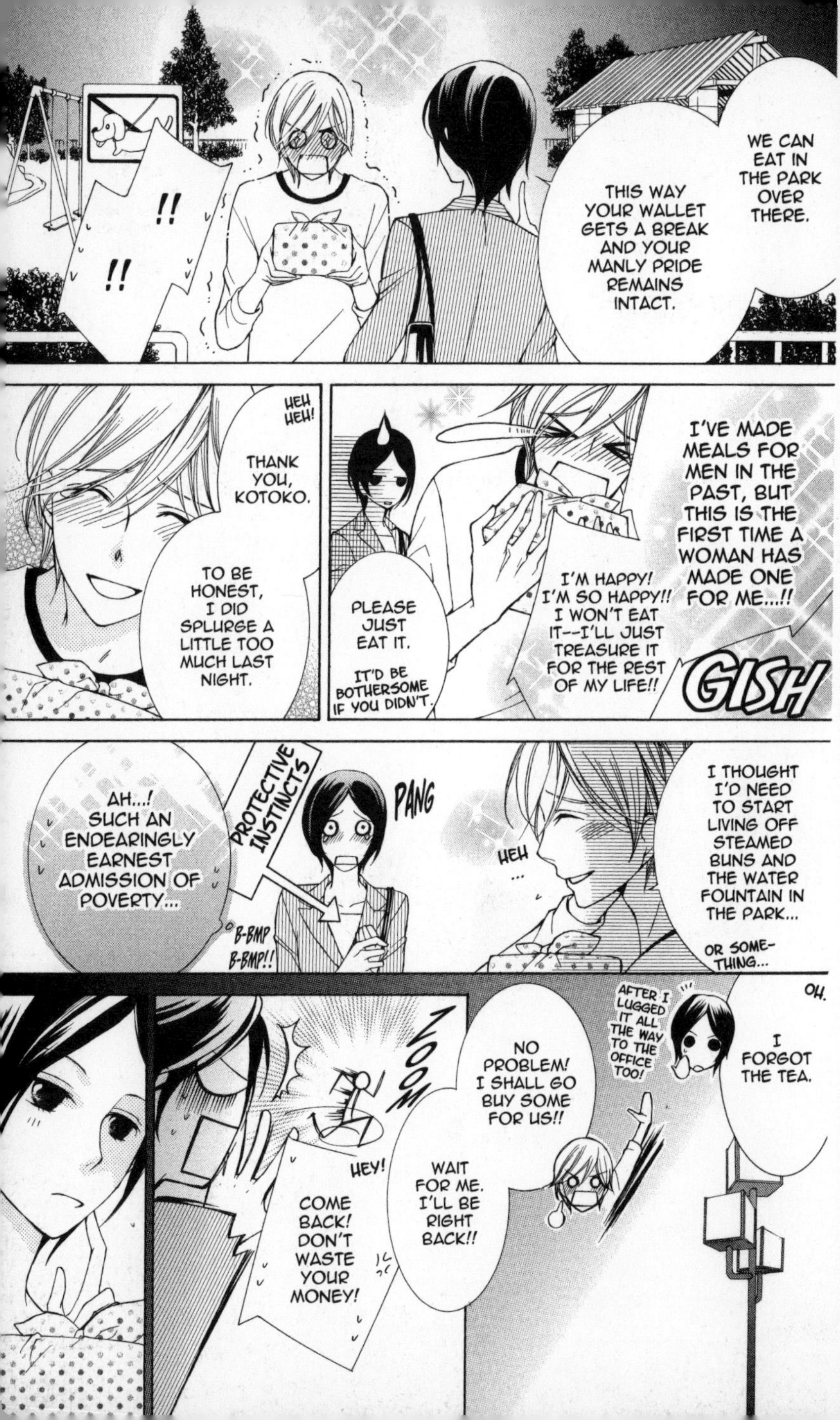
WE CAN EAT IN THE PARK OVER THERE.
THIS WAY YOUR WALLET GETS A BREAK AND YOUR MANLY PRIDE REMAINS INTACT.
!!
!!
I'VE MADE MEALS FOR MEN IN THE PAST, BUT THIS IS THE FIRST TIME A WOMAN HAS MADE ONE FOR ME...!!
GISH
I'M HAPPY! I'M SO HAPPY!! I WON'T EAT IT--I'LL JUST TREASURE IT FOR THE REST OF MY LIFE!!
PLEASE JUST EAT IT.
IT'D BE BOTHERSOME IF YOU DIDN'T.
HEH HEH!
THANK YOU, KOTOKO.
TO BE HONEST, I DID SPLURGE A LITTLE TOO MUCH LAST NIGHT.
I THOUGHT I'D NEED TO START LIVING OFF STEAMED BUNS AND THE WATER FOUNTAIN IN THE PARK...
OR SOMETHING...
HEH ...
PANG
PROTECTIVE INSTINCTS
AH...! SUCH AN ENDEARINGLY EARNEST ADMISSION OF POVERTY...
B-BMP B-BMP!!
OH.
I FORGOT THE TEA.
AFTER I LUGGED IT ALL THE WAY TO THE OFFICE TOO!
NO PROBLEM! I SHALL GO BUY SOME FOR US!!
ZOOOM
WAIT FOR ME. I'LL BE RIGHT BACK!!
HEY!
COME BACK! DON'T WASTE YOUR MONEY!

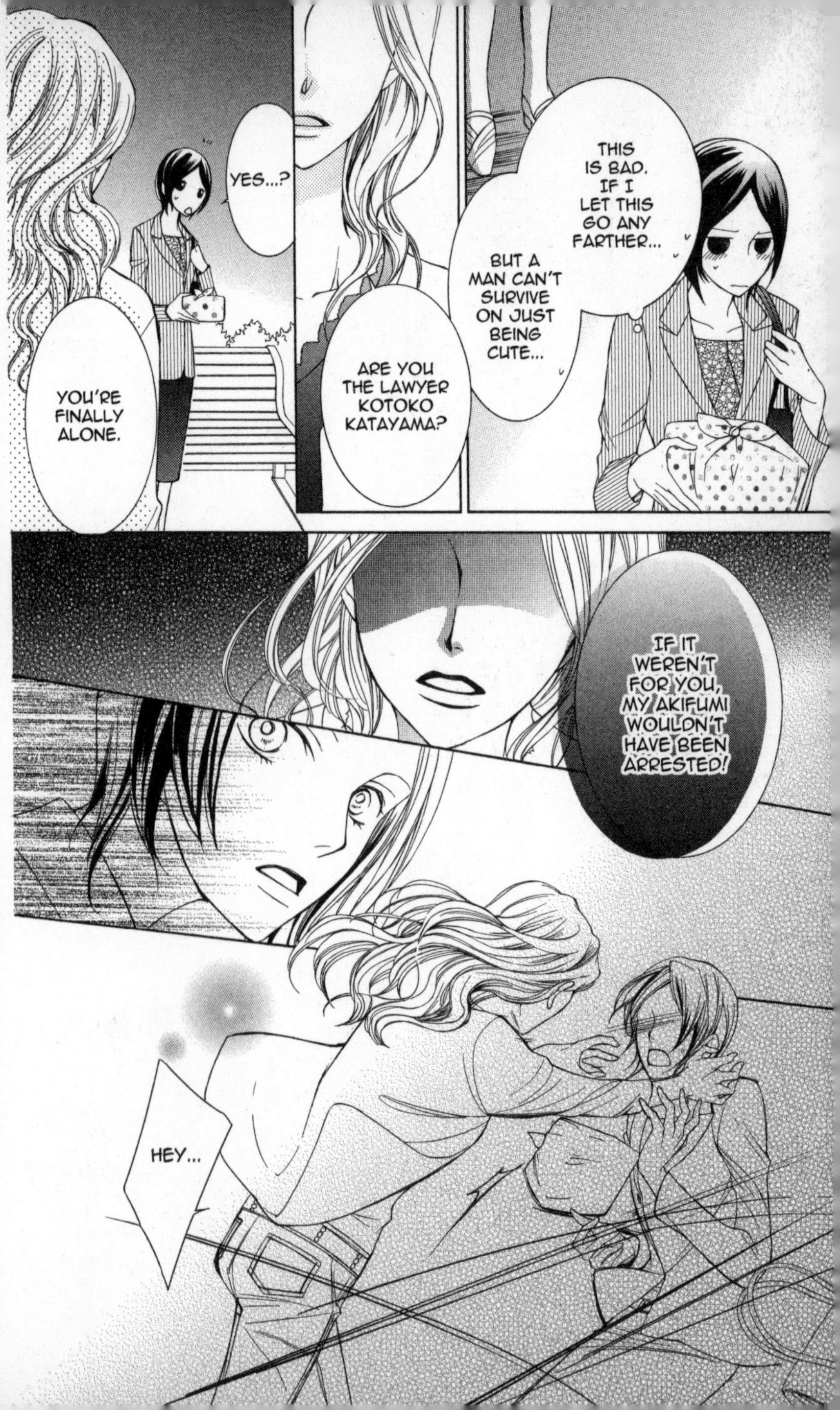

THIS IS BAD. IF I LET THIS GO ANY FARTHER...
BUT A MAN CAN'T SURVIVE ON JUST BEING CUTE...
ARE YOU THE LAWYER KOTOKO KATAYAMA?
YES...?
YOU'RE FINALLY ALONE.
IF IT WEREN'T FOR YOU, MY AKIFUMI WOULDN'T HAVE BEEN ARRESTED!
HEY...

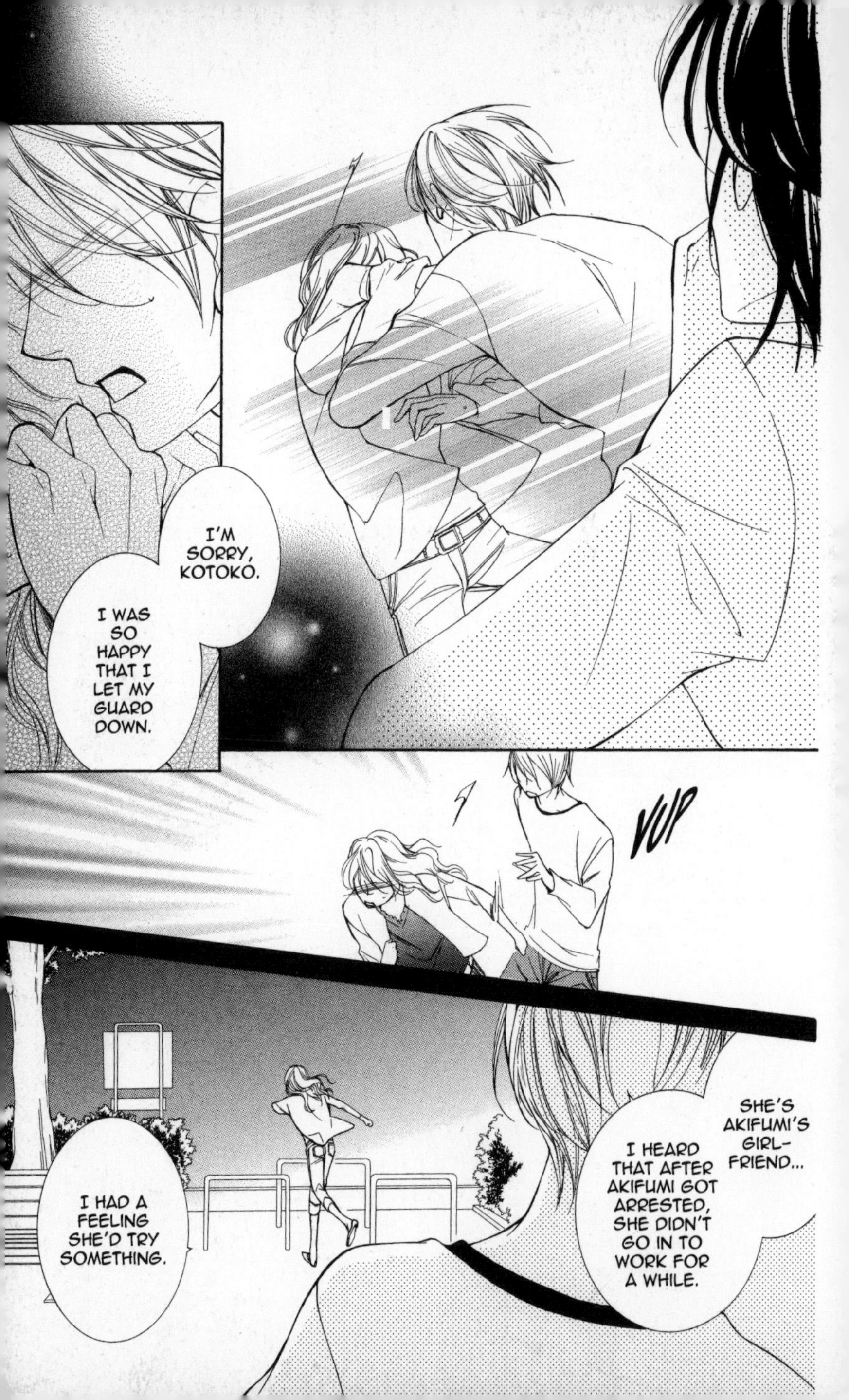
I'M SORRY, KOTOKO.
I WAS SO HAPPY THAT I LET MY GUARD DOWN.
VUP
SHE'S AKIFUMI'S GIRL-FRIEND...
I HEARD THAT AFTER AKIFUMI GOT ARRESTED, SHE DIDN'T GO IN TO WORK FOR A WHILE.
I HAD A FEELING SHE'D TRY SOMETHING.

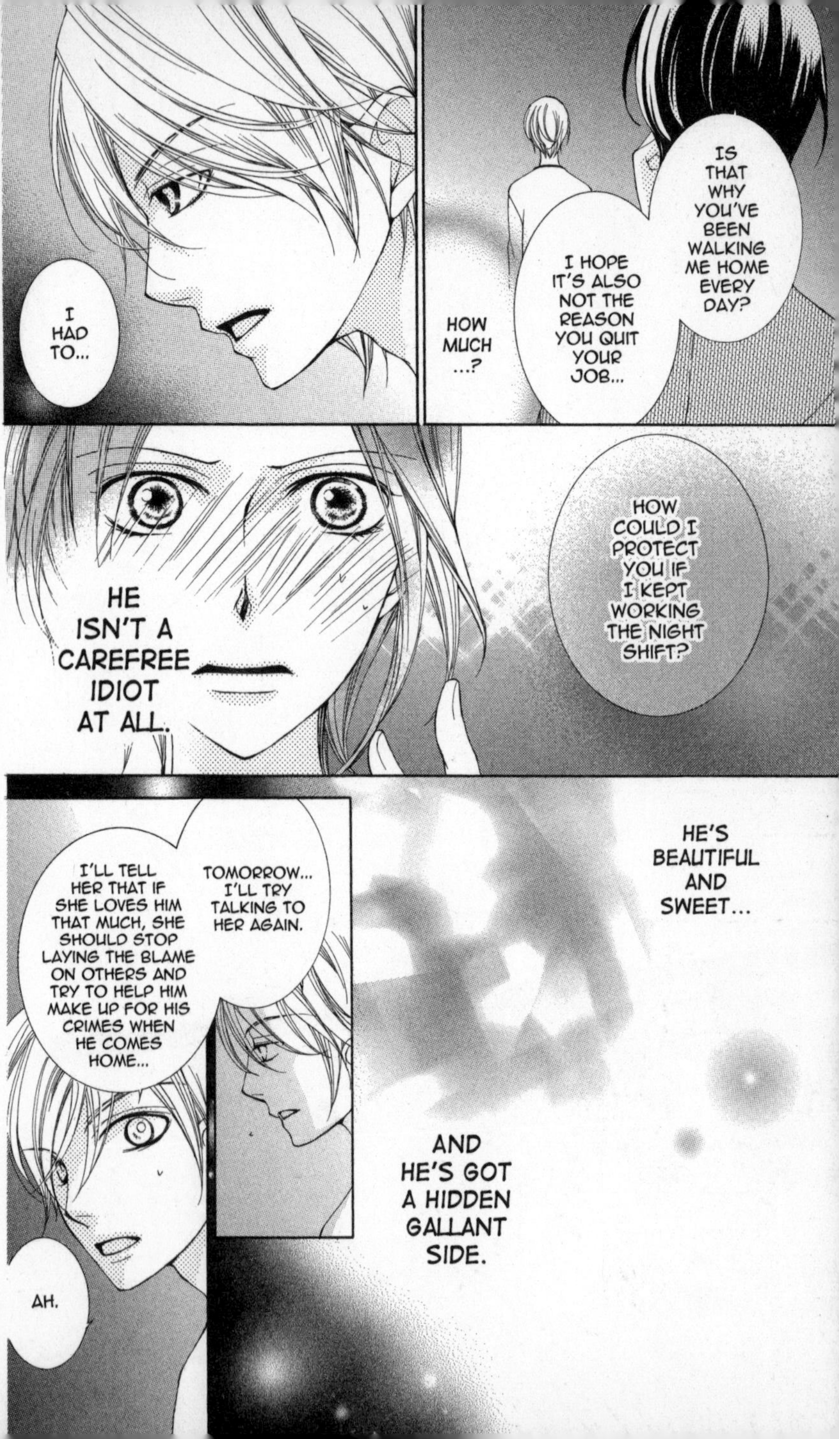
IS THAT WHY YOU'VE BEEN WALKING ME HOME EVERY DAY?
I HOPE IT'S ALSO NOT THE REASON YOU QUIT YOUR JOB...
HOW MUCH ...?
I HAD TO...
HOW COULD I PROTECT YOU IF I KEPT WORKING THE NIGHT SHIFT?
HE ISN'T A CAREFREE IDIOT AT ALL.
HE'S BEAUTIFUL AND SWEET...
AND HE'S GOT A HIDDEN GALLANT SIDE.
TOMORROW... I'LL TRY TALKING TO HER AGAIN.
I'LL TELL HER THAT IF SHE LOVES HIM THAT MUCH, SHE SHOULD STOP LAYING THE BLAME ON OTHERS AND TRY TO HELP HIM MAKE UP FOR HIS CRIMES WHEN HE COMES HOME...
AH.

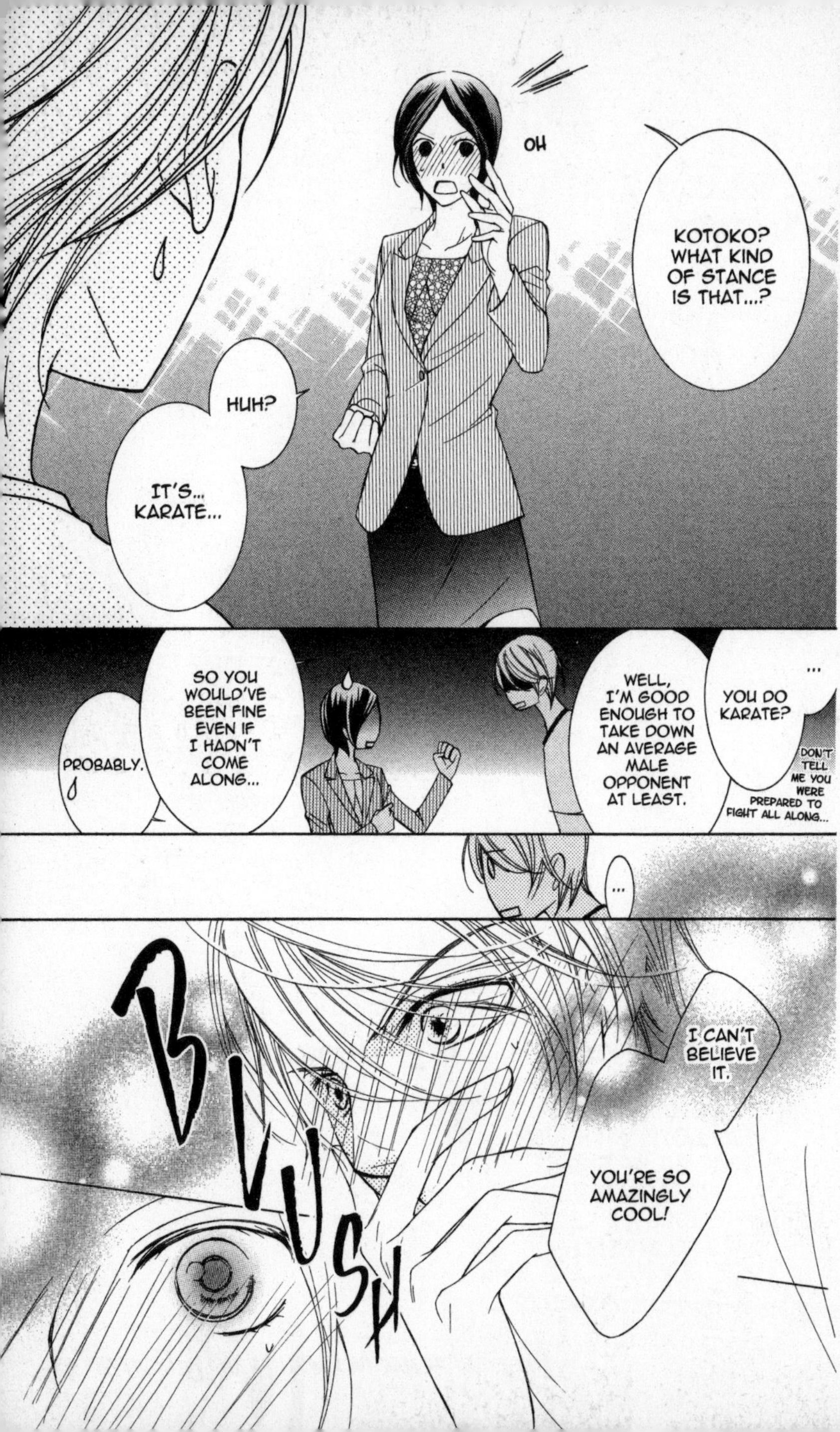
KOTOKO? WHAT KIND OF STANCE IS THAT...?
OH
HUH?
IT'S... KARATE...
...
YOU DO KARATE?
DON'T TELL ME YOU WERE PREPARED TO FIGHT ALL ALONG...
WELL, I'M GOOD ENOUGH TO TAKE DOWN AN AVERAGE MALE OPPONENT AT LEAST.
SO YOU WOULD'VE BEEN FINE EVEN IF I HADN'T COME ALONG...
PROBABLY.
...
I CAN'T BELIEVE IT.
YOU'RE SO AMAZINGLY COOL!
BLUSH

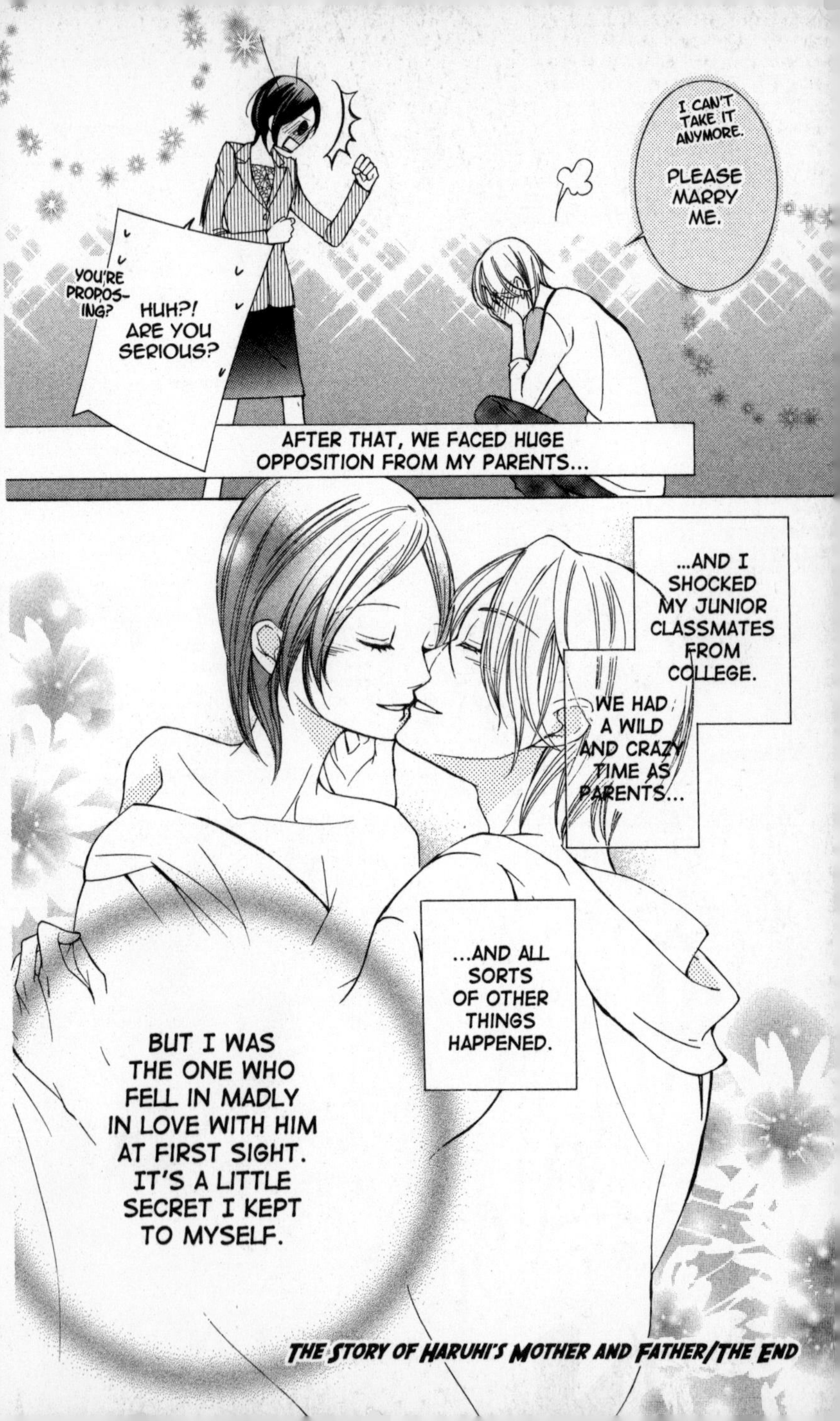
I CAN'T TAKE IT ANYMORE.
PLEASE MARRY ME.
HUH?! ARE YOU SERIOUS?
YOU'RE PROPOS-ING?
AFTER THAT, WE FACED HUGE OPPOSITION FROM MY PARENTS...
...AND I SHOCKED MY JUNIOR CLASSMATES FROM COLLEGE.
WE HAD A WILD AND CRAZY TIME AS PARENTS...
...AND ALL SORTS OF OTHER THINGS HAPPENED.
BUT I WAS THE ONE WHO FELL IN MADLY IN LOVE WITH HIM AT FIRST SIGHT. IT'S A LITTLE SECRET I KEPT TO MYSELF.
THE STORY OF HARUHI'S MOTHER AND FATHER/THE END

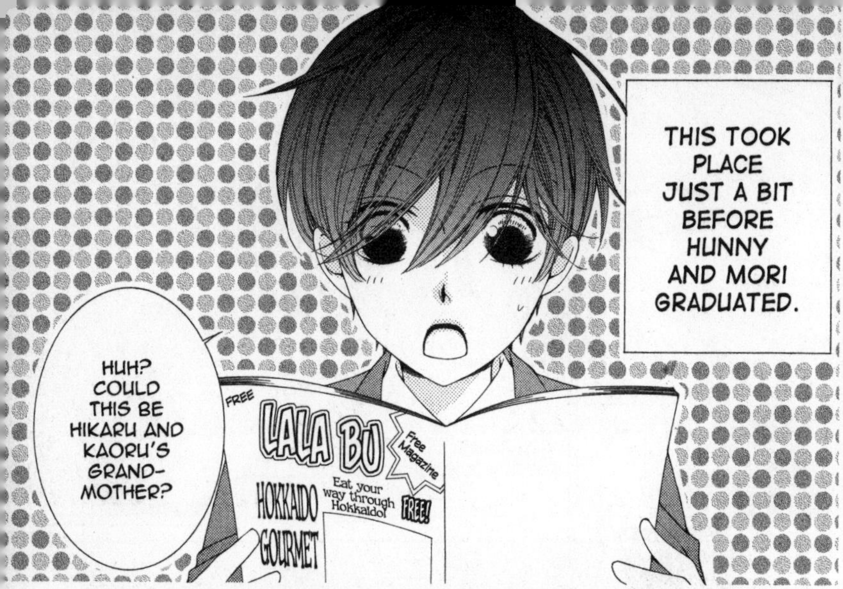
THIS TOOK PLACE JUST A BIT BEFORE HUNNY AND MORI GRADUATED.
HUH? COULD THIS BE HIKARU AND KAORU'S GRAND-MOTHER?
FREE
LALA BU
Free Magazine
HOKKAIDO GOURMET
Eat your way through Hokkaido!
FREE!

OURAN HIGH SCHOOL HOST CLUB

EXTRA EPISODE

THE HITACHIIN FAMILY PRECEPT

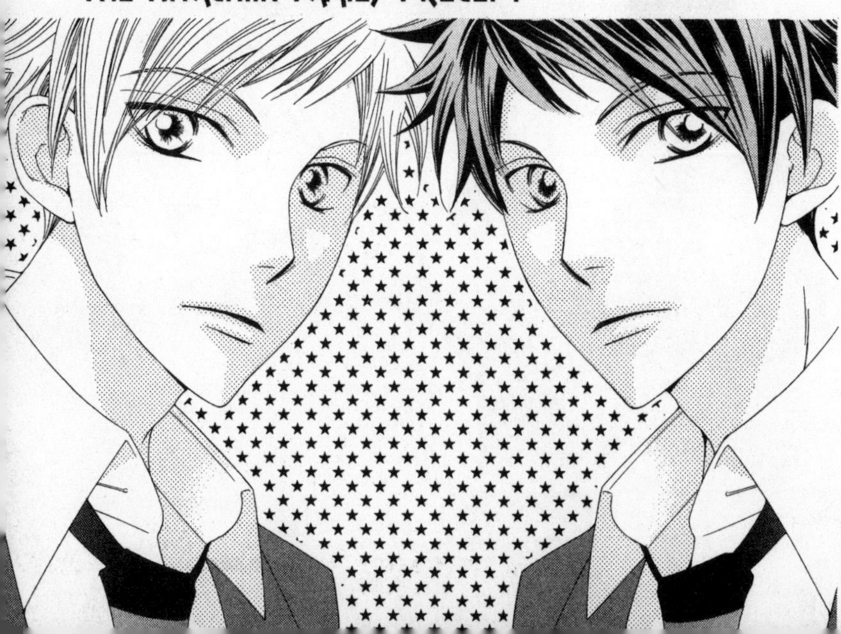

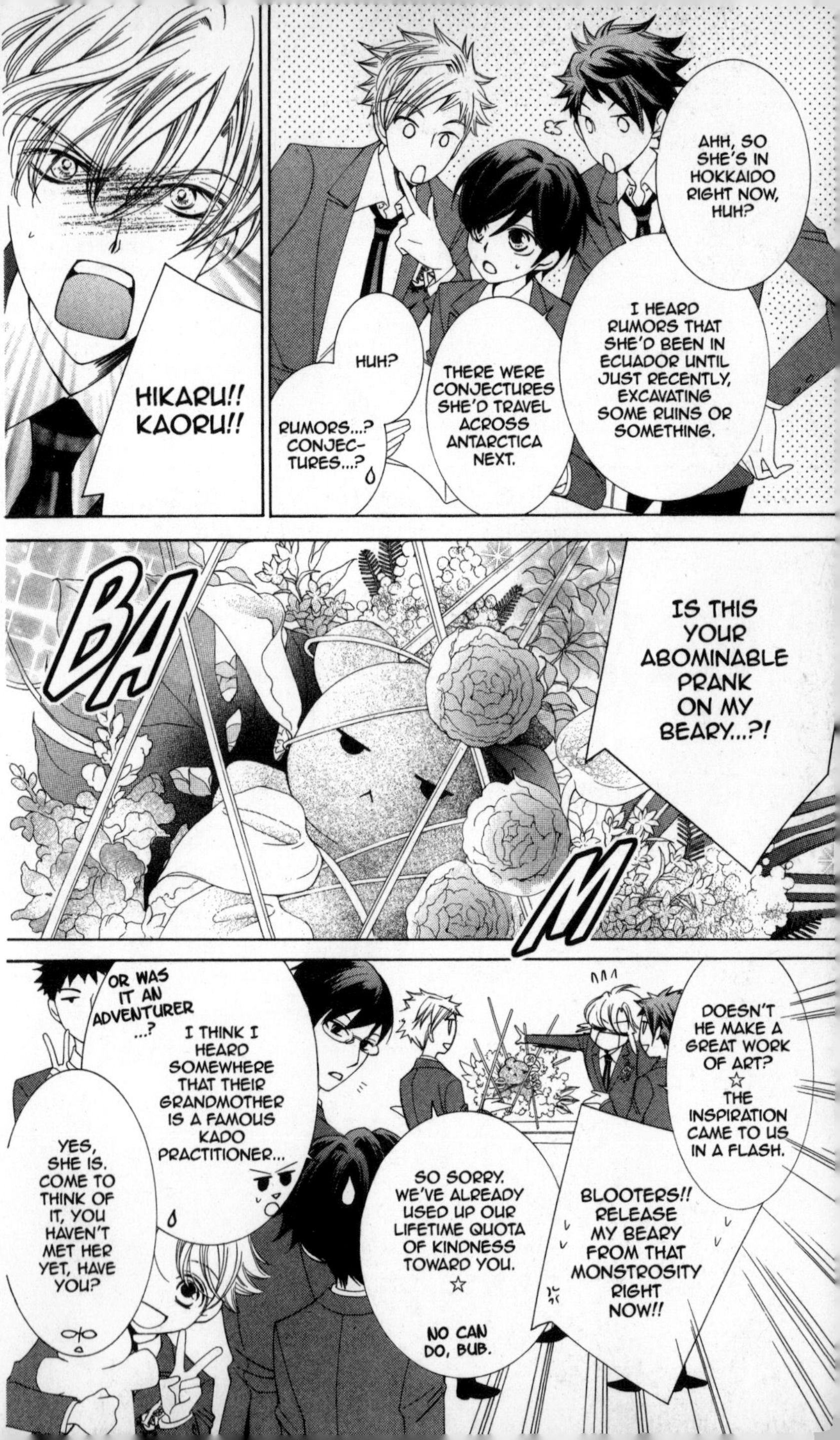
AHH, SO SHE'S IN HOKKAIDO RIGHT NOW, HUH?
I HEARD RUMORS THAT SHE'D BEEN IN ECUADOR UNTIL JUST RECENTLY, EXCAVATING SOME RUINS OR SOMETHING.
THERE WERE CONJECTURES SHE'D TRAVEL ACROSS ANTARCTICA NEXT.
HUH?
RUMORS...? CONJEC-TURES...?
HIKARU!! KAORU!!
IS THIS YOUR ABOMINABLE PRANK ON MY BEARY...?!
BA
M
DOESN'T HE MAKE A GREAT WORK OF ART? ☆ THE INSPIRATION CAME TO US IN A FLASH.
BLOOTERS!! RELEASE MY BEARY FROM THAT MONSTROSITY RIGHT NOW!!
SO SORRY. WE'VE ALREADY USED UP OUR LIFETIME QUOTA OF KINDNESS TOWARD YOU. ☆
NO CAN DO, BUB.
I THINK I HEARD SOMEWHERE THAT THEIR GRANDMOTHER IS A FAMOUS KADO PRACTITIONER...
OR WAS IT AN ADVENTURER ...?
YES, SHE IS. COME TO THINK OF IT, YOU HAVEN'T MET HER YET, HAVE YOU?

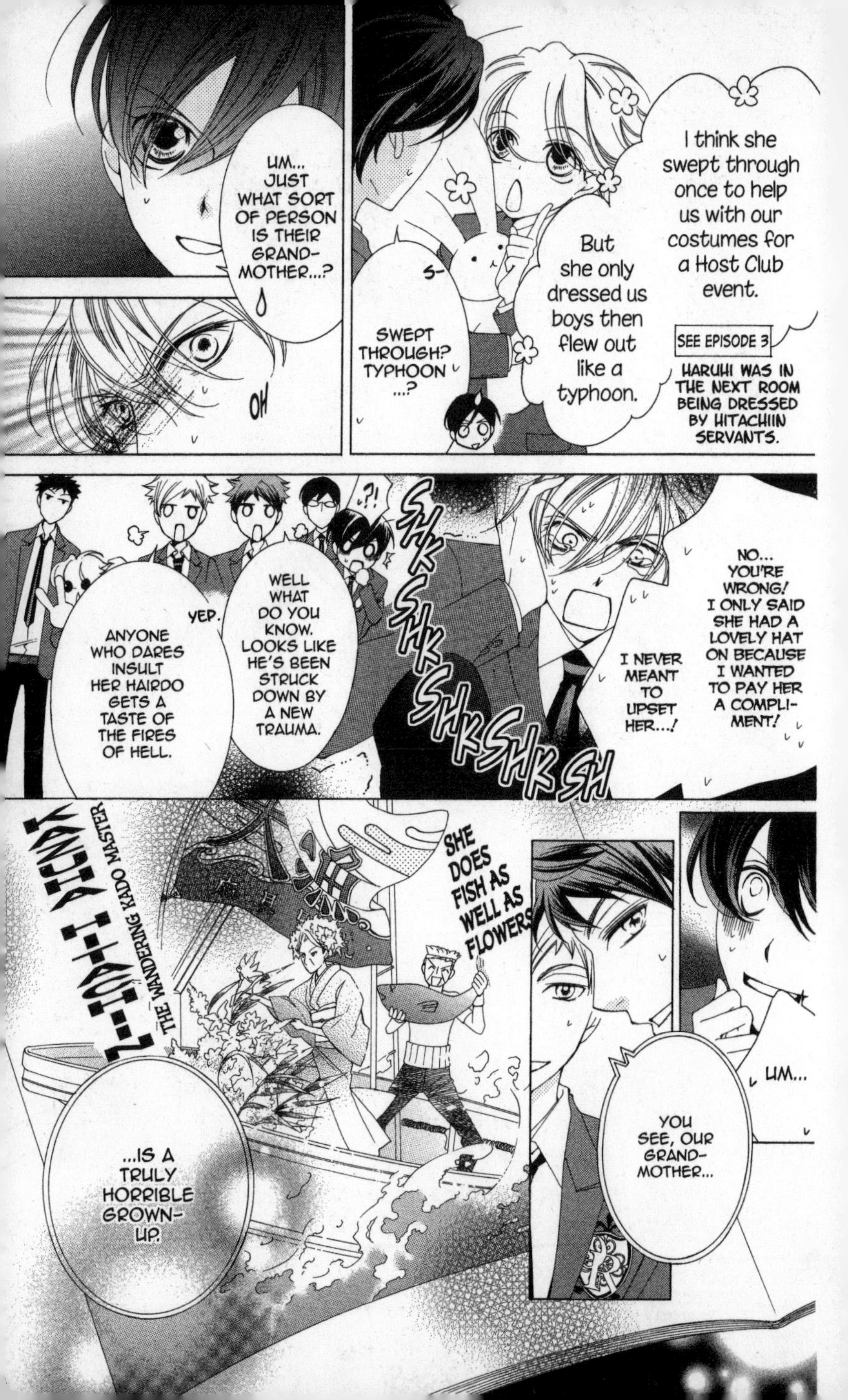
I think she swept through once to help us with our costumes for a Host Club event.
SEE EPISODE 3
HARUHI WAS IN THE NEXT ROOM BEING DRESSED BY HITACHIIN SERVANTS.
But she only dressed us boys then flew out like a typhoon.
S-
SWEPT THROUGH? TYPHOON ...?
UM... JUST WHAT SORT OF PERSON IS THEIR GRAND-MOTHER...?
OH
NO... YOU'RE WRONG! I ONLY SAID SHE HAD A LOVELY HAT ON BECAUSE I WANTED TO PAY HER A COMPLI-MENT!
I NEVER MEANT TO UPSET HER...!
SHK SHK SHK SHK SHK SH
?!
WELL WHAT DO YOU KNOW. LOOKS LIKE HE'S BEEN STRUCK DOWN BY A NEW TRAUMA.
YEP.
ANYONE WHO DARES INSULT HER HAIRDO GETS A TASTE OF THE FIRES OF HELL.
UM...
YOU SEE, OUR GRAND-MOTHER...
SHE DOES FISH AS WELL AS FLOWERS
THE WANDERING KADO MASTER
...IS A TRULY HORRIBLE GROWN-UP.

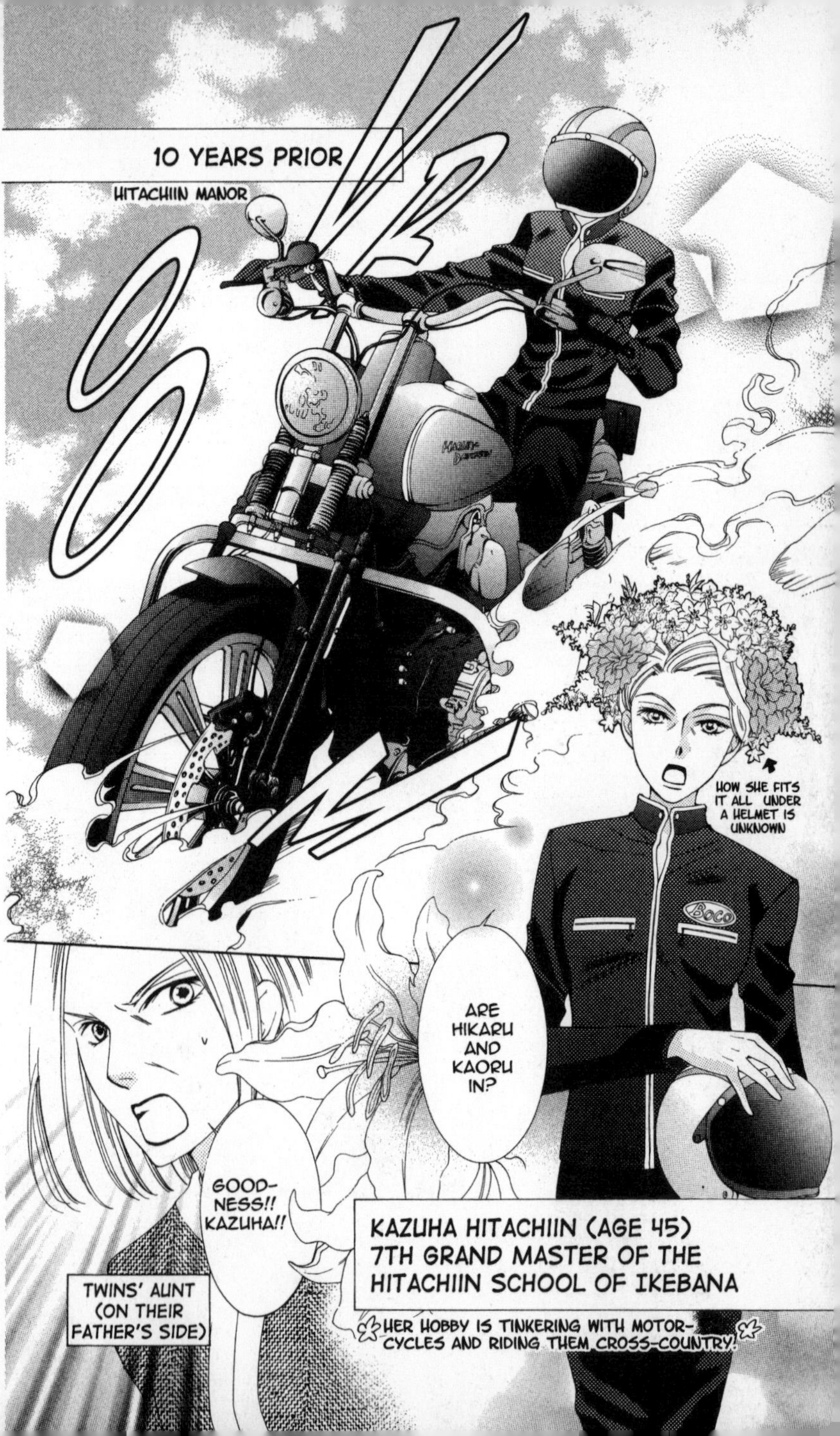
10 YEARS PRIOR
HITACHIIN MANOR
HOW SHE FITS IT ALL UNDER A HELMET IS UNKNOWN
ARE HIKARU AND KAORU IN?
KAZUHA HITACHIIN (AGE 45)
7TH GRAND MASTER OF THE HITACHIIN SCHOOL OF IKEBANA
HER HOBBY IS TINKERING WITH MOTOR-CYCLES AND RIDING THEM CROSS-COUNTRY!
GOOD-NESS!! KAZUHA!!
TWINS' AUNT (ON THEIR FATHER'S SIDE)

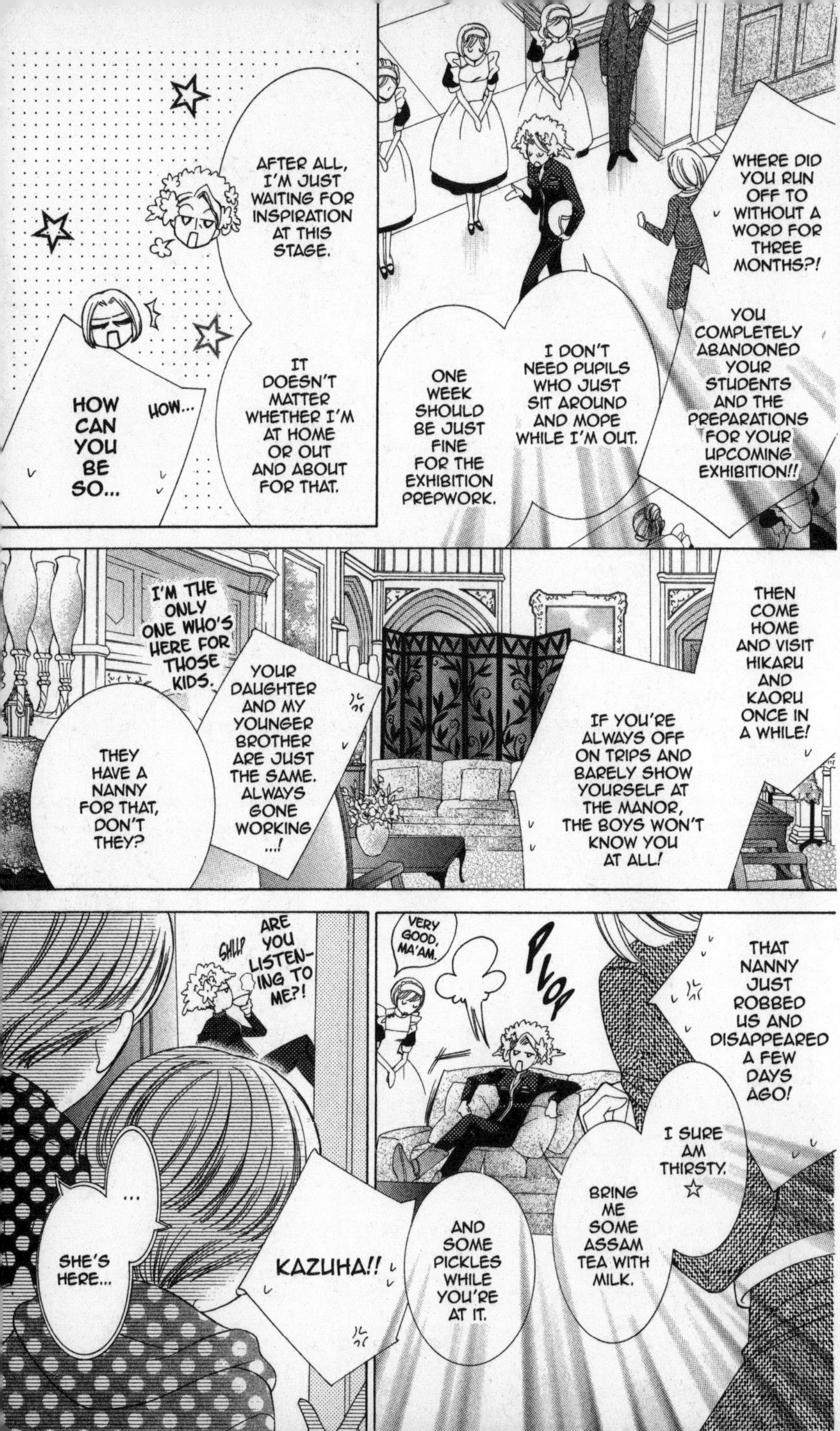
WHERE DID YOU RUN OFF TO WITHOUT A WORD FOR THREE MONTHS?!
YOU COMPLETELY ABANDONED YOUR STUDENTS AND THE PREPARATIONS FOR YOUR UPCOMING EXHIBITION!!
I DON'T NEED PUPILS WHO JUST SIT AROUND AND MOPE WHILE I'M OUT.
ONE WEEK SHOULD BE JUST FINE FOR THE EXHIBITION PREPWORK.
AFTER ALL, I'M JUST WAITING FOR INSPIRATION AT THIS STAGE.
IT DOESN'T MATTER WHETHER I'M AT HOME OR OUT AND ABOUT FOR THAT.
HOW...
HOW CAN YOU BE SO...
THEN COME HOME AND VISIT HIKARU AND KAORU ONCE IN A WHILE!
IF YOU'RE ALWAYS OFF ON TRIPS AND BARELY SHOW YOURSELF AT THE MANOR, THE BOYS WON'T KNOW YOU AT ALL!
I'M THE ONLY ONE WHO'S HERE FOR THOSE KIDS.
YOUR DAUGHTER AND MY YOUNGER BROTHER ARE JUST THE SAME. ALWAYS GONE WORKING ...!
THEY HAVE A NANNY FOR THAT, DON'T THEY?
THAT NANNY JUST ROBBED US AND DISAPPEARED A FEW DAYS AGO!
I SURE AM THIRSTY.
BRING ME SOME ASSAM TEA WITH MILK.
VERY GOOD, MA'AM.
AND SOME PICKLES WHILE YOU'RE AT IT.
KAZUHA!!
ARE YOU LISTENING TO ME?!
SHLLP
...
SHE'S HERE...

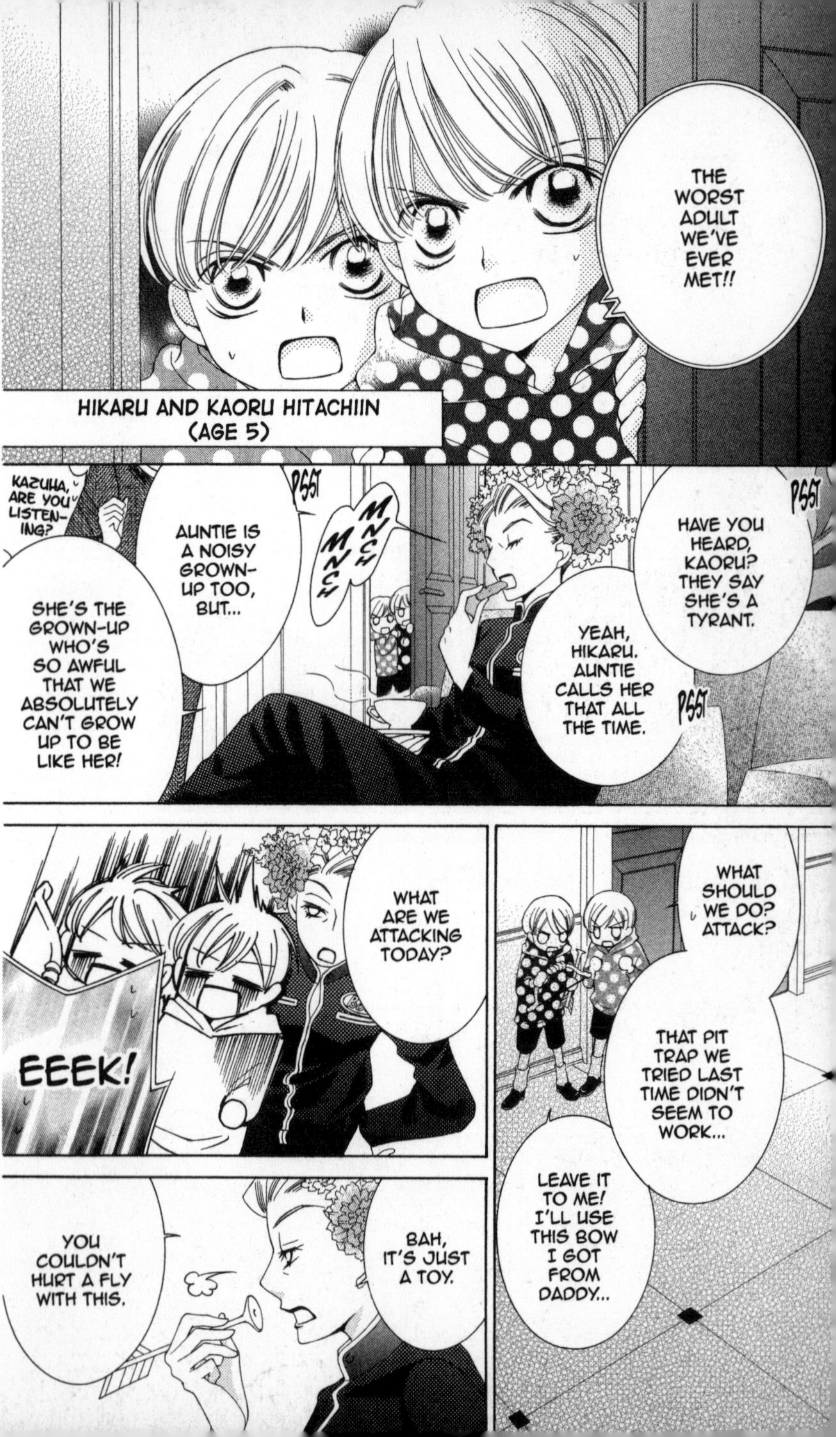
THE WORST ADULT WE'VE EVER MET!!
HIKARU AND KAORU HITACHIIN (AGE 5)
PSST
HAVE YOU HEARD, KAORU? THEY SAY SHE'S A TYRANT.
PSST
YEAH, HIKARU. AUNTIE CALLS HER THAT ALL THE TIME.
MNCH MNCH MNCH
PSST
AUNTIE IS A NOISY GROWN-UP TOO, BUT...
SHE'S THE GROWN-UP WHO'S SO AWFUL THAT WE ABSOLUTELY CAN'T GROW UP TO BE LIKE HER!
KAZUHA, ARE YOU LISTENING?
WHAT SHOULD WE DO? ATTACK?
THAT PIT TRAP WE TRIED LAST TIME DIDN'T SEEM TO WORK...
LEAVE IT TO ME! I'LL USE THIS BOW I GOT FROM DADDY...
WHAT ARE WE ATTACKING TODAY?
EEEK!
BAH, IT'S JUST A TOY.
YOU COULDN'T HURT A FLY WITH THIS.

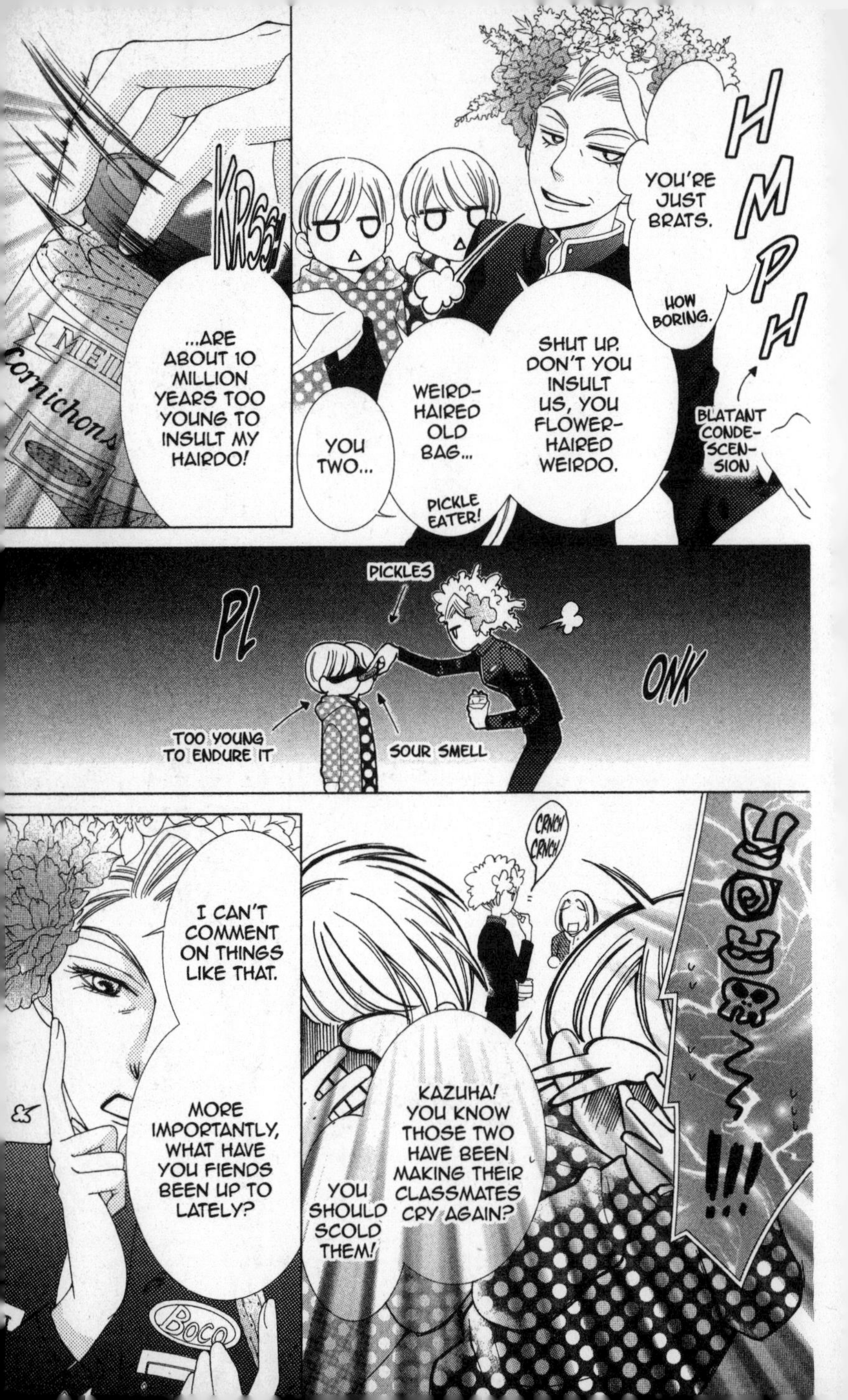
HMPH
YOU'RE JUST BRATS.
HOW BORING.
BLATANT CONDESCENSION
SHUT UP. DON'T YOU INSULT US, YOU FLOWER-HAIRED WEIRDO.
WEIRD-HAIRED OLD BAG...
PICKLE EATER!
YOU TWO...
KRSSH
...ARE ABOUT 10 MILLION YEARS TOO YOUNG TO INSULT MY HAIRDO!
Cornichons
PICKLES
PL
ONK
SOUR SMELL
TOO YOUNG TO ENDURE IT
!!!
CRNCH CRNCH
KAZUHA! YOU KNOW THOSE TWO HAVE BEEN MAKING THEIR CLASSMATES CRY AGAIN?
YOU SHOULD SCOLD THEM!
I CAN'T COMMENT ON THINGS LIKE THAT.
MORE IMPORTANTLY, WHAT HAVE YOU FIENDS BEEN UP TO LATELY?
Boco

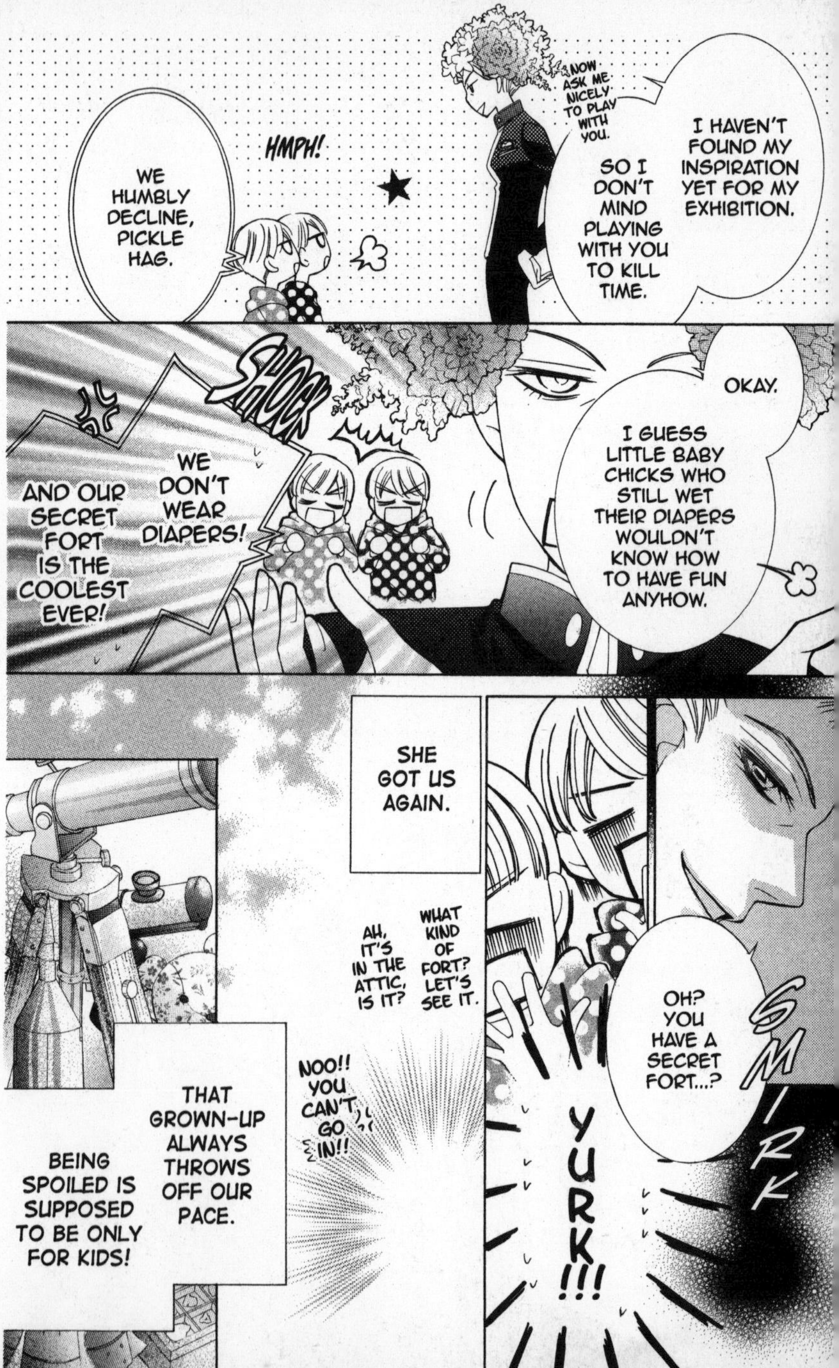
I HAVEN'T FOUND MY INSPIRATION YET FOR MY EXHIBITION.
SO I DON'T MIND PLAYING WITH YOU TO KILL TIME.
NOW ASK ME NICELY TO PLAY WITH YOU.
HMPH!
WE HUMBLY DECLINE, PICKLE HAG.
OKAY.
I GUESS LITTLE BABY CHICKS WHO STILL WET THEIR DIAPERS WOULDN'T KNOW HOW TO HAVE FUN ANYHOW.
SHOCK
WE DON'T WEAR DIAPERS!
AND OUR SECRET FORT IS THE COOLEST EVER!
OH? YOU HAVE A SECRET FORT...?
SMIRK
YURK!!!
SHE GOT US AGAIN.
WHAT KIND OF FORT? LET'S SEE IT.
AH, IT'S IN THE ATTIC, IS IT?
NOO!! YOU CAN'T GO IN!!
THAT GROWN-UP ALWAYS THROWS OFF OUR PACE.
BEING SPOILED IS SUPPOSED TO BE ONLY FOR KIDS!

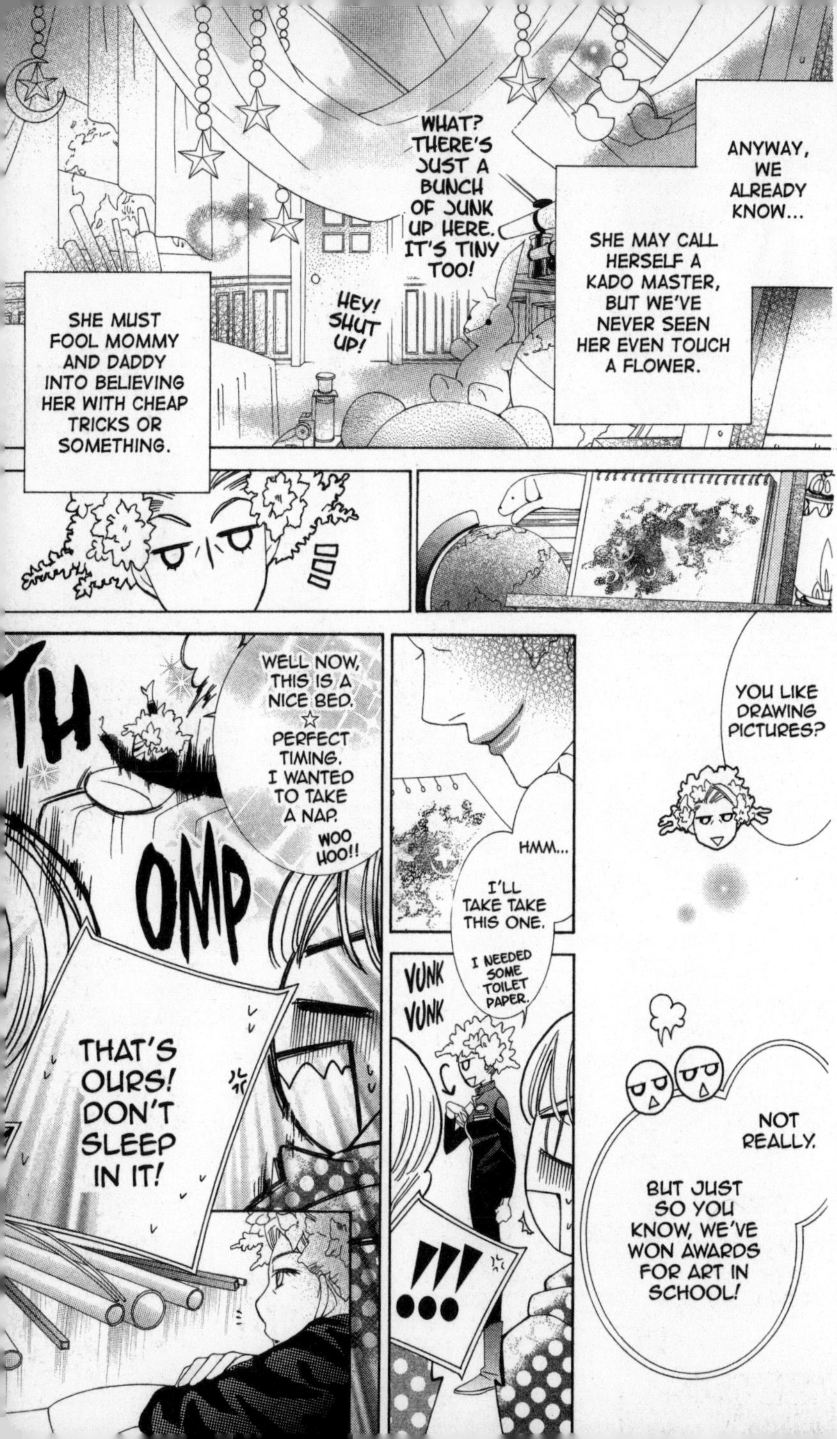
ANYWAY, WE ALREADY KNOW...
SHE MAY CALL HERSELF A KADO MASTER, BUT WE'VE NEVER SEEN HER EVEN TOUCH A FLOWER.
WHAT? THERE'S JUST A BUNCH OF JUNK UP HERE. IT'S TINY TOO!
HEY! SHUT UP!
SHE MUST FOOL MOMMY AND DADDY INTO BELIEVING HER WITH CHEAP TRICKS OR SOMETHING.
YOU LIKE DRAWING PICTURES?
NOT REALLY.
BUT JUST SO YOU KNOW, WE'VE WON AWARDS FOR ART IN SCHOOL!
HMM...
I'LL TAKE TAKE THIS ONE.
I NEEDED SOME TOILET PAPER.
VUNK
VUNK
!!!
WELL NOW, THIS IS A NICE BED. ☆ PERFECT TIMING. I WANTED TO TAKE A NAP.
WOO HOO!!
THOMP
THAT'S OURS! DON'T SLEEP IN IT!

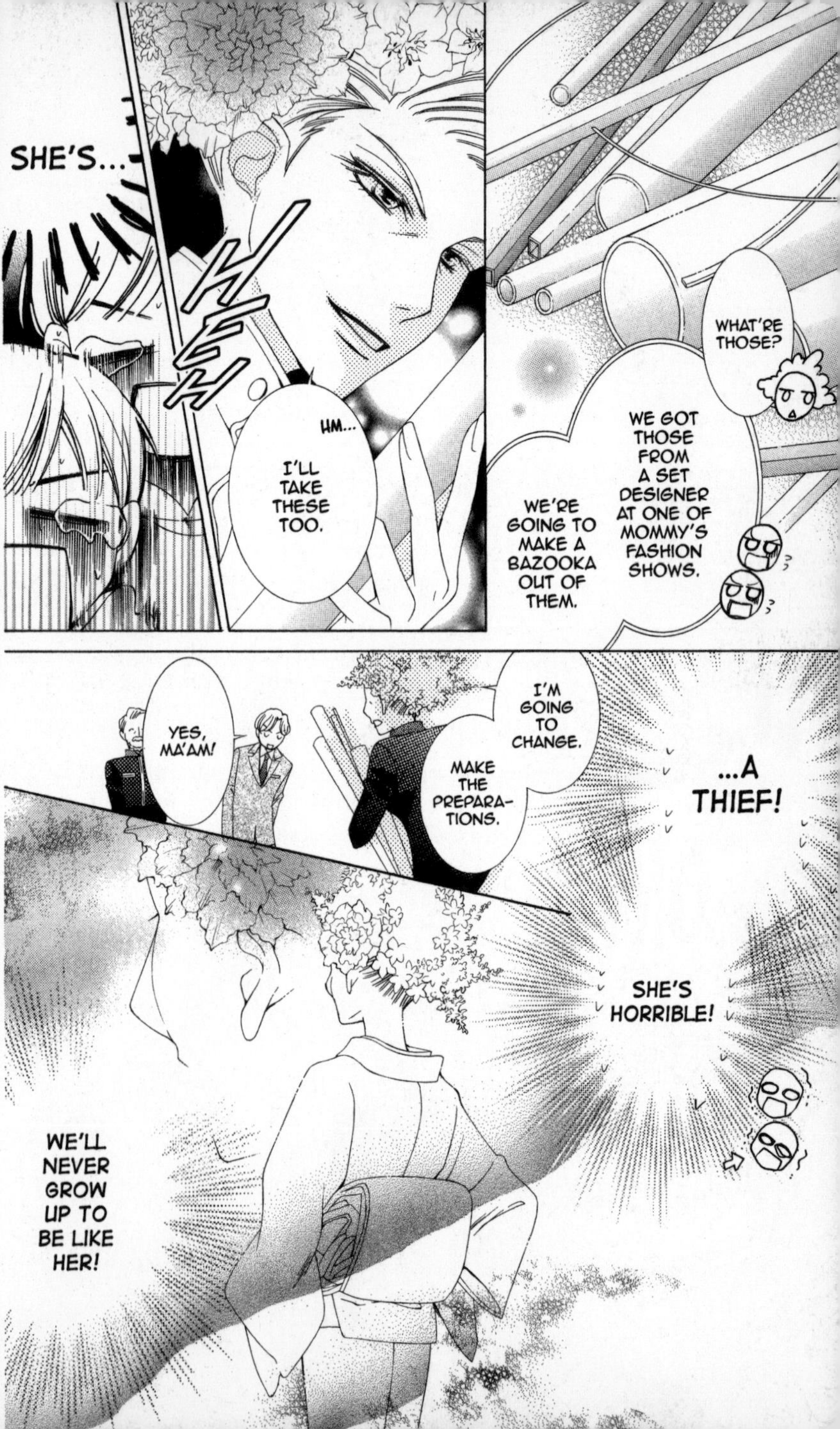
WHAT'RE THOSE?
WE GOT THOSE FROM A SET DESIGNER AT ONE OF MOMMY'S FASHION SHOWS.
WE'RE GOING TO MAKE A BAZOOKA OUT OF THEM.
HM...
I'LL TAKE THESE TOO.
SHE'S...
I'M GOING TO CHANGE.
MAKE THE PREPARATIONS.
YES, MA'AM!
...A THIEF!
SHE'S HORRIBLE!
WE'LL NEVER GROW UP TO BE LIKE HER!

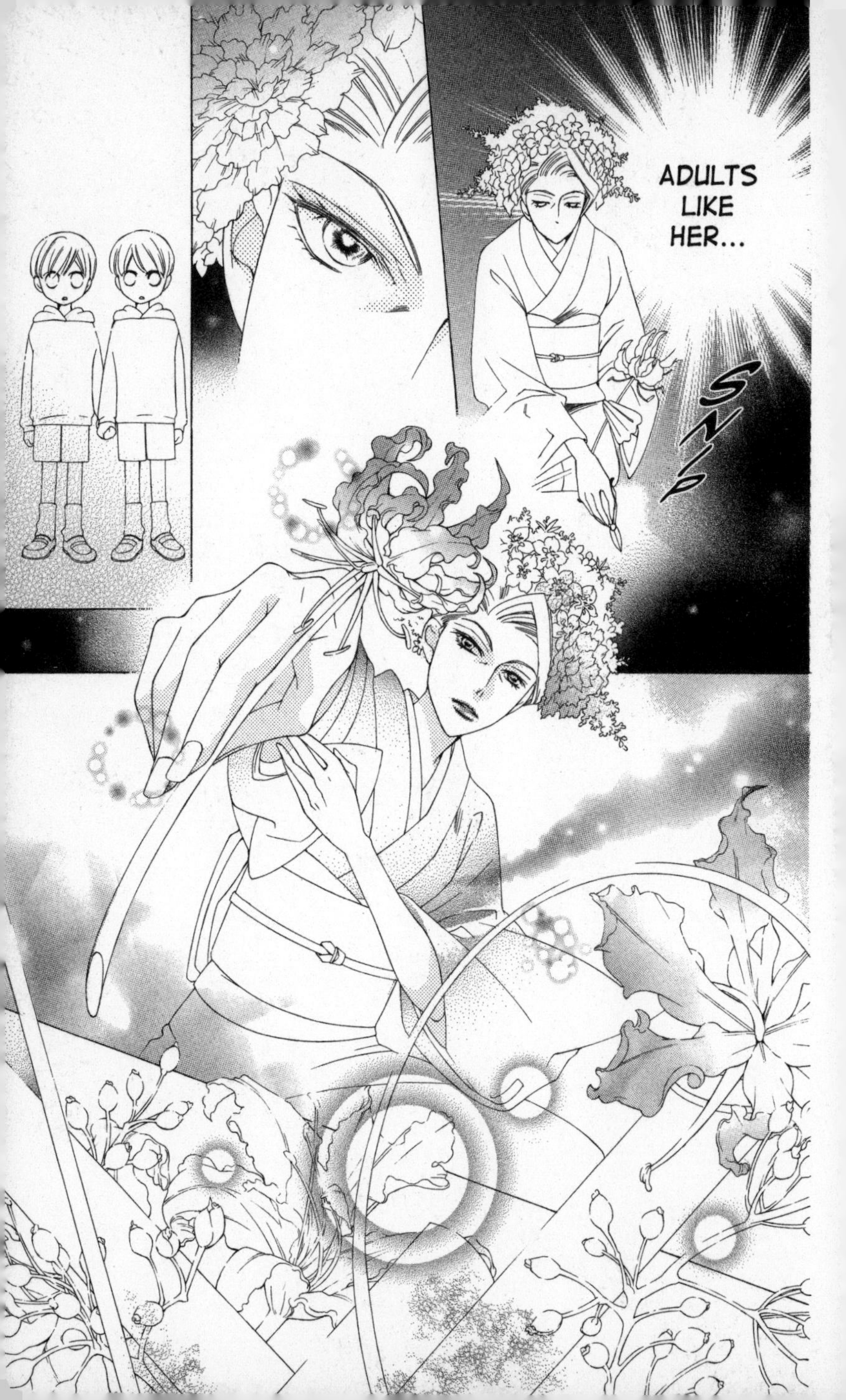
ADULTS LIKE HER...
SNIP

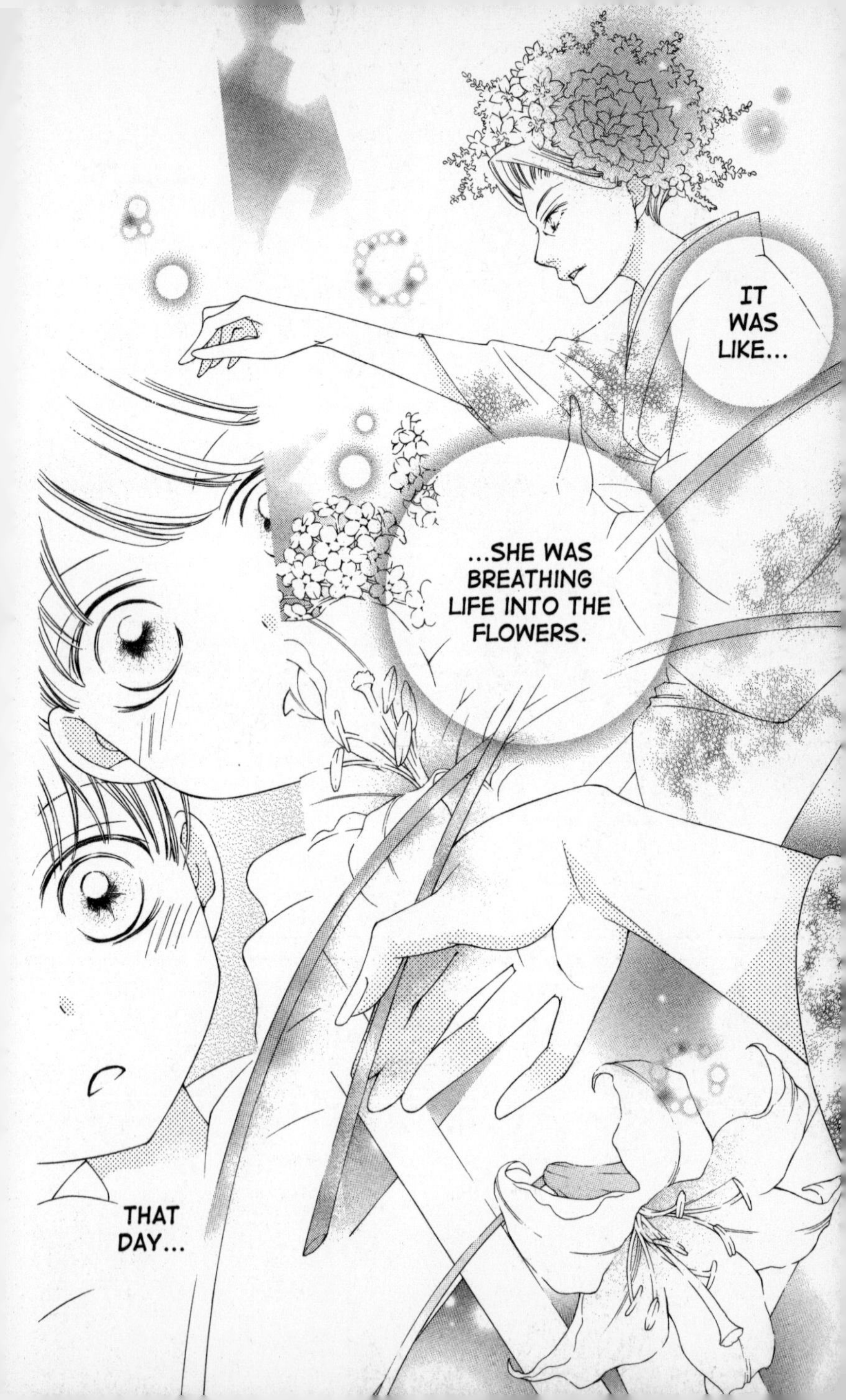
IT WAS LIKE...
...SHE WAS BREATHING LIFE INTO THE FLOWERS.
THAT DAY...

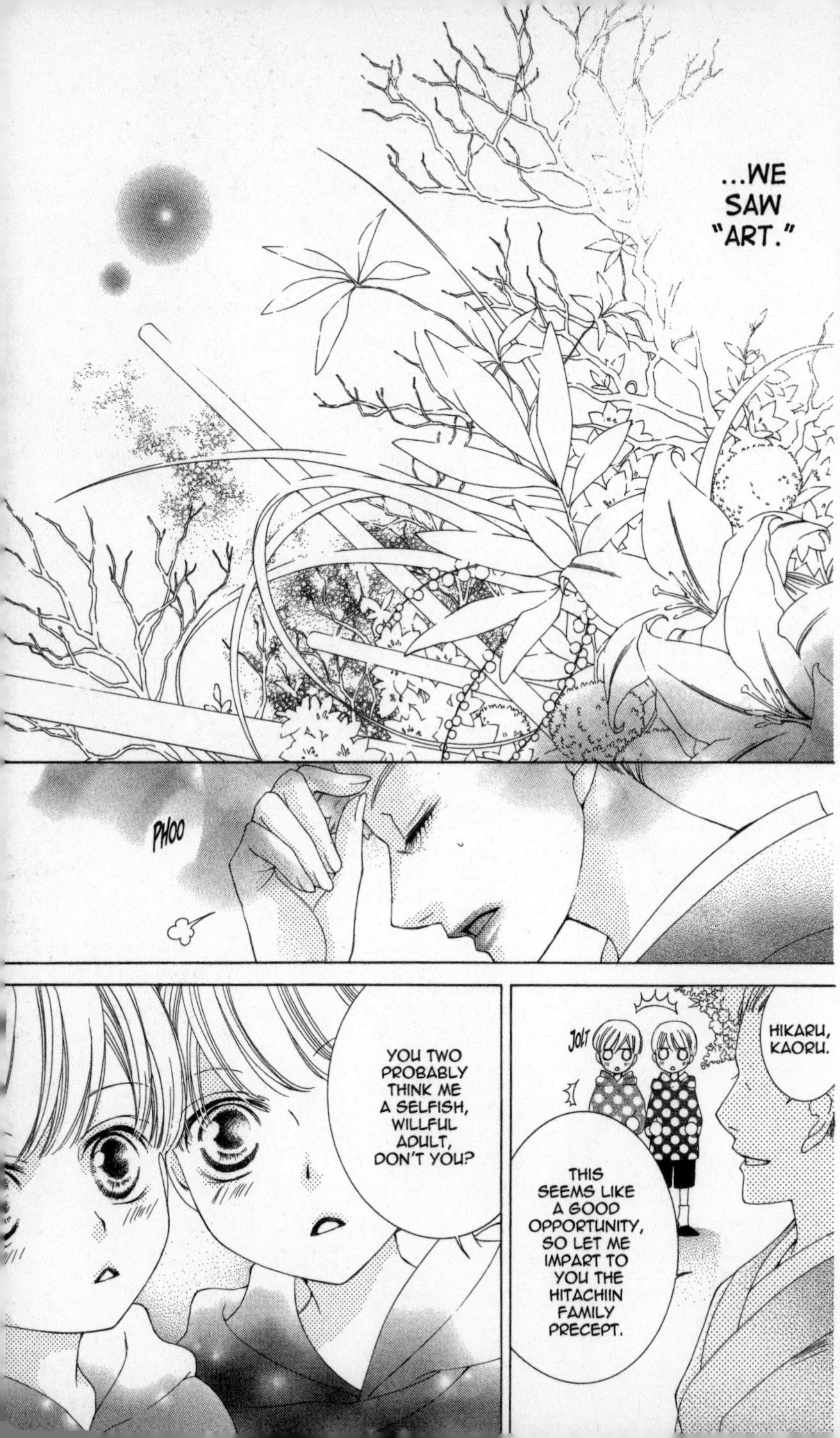
...WE SAW "ART."
PHOO
HIKARU, KAORU.
JOLT
THIS SEEMS LIKE A GOOD OPPORTUNITY, SO LET ME IMPART TO YOU THE HITACHIIN FAMILY PRECEPT.
YOU TWO PROBABLY THINK ME A SELFISH, WILLFUL ADULT, DON'T YOU?

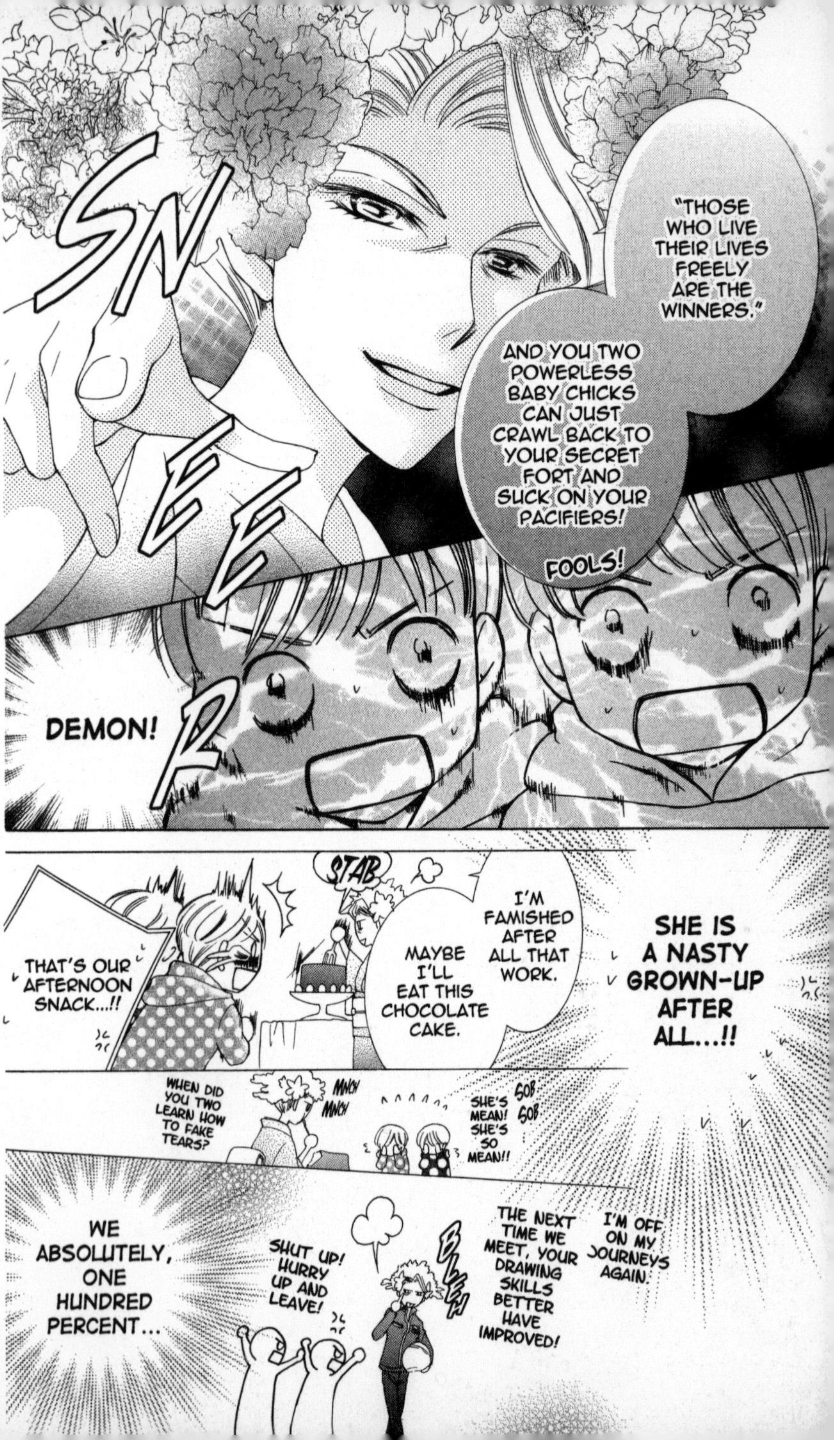
"THOSE WHO LIVE THEIR LIVES FREELY ARE THE WINNERS."
AND YOU TWO POWERLESS BABY CHICKS CAN JUST CRAWL BACK TO YOUR SECRET FORT AND SUCK ON YOUR PACIFIERS!
FOOLS!
SNEEER
DEMON!
SHE IS A NASTY GROWN-UP AFTER ALL...!!
I'M FAMISHED AFTER ALL THAT WORK.
MAYBE I'LL EAT THIS CHOCOLATE CAKE.
STAB
THAT'S OUR AFTERNOON SNACK...!!
SOB SOB
SHE'S MEAN! SHE'S SO MEAN!!
MNCH MNCH
WHEN DID YOU TWO LEARN HOW TO FAKE TEARS?
I'M OFF ON MY JOURNEYS AGAIN.
THE NEXT TIME WE MEET, YOUR DRAWING SKILLS BETTER HAVE IMPROVED!
BLEH
SHUT UP! HURRY UP AND LEAVE!
WE ABSOLUTELY, ONE HUNDRED PERCENT...

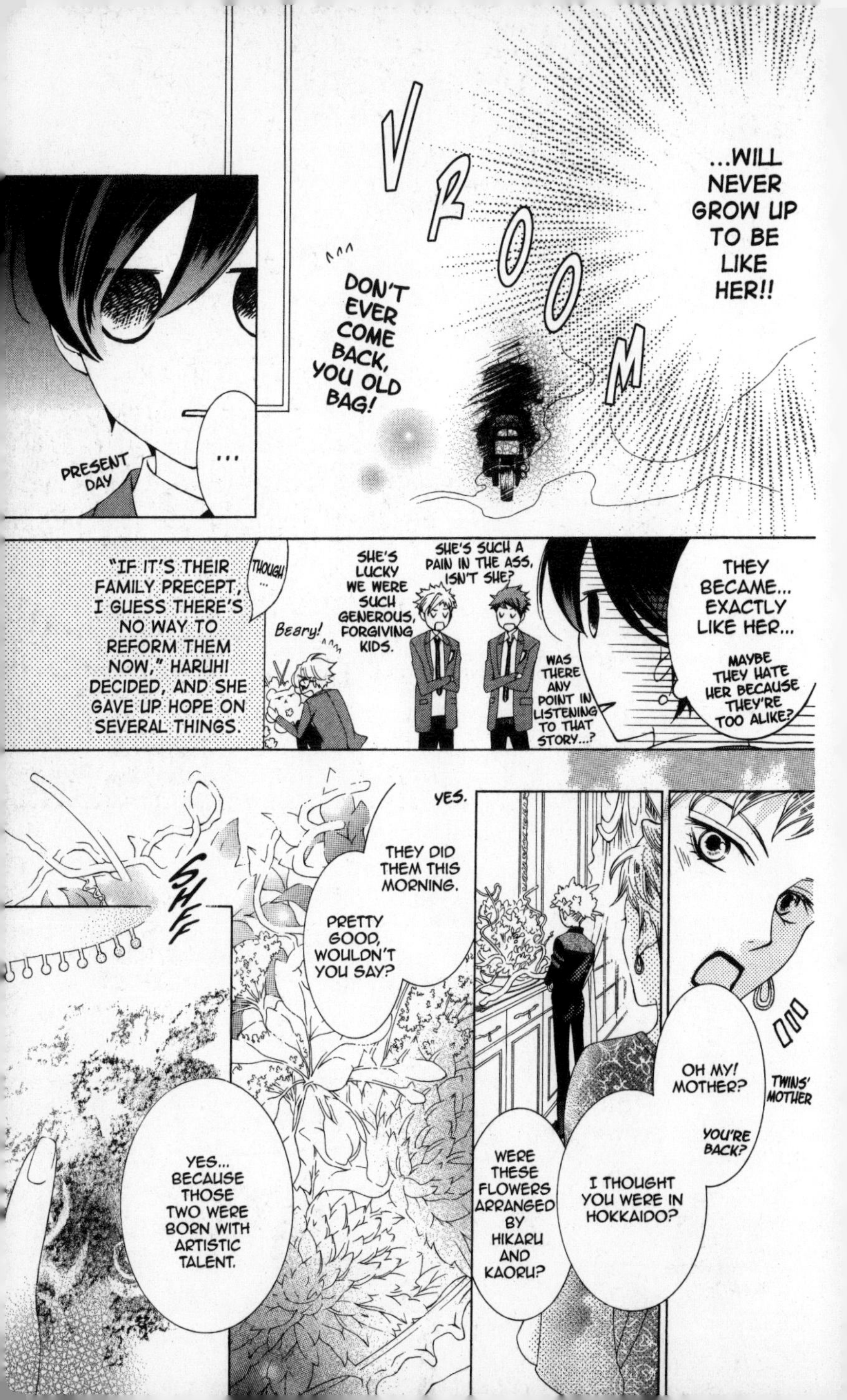
...WILL NEVER GROW UP TO BE LIKE HER!!
DON'T EVER COME BACK, YOU OLD BAG!
VROOM
PRESENT DAY
...
THEY BECAME... EXACTLY LIKE HER...
MAYBE THEY HATE HER BECAUSE THEY'RE TOO ALIKE?
WAS THERE ANY POINT IN LISTENING TO THAT STORY...?
SHE'S SUCH A PAIN IN THE ASS, ISN'T SHE?
SHE'S LUCKY WE WERE SUCH GENEROUS, FORGIVING KIDS.
Beary!
THOUGH...
"IF IT'S THEIR FAMILY PRECEPT, I GUESS THERE'S NO WAY TO REFORM THEM NOW," HARUHI DECIDED, AND SHE GAVE UP HOPE ON SEVERAL THINGS.
TWINS' MOTHER
OH MY! MOTHER?
YOU'RE BACK?
I THOUGHT YOU WERE IN HOKKAIDO?
WERE THESE FLOWERS ARRANGED BY HIKARU AND KAORU?
YES.
THEY DID THEM THIS MORNING.
PRETTY GOOD, WOULDN'T YOU SAY?
SHFF
YES... BECAUSE THOSE TWO WERE BORN WITH ARTISTIC TALENT.

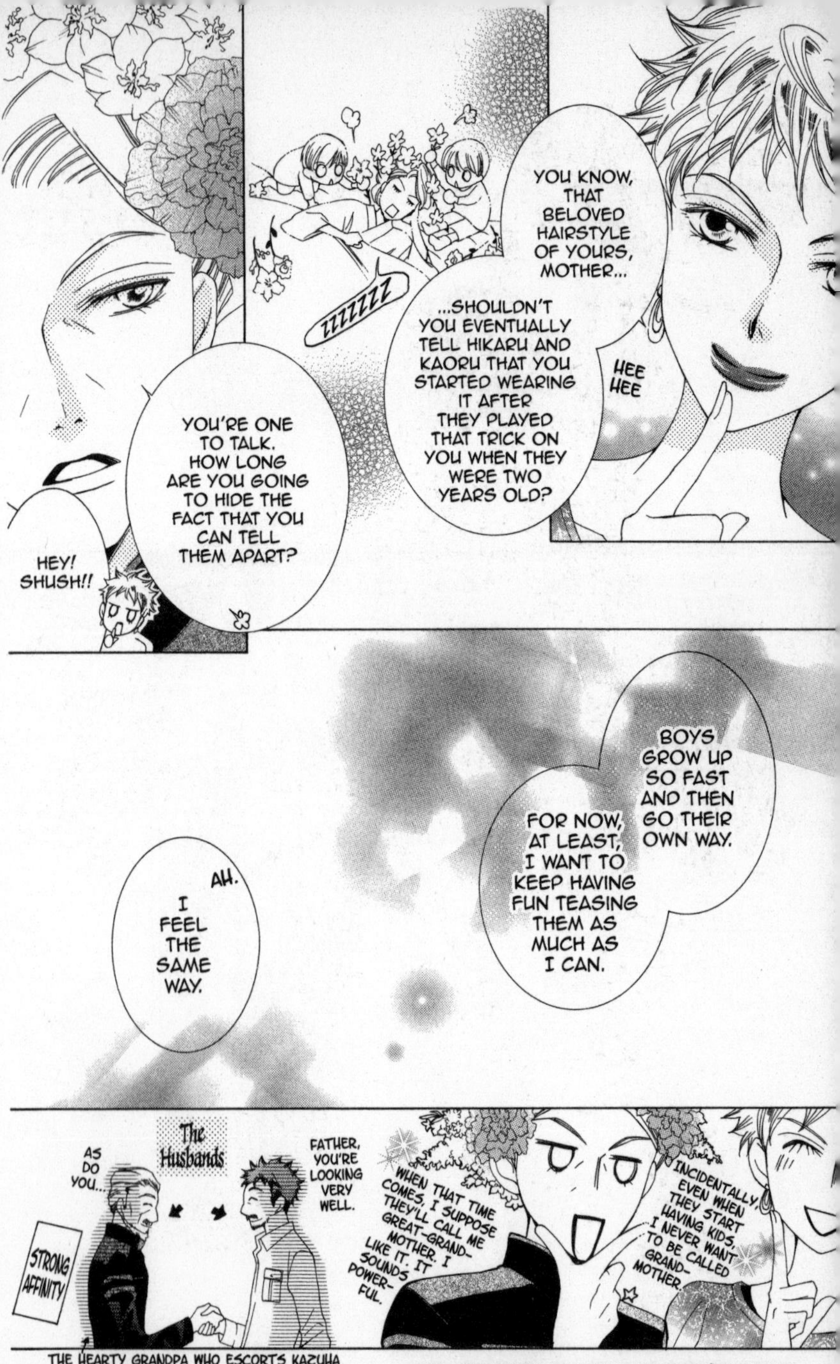
YOU KNOW, THAT BELOVED HAIRSTYLE OF YOURS, MOTHER...
HEE HEE
ZZZZZZZ
...SHOULDN'T YOU EVENTUALLY TELL HIKARU AND KAORU THAT YOU STARTED WEARING IT AFTER THEY PLAYED THAT TRICK ON YOU WHEN THEY WERE TWO YEARS OLD?
YOU'RE ONE TO TALK. HOW LONG ARE YOU GOING TO HIDE THE FACT THAT YOU CAN TELL THEM APART?
HEY! SHUSH!!
BOYS GROW UP SO FAST AND THEN GO THEIR OWN WAY.
FOR NOW, AT LEAST, I WANT TO KEEP HAVING FUN TEASING THEM AS MUCH AS I CAN.
AH. I FEEL THE SAME WAY.
INCIDENTALLY, EVEN WHEN THEY START HAVING KIDS, I NEVER WANT TO BE CALLED GRAND-MOTHER.
WHEN THAT TIME COMES, I SUPPOSE THEY'LL CALL ME GREAT-GRAND-MOTHER. I LIKE IT. IT SOUNDS POWER-FUL.
FATHER, YOU'RE LOOKING VERY WELL.
The Husbands
AS DO YOU...
STRONG AFFINITY

THE HEARTY GRANDPA WHO ESCORTS KAZUHA ON ALL HER JOURNEYS.

THE HITACHIIN FAMILY PRECEPT/THE END

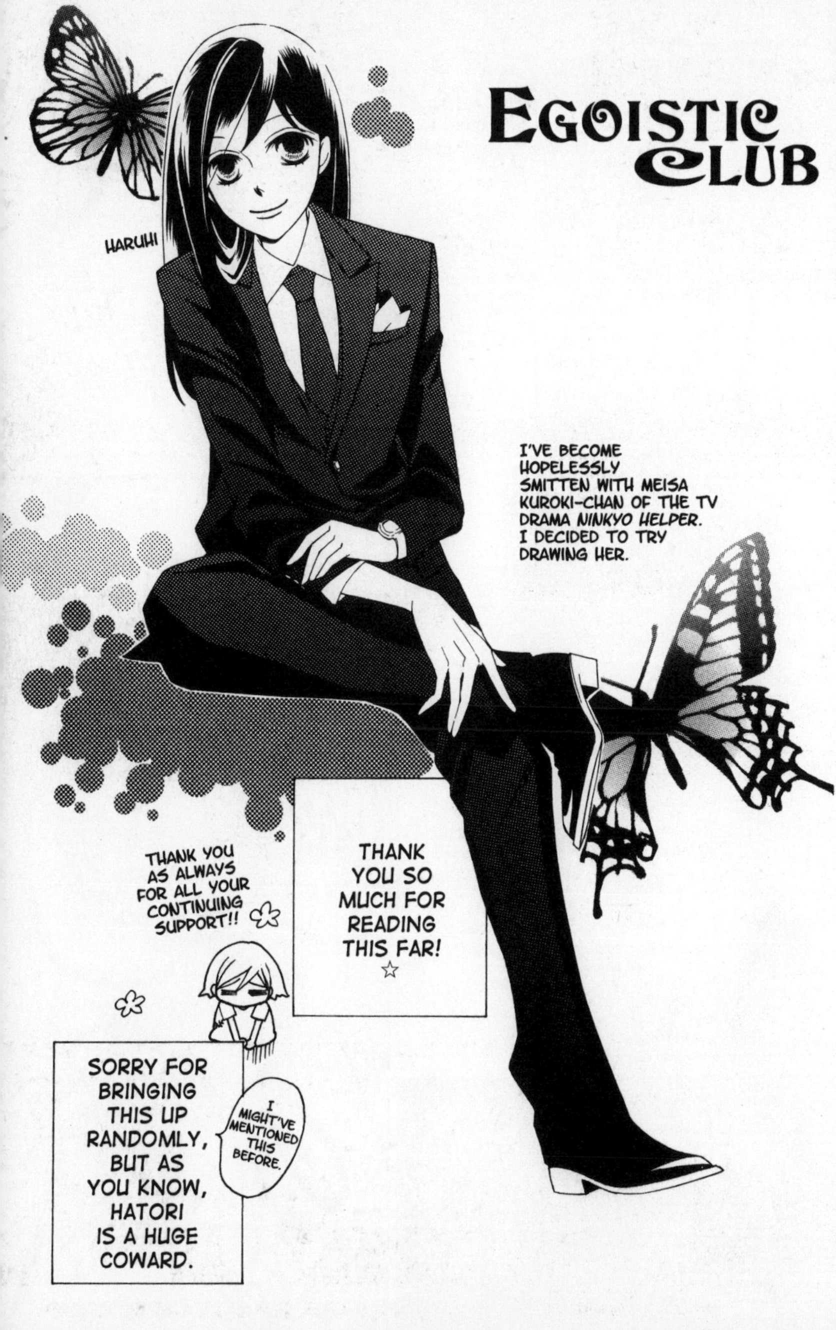
EGOISTIC CLUB
I'VE BECOME HOPELESSLY SMITTEN WITH MEISA KUROKI-CHAN OF THE TV DRAMA NINKYO HELPER. I DECIDED TO TRY DRAWING HER.
HARUHI
THANK YOU SO MUCH FOR READING THIS FAR! ☆
THANK YOU AS ALWAYS FOR ALL YOUR CONTINUING SUPPORT!!
SORRY FOR BRINGING THIS UP RANDOMLY, BUT AS YOU KNOW, HATORI IS A HUGE COWARD.
I MIGHT'VE MENTIONED THIS BEFORE.

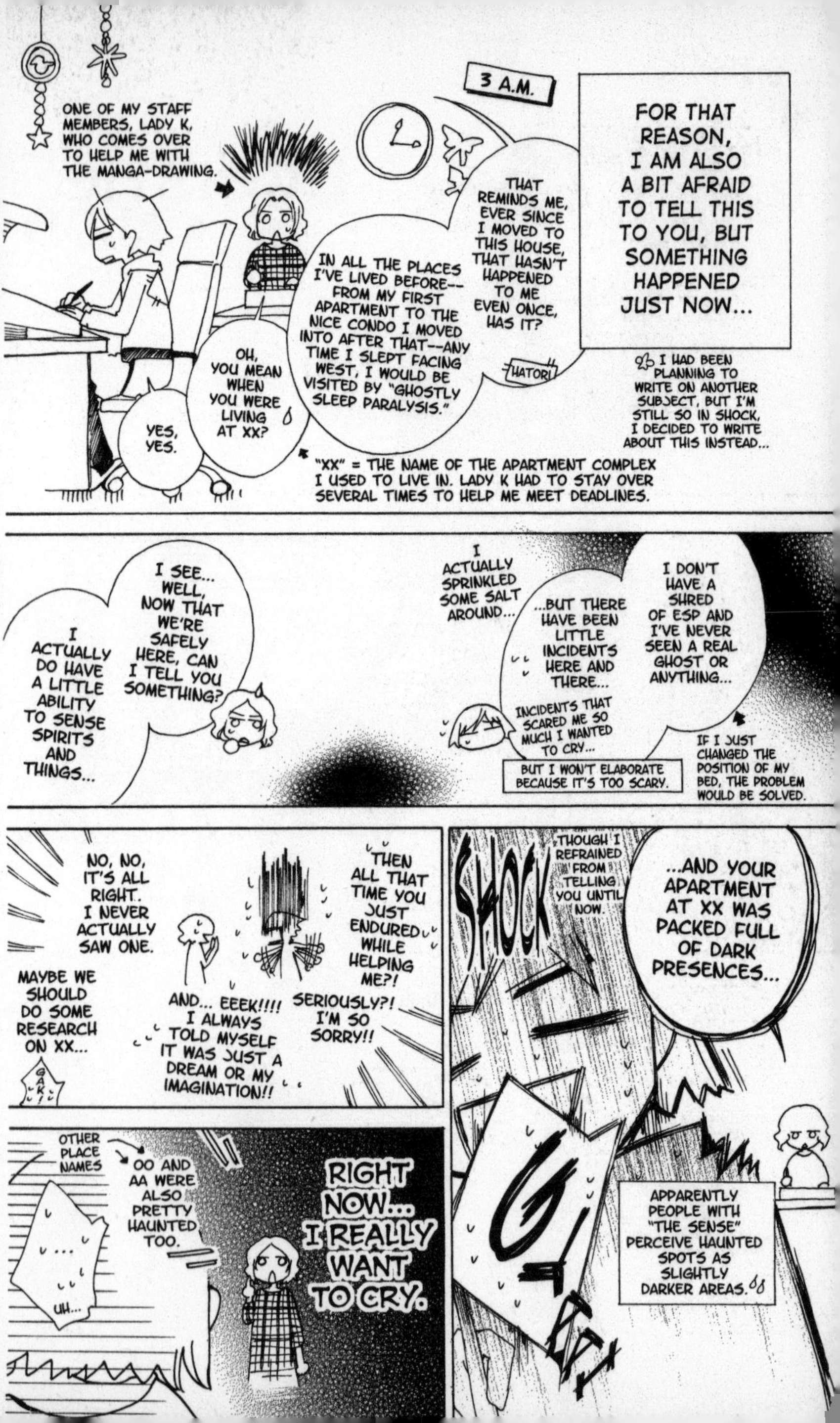

FOR THAT REASON, I AM ALSO A BIT AFRAID TO TELL THIS TO YOU, BUT SOMETHING HAPPENED JUST NOW...
I HAD BEEN PLANNING TO WRITE ON ANOTHER SUBJECT, BUT I'M STILL SO IN SHOCK, I DECIDED TO WRITE ABOUT THIS INSTEAD...
3 A.M.
THAT REMINDS ME, EVER SINCE I MOVED TO THIS HOUSE, THAT HASN'T HAPPENED TO ME EVEN ONCE, HAS IT?
HATORI
IN ALL THE PLACES I'VE LIVED BEFORE-- FROM MY FIRST APARTMENT TO THE NICE CONDO I MOVED INTO AFTER THAT--ANY TIME I SLEPT FACING WEST, I WOULD BE VISITED BY "GHOSTLY SLEEP PARALYSIS."
OH, YOU MEAN WHEN YOU WERE LIVING AT XX?
YES, YES.
"XX" = THE NAME OF THE APARTMENT COMPLEX I USED TO LIVE IN. LADY K HAD TO STAY OVER SEVERAL TIMES TO HELP ME MEET DEADLINES.
ONE OF MY STAFF MEMBERS, LADY K, WHO COMES OVER TO HELP ME WITH THE MANGA-DRAWING.
I DON'T HAVE A SHRED OF ESP AND I'VE NEVER SEEN A REAL GHOST OR ANYTHING...
IF I JUST CHANGED THE POSITION OF MY BED, THE PROBLEM WOULD BE SOLVED.
...BUT THERE HAVE BEEN LITTLE INCIDENTS HERE AND THERE...
I ACTUALLY SPRINKLED SOME SALT AROUND...
INCIDENTS THAT SCARED ME SO MUCH I WANTED TO CRY...
BUT I WON'T ELABORATE BECAUSE IT'S TOO SCARY.
I SEE... WELL, NOW THAT WE'RE SAFELY HERE, CAN I TELL YOU SOMETHING?
I ACTUALLY DO HAVE A LITTLE ABILITY TO SENSE SPIRITS AND THINGS...
...AND YOUR APARTMENT AT XX WAS PACKED FULL OF DARK PRESENCES...
THOUGH I REFRAINED FROM TELLING YOU UNTIL NOW.
SHOCK
GAK
APPARENTLY PEOPLE WITH "THE SENSE" PERCEIVE HAUNTED SPOTS AS SLIGHTLY DARKER AREAS.
THEN ALL THAT TIME YOU JUST ENDURED WHILE HELPING ME?!
SERIOUSLY?! I'M SO SORRY!!
AND... EEEK!!!! I ALWAYS TOLD MYSELF IT WAS JUST A DREAM OR MY IMAGINATION!!
NO, NO, IT'S ALL RIGHT. I NEVER ACTUALLY SAW ONE.
MAYBE WE SHOULD DO SOME RESEARCH ON XX...
GAK!
RIGHT NOW... I REALLY WANT TO CRY.
OTHER PLACE NAMES
OO AND AA WERE ALSO PRETTY HAUNTED TOO.
...
UH...

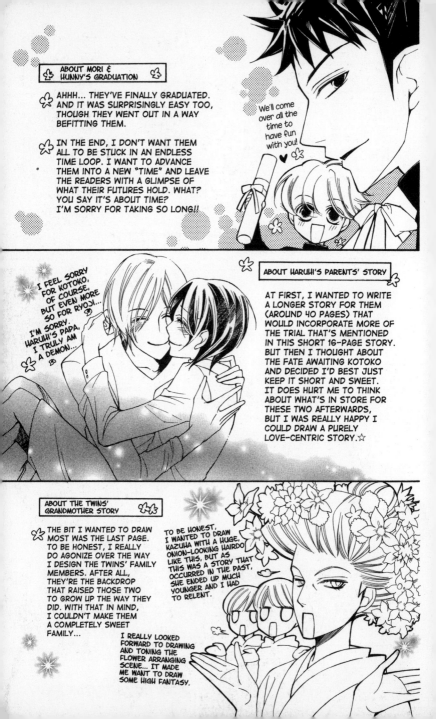

ABOUT MORI & HUNNY'S GRADUATION

AHHH... THEY'VE FINALLY GRADUATED. AND IT WAS SURPRISINGLY EASY TOO, THOUGH THEY WENT OUT IN A WAY BEFITTING THEM.

IN THE END, I DON'T WANT THEM ALL TO BE STUCK IN AN ENDLESS TIME LOOP. I WANT TO ADVANCE THEM INTO A NEW "TIME" AND LEAVE THE READERS WITH A GLIMPSE OF WHAT THEIR FUTURES HOLD. WHAT? YOU SAY IT'S ABOUT TIME? I'M SORRY FOR TAKING SO LONG!!

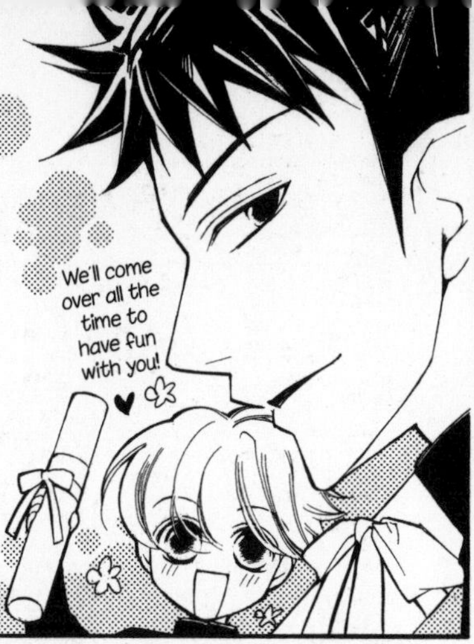
We'll come over all the time to have fun with you! ♥

ABOUT HARUHI'S PARENTS' STORY

AT FIRST, I WANTED TO WRITE A LONGER STORY FOR THEM (AROUND 40 PAGES) THAT WOULD INCORPORATE MORE OF THE TRIAL THAT'S MENTIONED IN THIS SHORT 16-PAGE STORY. BUT THEN I THOUGHT ABOUT THE FATE AWAITING KOTOKO AND DECIDED I'D BEST JUST KEEP IT SHORT AND SWEET. IT DOES HURT ME TO THINK ABOUT WHAT'S IN STORE FOR THESE TWO AFTERWARDS, BUT I WAS REALLY HAPPY I COULD DRAW A PURELY LOVE-CENTRIC STORY.☆

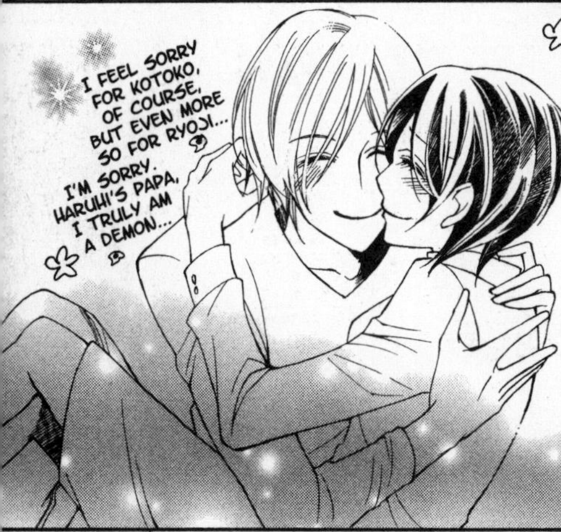
I FEEL SORRY FOR KOTOKO, OF COURSE, BUT EVEN MORE SO FOR RYOJI...
I'M SORRY. HARUHI'S PAPA, I TRULY AM A DEMON...

ABOUT THE TWINS' GRANDMOTHER STORY

THE BIT I WANTED TO DRAW MOST WAS THE LAST PAGE. TO BE HONEST, I REALLY DO AGONIZE OVER THE WAY I DESIGN THE TWINS' FAMILY MEMBERS. AFTER ALL, THEY'RE THE BACKDROP THAT RAISED THOSE TWO TO GROW UP THE WAY THEY DID. WITH THAT IN MIND, I COULDN'T MAKE THEM A COMPLETELY SWEET FAMILY...

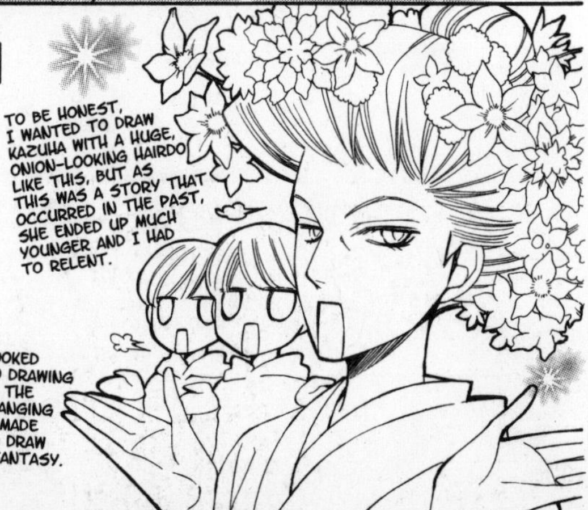
TO BE HONEST, I WANTED TO DRAW KAZUHA WITH A HUGE, ONION-LOOKING HAIRDO LIKE THIS, BUT AS THIS WAS A STORY THAT OCCURRED IN THE PAST, SHE ENDED UP MUCH YOUNGER AND I HAD TO RELENT.
I REALLY LOOKED FORWARD TO DRAWING AND TONING THE FLOWER ARRANGING SCENE... IT MADE ME WANT TO DRAW SOME HIGH FANTASY.

A KYOYA-LOOKING CHARACTER WHO'S JUST COME OUT OF THE BATH IS BEING TEASED BY A HARUHI-LOOKING CHARACTER AS THEY PLAY THE "POCKY GAME" TOGETHER.

IT'S KIND OF LIKE THE CONTINUATION OF THE FLIRTATIOUS DRAWING FROM VOLUME 3.

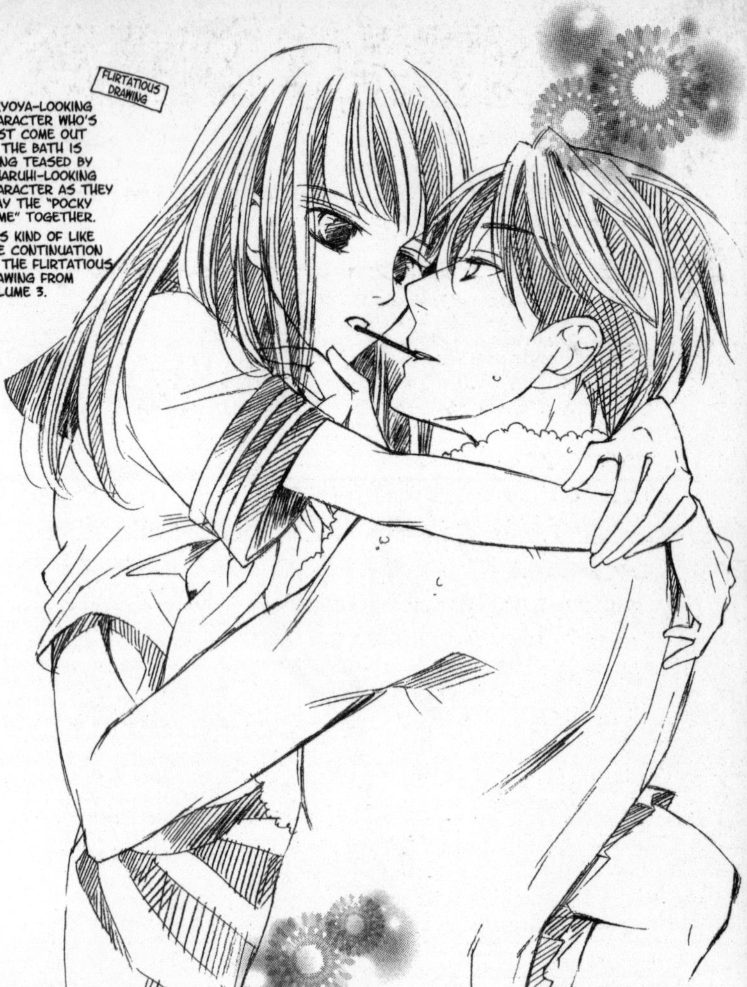
FLIRTATIOUS DRAWING

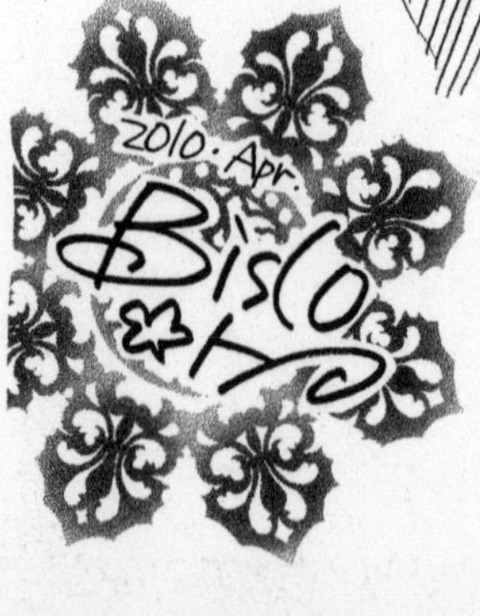
2010・Apr.
Bisco

Special Thanks!!

- SHIKAWA-SAMA AND MISS T
- EVERYONE AT THE COMPILATION OFFICE AND EVERYONE INVOLVED IN THE PRODUCTION OF THIS BOOK
- ATTORNEY-AT-LAW KONAMI KATASE
- ALL MY STAFF: YUI NATSUKI, RIKU, AYA AOMURA, YUTORI HIZAKURA, SHIZURU ONDA, UMEKO, AND BISCO'S MOM
- ALL MY EXTRA HELPERS: NATSUMI SATOU, SHIGEYOSHI TAKAGI, CHIAKI KARAZAWA AND HAZUKI.
- AND TO ALL OF YOU WHO READ THIS BOOK!! THANK YOU SO VERY MUCH!

EGOISTIC CLUB/THE END

EDITOR'S NOTES

EPISODE 72
Page 11: *Mitsumame* is a Japanese dessert consisting of boiled red peas, jelly cubes, fruit pieces, and molasses.

Page 32: *Anmitsu* has the same ingredients as mitsumame, but also includes sweet bean paste.

EPISODE 73
Page 76: *Gap moe* refers to two seemingly contradictory traits in the same character that fans find appealing.

EPISODE 74
Page 105: *Tsujigahana* is a type of textile art that involves dyeing, painting, and embroidering materials.

EXTRA EPISODE
Page 164: *Kado* is the traditional Japanese art of flower arranging.

Author Bio

Bisco Hatori made her manga debut with *Isshun kan no Romance* (A Moment of Romance) in *LaLa DX* magazine. The comedy *Ouran High School Host Club* is her breakout hit. When she's stuck thinking up characters' names, she gets inspired by loud, upbeat music (her radio is set to NACK5 FM). She enjoys reading all kinds of manga, but she's especially fond of the sci-fi drama *Please Save My Earth* and *Slam Dunk*, a basketball classic.

OURAN HIGH SCHOOL HOST CLUB
Vol. 16
Shojo Beat Edition

STORY AND ART BY BISCO HATORI

Translation/Su Mon Han
Touch-up Art & Lettering/Gia Cam Luc
Graphic Design/Amy Martin
Editor/Nancy Thistlethwaite

Ouran Koko Host Club by Bisco Hatori © Bisco Hatori 2010. All rights reserved.
First published in Japan in 2010 by HAKUSENSHA, Inc., Tokyo. English language
translation rights arranged with HAKUSENSHA, Inc., Tokyo.

The rights of the author(s) of the work(s) in this publication to be so identified have
been asserted in accordance with the Copyright, Designs and Patents Act 1988. A CIP
catalogue record for this book is available from the British Library.

The stories, characters and incidents mentioned in this publication
are entirely fictional.

No portion of this book may be reproduced or transmitted in any form or by any means
without written permission from the copyright holders.

Printed in the U.S.A.

Published by VIZ Media, LLC
P.O. Box 77010
San Francisco, CA 94107

10 9 8 7 6 5 4 3 2 1
First printing, June 2011

www.viz.com   www.shojobeat.com

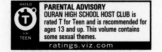

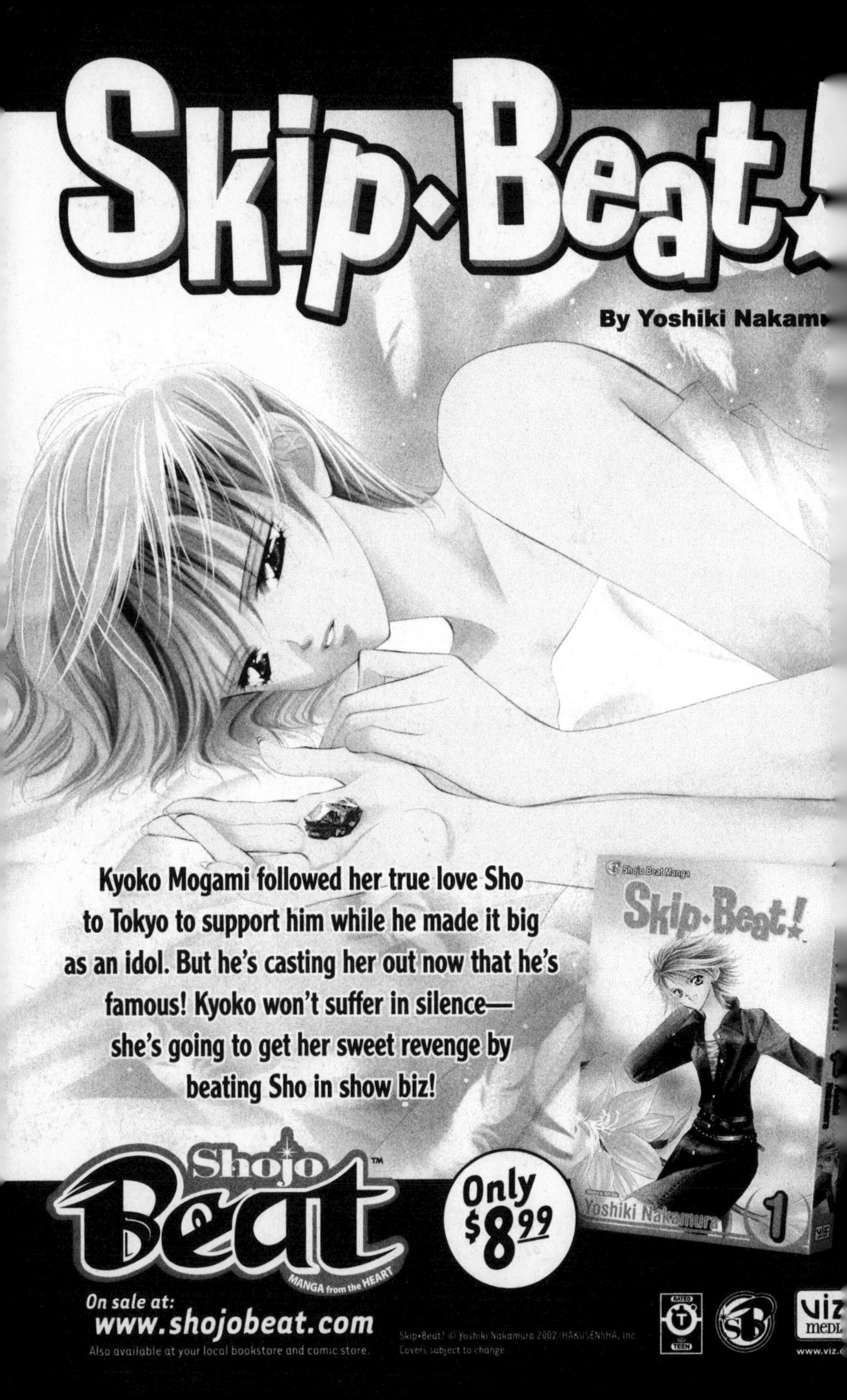
Skip·Beat!
By Yoshiki Nakam
Kyoko Mogami followed her true love Sho to Tokyo to support him while he made it big as an idol. But he's casting her out now that he's famous! Kyoko won't suffer in silence—she's going to get her sweet revenge by beating Sho in show biz!
Shojo Beat Manga
Skip·Beat!
Yoshiki Nakamura
1
Shojo Beat
MANGA from the HEART
Only $8.99
On sale at:
www.shojobeat.com
Also available at your local bookstore and comic store.
Skip•Beat! © Yoshiki Nakamura 2002/HAKUSENSHA, Inc.
Covers subject to change.
RATED T TEEN
VIZ MEDIA
www.viz.c

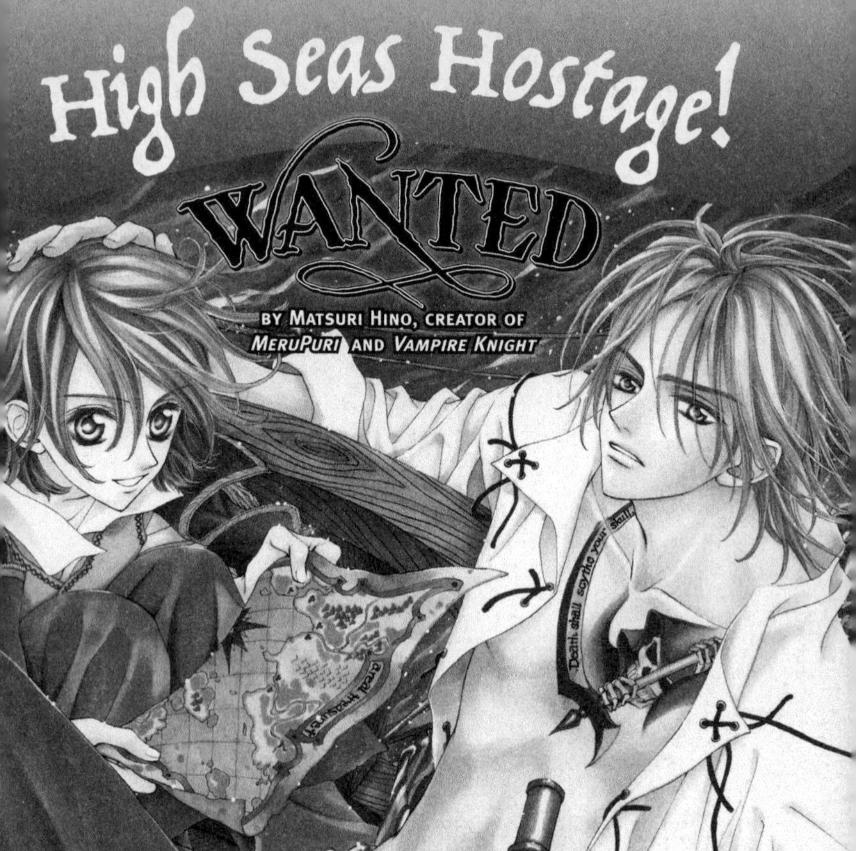
High Seas Hostage!
WANTED
BY MATSURI HINO, CREATOR OF
MERUPURI AND VAMPIRE KNIGHT
Death shall scythe your skull

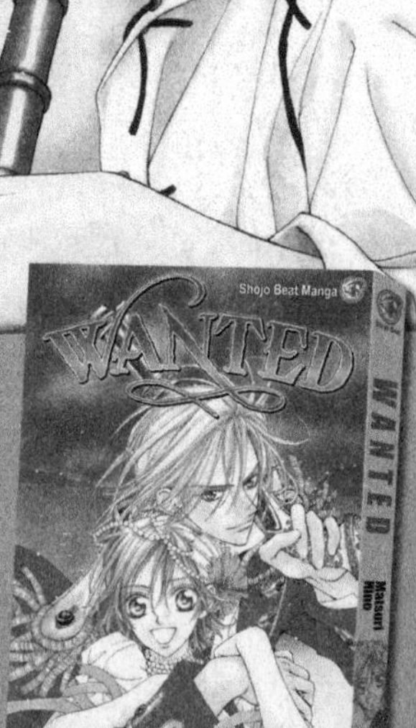
Shojo Beat Manga
WANTED
WANTED
Matsuri Hino
Matsuri Hino

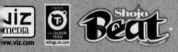

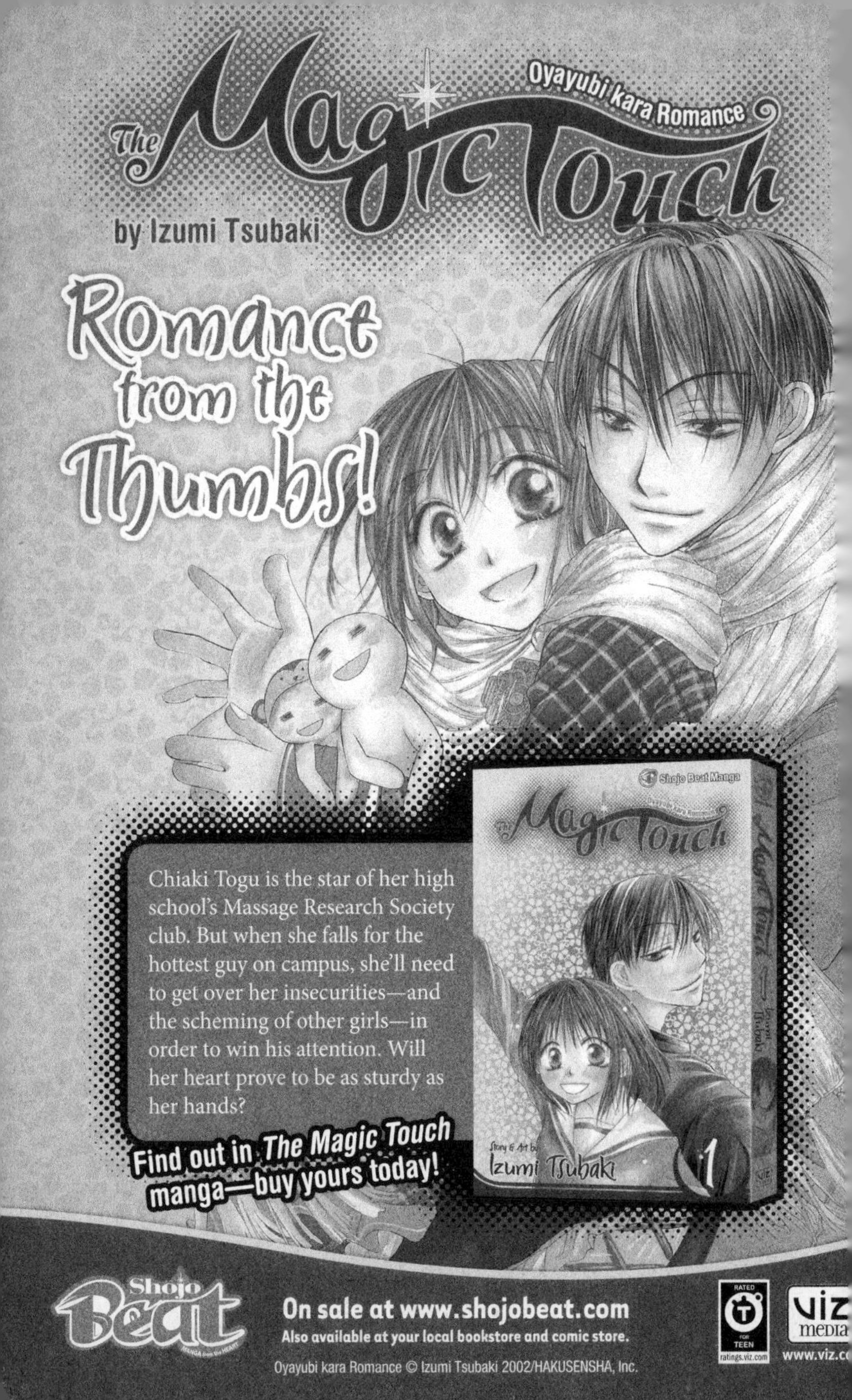
The Magic Touch
Oyayubi kara Romance
by Izumi Tsubaki
Romance from the Thumbs!
Chiaki Togu is the star of her high school's Massage Research Society club. But when she falls for the hottest guy on campus, she'll need to get over her insecurities—and the scheming of other girls—in order to win his attention. Will her heart prove to be as sturdy as her hands?
Find out in The Magic Touch manga—buy yours today!
Shojo Beat Manga
The Magic Touch
Story & Art by Izumi Tsubaki
1
Shojo Beat
On sale at www.shojobeat.com
Also available at your local bookstore and comic store.
Oyayubi kara Romance © Izumi Tsubaki 2002/HAKUSENSHA, Inc.
RATED T FOR TEEN
ratings.viz.com
VIZ media
www.viz.c

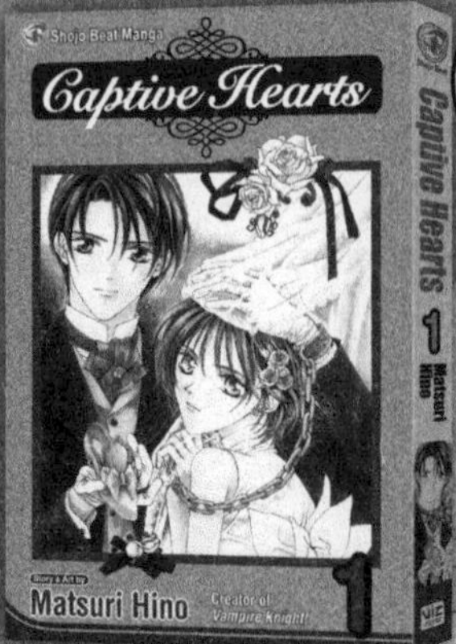

Shojo Beat Manga
Captive Hearts
Captive Hearts
1
Matsuri Hino
Matsuri Hino

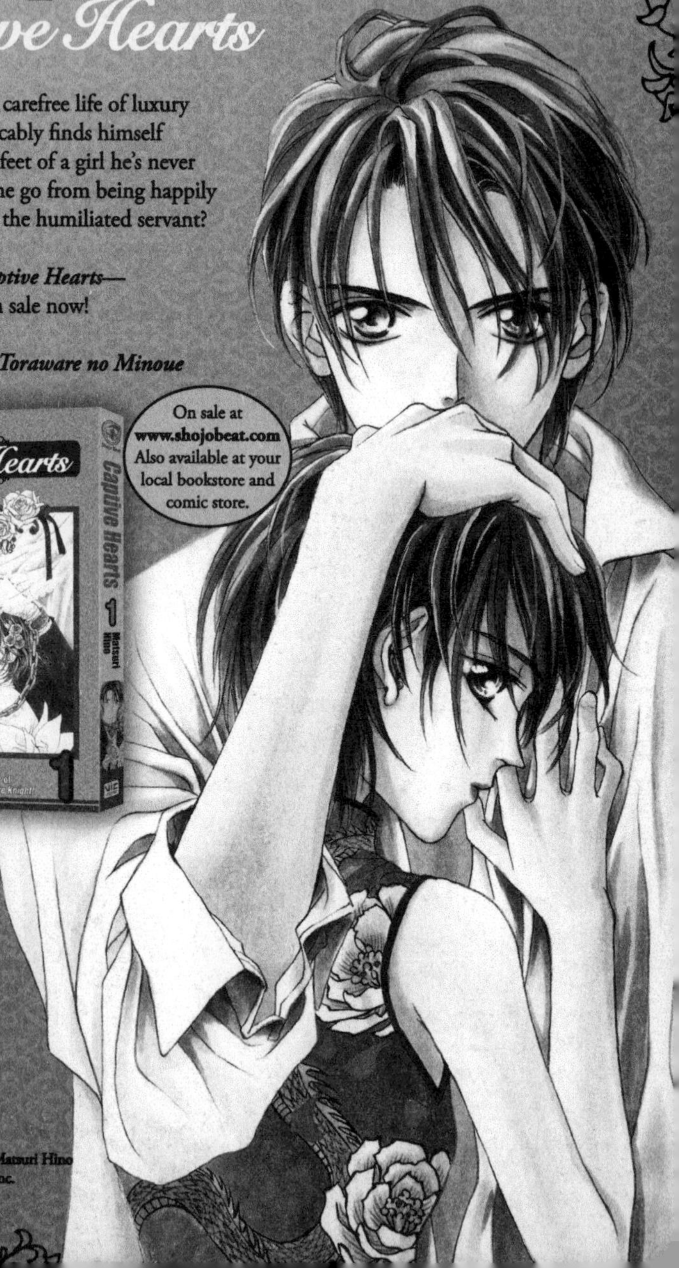

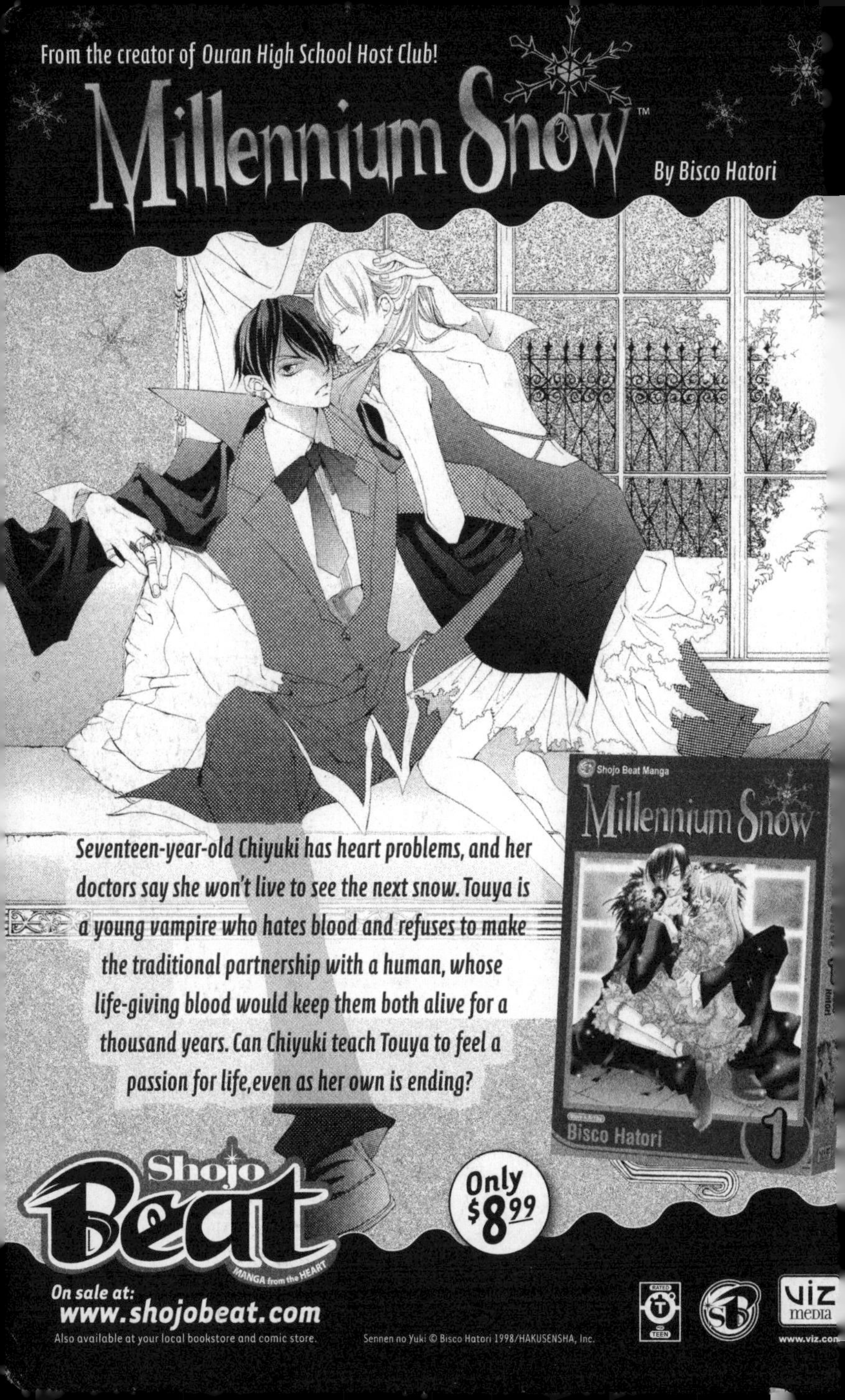
From the creator of Ouran High School Host Club!
Millennium Snow™
By Bisco Hatori
Shojo Beat Manga
Millennium Snow
Bisco Hatori
1
Seventeen-year-old Chiyuki has heart problems, and her doctors say she won't live to see the next snow. Touya is a young vampire who hates blood and refuses to make the traditional partnership with a human, whose life-giving blood would keep them both alive for a thousand years. Can Chiyuki teach Touya to feel a passion for life,even as her own is ending?
Shojo Beat
MANGA from the HEART
Only $8.99
On sale at:
www.shojobeat.com
Also available at your local bookstore and comic store.
Sennen no Yuki © Bisco Hatori 1998/HAKUSENSHA, Inc.
RATED T TEEN
VIZ media
www.viz.com